FIFTEEN DECISIVE BATTLES
OF THE WORLD

CREASY

One of

The Military Classics

SIR EDWARD S. CREASY

Edward Shepherd Creasy was born in 1812 in Kent. Educated at Eton and Cambridge, he became a Fellow of King's College in 1834 and in 1837 a member of the bar. He was called to the faculty of London University in 1840, as Professor of Modern and Ancient History.

Until 1860 he practiced law, and served as assistant-judge of the Westminster Sessions Court. In that year he was appointed Chief Justice of Ceylon and knighted. He remained in Ceylon for a decade, returned to England and retired on account of ill health. London was the place of his death, on January 27, 1872.

Sir Edward wrote voluminously, learnedly, and with brilliance, chiefly on historical subjects, but none of his books attained the popularity and earned him the enduring fame that did his *Fifteen Decisive Battles of the World.*

FIFTEEN DECISIVE BATTLES OF THE WORLD

By

SIR EDWARD S. CREASY

A Military Classic

MARATHON—SYRACUSE—ARBELA—METAURUS—
ARMINIUS—CHALONS—TOURS—HASTINGS—
ORLEANS—ARMADA—BLENHEIM—
PULTOWA—SARATOGA—
VALMY—WATERLOO

MILITARY SERVICE DIVISION
THE STACKPOLE COMPANY
Harrisburg, Pennsylvania

Printed in the United States of America
by
THE TELEGRAPH PRESS
Established 1831
Harrisburg, Pennsylvania

Publisher's Foreword

Although more than a century has passed since the appearance of Sir Edward Creasy's *Fifteen Decisive Battles of the World*, the skill with which Sir Edward threaded various geographical, logistical, and psychological factors into a colorful, realistic report of these battles makes his work as instructive and necessary for today's military student as when Creasy first wrote it. As an historical work it has more than stood the test of time, and today ranks as a military classic.

Creasy's list of *the* fifteen most decisive battles of the world ended with Waterloo, since this was the last great battle he knew of when he wrote (1850). If he were writing today he would undoubtedly have included in his list several of the crucial encounters of the last 100 years. Recognizing this, this company in 1943 published a book under the title of *Decisive Battles of the World* (Creasy-Murray), which projected Creasy's list into the 20th century. In addition to Creasy's original 15 battles, this book included 9 others which had either taken place after Creasy's time, or which modern historians felt ought to rank at least on a par with Creasy's 15.

This present book, *Fifteen Decisive Battles of the World*, is a revision of *Decisive Battles* with all post-Creasy battles deleted. The elimination of these later encounters was decided upon because it would now be necessary to include several World War I and II battles and possibly Korea, which in our opinion would have seriously overbalanced Creasy and impaired the book's original character. In this revision, we have, however, retained the contributions of the late Robert Hammond Murray, who went to great efforts in the 1943 edition to bring Creasy's involved style into conformity with modern reading tastes, and to delete dissertations and comments which in the passage of a century had lost their original pertinency. In the account of the destruction of the Spanish Armada, Murray also deleted Creasy's extracts from the English historian Hakluyt and substituted parts of the more colorful and detailed story of the great Armada by James Anthony Froude.

In an effort to retain as much of the original flavor of Creasy as possible, Murray in his original edit used Creasy's British spellings (and in some cases medieval and ancient spellings) where they did not hinder an understanding of the text, and in this revision we have continued these.

The Military Classics

A series of military masterpieces on various phases of war.

THE ART OF WAR, *by Sun Tzu.*

THE ART OF WAR ON LAND, *by Colonel A. H. Burne.*

ARMORED WARFARE, *by Major General J. F. C. Fuller.*

BATTLE STUDIES, *by Colonel Ardant du Picq.*

CAESAR'S GALLIC CAMPAIGNS, *by Lieutenant Colonel S. G. Brady.*

DEFENSE, *by Field Marshal Ritter von Leeb.*

FIFTEEN DECISIVE BATTLES OF THE WORLD, *by Sir Edward S. Creasy.*

FREDERICK THE GREAT—*Instructions to his Generals, translated by Brigadier General Thomas R. Phillips.*

JOMINI'S ART OF WAR, *edited by Brigadier General J. D. Hittle.*

MILITARY INSTITUTIONS OF THE ROMANS, *by Flavius Vegetius Renatus.*

NAPOLEON AND MODERN WAR, *by Colonel Conrad H. Lanza.*

THE POWER OF PERSONALITY IN WAR, *by Major General Baron von Freytag-Loringhoven.*

PRINCIPLES OF WAR, *by General Carl von Clausewitz.*

REVERIES ON THE ART OF WAR, *by Marshal Maurice de Saxe.*

SURPRISE, *by General Waldemar Erfurth.*

Creasy's Preface to the First Edition

(Written in 1851)

IT IS an honourable characteristic of the Spirit of this Age, that projects of violence and warfare are regarded among civilised states with gradually increasing aversion. The Universal Peace Society certainly does not, and probably never will, enrol the majority of statesmen among its members.

But even those who look upon the Appeal of Battle as occasionally unavoidable in international controversies, concur in thinking it a deplorable necessity, only to be resorted to when all peaceful modes of arrangement have been vainly tried; and when the law of self-defence justifies a State, like an individual, in using force to protect itself from imminent and serious injury.

For a writer, therefore, of the present day to choose battles for his favourite topic, merely because they were battles; merely because so many myriads of troops were arrayed in them, and so many hundreds or thousands of human beings stabbed, hewed, or shot each other to death during them, would argue strange weakness or depravity of mind. Yet it cannot be denied that a fearful and wonderful interest is attached to these scenes of carnage. There is undeniable greatness in the disciplined courage, and in the love of honour, which make the combatants confront agony and destruction. And the powers of the human intellect are rarely more strongly displayed than they are in the Commander, who regulates, arrays, and wields at his will these masses of armed disputants; who, cool yet daring, in the midst of peril, reflects on all, and provides for all, ever ready with fresh resources and designs, as the vicissitudes of the storm of slaughter require.

But these qualities, however high they may appear, are to be found in the basest as well as in the noblest of mankind. Catiline was as brave a soldier as Leonidas, and a much better officer. Alva surpassed the Prince of Orange in the field; and Suvorov was the military superior of Kosciusko. To adopt the emphatic words of Byron:—

> " 'Tis the Cause makes all,
> Degrades or hallows courage in its fall."

There are some battles, also, which claim our attention, independently of the moral worth of the combatants, on account of their enduring importance, and by reason of the practical influence on our own social and political condition, which we can trace up to the results of those engagements. They have for us an abiding and actual interest, both while we investigate the chain of causes and effects, by which they have helped to make us what we are; and also while we speculate on what we probably should have been, if any one of those battles had come to a different termination.

Hallam has admirably expressed this in his remarks on the victory gained by Charles Martel, between Tours and Poictiers, over the invading Saracens.

He says of it, that "it may justly be reckoned among those few battles of which a contrary event would have essentially varied the drama of the world in all its subsequent scenes, with Marathon, Arbela, the Metaurus, Chalons, and Leipzig." It was the perusal of this note of Hallam's that first led me to the consideration of my present subject.

I certainly differ from that great historian as to the comparative importance of some of the battles which he thus enumerates, and also of some which he omits. It is probable, indeed, that no two historical inquirers would entirely agree in their lists of the Decisive Battles of the World. Different minds will naturally vary in the impressions which particular events make on them; and in the degree of interest with which they watch the career, and reflect on the importance of different historical personages.

But our concurrence in our catalogue is of little moment, provided we learn to look on these great historical events in the spirit which Hallam's observations indicate. Those remarks should teach us to watch how the interests of many states are often involved in the collisions between a few; and how the effect of those collisions is not limited to a single age, but may give an impulse which will sway the fortunes of successive generations of mankind. Most valuable also is the mental discipline which is thus acquired, and by which we are trained not only to observe what has been, and what is, but also to ponder on what might have been.

We thus learn not to judge of the wisdom of measures too exclusively by the results. We learn to apply the juster standard of seeing what the circumstances and the probabilities were that surrounded a statesman or a general at the time when he decided on his plan: we value him not by his fortune, but by his qualities, the outcome of his plan.

The reasons why each of the following Fifteen Battles has been selected will, I trust, appear when it is described. But it may be well to premise a few remarks on the negative tests which have led me to reject others, which at first sight may appear equal in magnitude and importance to the chosen Fifteen.

I need hardly remark that it is not the number of killed and wounded in a battle that determines its general historical importance. It is not because only a few hundreds fell in the battle by which Joan of Arc captured the Tourelles and raised the siege of Orleans, that the effect of that crisis is to be judged: nor would a full belief in the largest number which Eastern historians state to have been slaughtered in any of the numerous conflicts between Asiatic rulers, make me regard the engagement in which they fell as one of paramount importance to mankind.

But, besides battles of this kind, there are many of great consequence, and attended with circumstances which powerfully excite our feelings, and rivet our attention, and yet which appear to me of mere secondary rank, inasmuch as either their effects were limited in area, or they themselves merely confirmed some great tendency or bias which an earlier battle had originated.

For example, the encounters between the Greeks and Persians, which followed Marathon, seem to me not to have been phenomena of primary impulse. Greek superiority had been already asserted, Asiatic ambition had already been checked, before Salamis [island southwest of Athens, off which Themistocles and his Greeks won over the Persians of Xerxes, 480 B. C.] and Plataea [ancient Grecian city, where the Persians were defeated severely, 479 B. C.] confirmed the superiority of European free states over Oriental despotism. So, Ægos-Potamos, [a Thracian stream, at the mouth of which the Peloponnesian War was ended by the defeat of the Athenian fleet by Lysander and his Spartans, 405 B. C.] which finally crushed the maritime power of Athens, seems to me inferior in interest to the defeat before Syracuse, where Athens received her first fatal check, and after which she only struggled to retard her downfall. I think similarly of Zama [town in north Africa, where Scipio Africanus overwhelmed Hannibal, 202 B. C., ending the Second Punic War] with respect to Carthage, as compared with the Metaurus; and, on the same principle, the subsequent great battles of the

French Revolution appear to me inferior in their importance to Valmy, which first determined the military character and career of the Revolution.

I am aware that a little activity of imagination, and a slight exercise of metaphysical ingenuity, may amuse us by showing how the chain of circumstances is so linked together that the smallest skirmish, or the slightest occurrence of any kind, that ever occurred, may be said to have been essential, in its actual termination, to the whole order of subsequent events.

But when I speak of Causes and Effects, I speak of the obvious and important agency of one fact upon another, and not of remote and fancifully infinitesimal influences. I am aware that, on the other hand, the reproach of Fatalism is justly incurred by those, who, like the writers of a certain school in a neighbouring country, recognise in history nothing more than a series of necessary phenomena, which follow inevitably one upon the other. But when, in this work, I speak of probabilities, I speak of human probabilities only. When I speak of Cause and Effect, I speak of those general laws only, by which we perceive the sequence of human affairs to be usually regulated; and in which we recognize emphatically the wisdom and power of the Supreme Lawgiver, the design of The Designer.

MITRE COURT CHAMBERS, TEMPLE,
June 26, 1851.

Contents

Chapter I

-{ ONE }-

Marathon, 490 B. C.

WHY DECISIVE: *"The day of Marathon . . . broke forever
the spell of Persian invincibility, which had paralyzed men's
minds. It generated among the Greeks the spirit which beat
back Xerxes and afterwards led on Xenephon, Agesilaus and
Alexander in terrible retaliation through their Asiatic campaigns. It secured for mankind the intellectual treasures of
Athens, the growth of free institutions, the liberal enlightenment of the western world and the gradual ascendancy for
many ages of the great principles of European civilization."*
[Creasy.]

I

Two thousand three hundred and forty years ago (in 1850;
2445 years in 1955), a council of Athenian officers was summoned on the slope of one of the mountains that look over the
plain of Marathon, on the eastern coast of Attica. The immediate subject of their meeting was to consider whether they
should give battle to an enemy that lay encamped on the shore
beneath them; but on the result of their deliberations depended,
not merely the fate of two armies, but the whole future progress
of human civilisation.

There were eleven members of that council of war. Ten
were the generals, who were then annually elected at Athens,
one for each of the local tribes into which the Athenians were
divided. Each general led the men of his own tribe, and each
was invested with equal military authority. One also of the
Archons (chief magistrate) was associated with them in the
joint command of the collective force. This magistrate was
termed the Polemarch or War-Ruler: he had the privilege of
leading the right wing of the army in battle, and of taking
part in all councils of war. A noble Athenian, named Callimachus, was the War-Ruler of this year; and, as such, stood
listening to the earnest discussion of the ten generals. They
had, indeed, deep matter for anxiety, though little aware how
momentous to mankind were the votes they were about to give,
or how the generations to come would read with interest the
record of their debate. They saw before them the invading

forces of a mighty empire, which had in the last fifty years shattered and enslaved nearly all the kingdoms and principalities of the then known world. They knew that all the resources of their own country were comprised in the little army entrusted to their guidance. They saw before them a chosen host of the Great King (Darius of Persia), sent to wreak his special wrath on that country, and on the other insolent little Greek community, which had dared to aid his rebels and burn the capital of one of his provinces.

That victorious host had already fulfilled half its mission of vengeance. Eretria, the confederate of Athens in the bold march against Sardis nine years before, had fallen in the last few days; and the Athenian generals could discern from the heights the island of Ægilia, in which the Persians had deposited their Eretrian prisoners, whom they had reserved to be led away captives into Upper Asia, there to hear their doom from the lips of King Darius himself. Moreover, the men of Athens knew that in the camp before them was their own banished tyrant, Hippias, who was seeking to be reinstated by foreign scimitars in despotic sway over any remnant of his countrymen that might survive the sack of their town, and might be left behind as too worthless for leading away into Median bondage.

The numerical disparity between the force which the Athenian commanders had under them, and that which they were called on to encounter, was fearfully apparent to some of the council. The historians who wrote nearest to the time of the battle do not pretend to give any detailed statements of the numbers engaged, but there are sufficient data for our making a general estimate. Every free Greek was trained to military duty: and, from the incessant border wars between the different states, few Greeks reached the age of manhood without having seen some service. But the muster-roll of free Athenian citizens of an age fit for military duty never exceeded thirty thousand, and at this epoch probably did not amount to two-thirds of that number. Moreover, the poorer portion of these were unprovided with the equipments, and untrained to the operations of the regular infantry. Some detachments of the best-armed troops would be required to garrison the city itself, and man the various fortified posts in the territory; so that it is impossible to reckon the fully equipped force that marched from Athens to Marathon, when the news of the Persian landing arrived, at higher than ten thousand men.

With one exception, the other Greeks held back from aiding them. Sparta had promised assistance; but the Persians had landed on the sixth day of the moon, and a religious scruple delayed the march of Spartan troops till the moon should have reached its full. From one quarter only, and that a most unexpected one, did Athens receive aid at the moment of her great peril.

For some years before this time, the little state of Platæa in Bœotia, being hard pressed by her powerful neighbour, Thebes, had asked the protection of Athens, and had owed to an Athenian army the rescue of her independence. Now when it was noised over Greece that the Mede had come from the uttermost parts of the earth to destroy Athens, the brave Platæans, unsolicited, marched with their whole force to assist in the defence, and to share the fortunes of their benefactors. The general levy of the Platæans only amounted to a thousand men; and this little column, marching from their city along the southern ridge of Mount Cithæron, and thence across the Attic territory, joined the Athenian forces above Marathon almost immediately before the battle. The reinforcement was numerically small; but the gallant spirit of the men who composed it must have made it of tenfold value to the Athenians: and its presence must have gone far to dispel the cheerless feeling of being deserted and friendless, which the delay of the Spartan succours was calculated to create among the Athenian ranks.

This generous daring of their weak, but true-hearted ally was never forgotten at Athens. The Platæans were made the fellow-countrymen of the Athenians, except the right of exercising certain political functions; and from that time forth in the solemn sacrifices at Athens, the public prayers were offered up for a joint blessing from Heaven upon the Athenians, and the Platæans also.

II

After the junction of the column from Platæa, the Athenian commanders must have had under them about eleven thousand full-armed and disciplined infantry, and probably a larger number of irregular light-armed troops; as, besides the poorer citizens who went to the field armed with javelins, cutlasses, and targets, each regular heavy-armed soldier was attended in the camp by one or more slaves, who were armed like the inferior freemen. Cavalry or archers the Athenians (on this occasion) had none: and the use in the field of military engines was not at that period introduced into ancient warfare.

Contrasted with their own scanty forces, the Greek commanders saw stretched before them, along the shores of the winding bay, the tents and shipping of the varied nations, that marched to do the bidding of the king of the eastern world. The difficulty of finding transports and of securing provisions would form the only limit to the numbers of a Persian army. Nor is there any reason to suppose the estimate of Justin exaggerated, who rates at a hundred thousand the force, which on this occasion had sailed, under the satraps Datis and Artaphernes, from the Cilician (southeastern Asia Minor) shores, against the devoted coasts of Eubœa and Attica. And after largely deducting from this total, so as to allow for mere mariners and camp followers, there must still have remained fearful odds against the national levies of the Athenians.

Nor could Greek generals then feel that confidence in the superior quality of their troops, which ever since the battle of Marathon has animated Europeans in conflicts with Asiatics; as, for instance, in the after struggles between Greece and Persia, or when the Roman legions encountered the myriads of Mithridates and Tigranes, or as is the case in the Indian campaigns of our own (British) regiments. On the contrary, up to the day of Marathon the Medes and Persians were reputed invincible. They had more than once met Greek troops in Asia Minor, in Cyprus, in Egypt, and had invariably beaten them.

Nothing can be stronger than the expressions used by the early Greek writers respecting the terror which the name of the Medes inspired, and the prostration of men's spirits before the apparently resistless career of the Persian arms. It is, therefore, little to be wondered at, that five of the ten Athenian generals shrank from the prospect of fighting a pitched battle against an enemy so superior in numbers and so formidable in military renown. Their own position on the heights was strong, and offered great advantages to a small defending force against assailing masses. They deemed it mere foolhardiness to descend into the plain to be trampled down by the Asiatic horse, overwhelmed with the archery, or cut to pieces by the invincible veterans of Cambyses and Cyrus (Kings

of Persia, predecessors of Darius). Moreover, Sparta, the great
war-state of Greece, had been applied to, and had promised
succor to Athens, though the religious observance which the
Dorians paid to certain times and seasons had for the present
delayed their march. Was it not wise, at any rate, to wait till
the Spartans came up, and to have the help of the best troops
in Greece before they exposed themselves to the shock of the
dreaded Medes?

Specious as these reasons might appear, the other five generals
were for speedier and bolder operations. And, fortunately for
Athens and for the world, one of them was a man, not only
of the highest military genius, but also of that energetic character
which impresses its own type and ideas upon spirits feebler in
conception.

III

Miltiades was the head of one of the noblest houses at
Athens: he ranked the Æacidæ (in Greek mythology, descendants
of the Myrmidons, ants changed into men by Zeus) among his
ancestry, and the blood of Achilles flowed in the veins of the
hero of Marathon. One of his immediate ancestors had acquired
the dominion of the Thracian Chersonese (the present peninsula of the Dardanelles or Gallipoli), and thus the family became at the same time Athenian citizens and Thracian princes.
This occurred at the time when Pisistratus was tyrant of Athens.
Two of the relatives of Miltiades—an uncle of the same name,
and a brother named Stesagoras—had ruled the Chersonese before Miltiades became its prince. He had been brought up at
Athens in the house of his father Cimon, who was renowned
throughout Greece for his victories in the Olympic chariot-
races, and who must have been possessed of great wealth. The
sons of Pisistratus, who succeeded their father in the tyranny
at Athens, caused Cimon to be assassinated, but they treated the
young Miltiades with favour and kindness; and when his
brother Stesagoras died in the Chersonese they sent him out
there as lord of the principality.

This was about twenty-eight years before the battle of
Marathon, and it is with his arrival in the Chersonese that our
first knowledge of the career and character of Miltiades commences. We find, in the first act recorded of him, proof of
the same resolute and unscrupulous spirit that marked his

mature age. His brother's authority in the principality had
been shaken by war and revolt; Miltiades determined to rule
more securely. On his arrival he kept close within his house,
as if he was mourning for his brother. The principal men of
the Chersonese, hearing of this, assembled from all the towns
and districts, and went together to the house of Miltiades on a
visit of condolence. As soon as he had thus got them in his
power, he made them all prisoners. He then asserted and
maintained his own absolute authority in the peninsula, taking
into his pay a body of five hundred regular troops, and
strengthening his interest by marrying the daughter of the king
of the neighbouring Thracians.

When the Persian power was extended to the Hellespont
and its neighbourhood, Miltiades, as prince of the Chersonese,
submitted to King Darius; and he was one of the numerous
tributary rulers, who led their contingents of men to serve in
the Persian army in the expedition against Scythia. Miltiades
and the vassal Greeks of Asia Minor were left by the Persian
king in charge of the bridge across the Danube, when the invading army crossed that river, and plunged into the wilds
of the country that now is Russia in vain pursuit of the ancestors of the modern Cossacks.

On learning the reverses that Darius met with in the
Scythian wilderness, Miltiades proposed to his companions that
they should break the bridge down, and leave the Persian king
and his army to perish by famine and the Scythian arrows. The
rulers of the Asiatic Greek cities whom Miltiades addressed,
shrank from this bold and ruthless stroke against the Persian
power, and Darius returned in safety. But it was known what
advice Miltiades had given; and the vengeance of Darius was
thenceforth specially directed against the man who had counselled such a deadly blow against his empire and his person.

The occupation of the Persian arms in other quarters left
Miltiades for some years after this in possession of the Chersonese; but it was precarious and interrupted. He, however,
availed himself of the opportunity which his position gave him
of conciliating the goodwill of his fellow-countrymen at Athens,
by conquering and placing under Athenian authority the islands
of Lemnos and Imbros, to which Athens had ancient claims,
but which she had never previously been able to bring into
complete subjection. At length, in 494 B.C., the complete sup-

pression of the Ionian revolt by the Persians left their armies and fleets at liberty to act against the enemies of the Great King to the west of the Hellespont. A strong squadron of Phœnician galleys was sent against the Chersonese.

Miltiades knew that resistance was hopeless; and while the Phœnicians were at Tenedos, he loaded five galleys with all the treasure that he could collect and sailed away for Athens. The Phœnicians (from the coast of ancient Syria) fell in with him, and chased him hard along the north of the Ægean. One of his galleys, on board of which was his eldest son, Metiochus, was actually captured; but Miltiades, with the other four, succeeded in reaching the friendly coast of Imbros in safety. Thence he afterwards proceeded to Athens, and resumed his station as a free citizen of the Athenian commonwealth.

The Athenians at this time had recently expelled Hippias, the son of Pisistratus, the last of their tyrants. They were in the full glow of their newly-recovered liberty and equality; and the constitutional changes of Cleisthenes had inflamed their republican zeal to the utmost. Miltiades had enemies at Athens; and these, availing themselves of the state of popular feeling, brought him to trial for his life for having been tyrant of the Chersonese. The charge did not necessarily import any acts of cruelty or wrong to individuals; it was founded on no specific law, but it was based on the horror with which the Greeks of that age regarded every man who made himself compulsory master of his fellow-men, and exercised irresponsible dominion over them. The fact of Miltiades having so ruled in the Chersonese was undeniable; but the question which the Athenians, assembled in judgment, must have tried, was, whether Miltiades, by becoming tyrant of the Chersonese, deserved punishment as an Athenian citizen. The eminent service that he had done the state in conquering Lemnos and Imbros for it, pleaded strongly in his favour. The people refused to convict him. He stood high in public opinion; and when the coming invasion of the Persians was known the people wisely elected him one of their generals for the year.

IV

Two other men of signal eminence in history, though their renown was achieved at a later period than that of Miltiades, were also among the ten Athenian generals at Marathon. One

was Themistocles, the future founder of the Athenian navy and
the destined victor of Salamis (over the fleet of Xerxes, 480
B.C., ten years after Marathon); the other was Aristides, who
afterwards led the Athenian troops at Platæa, and whose integrity and just popularity acquired for his country, when the
Persians had finally been repulsed, the advantageous pre-eminence of being acknowledged by half of the Greeks as their
impartial leader and protector.

It is not recorded what part either Themistocles or Aristides
took in the debate of the council of war at Marathon. But from
the character of Themistocles, his boldness, and his intuitive
genius for extemporising the best measures in every emergency
(a quality which the greatest of historians ascribes to him beyond all his contemporaries), we may well believe that the vote
of Themistocles was for prompt and decisive action. On the
vote of Aristides it may be more difficult to speculate. His
predilection for the Spartans may have made him wish to wait
till they came up; but, though circumspect, he was neither
timid as a soldier nor as a politician; and the bold advice of
Miltiades may probably have found in Aristides a willing, and
most assuredly a candid hearer.

Miltiades felt no hesitation as to the course which the Athenian army ought to pursue: and earnestly did he press his opinion
on his brother-generals. Practically acquainted with the organization of the Persian armies, Miltiades was convinced of
the superiority of the Greek troops, if properly handled; he saw
with the military eye of a great general the advantage which
the position of the forces gave him for a sudden attack, and as
a profound politician he felt the perils of remaining inactive,
and of giving treachery time to ruin the Athenian cause.

One officer in the council of war had not yet voted. This
was Callimachus, the War-Ruler. The votes of the generals
were five and five, so that the voice of Callimachus would be
decisive.

On that vote, in all human probability, the destiny of all the
nations of the world depended. Miltiades turned to him, and in
simple soldierly eloquence, the substance of which we may read
faithfully reported in Herodotus, who had conversed with the
veterans of Marathon, the great Athenian thus adjured his
countryman to vote for giving battle:—

"It now rests with you, Callimachus, either to enslave Athens, or, by assuring her freedom, to win yourself an immortality of fame, such as not even Harmodius and Aristogeiton have acquired. For never, since the Athenians were a people, were they in such danger as they are in at this moment. If they bow the knee to these Medes, they are to be given up to Hippias, and you know what they then will have to suffer. But if Athens comes victorious out of this contest, she has it in her to become the first city of Greece. Your vote is to decide whether we are to join battle or not. If we do not bring on a battle presently, some factious intrigue will disunite the Athenians, and the city will be betrayed to the Medes. But if we fight, before there is anything rotten in the state of Athens, I believe that, provided the gods will give fair play and no favour, we are able to get the best of it in the engagement."

The vote of the brave War-Ruler was gained; the council determined to give battle; and such was the ascendancy and military eminence of Miltiades, that his brother-generals, one and all, gave up their days of command to him, and cheerfully acted under his orders. Fearful, however, of creating any jealousy, and of so failing to obtain the co-operation of all parts of his small army, Miltiades waited till the day when the chief command would have come round to him in regular rotation before he led the troops against the enemy.

The inaction of the Asiatic commanders, during this interval, appears strange at first sight; but Hippias was with them, and they and he were aware of their chance of a bloodless conquest through the machinations of his partisans among the Athenians. The nature of the ground also explains, in many points, the tactics of the opposite generals before the battle, as well as the operations of the troops during the engagement.

V

The plain of Marathon, which is about twenty-two miles distant from Athens, lies along the bay of the same name on the north-eastern coast of Attica. The plain is nearly in the form of a crescent, and about six miles in length. It is about two miles broad in the centre, where the space between the mountains and the sea is greatest, but it narrows towards either extremity, the mountains coming close down to the water at the horns of the bay. There is a valley trending inwards from the middle of the plain, and a ravine comes down to it to the southward. Elsewhere it is closely girt round on the land side by rugged limestone mountains, which are thickly studded with pines, olive-trees, and cedars, and overgrown with the myrtle,* arbutus, and the other low odoriferous shrubs that everywhere perfume the Attic air. The level of the ground is now varied by the mound raised over those who fell in the battle, but it was an unbroken plain when the Persians encamped on it. There are marshes at each end, which are dry in spring and summer, and then offer no obstruction to the horseman, but are commonly flooded with rain and so rendered impracticable for cavalry in the autumn, the time of year at which the action took place.

The Greeks, lying encamped on the mountains, could watch every movement of the Persians on the plain below, while they were enabled completely to mask their own. Miltiades also had, from his position, the power of giving battle whenever he pleased, or of delaying it at his discretion, unless Datis were to attempt the perilous operation of storming the heights.

VI

If we turn to the map of the old world, to test the comparative territorial resources of the two states whose armies were now about to come into conflict, the immense preponderance of the material power of the Persian king over that of the Athenian republic, is more striking than any similar contrast which history can supply. It has been truly remarked, that, in estimating mere areas, Attica, containing on its whole surface only seven hundred square miles, shrinks into insignificance if compared with many a baronial fief of the middle ages, or many a colonial allotment of modern times. Its antagonist, the Persian empire, comprised the whole of modern Asiatic and much of modern European Turkey, the modern kingdom of Persia, and the countries of modern Georgia, Armenia, Balkh, the Punjab, Afghanistan, Baluchistan, Egypt, and Tripoli.

Nor could a European, in the beginning of the fifth century before our era, look upon this huge accumulation of power beneath the sceptre of a single Asiatic ruler, with the indifference with which we now observe on the map the extensive dominions of modern Oriental sovereigns. For, as has been already remarked, before Marathon was fought, the prestige of success and of supposed superiority of race was on the side of the Asiatic against the European.

Asia was the original seat of human societies; and long before any trace can be found of the inhabitants of the rest of the world having emerged from the rudest barbarism, we can perceive that mighty and brilliant empires flourished in the Asiatic continent. They appear before us through the twilight of primeval history, dim and indistinct, but massive and majestic, like mountains in the early dawn.

Instead, however, of the infinite variety and restless change, which have characterised the institutions and fortunes of European states ever since the commencement of the civilisation of our continent, a monotonous uniformity pervades the histories of nearly all Oriental empires, from the most ancient down to the most recent times. They are characterised by the rapidity of their early conquests; by the immense extent of the dominions comprised in them; by the establishment of a satrap or pasha system of governing the provinces; by an invariable and speedy degeneracy in the princes of the royal house, the effeminate nurslings of the seraglio succeeding to the warrior-sovereigns reared in the camp; and by the internal anarchy and insurrections, which indicate and accelerate the decline and fall of these unwieldy and ill-organized fabrics of power. It is also a striking fact that the governments of all the great Asiatic empires have in all ages been absolute despotisms. And Heeren is right in connecting this with another great fact, which is important from its influence both on the political and the social life of Asiatics:

"Among all the considerable nations of inner Asia, the paternal government of every household was corrupted by polygamy: where that custom exists, a good political constitution is impossible. Fathers being converted into domestic despots, are ready to pay the same abject obedience to their sovereign which they exact from their family and dependents in their domestic economy."

We should bear in mind also the inseparable connection between the state religion and all legislation, which has always prevailed in the East, and the constant existence of a powerful sacerdotal body, exercising some check, although precarious and irregular, over the throne itself, grasping at all civil administration, claiming the supreme control of education, stereotyping the lines in which literature and science must move, and limiting the extent to which it shall be lawful for the human mind to prosecute its inquiries.

With these general characteristics rightly felt and understood, it becomes a comparatively easy task to investigate and appreciate the origin, progress, and principles of Oriental empires in general, as well as of the Persian monarchy in particular. And we are thus better enabled to appreciate the repulse which Greece gave to the arms of the East, and to judge of the probable consequences to human civilisation, if the Persians had succeeded in bringing Europe under their yoke, as they had already subjugated the fairest portions of the rest of the then known world.

The Greeks, from their geographical position, formed the natural vanguard of European liberty against Persian ambition; and they pre-eminently displayed the salient points of distinctive national character, which have rendered European civilisation so far superior to Asiatic. The nations that dwelt in ancient times around and near the northern shores of the Mediterranean sea, were the first in our continent to receive from the East the rudiments of art and literature, and the germs of social and political organisation. Of these nations, the Greeks, through their vicinity to Asia Minor, Phœnicia, and Egypt, were among the very foremost in acquiring the principles and habits of civilised life; and they also at once imparted a new and wholly original stamp on all which they received. Thus, in their religion they received from foreign settlers the names of all their deities and many of their rites, but they discarded the loathsome monstrosities of the Nile, the Orontes, and the Ganges; they nationalised their creed; and their own poets created their beautiful mythology. No sacerdotal caste ever existed in Greece.

So, in their governments they lived long under hereditary kings, but never endured the permanent establishment of absolute monarchy. Their early kings were constitutional rulers, governing with defined prerogatives. And long before the Persian invasion the kingly form of government had given way in almost all the Greek states to republican institutions, presenting infinite varieties of the balancing or the alternate predominance of the oligarchial and democratical principles.

In literature and science the Greek intellect followed no beaten track, and acknowledged no limitary rules. The Greeks thought their subjects boldly out; and the novelty of a speculation invested it in their minds with interest and not with criminality.

Versatile, restless, enterprising and self-confident, the Greeks presented the most striking contrast to the habitual quietude and submissiveness of the Orientals. And, of all the Greeks, the Athenians exhibited these national characteristics in the strongest degree. This spirit of activity and daring, joined to a generous sympathy for the fate of their fellow-Greeks in Asia, had led them to join in the last Ionian war; and now, mingling with their abhorrence of the usurping family of their own citizens, which for a period had forcibly seized on and exercised despotic power at Athens, it nerved them to defy the wrath of King Darius, and to refuse to receive back at his bidding the tyrant, whom they had some years before driven from their land.

Inscriptions in a character termed the arrow-headed, or cuneiform, had long been known to exist on the marble monuments at Persepolis, near the site of the ancient Susa, and on the faces of rocks in other places formerly ruled over by the early Persian kings. But for thousands of years they had been mere unintelligible enigmas to the curious, but baffled beholder; and they were often referred to as instances of the folly of human pride, which could indeed write its own praises in the solid rock, but only for the rock to outlive the language as well as the memory of the vainglorious inscribers.

Major Rawlinson, of the East India Company's service, after years of labour, at last accomplished the glorious achievement of fully revealing the alphabet and the grammar of this long unknown tongue. He fully deciphered and expounded the inscriptions on the sacred rock of Behistun, on the western frontiers of Media. These records of the Achæmenidæ at length found their interpreter; and Darius himself speaks to us from the consecrated mountain, and tells us the names of the nations that obeyed him, the revolts that he suppressed, his victories, his piety, and his glory.

Kings who thus seek the admiration of posterity are little likely to dim the record of their successes by the mention of their occasional defeats; and it throws no suspicion on the narrative of the Greek historians, that we find these inscriptions silent respecting the overthrow of Datis and Artaphernes, as well as respecting the reverses which Darius sustained in person during his Scythian campaigns. But these indisputable monuments of Persian fame confirm, and even increase, the opinion with which Herodotus inspires us, of the vast power which Cyrus founded and Cambyses increased; which Darius augmented by Indian and Arabian conquests and seemed likely, when he directed his arms against Europe, to become the predominant monarchy of the world.

With the exception of the Chinese empire, in which, throughout all ages down to the last (relatively) few years, one-third of the human race dwelt almost unconnected with the other portions, all the great kingdoms, which we know to have existed in ancient Asia, were, in Darius's time, blended with the Persian. The northern Indians, the Assyrians, the Syrians, the Babylonians, the Chaldees, the Phœnicians, the nations of Palestine, the Armenians, the Bactrians, the Lydians, the Phrygians, the Parthians, and the Medes,—all obeyed the sceptre of the Great King: the Medes standing next to the native Persians in honour, and the empire being frequently spoken of as that of the Medes, or as that of the Medes and Persians.

Egypt and Cyrene were Persian provinces; the Greek colonists in Asia Minor and the islands of the Ægean were Darius's subjects; and their gallant, but unsuccessful attempts to throw off the Persian yoke had only served to rivet it more strongly and to increase the general belief that the Greeks could not stand before the Persians in a field of battle. Darius's Scythian war, although unsuccessful in its immediate object, had brought about the subjugation of Thrace and the submission of Macedonia. From the Indus to the Peneus, (a river in Thessaly) all was his.

VII

We may imagine the wrath with which the lord of so many nations must have heard, nine years before the battle of Marathon, that a strange nation towards the setting sun, called the Athenians, had dared to help his rebels in Ionia against him, and that they had plundered and burnt the capital of one of his provinces. Before the burning of Sardis,

Darius seems never to have heard of the existence of **Athens**; but his satraps in Asia Minor had for some time seen **Athenian** refugees at their provincial courts imploring assistance against their fellow-countrymen.

When Hippias was driven away from Athens, and the tyrannic dynasty of the Pisistratidæ finally overthrown in 510 B.C., the banished tyrant and his adherents, after vainly seeking to be restored by Spartan intervention, had betaken themselves to Sardis, the capital city of the satrapy of Artaphernes. There Hippias (in the expressive words of Herodotus) began every kind of agitation, slandering the Athenians before Artaphernes, and doing all he could to induce the satrap to place Athens in subjection to him, as the tributary vassal of King Darius. When the Athenians heard of his practices, they sent envoys to Sardis to remonstrate with the Persians against taking up the quarrel of the Athenian refugees. But Artaphernes gave them in reply a menacing command to receive Hippias back again if they looked for safety. The Athenians were resolved not to purchase safety at such a price; and after rejecting the satrap's terms, they considered that they and the Persians were declared enemies. At this very crisis the Ionian Greeks implored the assistance of their European brethren, to enable them to recover their independence from Persia. Athens, and the city of Eretria in Eubœa alone consented.

Twenty Athenian galleys, and five Eretrian, crossed the Ægean Sea; and by a bold and sudden march upon Sardis the Athenians and their allies succeeded in capturing the capital city of the haughty satrap, who had recently menaced them with servitude or destruction. The Persian forces were soon rallied, and the Greeks were compelled to retire. They were pursued, and defeated on their return to the coast, and Athens took no further part in the Ionian war. But the insult that she had put upon the Persian power was speedily made known throughout that empire, and was never to be forgiven or forgotten. In the emphatic simplicity of the narrative of Herodotus, the wrath of the Great King is thus described:

"Now when it was told to King Darius that Sardis had been taken and burnt by the Athenians and Ionians, he took small heed of the Ionians, well knowing who they were, and that their revolt would soon be put down; but he asked who, and what manner of men, the Athenians were. And when he had been told, he called for his bow; and, having taken it, and placed an arrow on the string, he let the arrow fly towards heaven; and as he shot it into the air, he said, 'O Supreme God! grant me that I may avenge myself on the Athenians.' And when he had said this, he appointed one of his servants to say to him every day as he sat at meat, 'Sire, remember the Athenians.'"

Some years were occupied in the complete reduction of Ionia. But when this was effected, Darius ordered his victorious forces to proceed to punish Athens and Eretria, and to conquer European Greece. The first armament sent for this purpose was shattered by shipwreck, and nearly destroyed off Mount Athos. But the purpose of King Darius was not easily shaken. A large army was ordered to be collected in Cilicia; and requisitions were sent to all the maritime cities of the Persian empire for ships of war, and for transports of sufficient size for carrying cavalry as well as infantry across the Ægean.

While these preparations were being made, Darius sent heralds round to the Grecian cities demanding their submission to Persia. It was proclaimed in the market-place of each little Hellenic state (some with territories not larger than the Isle of Wight), that King Darius, the lord of all men, from the rising to the setting sun, required earth and water to be delivered to his heralds, as a symbolical acknowledgment that he was head and master of the country.

Terror-stricken at the power of Persia and at the severe punishment that had recently been inflicted on the refractory Ionians, many of the continental Greeks and nearly all the islanders submitted, and gave the required tokens of vassalage. At Sparta and Athens an indignant refusal was returned, a refusal which was disgraced by outrage and violence against the persons of the Asiatic heralds.

VIII

Fresh fuel was thus added to the anger of Darius against Athens, and the Persian preparations went on with renewed vigour. In the summer of 490 B.C., the army destined for the invasion was assembled in the Aleian plain of Cilicia, near the sea. A fleet of six hundred galleys and numerous transports was collected on the coast for the embarkation of troops, horse as well as foot. A Median general named Datis and Artaphernes, the son of the satrap of Sardis, and who was also nephew of Darius, were placed in titular joint command of the expedition.

That the real supreme authority was given to Datis alone is probable, from the way in which the Greek writers speak of him. We know no details of the previous career of this officer; but there is every reason to believe that his abilities and bravery had been proved by experience, or his Median birth would have prevented his being placed in high command by Darius. He appears to have been the first Mede who was thus trusted by the Persian kings after the overthrow of the conspiracy of the Median Magi against the Persians immediately before Darius obtained the throne. Datis received instructions to complete the subjugation of Greece, and especial orders were given him with regard to Eretria and Athens. He was to take these two cities; and he was to lead the inhabitants away captive, and bring them as slaves into the presence of the Great King.

Datis embarked his forces in the fleet that awaited them; and coasting along the shores of Asia Minor till he was off Samos, he thence sailed due westward through the Ægean Sea for Greece, taking the islands in his way. The Naxians had, ten years before, successfully stood a siege against a Persian armament, but they now were too terrified to offer any resistance, and fled to the mountain-tops, while the enemy burnt their town and laid waste their lands. Thence Datis, compelling the Greek islanders to join him with their ships and men, sailed onward to the coast of Eubœa. The little town of Carystus essayed resistance, but was quickly overpowered. He next attacked Eretria.

The Athenians sent four thousand men to its aid. But treachery was at work among the Eretrians; and the Athenian force received timely warning from one of the leading men of the city to retire to aid in saving their own country, instead of remaining to share in the inevitable destruction of Eretria. Left to themselves, the Eretrians repulsed the assaults of the Persians against their walls for six days; on the seventh day they were betrayed by two of their chiefs, and the Persians occupied the city. The temples were burnt in revenge for the burning of Sardis, and the inhabitants were bound and placed as prisoners in the neighboring islet of Ægylia, to wait there till Datis should bring the Athenians to join them in captivity, when both populations were to be led into Upper Asia, there to learn their doom from the lips of King Darius himself.

Flushed with success, and with half his mission thus accomplished, Datis re-embarked his troops, and crossing the little channel that separates Eubœa from the mainland, he encamped his troops on the Attic coast at Marathon, drawing up his galleys on the shelving beach, as was the custom with the navies of antiquity. The conquered islands behind him served as places of deposit for his provisions and military stores. His position at Marathon seemed to him in every respect advantageous and the level nature of the ground on which he camped was favourable for the employment of his cavalry, if the Athenians should venture to engage him.

Hippias, who accompanied him, and acted as the guide of the invaders, had pointed out Marathon as the best place for a landing, for this very reason. Probably Hippias was also influenced by the recollection that forty-seven years previously he, with his father Pisistratus, had crossed with an army from Eretria to Marathon, and had won an easy victory over their Athenian enemies on that very plain, which had restored them to tyrannic power. The omen seemed cheering. The place was the same; but Hippias soon learned to his cost how great a change had come over the spirit of the Athenians.

But though "the fierce democracy" of Athens was zealous and true against foreign invader and domestic tyrant, a faction existed in Athens, as at Eretria, of men willing to purchase a party-triumph over their fellow-citizens at the price of their country's ruin. Communications were opened between these men and the Persian camp, which would have led to a catastrophe like that of Eretria if Miltiades had not resolved, and had not persuaded his colleagues to resolve, on fighting at all hazards.

IX

When Miltiades arrayed his men for action, he staked on the arbitrament of one battle not only the fate of Athens, but that of all Greece; for if Athens had fallen, no other Greek state, except Lacedæmon, would have had the courage to resist; and the Lacedæmonians (Spartans), though they would

probably have died in their ranks to the last man, never could
have successfully resisted the victorious Persians, and the numerous Greek troops, which would have soon marched under the
Persian satraps, had they prevailed over Athens.

Nor was there any power to the westward of Greece that
could have offered an effectual opposition to Persia, had she
once conquered Greece, and made that country a basis for
future military operations. Rome was. at this time in her
season of utmost weakness. Her dynasty of powerful Etrus-
can kings had been driven out, and her infant commonwealth
was reeling under the attacks of the Etruscans and Volscians
from without, and the fierce dissensions between the patricians
and plebeians within. Etruria, with her Lucumos and serfs,
was no match for Persia. Samnium (in central Italy) had not
grown into the might which she afterwards put forth: nor
could the Greek colonies in South Italy and Sicily hope to
survive when their parent states had perished. Carthage had
escaped the Persian yoke in the time of Cambyses, through the
reluctance of the Phœnician mariners to serve against their
kinsmen. But such forbearance could not long have been relied
on, and the future rival of Rome would have become as submissive a minister of the Persian power as were the Phœnician cities themselves.

If we turn to Spain, or if we pass the great mountain-chain,
which prolonged through the Pyrenees, the Cevennes, the Alps,
and the Balkan, divides northern from southern Europe, we
shall find nothing at that period but mere savage Finns, Celts,
Slavs and Teutons. Had Persia beaten Athens at Marathon,
she could have found no obstacle to prevent Darius, the chosen
servant of Ormuzd, from advancing his sway over all the known
Western races of mankind. The infant energies of Europe
would have been trodden out beneath universal conquest; and
the history of the world, like the history of Asia, would have
become a mere record of the rise and fall of despotic dynasties,
of the incursions of barbarous hordes, and of the mental and
political prostration of millions beneath the diadem, the tiara
and the sword.

Great as the preponderance of the Persian over the Athenian
power at that crisis seems to have been, it would be unjust
to impute wild rashness to the policy of Miltiades, and those
who voted with him in the Athenian council of war, or to

look on the after-current of events as the mere result of successful indiscretion. As before has been remarked, Miltiades, whilst prince of the Chersonese, had seen service in the Persian armies and he knew by personal observation how many elements of weakness lurked beneath their imposing aspect of strength. He knew that the bulk of their troops no longer consisted of the hardy shepherds and mountaineers from Persia proper and Kurdistan, who won Cyrus's battles, but that unwilling contingents from conquered nations now largely filled up the Persian muster-rolls, fighting more from compulsion than from any zeal in the cause of their masters. He had also the sagacity and the spirit to appreciate the superiority of the Greek armour and organization over the Asiatic, notwithstanding former reverses. Above all, he felt and worthily trusted the enthusiasm of the men under his command.

The Athenians, whom he led, had proved by their newborn valour in recent wars against the neighbouring states, that "Liberty and Equality of civic rights are brave spirit-stirring things: and they who, while under the yoke of a despot, had been no better men of war than any of their neighbours, as soon as they were free, became the foremost men of all; for each felt that in fighting for a free commonwealth, he fought for himself and whatever he took in hand, he was zealous to do the work thoroughly."

So the nearly contemporaneous historian (Herodotus) describes the change of spirit that was seen in the Athenians after their tyrants were expelled; and Miltiades knew that in leading them against the invading army, where they had Hippias, the foe they most hated, before them, he was bringing into battle no ordinary men, and could calculate on no ordinary heroism. As for traitors, he was sure, that whatever treachery might lurk among some of the higher-born and wealthier Athenians, the rank and file whom he commanded were ready to do their utmost in his and their own cause. With regard to future attacks from Asia, he might easily hope that one victory would inspire all Greece to combine against the common foe; and that the latent seeds of revolt and disunion in the Persian empire would soon burst forth and paralyse its energies, so as to leave Greek independence secure.

X

With these hopes and risks, Miltiades, on the afternoon of a September day, 490 B.C., gave the word for the Athenian army to prepare for battle. There were many local associations connected with those mountain heights, which were calculated powerfully to excite the spirits of the men, and of which the commanders well knew how to avail themselves in their exhortations to their troops before the encounter.

Marathon itself was a region sacred to Hercules. Close to them was the fountain of Macaria, who had in days of yore devoted herself to death for the liberty of her people. The very plain on which they were to fight was the scene of the exploits of their national hero, Theseus; and there, too, as old legends told, the Athenians and the Heraclidæ had routed the invader, Eurystheus. These traditions were not mere cloudy myths, or idle fictions, but matters of implicit, earnest faith to the men of that day; and many a fervent prayer arose from the Athenian ranks to the heroic spirits, who while on earth had striven and suffered on that very spot, and who were believed to be now heavenly powers, looking down with interest on their still beloved country, and capable of interposing with superhuman aid in its behalf.

According to old national custom, the warriors of each tribe were arrayed together; neighbour thus fighting by the side of neighbour, friend by friend, and the spirit of emulation and the consciousness of responsibility excited to the very utmost. The War-Ruler, Callimachus, had the leading of the right wing; the Platæans formed the extreme left; and Themistocles and Aristides commanded the centre. The line consisted of the heavy-armed spearmen only. For the Greeks (until the time of Iphicrates) took little or no account of light-armed soldiers in a pitched battle, using them only in skirmishes or for the pursuit of a defeated enemy. The panoply of the regular infantry consisted of a long spear, of a shield, helmet, breast-plate, greaves, and short sword. Thus equipped, they usually advanced slowly and steadily into action in a uniform phalanx of about eight spears deep.

But the military genius of Miltiades led him to deviate on this occasion from the commonplace tactics of his countrymen. It was essential for him to extend his line so as to cover all the practicable ground, and to secure himself from being outflanked and charged in the rear by the Persian horse. This extension involved the weakening of his line. Instead of a uniform reduction of its strength, he determined on detaching principally from his centre, which, from the nature of the ground, would have the best opportunities for rallying if broken; and on strengthening his wings, so as to insure advantage at those points; and he trusted to his own skill, and to his soldiers' discipline, for the improvement of that advantage into decisive victory. It is remarkable that there is no other instance of a Greek general deviating from the ordinary mode of bringing a phalanx of spearmen into action, until the battles of Leuctra and Mantinea, more than a century after Marathon, when Epaminondas introduced the tactics (which Alexander the Great in ancient times, and Frederick the Great in modern times, made so famous) of concentrating an overpowering force on some decisive point of the enemy's line, while he kept back, or, in military phrase, refused the weaker part of his own.

In this order, and availing himself probably of the inequalities of the ground, so as to conceal his preparations from the enemy till the last possible moment, Miltiades drew up the eleven thousand infantry, whose spears were to decide this crisis in the struggle between the European and the Asiatic worlds. The sacrifices, by which the favour of Heaven was sought, and its will consulted, were announced to show propitious omens.

The trumpet sounded for action, and, chanting the hymn of battle, the little army bore down upon the host of the foe. Then, too, along the mountain slopes of Marathon must have resounded the mutual exhortation which Æschylus, who fought in both battles, tells us was afterwards heard over the waves of Salamis: "On, sons of the Greeks! Strike for the freedom of your country! Strike for the freedom of your children and of your wives—for the shrines of your fathers' gods, and for the sepulchres of your sires! All—all are now staked upon the strife!"

Instead of advancing at the usual slow pace of the phalanx, Miltiades brought his men on at a run. They were all trained in the exercises of the palæstra, (wrestling school gymnasium), so that there was no fear of their ending the charge in breath-

less exhaustion: and it was of the deepest importance for him
to traverse as rapidly as possible the space of about a mile of
level ground, that lay between the mountain foot and the
Persian outposts, and so to get his troops into close action before
the Asiatic cavalry could mount, form, and manœuvre against
him, or their archers keep him long under bow-shot, and before
the enemy's generals could fairly deploy their masses.

"When the Persians," says Herodotus, "saw the Athenians
running down on them, without horse or bowmen, and scanty
in numbers, they thought them a set of madmen rushing
upon certain destruction." They began, however, to prepare
to receive them, and the Eastern chiefs arrayed, as quickly
as time and place allowed, the varied races who served in
their motley ranks.

Mountaineers from Hyrcania and Afghanistan, wild horsemen from the steppes of Khorassan, the black archers of
Ethiopia, swordsmen from the banks of the Indus, the Oxus,
the Euphrates and the Nile, made ready against the enemies
of the Great King. But no national cause inspired them, except the division of native Persians; and in the large host there
was no uniformity of language, creed, race, or military system.
Still, among them there were many gallant men, under a
veteran general; they were familiarized with victory and in
contemptuous confidence, their infantry, which alone had time
to form, awaited the Athenian charge.

On came the Greeks, with one unwavering line of levelled
spears, against which the light targets, the short lances and
scimitars of the Orientals offered weak defense. The front rank
of the Asiatics must have gone down to a man at the first
shock. Still they recoiled not, but strove by individual gallantry,
and by the weight of numbers, to make up for the disadvantages
of weapons and tactics, and to bear back the shallow line of
the Europeans.

In the centre, where the native Persians and the Sacæ fought,
they succeeded in breaking through the weaker part of the
Athenian phalanx; and the tribes led by Aristides and Themistocles were, after a brave resistance, driven back over the plain,
and chased by the Persians up the valley towards the inner
country. There the nature of the ground gave the opportunity
of rallying and renewing the struggle: and meanwhile, the
Greek wings, where Miltiades had concentrated his chief

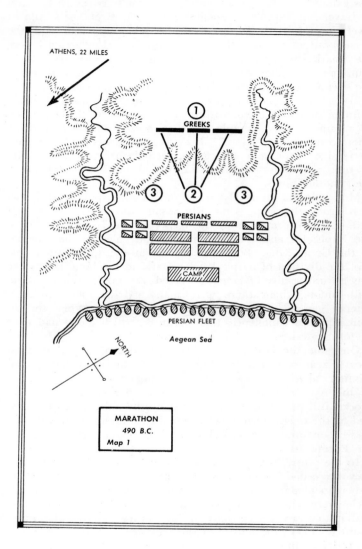

ATHENS, 22 MILES

GREEKS

PERSIANS

CAMP

PERSIAN FLEET

Aegean Sea

NORTH

MARATHON
490 B.C.
Map 1

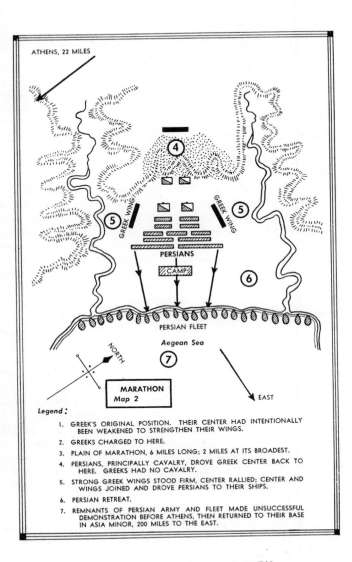

ATHENS, 22 MILES

GREEK WING

GREEK WING

PERSIANS

CAMP

PERSIAN FLEET

Aegean Sea

NORTH

MARATHON
Map 2

EAST

Legend :

1. GREEK'S ORIGINAL POSITION. THEIR CENTER HAD INTENTIONALLY BEEN WEAKENED TO STRENGTHEN THEIR WINGS.

2. GREEKS CHARGED TO HERE.

3. PLAIN OF MARATHON, 6 MILES LONG; 2 MILES AT ITS BROADEST.

4. PERSIANS, PRINCIPALLY CAVALRY, DROVE GREEK CENTER BACK TO HERE. GREEKS HAD NO CAVALRY.

5. STRONG GREEK WINGS STOOD FIRM, CENTER RALLIED; CENTER AND WINGS JOINED AND DROVE PERSIANS TO THEIR SHIPS.

6. PERSIAN RETREAT.

7. REMNANTS OF PERSIAN ARMY AND FLEET MADE UNSUCCESSFUL DEMONSTRATION BEFORE ATHENS, THEN RETURNED TO THEIR BASE IN ASIA MINOR, 200 MILES TO THE EAST.

strength, had routed the Asiatics opposed to them, and the Athenian and Platæan officers, instead of pursuing the fugitives, kept their troops well in hand, and wheeling round they formed the two wings together.

Miltiades instantly led them against the Persian centre, which had hitherto been triumphant, but which now fell back, and prepared to encounter these new and unexpected assailants. Aristides and Themistocles renewed the fight with their re-organized troops, and the full force of the Greeks was brought into close action with the Persian and Sacian divisions of the enemy. Datis's veterans strove hard to keep their ground, and evening was approaching before the stern encounter was decided.

But the Persians, with their slight wicker shields, destitute of body-armour, and never taught by training to keep the even front and act with the regular movement of the Greek infantry, fought at grievous disadvantage with their shorter and feebler weapons against the compact array of well-armed Athenian and Platæan spearmen, all perfectly drilled to perform each necessary evolution in concert and to preserve a uniform and unwavering line in battle. In personal courage and in bodily activity, the Persians were not inferior to their adversaries. Their spirits were not yet cowed by the recollection of former defeats; and they lavished their lives freely, rather than forfeit the fame which they had won by so many victories.

While their rear-ranks poured an incessant shower of arrows over the heads of their comrades, the foremost Persians kept rushing forward, sometimes singly, sometimes in desperate groups of twelve or ten upon the projecting spears of the Greeks, striving to force a lane into the phalanx, and to bring their scimitars and daggers into play. But the Greeks felt their superiority, and though the fatigue of the long-continued action told heavily on their inferior numbers, the sight of the carnage that they dealt amongst their assailants nerved them to fight still more fiercely on.

At last the previously unvanquished lords of Asia turned their backs and fled, and the Greeks followed, striking them down, to the water's edge, where the invaders were now hastily launching their galleys, and seeking to embark and fly. Flushed with success, the Athenians dashed at the fleet.

"Bring fire, bring fire," was their cry, and they began to lay hold of the ships. But here the Asiatics resisted desperately, and the principal loss sustained by the Greeks was in the assault on the fleet. Here fell the brave War Ruler Callimachus, the general Stesilaus, and other Athenians of note. Conspicuous among them was Cynægeirus, the brother of the tragic poet Æschylus. He had grasped the ornamental work on the stern of one of the galleys, and had his hand struck off by an axe.

Seven galleys were captured, but the Persians succeeded in saving the rest. They pushed off from the fatal shore, but even here the skill of Datis did not desert him and he sailed round to the western coast of Attica, in hopes to find the city unprotected and to gain possession of it from some of the partisans of Hippias.

Miltiades, however, saw and counteracted his manœuvre. Leaving Aristides, and the troops of his tribe, to guard the spoil and the slain, the Athenian commander led his conquering army by a rapid night-march back across the country to Athens. And when the Persian fleet had doubled the Cape of Sunium and sailed up to the Athenian harbour in the morning, Datis saw arrayed on the heights above the city the troops, before whom his men had fled on the preceding evening. All hope of further conquest in Europe for the time was abandoned, and the baffled armada returned to the Asiatic coasts.

After the battle had been fought, but while the dead bodies were yet on the ground, the promised reinforcement from Sparta arrived. Two thousand Lacedæmonian spearmen, starting immediately after the full moon, had marched the hundred and fifty miles between Athens and Sparta in the wonderfully short time of three days. Though too late to share in the glory of the action, they requested to be allowed to march to the battle-field to behold the Medes. They proceeded thither, gazed on the dead bodies of the invaders; and then, praising the Athenians and what they had done, they returned to Lacedæmon.

The number of the Persian dead was six thousand four hundred; of the Athenians, a hundred and ninety-two. The number of Platæans who fell is not mentioned, but as they fought in the part of the army which was not broken, it cannot have been large.

The apparent disproportion between the losses of the two

armies is not surprising, when we remember the armour of
the Greek spearmen, and the impossibility of heavy slaughter
being inflicted by sword or lance on troops so armed, so long
as they kept firm in their ranks.

XI

The Athenian slain were buried on the field of battle.
This was contrary to the usual custom, according to which
the bones of all who fell fighting for their country in each
year were deposited in a public sepulchre in the suburb of
Athens called the Cerameicus. But it was felt that a distinction ought to be made in the funeral honours paid to
the men of Marathon, even as their merit had been distinguished over that of all other Athenians. A lofty mound
was raised on the plain of Marathon, beneath which the
remains of the men of Athens who fell in the battle were
deposited. Ten columns were erected on the spot, one for
each of the Athenian tribes; and on the monumental column
of each tribe were graven the names of those of its members
whose glory it was to have fallen in the great battle of
liberation. The antiquarian Pausanias read those names there
six hundred years after the time when they were first graven.
The columns have long perished, but the mound still marks
the spot where the noblest heroes of antiquity repose.

A separate tumulus was raised over the bodies of the slain
Platæans, and another over the light-armed slaves who had
taken part and had fallen in the battle. It is probable that the
Greek light-armed irregulars were active in the attack on the
Persian ships, and it was in this attack that the Greeks suffered
their principal loss. There was also a distinct sepulchral monument to the general to whose genius the victory was mainly due.

XII

Miltiades did not live long after his achievement at Marathon, but he lived long enough to experience a lamentable
reverse of his popularity and good fortune. As soon as the
Persians had quitted the western coast of the Ægean, he proposed
to an assembly of the Athenian people that they should fit out
seventy galleys, with a proportionate force of soldiers and military stores, and place them at his disposal; not telling them

whither he meant to proceed, but promising them that if they would equip the force he asked for, and give him discretionary powers, he would lead it to a land where there was gold in abundance to be won with ease. The Greeks of that time believed in the existence of Eastern realms teeming with gold, as firmly as the Europeans of the sixteenth century believed in Eldorado of the West. The Athenians probably thought that the recent victor of Marathon, and former officer of Darius, was about to guide them on a secret expedition against some wealthy and unprotected 'cities of treasure in the Persian dominions.

The armament was voted and equipped, and sailed eastward from Attica, no one but Miltiades knowing its destination, until the Greek isle of Paros was reached, when his true object appeared. In former years, while connected with the Persians as prince of the Chersonese, Miltiades had been involved in a quarrel with one of the leading men among the Parians, who had injured his credit and caused some slights to be put upon him at the court of the Persian satrap, Hydarnes. The feud had ever since rankled in the heart of the Athenian chief, and he now attacked Paros for the sake of avenging himself on his ancient enemy. His pretext, as general of the Athenians, was, that the Parians had aided the armament of Datis with a war-galley.

The Parians pretended to treat about terms of surrender, but used the time, which they thus gained, in repairing the defective parts of the fortifications of their city; and they then set the Athenians at defiance. So far, says Herodotus, the accounts of all the Greeks agree. But the Parians, in after years, told also a wild legend, how a captive priestess of a Parian temple of the Deities of the Earth promised Miltiades to give him the means of capturing Paros; how, at her bidding, the Athenian general went alone at night and forced his way into a holy shrine, near the city gate, but with what purpose it was not known; how a supernatural awe came over him, and in his flight he fell and fractured his leg; how an oracle afterwards forbade the Parians to punish the sacrilegious and traitorous priestess, "because it was fated that Miltiades should come to an ill end, and she was only the instrument to lead him to evil." Certain it was that Miltiades either dislocated or broke his leg during an unsuccessful siege of that city, and returned home in evil plight with his baffled and defeated forces.

The indignation of the Athenians was proportionate to the hope and excitement which his promises had raised. Xanthippus, the head of one of the first families in Athens, indicted him before the supreme popular tribunal for the capital offence of having deceived the people. His guilt was undeniable, and the Athenians passed their verdict accordingly. But the recollections of Lemnos and Marathon, and the sight of the fallen general, who lay stretched on a couch before them, pleaded successfully in mitigation of punishment, and the sentence was commuted from death to a fine of fifty talents. This was paid by his son, the afterwards illustrious Cimon, Miltiades dying soon after the trial of the injury which he had received at Paros.

The melancholy end of Miltiades, after his elevation to such a height of power and glory, must often have been recalled to the mind of the ancient Greeks, by the sight of one, in particular, of the memorials of the great battle which he won. This was the remarkable statue (minutely described by Pausanias) which the Athenians, in the time of Pericles, caused to be hewn out of a huge block of marble, which, it is believed, had been provided by Datis to form a trophy of the anticipated victory of the Persians. Phidias fashioned out of this a colossal image of the goddess Nemesis, the deity whose peculiar function was to visit the exuberant prosperity both of nations and individuals with sudden and awful reverses. This statue was placed in a temple of the goddess at Rhamnus, about eight miles from Marathon.

Athens herself contained numerous memorials of her primary great victory. Panenus, the cousin of Phidias, represented it in fresco on the walls of the painted porch; and, centuries afterwards, the figures of Miltiades and Callimachus at the head of the Athenians, were conspicuous in the fresco. The tutelary deities were exhibited taking part in the fray. In the background were seen the Phœnician galleys; and nearer to the spectator, the Athenians and the Platæans (distinguished by their leathern helmets) were chasing routed Asiatics into the marshes and the sea. The battle was sculptured also on the Temple of Victory in the Acropolis; and even now there may be traced on the frieze the figures of the Persian combatants with their lunar shields, their bows and quivers, their curved scimitars, their loose trousers, and Phrygian tiaras.

These and other memorials of Marathon were the product

of the meridian age of Athenian intellectual splendour—of the age of Phidias and Pericles. For it was not merely by the generation of men whom the battle liberated from Hippias and the Medes that the transcendent importance of their victory was gratefully recognised. Through the whole epoch of her prosperity, through the long Olympiads (periods of four years between the Olympian games) of her decay, through centuries after her fall, Athens looked back on the day of Marathon as the brightest of her national existence.

By a natural blending of patriotic pride with grateful piety, the very spirits of the Athenians who fell at Marathon were deified by their countrymen. The inhabitants of the districts of Marathon paid religious rites to them; and orators solemnly invoked them in their most impassioned adjurations before the assembled men of Athens. "Nothing was omitted that could keep alive the remembrance of a deed which had first taught the Athenian people to know its own strength, by measuring it with the power which had subdued the greater part of the known world. The consciousness thus awakened fixed its character, its station, and its destiny; it was the spring of its later actions and ambitious enterprises."

It was not indeed by one defeat, however signal, that the pride of Persia could be broken, and her dreams of universal empire be dispelled. Ten years afterwards she renewed her attempts upon Europe on a grander scale of enterprise, and was repulsed by Greece with greater and reiterated loss. Larger forces and heavier slaughter than had been seen at Marathon signalised the conflicts of Greeks and Persians at Artemisium, Salamis, Platæa, and the Eurymedon.

But mighty and momentous as these battles were, they rank not with Marathon in importance. They originated no new impulse. They turned back no current of fate. They were merely confirmatory of the already existing bias which Marathon had created. The day of Marathon is the critical epoch in the history of the two nations. It broke forever the spell of Persian invincibility, which had paralysed men's minds. It generated among the Greeks the spirit which beat back Xerxes, and afterwards led on Xenophon, Agesilaus, and Alexander, in terrible retaliation, through their Asiatic campaigns. It secured for mankind the intellectual treasures of Athens, the growth of free institutions, the liberal enlightenment of the Western world, and the gradual ascendancy for many ages of the great principles of European civilisation.

SYNOPSIS OF EVENTS BETWEEN THE BATTLE OF MARATHON, 490 B.C., AND THE DEFEAT OF THE ATHENIANS AT SYRACUSE, 413 B.C.

490 to 487 B.C. All Asia is filled with the preparations made by King Darius for a new expedition against Greece. Themistocles persuades the Athenians to leave off dividing the proceeds of their silver mines among themselves, and to employ the money in strengthening their navy.

487. Egypt revolts from the Persians, and delays the expedition against Greece.

485. Darius dies, and Xerxes his son becomes King of Persia in his stead.

484. The Persians recover Egypt.

480. Xerxes invades Greece. Indecisive actions between the Persians and Greek fleets at Artemisium. Destruction of the three hundred Spartans at Thermopylæ. The Athenians abandon Attica and go on shipboard. Great naval victory of the Greeks at Salamis. Xerxes returns to Asia, leaving a chosen army under Mardonius, to carry on the war against the Greeks.

478. Mardonius and his army destroyed by the Greeks at Platæa. The Greeks land in Asia Minor, and defeat a Persian force at Mycale. In this and the following years the Persians lose all their conquests in Europe, and many on the coast of Asia.

477. Many of the Greek maritime states take Athens as their leader, instead of Sparta.

466. Victories of Cimon over the Persians at the Eurymedon.

464. Revolt of the Helots against Sparta. Third Messenian war.

460. Egypt again revolts against Persia. The Athenians send a powerful armament to aid the Egyptians, which, after gaining some successes, is destroyed, and Egypt submits. This war lasted six years.

457. Wars in Greece between the Athenian and several Peloponnesian states. Immense exertions of Athens at this time. "There is an original inscription still preserved in the Louvre, which attests the energies of Athens at this crisis, when Athens, like England in modern wars, at once sought conquests abroad, and repelled enemies at home. At the period we now advert to . (457 B.C.), an Athenian armament of two hundred galleys was engaged in a bold though unsuccessful expedition against Egypt. The Athenian crews had landed, had won a battle; they had then re-embarked and sailed up the Nile, and were busily besieging the Persian garrison in Memphis. As the complement of a trireme galley was at least two hundred men, we cannot estimate the forces then employed by Athens against Egypt at less than forty thousand men. At the same time she kept squadrons on the coasts of Phœnicia and Cyprus, and yet maintained a home-

fleet that enabled her to defeat her Peloponnesian enemies at Cecryphalæ and Ægina, capturing in the last engagement seventy galleys. This last fact may give us some idea of the strength of the Athenian home-fleet that gained the victory; and by adopting the same ratio of multiplying whatever number of galleys we suppose to have been employed, by two hundred, so as to gain the aggregate number of the crews, we may form some estimate of the forces which this little Greek state then kept on foot. Between sixty and seventy thousand men must have served in her fleets during that year. Her tenacity of purpose was equal to her boldness of enterprise. Sooner than yield or withdraw from any of their expeditions the Athenians at this very time, when Corinth sent an army to attack their garrison at Megara, did not recall a single crew or a single soldier from Ægina or from abroad; but the lads and old men, who had been left to guard the city, fought and won a battle against these new assailants. The inscription which we have referred to, is graven on a votive tablet to the memory of the dead, erected in that year by the Erecthean tribe, one of the ten into which the Athenians were divided. It shows, as Thirlwall has remarked, 'that the Athenians were conscious of the greatness of their own effort'; and in it this little civic community of the ancient world still 'records to us with emphatic simplicity, that its slain fell in Cyprus, in Egypt, in Phœnicia, at Haliæ, in Ægina, and in Megara, in the same year.' "

445. A thirty years' truce concluded between Athens and Lacedæmon.

440. The Samians endeavour to throw off the supremacy of Athens. Samos completely reduced to subjection. Pericles is now sole director of the Athenian councils.

431. Commencement of the great Peloponnesian war, in which Sparta, at the head of nearly all the Peloponnesian states, and aided by the Bœotians and some of the other Greeks beyond the Isthmus, endeavours to reduce the power of Athens, and to restore independence to the Greek maritime states who were the subject allies of Athens. At the commencement of the war the Peloponnesian armies repeatedly invade and ravage Attica, but Athens herself is impregnable, and her fleets secure her the dominion of the sea.

430. Athens visited by a pestilence, which sweeps off large numbers of her population.

425. The Athenians gain great advantages over the Spartans at Sphacteria, and by occupying Cythera; but they suffer a severe defeat in Bœotia, and the Spartan general, Brasidas, leads an expedition to the Thracian coasts and conquers many of the most valuable Athenian possessions in those regions.

421. Nominal truce for thirty years between Athens and Sparta, but hostilities continue on the Thracian coast and in other quarters.

415. The Athenians send an expedition to conquer Sicily.

◄[TWO]►

The Athenian Defeat at Syracuse, Sicily, 413 B. C.

WHY DECISIVE: *"The Romans knew not, and could not know, how deeply the greatness of their own posterity, and the fate of the whole western world, were involved in the destruction of the fleet of Athens, in the harbor of Syracuse. Had [the Greeks] proved victorious the energies of Greece during the next eventful century would have found their field in the west no less than in the east; Greece and not Rome might have conquered Carthage; Greek instead of Latin might have been at this day the principal element of the language of Spain, of France and of Italy; and the laws of Athens, rather than those of Rome, might be the foundation of the law of the civilized world."* [Thomas Arnold.]

I

FEW cities have undergone more memorable sieges during ancient and mediæval times, than has the city of Syracuse. Athenian, Carthaginian, Roman, Vandal, Byzantine, Saracen, and Norman have in turns beleaguered her walls; and the resistance which she successfully opposed to some of her early assailants was of the deepest importance, not only to the fortunes of the generations then in being, but to all the subsequent current of human events. To adopt the eloquent expressions of Arnold respecting the check which she gave to the Carthaginian arms, "Syracuse was a breakwater, which God's providence raised up to protect the yet immature strength of Rome." And her triumphant repulse of the great Athenian expedition against her was of even more widespread and enduring importance. It forms a decisive epoch in the strife for universal empire, in which all the great states of antiquity successively engaged and failed.

The present city of Syracuse is a place of little or no military strength, as the fire of artillery from the neighbouring heights would almost completely command it. But in ancient warfare its position, and the care bestowed on its walls, rendered it formidably strong.against besieging armies.

The ancient city, in the time of the Peloponnesian (Peloponnesus, ancient name of the Morean peninsula, in southern Greece) war, was chiefly built on the knob of land which projects into the sea on the eastern coast of Sicily, between two bays; one of which, to the north, was called the bay of Thapsus, while the southern one formed the great harbour of the city of Syracuse itself. A small island, or peninsula (for such it soon was rendered), lies at the south-eastern extremity of this knob of land, stretching almost entirely across the mouth of the great harbour, and rendering it nearly land-locked.

This island comprised the original settlement of the first Greek colonists from Corinth, who founded Syracuse two thousand five hundred years ago (in 1850); and the modern city has shrunk again into these primary limits. But, in the fifth century before our era, the growing wealth and population of the Syracusans had led them to occupy and include within their city walls portion after portion of the mainland lying next to the little isle; so that at the time of the Athenian expedition the seaward part of the land between the two bays already spoken of was built over, and fortified from bay to bay; constituting the larger part of Syracuse.

The landward wall, therefore, of the city traversed this knob of land, which continues to slope upwards from the sea, and which to the west of the old fortifications (that is, towards the interior of Sicily) rises rapidly for a mile or two, but diminishes in width, and finally terminates in a long narrow ridge, between which and Mount Hybla a succession of chasms and uneven low ground extend. On each flank of this ridge the descent is steep and precipitous from its summits to the strips of level land that lie immediately below it.

The usual mode of assailing fortified towns in the time of the Peloponnesian war was to build a double wall around them, sufficiently strong to check any sally of the garrison from within, or any attack of a relieving force from without. The interval within the two walls of the circumvallation was roofed over and formed barracks, in which the besiegers posted themselves, and awaited the effects of want or treachery among the besieged in producing a surrender. And, in every Greek city of those days, as in every Italian republic of the Middle Ages, the rage of domestic sedition between aristocrats and democrats ran high.

Rancorous refugees swarmed in the camp of every invading enemy; and every blockaded city was sure to contain within its walls a body of intriguing malcontents, who were eager to purchase a party triumph at the expense of a national disaster. Famine and faction were the allies on whom besiegers relied. The generals of that time trusted to the operation of these sure confederates as soon as they could establish a complete blockade. They rarely ventured on the attempt to storm any fortified post. For the military engines of antiquity were feeble in breaching masonry, before the improvements which the first Dionysius effected in the mechanics of destruction; and the lives of the boldest and most highly trained spearmen would, of course, have been idly spent in charges against unshattered walls.

A city built close to the sea, like Syracuse, was impregnable, save by the combined operations of a superior hostile fleet, and a superior hostile army. And Syracuse, from her size, her population, and her military and naval resources, not unnaturally thought herself secure from finding in another Greek city a foe capable of sending a sufficient armament to menace her with capture and subjection. But in the spring of 414 B.C., the Athenian navy was mistress of her harbour and the adjacent seas; an Athenian army had defeated her troops, and cooped them within the town; and from bay to bay a blockading-wall was being rapidly carried across the strips of level ground and the high ridge outside the city (then termed Epipolæ), which, if completed, would have cut the Syracusans off from all succour from the interior of Sicily, and have left them at the mercy of the Athenian generals. The besiegers' works were, indeed, unfinished; but every day the unfortified interval in their lines grew narrower, and so diminished all apparent hope of safety for the beleaguered town.

Athens was now staking the flower of her forces, and the accumulated fruits of seventy years of glory, on one bold throw for the dominion of the Western world. As Napoleon from Mount Cœur de Lion pointed to St. Jean d'Acre, and told his staff that the capture of that town would decide his destiny and would change the face of the world, so the Athenian officers, from the heights of Epipolæ, must have looked on Syracuse, and felt that with its fall all the known powers of the earth would fall beneath them. They must have felt, also, that Athens, if repulsed there, must pause forever in her career of conquest and sink from an imperial republic into a ruined and subservient community.

II

At Marathon, the first in date of the great battles of the world, we beheld Athens struggling for self-preservation against the invading armies of the East. At Syracuse she appears as the ambitious and oppressive invader of others. In her, as in other republics of old and of modern times, the same energy that had inspired the most heroic efforts in defence of the national independence soon learned to employ itself in daring and unscrupulous schemes of self-aggrandisement at the expense of neighbouring nations. In the interval between the Persian and the Peloponnesian wars, she had rapidly grown into a conquering and dominant state, the chief of a thousand tributary cities, and the mistress of the largest and best-manned navy that the Mediterranean had yet beheld.

The occupations of her territory by Xerxes and Mardonius, in the second Persian war (480 B.C.) had forced her whole population to become mariners; and the glorious result of that struggle confirmed them in their zeal for their country's service at sea. The voluntary suffrage of the Greek cities of the coasts and islands of the Ægean first placed Athens at the head of the confederation formed for the further prosecution of the war against Persia. But this titular ascendancy was soon converted by her into practical and arbitrary dominion. She protected them from piracy and from the Persian power, which soon fell into decrepitude and decay; but she exacted in return implicit obedience to herself. She claimed and enforced a prerogative of taxing them at her discretion and proudly refused to be accountable for her mode of expending their supplies. Remonstrance against her assessments was treated as factious disloyalty and refusal to pay was promptly punished as revolt.

Permitting and encouraging her subject allies to furnish all their contingents in money, instead of part consisting of ships and men, the sovereign republic gained the double object of training her own citizens by constant and well-paid service in her fleets, and of seeing her confederates lose their skill and discipline by inaction, and become more and more passive and

powerless under her yoke. Their towns were generally dismantled, while the imperial city herself was fortified with the
greatest care and sumptuousness, the accumulated revenues from
her tributaries serving to strengthen and adorn to the utmost
her havens, her docks, her arsenals, her theatres and her shrines
and to array her in that plentitude of architectural magnificence,
the ruins of which still attest the intellectual grandeur of the
age and people, which produced a Pericles to plan and a
Phidias to execute.

All republics that acquire supremacy over other nations rule
them selfishly and oppressively. There is no exception to this
in either ancient or modern times. Carthage, Rome, Venice,
Genoa, Florence, Pisa, Holland and republican France, all
tyrannised over every province and subject state where they
gained authority. But none of them openly avowed their
system of doing so upon principle, with the candour which
the Athenian republicans displayed, when any remonstrance
was made against the severe exactions which they imposed
upon their vassal allies. They avowed that their empire was a
tyranny, and frankly stated that they solely trusted to force
and terror to uphold it. They appealed to what they called
"the eternal law of nature, that the weak should be coerced
by the strong."

Sometimes they stated, and not without some truth, that
the unjust hatred of Sparta against themselves forced them to
be unjust to others in self-defence. To be safe they must be
powerful; and to be powerful, they must plunder and coerce
their neighbours. They never dreamed of communicating any
franchise, or share in office to their dependents, but jealousy
monopolised every post of command, and all political and judicial power; exposing themselves to every risk with unflinching
gallantry, enduring cheerfully the laborious training and severe
discipline which their sea-service required; venturing readily
on every ambitious scheme and never suffering difficulty or
disaster to shake their tenacity of purpose. Their hope was
to acquire unbounded empire for the country, and the means
of maintaining each of the thirty thousand citizens who made
up the sovereign republic, in exclusive devotion to military
occupations, and to those brilliant sciences and arts, in which
Athens already had reached the meridian of intellectual
splendour.

Her great political dramatist (Thucydides) speaks of the
Athenian empire as comprehending a thousand states. The
language of the stage must not be taken too literally; but the
number of the dependencies of Athens, at the time when the
Peloponnesian confederacy attacked her, was undoubtedly very
great. With a few trifling exceptions, all the islands of the
Ægean, and all the Greek cities, which in that age fringed the
coasts of Asia Minor, the Hellespont, and Thrace, paid tribute
to Athens, and implicitly obeyed her orders. The Ægean Sea
was an Attic lake.

III

Westward of Greece, her influence, though strong, was not
equally predominant. She had colonies and allies among the
wealthy and populous Greek settlements in Sicily and South
Italy, but she had no organised system of confederates in those
regions and her galleys brought her no tribute from the western
seas. The extension of her empire over Sicily was the favourite
project of her ambitious orators and generals. While her great
statesman, Pericles, lived, his commanding genius kept his
countrymen under control, and forbade them to risk the fortunes of Athens in distant enterprises, while they had unsubdued
and powerful enemies at their own doors. He taught Athens
this maxim, but he also taught her to know and to use her
own strength, and when Pericles had departed, the bold spirit,
which he had fostered, overleaped the salutary limits which he
had prescribed.

When her bitter enemies, the Corinthians, succeeded, in 431
B.C., in inducing Sparta to attack her, and a confederacy was
formed of five-sixths of the continental Greeks, all animated
by anxious jealousy and bitter hatred of Athens; when armies
far superior in numbers and equipment to those which had
marched against the Persians, were poured into the Athenian
territory, and laid it waste to the city walls, the general opinion
was that Athens would, in two or three years at the farthest, be
reduced to submit to the requisitions of her invaders. But her
strong fortifications, by which she was girt and linked to her
principal haven, gave her, in those ages, almost all the advantages of an insular position. Pericles had made her trust
to her empire of the seas.

Every Athenian in those days was a practised seaman. A

state, indeed, whose members, of an age fit for service, at no time exceeded thirty thousand, and whose territorial extent did not equal half Sussex, could only have acquired such a naval dominion as Athens once held, by devoting, and zealously training, all its sons to service in its fleets. In order to man the numerous galleys which she sent out, she necessarily employed also large numbers of hired mariners and slaves at the oar, but the staple of her crews was Athenian, and all posts of command were held by native citizens. It was by reminding them of this, of their long practice in seamanship, and the certain superiority which their discipline gave them over the enemy's marine, that their great minister mainly encouraged them to resist the combined power of Lacedæmon and her allies. He taught them that Athens might thus reap the fruit of her zealous devotion to maritime affairs ever since the invasion of the Medes; "she had not, indeed, perfected herself; but the reward of her superior training was the rule of the sea—a mighty dominion, for it gave her the rule of much fair land beyond its waves, safe from the idle ravages with which the Lacedæmonians might harass Attica, but never could subdue Athens."

Athens accepted the war with which her enemies threatened her, rather than descend from her pride of place. And though the awful visitation of the plague came upon her, and swept away more of her citizens than the Dorian [Dorians, one of the three traditional branches of the Greeks, invaded Greece about the 10th century B.C. and settled there] spear laid low, she held her own gallantly against her foes. If the Peloponnesian armies in irresistible strength wasted every spring her corn lands, her vineyards and her olive groves with fire and sword, she retaliated on their coasts with her fleets which, if resisted, proved the pre-eminent skill and bravery of her seamen. Some of her subject-allies revolted, but the revolts were in general sternly and promptly quelled.

The genius of one enemy had, indeed, inflicted blows on her power in Thrace, which she was unable to remedy; but he fell in battle in the tenth year of the war; and with the loss of Brasidas the Lacedæmonians (Spartans) seemed to have lost all energy and judgment. Both sides at length grew weary of the war; and in 421 B.C. a truce of fifty years was concluded, which, though ill-kept, and though many of the confederates of Sparta refused to recognise it, and hostilities still continued in many parts of Greece, protected the Athenian territory from the ravages of enemies, and enabled Athens to accumulate large sums out of the proceeds of her annual revenues.

So also, as a few years passed by, the havoc which the pestilence and the sword had made in her population was repaired; and in 415 B.C. Athens was full of bold and restless spirits, who longed for some field of distant enterprise, wherein they might signalise themselves, and aggrandise the State; and who looked on the alarm of Spartan hostility as a mere old woman's tale. When Sparta had wasted their territory she had done her worst; and the fact of its always being in her power to do so, seemed a strong reason for seeking to increase the transmarine dominion of Athens.

The West was now the quarter towards which the thoughts of every aspiring Athenian were directed. From the very beginning of the war Athens had kept up an interest in Sicily and her squadrons had, from time to time, appeared on its coasts and taken part in the dissensions in which the Sicilian Greeks were universally engaged one against another. There were plausible grounds for a direct quarrel and an open attack by the Athenians upon Syracuse.

With the capture of Syracuse all Sicily, it was hoped, would be secured. Carthage and Italy were next to be assailed. With large levies of Iberian mercenaries (from Spain and Portugal) she then meant to overwhelm her Peloponnesian enemies. The Persian monarchy lay in hopeless imbecility, inviting Greek invasion; nor did the known world contain the power that seemed capable of checking the growing might of Athens, if Syracuse once could be hers.

The national historian of Rome has left us, as an episode of his great work, a disquisition on the probable effects that would have followed, if Alexander the Great had invaded Italy. Posterity has generally regarded that disquisition as proving Livy's patriotism more strongly than his impartiality or acuteness. Yet, right or wrong, the speculations of the Roman writer were directed to the consideration of a very remote possibility. To whatever age Alexander's life might have been prolonged, the East would have furnished full occupation for his martial ambition, as well as for those schemes of commercial grandeur and imperial amalgamation of nations, in which the truly great qualities of his mind loved to display themselves. With his death the dismemberment of his empire among his generals was certain, even as the dismemberment of Napoleon's empire, among his marshals, would certainly have ensued, if he had been cut off in the zenith of his power.

Rome, also, was far weaker when the Athenians were in Sicily, than she was a century afterwards in Alexander's time. There can be little doubt but that Rome would have been blotted out from the independent powers of the West, had she been attacked at the end of the fifth century B.C., by an Athenian army, largely aided by Spanish mercenaries, and flushed with triumphs over Sicily and Africa; instead of the collision between her and Greece having been deferred until the latter had sunk into decrepitude, and the Roman Mars had grown into full vigour.

IV

The armament which the Athenians equipped against Syracuse was in every way worthy of the state which formed such projects of universal empire; and it has been truly termed (by Thomas Arnold, English historian) "the noblest that ever yet had been sent forth by a free and civilised commonwealth." The fleet consisted of one hundred and thirty-four war-galleys, with a multitude of store-ships. A powerful force of the best heavy-armed infantry that Athens and her allies could furnish, was sent on board together with a smaller number of slingers and bowmen. The quality of the forces was even more remarkable than the number. The zeal of individuals vied with that of the republic in giving every galley the best possible crew, and every troop the most perfect accoutrements. And with private as well as public wealth eagerly lavished on all that could give splendour as well as efficiency to the expedition, the fated fleet began its voyage for the Silician shores in the summer of 415 B.C.

The Syracusans themselves, at the time of the Peloponnesian war, were a bold and turbulent democracy, tyrannising over the weaker Greek cities in Sicily, and trying to gain in that island the same arbitrary supremacy which Athens maintained along the eastern coast of the Mediterranean. In numbers and in spirit they were fully equal to the Athenians, but far inferior to them in military and naval discipline. When the probability of an Athenian invasion was first publicly discussed at Syracuse and efforts were made by some of the wiser citizens to improve the state of the national defences, and prepare for the impending danger, the rumours of coming war and the proposals for preparation were received by the mass of the Syracusans with scornful incredulity.

The speech of one of their popular orators is preserved to us in Thucydides. The Syracusan orator told his countrymen to dismiss with scorn the visionary terrors which a set of designing men among themselves strove to excite, in order to get power and influence thrown into their own hands. He told them that Athens knew her own interest too well to think of wantonly provoking their hostility: "Even if the enemies were to come," said he, "so distant from their resources, and opposed to such a power as ours, their destruction would be easy and inevitable. Their ships will have enough to do to get to our island at all, and to carry such stores of all sorts as will be needed. They cannot therefore carry, besides, an army large enough to cope with such a population as ours. They will have no fortified place from which to commence their operations, but must rest them on no better base than a set of wretched tents and such means as the necessities of the moment will allow them. But in truth I do not believe that they would even be able to effect a disembarkation. Let us, therefore, set at nought these reports as altogether of home manufacture; and be sure that if any enemy *does* come, the state will know how to defend itself in a manner worthy of the national honour."

Such assertions pleased the Syracusan assembly. But the invaders of Syracuse came; made good their landing in Sicily; and, if they had promptly attacked the city itself, instead of wasting nearly a year in desultory operations in other parts of the island, the Syracusans must have paid the penalty of their self-sufficient carelessness in submission to the Athenian yoke.

But, of the three generals who led the Athenian expedition, two only were men of ability, and one was most weak and incompetent. Fortunately for Syracuse, Alcibiades, the most skilful of the three, was soon deposed from his command by a factious and fanatic vote of his fellow-countrymen, and the other competent one, Lamachus, fell early in a skirmish; while, more fortunately still for her, the feeble and vacillating Nicias remained unrecalled and unhurt, to assume the undivided leadership of the Athenian army and fleet, and to mar, by alternate over-caution and over-carelessness, every chance of success which the early part of the operations offered. Still, even under him, the Athenians nearly won the town. They defeated the raw levies of the Syracusans, cooped them within the walls and, as before mentioned, almost effected continuous fortification from bay to bay over Epipolæ, the completion of which would certainly have been followed by a capitulation.

V

Alcibiades, the most complete example of genius without principle that history produces, the Bolingbroke (English statesman 1678-1751,) of antiquity, but with high military talents superadded to diplomatic and oratorical powers, on being summoned home from his command in Sicily to take his trial before the Athenian tribunal, had escaped to Sparta; and he exerted himself there with all the selfish rancour of a renegade to renew the war with Athens, and to send instant assistance to Syracuse.

When we read his words in the pages of Thucydides (who was himself an exile from Athens at this period, and may probably have been at Sparta, and heard Alcibiades speak), we are at loss whether most to admire or abhor his subtile and traitorous counsels. After an artful exordium, in which he tried to disarm the suspicions which he felt must be entertained of him, and to point out to the Spartans how completely his interests and theirs were identified, through hatred of the Athenian democracy, he thus proceeded:—

"Hear me, at any rate, on the matters which require your grave attention, and which I, from the personal knowledge that I have of them, can and ought to bring before you. We Athenians sailed to Sicily with the design of subduing, first the Greek cities there, and next those in Italy. Then we intended to make an attempt on the dominions of Carthage, and on Carthage itself. If all these projects succeeded (nor did we limit ourselves to them in these quarters), we intended to increase our fleet with the inexhaustible supplies of ship timber which Italy affords, to put in requisition the whole military force of the conquered Greek states, and also to hire large armies of the barbarians; of the Iberians, (Spanish infantry

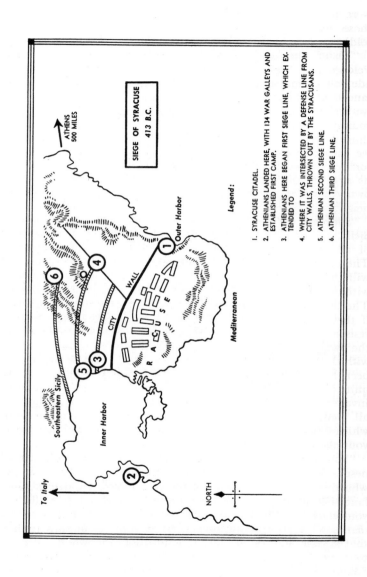

SIEGE OF SYRACUSE
413 B.C.

Legend:

1. SYRACUSE CITADEL.

2. ATHENIANS LANDED HERE, WITH 134 WAR GALLEYS AND ESTABLISHED FIRST CAMP.

3. ATHENIANS HERE BEGAN FIRST SIEGE LINE, WHICH EXTENDED TO

4. WHERE IT WAS INTERSECTED BY A DEFENSE LINE FROM CITY WALLS, THROWN OUT BY THE SYRACUSANS.

5. ATHENIAN SECOND SIEGE LINE.

6. ATHENIAN THIRD SIEGE LINE.

were the backbone of the armies of Carthage) and others in those regions, who are allowed to make the best possible soldiers.

"Then, when we had done all this, we intended to assail Peloponnesus with our collected force. Our fleets would blockade you by sea, and desolate your coasts; our armies would be landed at different points and assail your cities. Some of these we expected to storm, and others we meant to take by surrounding them with fortified lines. We thought that it would thus be an easy matter thoroughly to wear you down: and then we should become the masters of the whole Greek race. As for expense, we reckoned that each conquered state would give us supplies of money and provisions sufficient to pay for its own conquest, and furnish the means for the conquest of its neighbours.

"Such are the designs of the present Athenian expedition to Sicily, and you have heard them from the lips of the man who, of all men living, is most accurately acquainted with them. The other Athenian generals, who remain with the expedition, will endeavour to carry out these plans. And be sure that without your speedy interference they will all be accomplished. The Sicilian Greeks are deficient in military training, but still if they could be at once brought to combine in an organised resistance to Athens, they might even now be saved. But as for the Syracusans resisting Athens by themselves they have already with the whole strength of their population fought a battle and been beaten; they cannot face the Athenians at sea; and it is quite impossible for them to hold out against the force of their invaders. And if this city falls into the hands of the Athenians, all Sicily is theirs, and presently Italy also, and the danger which I warned you of from that quarter will soon fall upon yourselves.

"You must, therefore, in Sicily fight for the safety of Peloponnesus. Send some galleys thither instantly. Put men on board who can work their own way over, and who, as soon as they land, can do duty as regular troops. But above all, let one of yourselves, let a man of Sparta, go over to take the chief command, to bring into order and effective discipline the forces that are in Syracuse, and urge those, who at present hang back, to come forward and aid the Syracusans. The presence of a Spartan general at this crisis will do more to save the city, than a whole army." The renegade then proceeded to urge on them the necessity of encouraging their friends in Sicily, by showing that they themselves were earnest in hostility to Athens. He exhorted them not only to march their armies into Attica again, but to take up a permanent fortified position in the country: and he gave them in detail information of all that the Athenians most dreaded, and how his country might receive the most distressing and enduring injury at their hands.

The Spartans resolved to act on his advice. and appointed Gylippus to the Sicilian command. Gylippus was a man who, to the national bravery and military skill of a Spartan, united political sagacity that was worthy of his great fellow-country-man Brasidas; but his merits were debased by mean and sordid vice; and his is one of the cases in which history has been austerely just, and where little or no fame has been accorded to the successful, but venal soldier. But for the purpose for which he was required in Sicily, an abler man could not have been found in Lacedæmon. His country gave him neither men nor money, but she gave him her authority; and the influence of her name and of his own talents were speedily seen in the zeal with which the Corinthians and other Peloponnesian Greeks began to equip a squadron to act under him for the rescue of Sicily. As soon as four galleys were ready, he hurried over with them to the southern coast of Italy; and there, though he received such evil tidings of the state of Syracuse that he abandoned all hope of saving that city, he determined to remain on the coast, and do what he could in preserving the Italian cities from the Athenians.

VI

So nearly, indeed, had Nicias completed his beleaguering lines, and so utterly desperate had the state of Syracuse seemingly become, that an assembly of the Syracusans was actually convened, and they were discussing the terms on which they should offer to capitulate, when a galley was seen dashing into the great harbour, and making her way towards the town with all the speed that her rowers could supply. From her shunning the part of the harbour where the Athenian fleet lay, and making straight for the Syracusan side, it was clear that she was a friend; the enemy's cruisers, careless through confidence of success, made no attempt to cut her off. She touched the beach and a Corinthian captain springing on shore from her was eagerly conducted to the assembly of the Syracusan people, just in time to prevent the fatal vote being put for a surrender.

Providentially for Syracuse, Gongylus, the commander of the galley, had been prevented by an Athenian squadron from following Gylippus to south Italy, and he had been obliged to push direct for Syracuse from Greece.

The sight of actual succour, and the promise of more, revived the drooping spirits of the Syracusans. They felt that they were not left desolate to perish; and the tidings that a Spartan was coming to command them, confirmed their resolution to continue their resistance. Gylippus was already near the city. He had learned at Locri that the first report which had reached him of the state of Syracuse was exaggerated; and that there was an unfinished space in the besiegers' lines through which it was barely possible to introduce reinforcements into the town.

Crossing the straits of Messina, which the culpable negligence of Nicias had left unguarded, Gylippus landed on the northern coast of Sicily, and there began to collect from the Greek cities an army, of which the regular troops that he brought from Peloponnesus formed the nucleus. Such was the influence of Sparta, and such were his own abilities and activity, that he succeeded in raising a force of about two thousand fully-armed infantry, with a large number of irregular troops.

Nicias, as if infatuated, made no attempt to counteract his operations; nor, when Gylippus marched his little army towards Syracuse did the Athenian commander endeavour to check him. The Syracusans marched out to meet him; and while the Athenians were solely intent on completing their fortifications on the southern side towards the harbour, Gylippus turned their position by occupying the high ground in the extreme rear of Epipolæ. He then marched through the unfortified interval of Nicias's lines into the besieged town; and joining his troops with the Syracusan forces, after some engagements with varying success, gained the mastery over Nicias, drove the Athenians from Epipolæ, and hemmed them into a disadvantageous position in the low grounds near the great harbour.

The attention of all Greece was now fixed on Syracuse, and every enemy of Athens felt the importance of the opportunity now offered of checking her ambition, and, perhaps, of striking a deadly blow at her power. Large reinforcements from Corinth,

Thebes and other cities now reached the Syracusans, while the baffled and dispirited Athenian general earnestly besought his countrymen to recall him, and represented the further prosecution of the siege as hopeless.

But Athens had made it a maxim never to let difficulty or disaster drive her back from any enterprise once undertaken, so long as she possessed the means of making any effort, however desperate, for its accomplishment. With indomitable pertinacity she now decreed, instead of recalling her first armament from before Syracuse, to send out a second, though her enemies near home had now renewed open warfare against her, and by occupying a permanent fortification in her territory, had severely distressed her population, and were pressing her with almost all the hardships of an actual siege. She still was mistress of the sea, and she sent forth another fleet of seventy galleys and another army, which seemed to drain the very last reserves of her military population, to see if Syracuse could not yet be won and the honour of the Athenian arms be preserved from the stigma of a retreat. Hers was, indeed, a spirit that might be broken, but never would bend. At the head of this second expedition, she wisely placed her best general, Demosthenes, one of the most distinguished officers whom the long Peloponnesian war had produced, and who, if he had originally held the Sicilian command, would soon have brought Syracuse to submission.

The fame of Demosthenes the general, has been dimmed by the superior lustre of his great countryman, Demosthenes the orator. When the name of Demosthenes is mentioned, it is the latter alone that is thought of. The soldier has found no biographer. Yet out of the long list of the great men of the Athenian republic, there are few who deserve to stand higher than this brave, though finally unsuccessful, leader of her fleets and armies in the first half of the Peloponnesian war. In his first campaign in Ætolia he had shown some of the rashness of youth, and had received a lesson of caution, by which he profited throughout the rest of his career, but without losing any of his natural energy in enterprise or in execution. He had performed the eminent service of rescuing Naupactus from a powerful hostile armament in the seventh year of the war; he had then, at the request of the Acarnanian republics, taken on himself the office of commander-in-chief of all their forces, and at their head he had gained some important advantages over the enemies of Athens in western Greece. His most celebrated exploits had been the occupation of Pylos on the Messenian coast, the successful defence of that place against the fleet and armies of Lacedæmon, and the subsequent capture of the Spartan forces on the isle of Sphacteria, which was the severest blow dealt to Sparta throughout the war, and which had mainly caused her to humble herself to make the truce with Athens.

Demosthenes was as honourably unknown in the war of party politics at Athens, as he was eminent in the war against the foreign enemy. We read of no intrigues of his on either the aristocratic or democratic side. He was neither in the interest of Nicias, nor of Cleon. His private character was free from any of the stains which polluted that of Alcibiades. On all these points the silence of the comic dramatist is decisive evidence in his favour. He had also the moral courage, not always combined with physical, of seeking to do his duty to his country, irrespective of any odium that he himself might incur, and unhampered by any petty jealousy of those who were associated with him in command. There are few men named in ancient history, of whom posterity would gladly know more, or whom we sympathise with more deeply in the calamities that befell Athens than Demosthenes, the son of Alcishenes, who in the spring of the year 413 B.C. left Piræus at the head of the second Athenian expedition against Sicily.

His arrival was critically timed, for Gylippus had encouraged the Syracusans to attack the Athenians under Nicias by sea as well as by land, and by an able stratagem of Ariston, one of the admirals of the Corinthian auxiliary squadron, the Syracusans and their confederates had inflicted on the fleet of Nicias the first defeat that the Athenian navy had ever sustained from a numerically inferior foe. Gylippus was preparing to follow up his advantage by fresh attacks on the Athenians on both elements, when the arrival of Demosthenes completely changed the aspect of affairs, and restored the superiority to the invaders.

With seventy-three war galleys in the highest state of efficiency, and brilliantly equipped, with a force of five thousand picked men of the regular infantry of Athens and her allies, and a still larger number of bow-men, javelin-men, and slingers on board, Demosthenes rowed round the great harbour with loud cheers and martial music, as if in defiance of the Syracusans and their confederates. His arrival had indeed changed their newly-born hopes into the deepest consternation. The resources of Athens seemed inexhaustible, and resistance to her hopeless. They had been told that she was reduced to the last extremities, and that her territory was occupied by an enemy; and yet, here they saw her as if in prodigality of power, sending forth, to make foreign conquests, a second armament, not inferior to that with which Nicias had first landed on the Sicilian shores.

VII

With the intuitive decision of a great commander, Demosthenes at once saw that the possession of Epipolæ was the key to the possession of Syracuse, and he resolved to make a prompt and vigorous attempt to recover that position, while his force was unimpaired, and the consternation which its arrival had produced among the besieged, remained unabated. The Syracusans and their allies had run out an outwork along Epipolæ from the city walls, intersecting the fortified lines of circumvallation which Nicias had commenced, but from which he had been driven by Gylippus. Could Demosthenes succeed in storming this outwork, and in re-establishing the Athenian troops on the high ground, he might fairly hope to be able to resume the circumvallation of the city and become the conqueror of Syracuse for, when once the besiegers' lines were completed, the number of the troops with which Gylippus had garrisoned the place, would only tend to exhaust the stores of provisions and accelerate its downfall.

An easily repelled attack was first made on the outwork in the daytime, probably more with the view of blinding the besieged to the nature of the main operations, than with any expectation of succeeding in an open assault with every disadvantage of the ground to contend against. But, when darkness had set in, Demosthenes formed his men in columns, each soldier taking with him five days' provisions, and the engineers and workmen of the camp following the troops with their tools, and all portable implements of fortification, so as at once to secure any advantage of ground that the army might gain. Thus equipped and prepared, he led his men along by the foot of the southern flank of Epipolæ in a direction towards the interior of the island, till he came immediately below the narrow ridge that forms the extremity of the high ground looking westward. He then wheeled his vanguard to the right, sent them rapidly up the paths that wind along the face of the cliff, and succeeded in completely surprising the Syracusan outposts and in placing his troops fairly on the extreme summit of the all-important Epipolæ. Thence the Athenians marched eagerly down the slope towards the town, routing some Syracusan detachments that were quartered in their way, and vigorously assailing the unprotected part of the outwork.

All at first favoured them. The outwork was abandoned by its garrison, and the Athenian engineers began to dismantle it. In vain Gylippus brought up fresh troops to check the assault. The Athenians broke and drove them back and continued to press hotly forward, in the full confidence of victory. But, amid the general consternation of the Syracusans and their confederates, one body of infantry stood firm. This was a brigade of their Bœotian allies (from one of the small republics of eastern Greece), which was posted low down the slope of Epipolæ, outside the city walls. Coolly and steadily the Bœotian infantry formed their line, and, undismayed by the current of flight around them, advanced against the advancing Athenians. This was the crisis of the battle. But the Athenian van was disorganized by its own previous successes and, yielding to the unexpected charge thus made on it by troops in perfect order, and of the most obstinate courage, it was driven back in confusion upon the other divisions of the army, that still continued to press forward.

When once the tide was thus turned, the Syracusans passed rapidly from the extreme of panic to the extreme of vengeful daring, and with all their forces they now fiercely assailed the embarrassed and receding Athenians. In vain did the officers of the latter strive to re-form their line. Amid the din and the shouting of the fight, and the confusion inseparable upon a night engagement, especially one where many thousand combatants were pent and whirled together in a narrow and uneven area, the necessary manœuvres were impracticable. Although many companies still fought on desperately, wherever the moonlight showed them the semblance of a foe, they fought without concert or subordination, and not unfrequently amid the deadly chaos Athenian troops assailed each other. Keeping their ranks close, the Syracusans and their allies pressed on against the disorganized masses of the besiegers and at length drove them, with heavy slaughter, over the cliffs, which, scarce an hour before, they had scaled full of hope and apparently certain of success.

This defeat was decisive of the event of the siege. The Athenians afterwards struggled only to protect themselves from the vengeance which the Syracusans sought to wreak in the complete destruction of their invaders. Never, however, was vengeance more complete and terrible. A series of seafights followed, in which the Athenians galleys were utterly destroyed or captured. The mariners and soldiers who escaped death in disastrous engagements, and in a vain attempt to force a retreat into the interior of the island, became prisoners of war. Nicias and Demosthenes were put to death in cold blood and their men either perished miserably in the Syracusan dungeons, or were sold into slavery to the very persons whom, in their pride of power, they had crossed the seas to enslave.

All danger from Athens to the independent nations of the West was now for ever at an end. She, indeed, continued to struggle against her combined enemies and revolted allies with unparalleled gallantry; and many more years of varying warfare passed away before she surrendered to their arms. But no success in subsequent conquests could ever have restored her to the pre-eminence in enterprise, resources, and maritime skill, which she had acquired before her fatal reverses in Sicily. Nor among the rival Greek republics, whom her own rashness aided to crush her, was there any capable of reorganising her empire, or resuming her schemes of conquest. The dominion of western Europe was left for Rome and Carthage to dispute two centuries later, in conflicts still more terrible, and with even higher displays of military daring and genius, than Athens had witnessed either in her rise, her meridian or her fall.

[EDITOR'S NOTE: Syracuse was besieged by the Athenians for two years, from 415 to 413 B.C. The Allies, in July, 1943, took the city in a few hours. The modern city, with a population of 53,000, covers only a fraction of the area occupied by ancient Syracuse, which had several hundred thousand citizens.]

SYNOPSIS OF THE EVENTS BETWEEN THE DEFEAT OF THE ATHENIANS AT SYRACUSE, AND THE BATTLE OF ARBELA.

412 B.C. Many of the subject allies of Athens revolt from her, on her disasters before Syracuse being known; the seat of war is transferred to the Hellespont and eastern side of the Ægean.

410. The Carthaginians attempt to make conquests in Sicily.

407. Cyrus the Younger is sent by the king of Persia to take the government of all the maritime parts of Asia Minor, and with orders to help the Lacedæmonian fleet against the Athenian.

406. Agrigentum taken by the Carthaginians.

405. The last Athenian fleet destroyed by Lysander at Ægospotamos. Athens closely besieged. Rise of the power of Dionysius at Syracuse.

404. Athens surrenders. End of the Peloponnesian war. The ascendancy of Sparta complete throughout Greece.

403. Thrasybulus, aided by the Thebans and with the connivance of one of the Spartan kings, liberates Athens from the Thirty Tyrants, and restores the democracy.

401. Cyrus the Younger commences his expedition into Upper Asia to dethrone his brother Artaxerxes Memnon. He takes with him an auxiliary force of ten thousand Greeks. He is killed in battle at Cunaxa; and the Ten Thousand, led by Xenophon, effect their retreat in spite of the Persian armies and the natural obstacles of their march.

399. In this, and the five following years, the Lacedæmonians under Agesilaus and other commanders, carry on war against the Persian satraps in Asia Minor.

396. Syracuse is besieged by the Carthaginians, and successfully defended by Dionysius.

394. Rome makes her first great stride in the career of conquest by the capture of Veii.

393. The Athenian admiral, Conon, in conjunction with the Persian satrap Pharnabazus, defeats the Lacedæmonian fleet off Cnidus, and restores the fortifications of Athens. Several of the former allies of Sparta in Greece, carry on hostilities against her.

388. The nations of northern Europe now first appear in authentic history. The Gauls overrun great part of Italy and burn Rome. Rome recovers from the blow, but her old enemies, the Æquians and Volscians, are left completely crushed by the Gallic invaders.

387. The peace of Antalcidas is concluded among the Greeks by the mediation, and under the sanction, of the Persian king.

378 to 361. Fresh wars in Greece. Epaminondas raises Thebes to be the leading state of Greece, and the supremacy of Sparta is destroyed at the battle of Leuctra. Epaminondas is killed in gaining the victory of Mantinea, and the power of Thebes falls with him. The Athenians attempt a balancing system between Sparta and Thebes.

359. Philip becomes king of Macedon.

357. The Social War breaks out in Greece, and lasts three years. Its result checks the attempt of Athens to regain her old maritime empire.

56. Alexander the Great is born.

3. Rome begins her wars with the Samnites: they extend over a period of fifty years. The result of this obstinate contest is to secure for her the dominion of Italy.

340. Fresh attempts of the Carthaginians upon Syracuse. Timoleon defeats them with great slaughter.

338. Philip defeats the confederate armies of Athens and Thebes at Chæronea, and the Macedonian supremacy over Greece is firmly established.

336. Philip is assassinated, and Alexander the Great becomes king of Macedon. He gains several victories over the northern barbarians who had attacked Macedonia, and destroys Thebes, which, in conjunction with Athens, had taken up arms against the Macedonians.

334. Alexander passes the Hellespont.

-❮ THREE ❯-

Arbela, 331 B. C.

WHY DECISIVE: *"The ancient Persian empire, which once menaced all the nations of the earth with subjection, was irreparably crushed [at Arbela] when Alexander had won his crowning victory there."* [Creasy.] *"At every step [after Arbela] the Greek power took root and the language and the civilization of Greece were planted from the shores of the Aegean to the banks of the Indus, from the Caspian Sea and the great Hyrcanian plain [southeast of the Caspian] to the cataracts of the Nile; to exist actually for nearly a thousand years and in their effects to endure forever."* [Thomas Arnold.]

I

A LONG and not uninstructive list might be made out of illustrious men, whose characters have been vindicated during recent times from aspersions which for centuries had been thrown on them. The spirit of modern inquiry, and the tendency of modern scholarship, both of which are often said to be solely negative and destructive have, in truth, restored to splendour, and almost created anew, far more than they have assailed with censure or dismissed from consideration as unreal. The truth of many a brilliant narrative of brilliant exploits has of late years been triumphantly demonstrated; and the shallowness of the sceptical scoffs with which little minds have carped at the great minds of antiquity, has been in many instances decisively exposed. The laws, the politics, and the lines of action adopted or recommended by eminent men and powerful nations have been examined with keener investigation, and considered with more comprehensive judgment, than formerly were brought to bear on these subjects. The result has been at least as often favourable as unfavourable to the persons and the states so scrutinised; and many an oft-repeated slander against both measures and men has thus been silenced, we may hope for ever.

The name of the victor of Arbela has led to these reflections; for, although the rapidity and extent of Alexander's conquests have through all ages challenged admiration and amazement, the grandeur of genius, which he displayed in his schemes of commerce, civilisation, and of comprehensive union and unity amongst nations, has, until lately, been comparatively unhonoured. This long-continued depreciation was of early date. The ancient rhetoricians—a class of babblers, a school for lies and scandal, as Niebuhr justly termed them—chose, among the stock themes for their commonplaces, the character and exploits of Alexander. They had their followers in every age; and until a very recent period, all who wished to "point a moral or adorn a tale," about unreasoning ambition, extravagant pride, and the formidable frenzies of free will when leagued with free power, have never failed to blazon forth the so-called madman of Macedonia as one of the most glaring examples. Without doubt, many of these writers adopted with implicit credence traditional ideas, and supposed, with un-inquiring philanthropy, that in blackening Alexander, they were doing humanity good service. But also, without doubt, many of his assailants, like those of other great men, have been mainly instigated by "that strongest of all antipathies, the antipathy of a second-rate mind to a first-rate one," (Mme. de Staël) and by the envy which talent too often bears to genius.

Arrian, who wrote his history of Alexander, when Hadrian was emperor of the Roman world (117-138) and when the spirit of declamation and dogmatism was at its full height, but who was himself, unlike the dreaming pedants of the schools, a statesman and a soldier of practical and proved ability, well rebuked the malevolent aspersions which he heard con-tinually thrown upon the memory of the great conqueror of the East. He truly says, "Let the man who speaks evil of Alexander not merely bring forward those passages of Alexander's life which were really evil, but let him collect and review *all* the actions of Alexander, and then let him thoroughly consider first who and what manner of man he himself is, and what has been his own career; and then let him consider who and what manner of man Alexander was, and to what an eminence of human grandeur *he* arrived. Let him consider that Alexander was a king, and the undisputed lord of the two continents; and that his name is renowned throughout the whole earth. Let the evil speaker against Alexander bear all this in mind, and then let him reflect on his own insignificance, the pettiness of his own circumstances and affairs, and the blunders that he makes about these,

paltry and trifling as they are. Let him then ask himself
whether he is a fit person to censure and revile such a man
as Alexander. I believe that there was in his time no nation of
men, no city, nay, no single individual, with whom Alexander's
name had not become a familiar word. I therefore hold that
such a man, who was like no ordinary mortal, was not born
into the world without some special providence."

And one of the most distinguished soldiers and writers of
our own nation, Sir Walter Raleigh, though he failed to
estimate justly the full merits of Alexander, has expressed
his sense of the grandeur of the part played in the world by
"The Great Emathian Conqueror."

A higher authority than either Arrian or Raleigh may now
be referred to by those who wish to know the real merit of
Alexander as a general, and how far the commonplace assertions
are true, that his successes were the mere results of fortunate
rashness and unreasoning pugnacity. Napoleon selected Alexander as one of the seven greatest generals whose noble deeds
history has handed down to us, and from the study of whose
campaigns the principles of war are to be learned. The
critique of the greatest conqueror of modern times on the
military career of the great conqueror of the old world is no
less graphic than true.

"Alexander crossed the Dardanelles, 334 B.C., with an army
of about forty thousand men, of which one-eighth was cavalry;
he forced the passage of the Granicus in opposition to an
army under Memnon, the Greek, who commanded for Darius
on the coast of Asia, and he spent the whole of the year 333
in establishing his power in Asia Minor. He was seconded by
the Greek colonists, who dwelt on the borders of the Black
Sea, and on the Mediterranean, and in Smyrna, Ephesus, Tarsus,
Miletus, etc. The kings of Persia left their provinces and
towns to be governed according to their own particular laws.
Their empire was a union of confederated states, and did not
form one nation; this facilitated its conquest. As Alexander only
wished for the throne of the monarch, he easily effected the
change, by respecting the customs, manners, and laws of the
people, who experienced no change in their condition.

"In the year 332, he met with Darius at the head of sixty
thousand men, who had taken up a position near Tarsus,
on the banks of the Issus, in the province of Cilicia. He

defeated him, entered Syria, took Damascus, which contained all the riches of the Great King, and laid siege to Tyre. This superb metropolis of the commerce of the world detained him nine months. He took Gaza after a siege of two months; crossed the desert in seven days; entered Pelusium and Memphis, and founded Alexandria. In less than two years, after two battles and four or five sieges, the coasts of the Black Sea from Phasis to Byzantium, those of the Mediterranean as far as Alexandria, all Asia Minor, Syria, and Egypt, had submitted to his arms.

"In 331, he repassed the desert, encamped in Tyre, recrossed Syria, entered Damascus, passed the Euphrates and Tigris, and defeated Darius on the field of Arbela, when he was at the head of a still stronger army than that which he commanded on the Issus, and Babylon opened her gates to him. In 330, he overran Susa, and took that city, Persepolis, and Pasargada, which contained the tomb of Cyrus. In 329, he directed his course northward, entered Ecbatana, and extended his conquests to the coasts of the Caspian, punished Bessus, the cowardly assassin of Darius, penetrated into Scythia, and subdued the Scythians. In 328, he forced the passage of the Oxus, received sixteen thousand recruits from Macedonia, and reduced the neighbouring people to subjection.

"In 327, he crossed the Indus, vanquished Porus in a pitched battle, took him prisoner, and treated him as a king. He contemplated passing the Ganges, but his army refused. He sailed down the Indus, in the year 326, with eight hundred vessels; having arrived at the ocean, he sent Nearchus with a fleet to run along the coasts of the Indian Ocean and the Persian Gulf, as far as the mouth of the Euphrates. In 325, he took sixty days in crossing from Gedrosia, entered Keramania, returned to Pasargada, Persepolis, and Susa, and married Statira, the daughter of Darius. In 324, he marched once more to the north, passed Ecbatana, and terminated his career at Babylon."

II

The enduring importance of Alexander's conquests is to be estimated not by the duration of his own life and empire, or even by the duration of the kingdoms which his generals after his death formed out of the fragments of that mighty dominion. In every region of the world that he traversed, Alexander planted Greek settlements, and founded cities, in the populations of which the Greek element at once asserted its predominance. Among his successors, the Seleucidæ and the Ptolemies imitated their great captain in blending schemes of civilisation, of commercial intercourse, and of literary and scientific research with all their enterprises of military aggrandisement, and with all their systems of civil administration.

Such was the ascendancy of the Greek genius, so wonderfully comprehensive and assimilating was the cultivation which it introduced that, within thirty years after Alexander crossed the Hellespont, the language, the literature, and the arts of Hellas, enforced and promoted by the arms of semi-Hellenic Macedon, predominated in every country from the shores of that sea to the Indian waters. Even sullen Egypt acknowledged the intellectual supremacy of Greece; and the language of Pericles and Plato became the language of the statesmen and the sages who dwelt in the mysterious land of the Pyramids and the Sphinx. It is not to be supposed that this victory of the Greek tongue was so complete as to exterminate the Coptic, the Syrian, the Armenian, the Persian, or the other native languages of the numerous nations and tribes between the Ægean, the Iaxertes, the Indus, and the Nile. They survived as provincial dialects. Each probably was in use as the vulgar tongue of its own district.

But every person with the slightest pretence to education spoke Greek. Greek was universally the state language, and the exclusive language of all literature and science. It formed also for the merchant, the trader, and the traveller, as well as for the courtier, the government official, and the soldier, the organ of intercommunication among the myriads of mankind inhabiting these large portions of the Old World. Throughout Asia Minor, Syria, and Egypt, the Hellenic character that was thus imparted, remained in full vigour down to the time of the Mohammedan conquests. The infinite value of this to humanity in the highest and holiest point of view has been gratefully recognized by those who have observed how the early growth and progress of Christianity were aided by this diffusion of the Greek language and civilisation throughout Asia Minor, Syria, and Egypt, caused by the Macedonian conquest of the East.

In Upper Asia, beyond the Euphrates, the direct and material influence of Greek ascendancy was more short-lived. Yet, during the existence of the Hellenic kingdoms in these regions, especially of the Greek kingdom of Bactria, the modern Bokhara, very important effects were produced on the intellectual tendencies and tastes of the inhabitants of those countries and of the adjacent ones, by the animating contact of the Grecian spirit. Much of Hindu science and philosophy, much of the literature of the later Persian kingdom of the Arsacidæ, either originated from, or was largely modified by, Grecian influences. So, also, the learning and science of the Arabians were in a far less degree the result of original invention and genius, than the reproduction, in an altered form, of the Greek philosophy and the Greek lore, acquired by the Saracenic conquerors together with their acquisition of the provinces which Alexander had subjugated nearly a thousand years before the armed disciples of Mohammed commenced their career in the East.

It is well known that Western Europe in the Middle Ages drew its philosophy, its arts, and its science, principally from Arabian teachers. And thus we see how the intellectual influence of ancient Greece, poured on the Eastern world by Alexander's victories, and then brought back to bear on mediæval Europe by the spread of the Saracenic powers, has exerted its action on the elements of modern civilisation by this powerful, though indirect, channel, as well as by the more obvious effects of the remnants of classic civilisation which survived in Italy, Gaul, Britain, and Spain, after the irruption of the Germanic nations.

These considerations invest the Macedonian triumphs in the East with never-dying interest, such as the most showy and sanguinary successes of mere "low ambition and the pride of kings," however they may dazzle for a moment, can never retain with posterity. Whether the old Persian empire, which Cyrus founded, could have survived much longer than it did, even if Darius had been victorious at Arbela, may safely be disputed. That ancient dominion, like the Turkish at the present time, laboured under every cause of decay and dissolution. The satraps, like the modern pashas, continually rebelled against the central power, and Egypt in particular, was almost always in a state of insurrection against its nominal sovereign. There was no longer any effective central control, or any internal principle of unity fused through the huge mass of the empire, and binding it together. Persia was evidently about to fall; but had it not been for Alexander's invasion of Asia, she would most probably have fallen beneath some other Oriental power, as Media and Babylon had formerly fallen before herself, and as, in after times, the Parthian supremacy gave way to the revived ascendancy of Persia in the East, under the sceptres of the Arsacidæ. A revolution that merely substituted one Eastern power for another would have been utterly barren and unprofitable to mankind.

Alexander's victory at Arbela not only overthrew an Oriental dynasty, but established European rulers in its stead. It broke the monotony of the Eastern world by the impression of Western energy and superior civilisation.

III

Arbela, the city which has furnished its name to the decisive battle that gave Asia to Alexander, lies more than twenty miles from the actual scene of conflict. The little village then named Gaugamela is close to the spot where the armies met, but has ceded the honour of naming the battle to its more euphonious neighbour. Gaugamela is situated in one of the wide plains that lie between the Tigris and the mountains of Kurdistan. A few undulating hillocks diversify the surface of this sandy tract, but the ground is generally level, and admirably qualified for the evolutions of cavalry, and also calculated to give the larger of two armies the full advantage of numerical superiority.

The Persian king (who, before he came to the throne, had proved his personal valour as a soldier, and his skill as a general) had wisely selected this region for the third and decisive encounter between his forces and the invaders. The previous defeats of his troops, however severe they had been, were not looked on as irreparable. The battle of Granicus (ancient name of a small river in Asia Minor) had been fought by his generals rashly and without mutual concert. And, though Darius himself had commanded and been beaten at Issus, that defeat might be attributed to the disadvantageous nature of the ground; where, cooped up between the mountains, the river, and the sea, the numbers of the Persians confused and

clogged alike the general's skill and the soldiers' prowess, so
that their very strength became their weakness. Here, on the
broad plains of Kurdistan, there was scope for Asia's largest
host to array ,its lines, to wheel, to skirmish, to condense or
expand its squadrons, to manœuvre, and to charge at will.
Should Alexander and his scanty band dare to plunge into
that living sea of war, their destruction seemed inevitable.

Darius felt, however, the critical nature to himself as well
as to his adversary of the coming encounter. He could not
hope to retrieve the consequences of a third overthrow. The
great cities of Mesopotamia and Upper Asia, the central provinces of the Persian empire, were certain to be at the mercy
of the victor. Darius knew also the Asiatic character well
enough to be aware how it yields to the prestige of success
and the apparent career of destiny. He felt that the diadem
was now either to be firmly replaced on his own brow, or
to be irrevocably transferred to the head of his European
conquerer. He, therefore, during the long interval left him
after the battle of Issus, while Alexander was subjugating
Syria and Egypt, assiduously busied himself in selecting the
best troops which his vast empire supplied and in training
his varied forces to act together with some uniformity of discipline and system.

The hardy mountaineers of Afghanistan, Bokhara, Khiva,
and Tibet, were then, as at present, far different from the
generality of Asiatics in warlike spirit and endurance. From
these districts Darius collected large bodies of admirable infantry; and the countries of the modern Kurds and Turkomans
supplied, as they do now, squadrons of horsemen, strong, skilful,
bold, and trained to a life of constant activity and warfare.
It is not uninteresting to notice that the ancestors of the Sikhs
of India served as allies of Darius against the Macedonians.
They are spoken of in Arrian as Indians who dwelt near
Bactria. They were attached to the troops of that satrapy, and
their cavalry was one of the most formidable forces in the
whole Persian army.

Besides these picked troops, contingents also came in from
the numerous other provinces that yet obeyed the Great King.
Altogether, the horses are said to have been forty thousand,
the scythe-bearing chariots two hundred, and the armed elephants fifteen in number. The amount of the infantry is

uncertain; but the knowledge which both ancient and modern times supply of the usual character of Oriental armies, and of their populations of camp-followers, may warrant us in believing that many myriads (anciently 10,000 persons) were prepared to fight, or to encumber those who fought for the last Darius.

The position of the Persian king near Mesopotamia was chosen with great military skill. It was certain that Alexander on his return from Egypt must march northward along the Syrian coast, before he attacked the central provinces of the Persian empire. A direct eastward march from the lower part of Palestine across the great Syrian desert was then, as now, utterly impracticable. Marching eastward from Syria, Alexander would, on crossing the Euphrates, arrive at the vast Mesopotamian plains. The wealthy capitals of the empire, Babylon, Susa, and Persepolis, would then lie to his south; and if he marched down through Mesopotamia to attack them, Darius might reasonably hope to follow the Macedonians with his immense force of cavalry, and without even risking a pitched battle, to harass and finally overwhelm them. We may remember that three centuries afterwards a Roman army under Crassus was thus actually destroyed by the Oriental archers and horsemen on these very plains; and that the ancestors of the Parthians who thus vanquished the Roman legions, served by thousands under King Darius.

If, on the contrary, Alexander should defer his march against Babylon, and first seek an encounter with the Persian army, the country on each side of the Tigris in this latitude was highly advantageous for such an army as Darius commanded; and he had close in his rear the mountainous districts of northern Media, where he himself had in early life been satrap, where he had acquired reputation as a soldier ‘and a general, and where he justly expected to find loyalty to his person, and a safe refuge in case of defeat.

His great antagonist came on across the Euphrates against him, at the head of an army which Arrian, copying from the journals of the Macedonian officers, states to have consisted of forty thousand foot, and seven thousand horse. In studying the campaigns of Alexander, we possess the peculiar advantage of deriving our information from two of Alexander's generals of division, who bore an important part in all his enterprises. Aristobulus and Ptolemy (who afterwards became king of

Egypt) kept regular journals of the military events which they witnessed; and these journals were in the possession of Arrian, when he drew up his history of Alexander's expedition. The high character of Arrian for integrity makes us confident that he used them fairly, and his comments on the occasional discrepancies between the two Macedonian narratives prove that he used them sensibly. He frequently quotes the very words of his authorities and his history thus acquires a charm such as very few ancient or modern military narratives possess. The anecdotes and expressions which he records, we fairly believe to be genuine, and not to be the coinage of a rhetorician, like those in Curtius. In fact, in reading Arrian, we read General Aristobulus and General Ptolemy on the campaigns of the Macedonians; and it is like reading General Jomini or General Foy on the campaigns of the French.

IV

The estimate which we find in Arrian of the strength of Alexander's army, seems reasonable, when we take into account both the losses which he had sustained, and the reinforcements which he had received since he left Europe. Indeed, to Englishmen, who know with what mere handfuls of men our own generals have, at Plassy, at Assaye, at Meeanee, and other Indian battles, routed large hosts of Asiatics, the disparity of numbers that we read of in the victories won by the Macedonians over the Persians, presents nothing incredible. The army which Alexander now led was wholly composed of veteran troops in the highest possible state of equipment and discipline, enthusiastically devoted to their leader, and full of confidence in his military genius and his victorious destiny.

The celebrated Macedonian phalanx formed the main strength of his infantry. This force had been raised and organised by his father Philip, who on his accession to the Macedonian throne needed a numerous and quickly-formed army, and who by lengthening the spear of the ordinary Greek phalanx and increasing the depth of the files, brought the tactic of armed masses to the greatest efficiency of which it was capable with such materials as he possessed. He formed his men sixteen deep, and placed in their grasp the *sarissa,* as the Macedonian pike was called, which was four-and-twenty feet in length, and when couched for action, reached eighteen feet in front of the soldier: so that, as a space of about two feet was allowed between the ranks, the spears of the five files behind him projected in advance of each front-rank man. The phalangite soldier was fully equipped in the defensive armour of the regular Greek infantry.

Thus the phalanx presented a ponderous and bristling mass, which, so long as its order was kept compact, was sure to bear down all opposition. The defects of such an organisation are obvious, and were proved in after years, when the Macedonians were opposed to the Roman legions. But it is clear that, under Alexander, the phalanx was not the cumbrous unwieldy body which it was at Cynoscephalæ and Pydna. His men were veterans and he could obtain from them an accuracy of movement and steadiness of evolution, such as probably the recruits of his father would only have floundered in attempting, and such as certainly were impracticable in the phalanx when handled by his successors; especially as under them it ceased to be a standing force, and became only a militia.

Under Alexander the phalanx consisted of an aggregate of eighteen thousand men, who were divided into six brigades of three thousand each. These were again subdivided into regiments and companies; and the men were carefully trained to wheel, to face about, to take more ground, or to close up, as the emergencies of the battle required. Alexander also arrayed, in the intervals of the regiments of his phalangites, troops armed in a different manner which could prevent their line from being pierced, and their companies taken in flank, when the nature of the ground prevented a close formation; and which could be withdrawn, when a favourable opportunity arrived for closing up the phalanx or any of its brigades for a charge, or when it was necessary to prepare to receive cavalry.

Besides the phalanx, Alexander had a considerable force of infantry who were called shield-bearers; they were not so heavily armed as the phalangites, or as was the case with the Greek regular infantry in general, but they were equipped for close fight, as well as for skirmishing, and were far superior to the ordinary irregular troops of Greek warfare. They were about six thousand strong. Besides these, he had several bodies of Greek regular infantry, and he had archers, slingers and javelin-men, who fought also with broadsword and target. They were principally supplied to him by the highlanders of Illyria and

Thracia. The main strength of his cavalry consisted of two chosen corps of cuirassiers, one Macedonian, and one Thessalian, each of which were about fifteen hundred strong. They were provided with long lances and heavy swords, and horse as well as man was fully equipped with defensive armour. Other regiments of regular cavalry were less heavily armed, and there were several bodies of light horsemen, whom Alexander's conquests in Egypt and Syria had enabled him to mount superbly.

V

A little before the end of August, Alexander crossed the Euphrates at Thapsacus, a small corps of Persian cavalry under Mazæus retiring before him. Alexander was too prudent to march down through the Mesopotamian deserts, and continued to advance eastward with the intention of passing the Tigris, and then, if he was unable to find Darius and bring him to action, of marching southward on the left side of that river along the skirts of a mountainous district, where his men would suffer less from heat and thirst, and where provisions would be more abundant.

Darius, finding that his adversary was not to be enticed into the march through Mesopotamia against his capital, determined to remain on the battle-ground, which he had chosen on the left of the Tigris; where, if his enemy met a defeat or a check, the destruction of the invaders would be certain with two such rivers as the Euphrates and the Tigris in their rear. The Persian king availed himself to the utmost of every advantage in his power. He caused a large space of ground to be carefully levelled for the operation of his scythe-armed chariots; and he deposited his military stores in the strong town of Arbela, about twenty miles in his rear. The rhetoricians of after ages have loved to describe Darius Codomannus as a second Xerxes in ostentation and imbecility; but a fair examination of his generalship in this his last campaign, shows that we was worthy of bearing the same name as his great predecessor, the royal son of Hystaspes.

On learning that Darius was with a large army on the left of the Tigris, Alexander hurried forward and crossed that river without opposition. He was at first unable to procure any certain intelligence of the precise position of the enemy, and after giving his army a short interval of rest, he marched for four days down the left bank of the river. A moralist may pause upon the fact that Alexander must in this march have passed within a few miles of the remains of Nineveh, the great city of the primeval conquerers of the human race. Neither the Macedonian king nor any of his followers knew what those vast mounds had once been. They had already become nameless masses of grass-grown ruins; and it is only within the past few years that the intellectual energy of one of our own countrymen has rescued Nineveh from its long centuries of oblivion. (Sir Austen Henry Layard).

On the fourth day of Alexander's southward march his advanced guard reported that a body of the enemy's cavalry was in sight. He instantly formed his army in order for battle and directing them to advance steadily, he rode forward at the head of some squadrons of cavalry and charged the Persian horse whom he found before him. This was a mere reconnoitering party, and they broke and fled immediately; but the Macedonians made some prisoners, and from them Alexander found that Darius was posted only a few miles off and learned the strength of the army that he had with him. On receiving this news, Alexander halted and gave his men repose for four days, so that they should go into action fresh and vigorous. He also fortified his camp, and deposited in it all his military stores, and his sick and disabled soldiers; intending to advance upon the enemy with the serviceable part of his army perfectly unencumbered.

After this halt, he moved forward, while it was yet dark, with the intention of reaching the enemy, and attacking them at break of day. About half-way between the camps there were some undulations of the ground, which concealed the two armies from each other's view. But on Alexander arriving at their summit, he saw by the early light the Persian host arrayed before him; and he probably also observed traces of some engineering operation having been carried on along part of the ground in front of them. Not knowing that these marks had been caused by the Persians having levelled the ground for the free use of their war-chariots, Alexander suspected that hidden pitfalls had been prepared with a view of disordering the approach of his cavalry. He summoned a council of war forthwith. Some of the officers were for attacking instantly at all hazards, but the more prudent opinion of Parmenio prevailed, and it was determined not to advance farther till the battle-ground had been carefully surveyed.

Alexander halted his army on the heights; and taking with him some light-armed infantry and some cavalry he passed part of the day in reconnoitring the enemy, and observing the nature of the ground which he had to fight on. Darius wisely refrained from moving from his position to attack the Macedonians on the eminences which they occupied, and the two armies remained until night without molesting each other. On Alexander's return to his headquarters, he summoned his generals and superior officers together, and telling them that he well knew that *their* zeal wanted no exhortation he besought them to do their utmost in encouraging and instructing those whom each commanded to do their best in the next day's battle. They were to remind them that they were now not going to fight for a province, as they had hitherto fought, but they were about to decide by their swords the dominion of all Asia. Each officer ought to impress this upon his subalterns, and they should urge it on their men. Their natural courage required no long words to excite its ardour, but they should be reminded of the paramount importance of steadiness in action. The silence in the ranks must be unbroken as long as silence was proper; but when the time came for the charge, the shout and the cheer must be full of terror for the foe. The officers were to be alert in receiving and communicating orders; and every one was to act as if he felt that the whole result of the battle depended on his own single good conduct.

Having thus briefly instructed his generals, Alexander ordered that the army should sup, and take their rest for the night.

Darkness had closed over the tents of the Macedonians when Alexander's veteran general, Parmenio, came to him and proposed that they should make a night attack on the Persians. The king is said to have answered, that he scorned to filch a victory, and that Alexander must conquer openly and fairly. Arrian justly remarks that Alexander's resolution was as wise as it was spirited. Besides the confusion and uncertainty which are inseparable from night engagements the value of Alexander's victory would have been impaired, if gained under circumstances which might supply the enemy with any excuse for his defeat, and encourage him to renew the contest. It was necessary for Alexander not only to beat Darius, but to gain such a victory as should leave his rival without apology for defeat, and without hope of recovery.

The Persians, in fact, expected and were prepared to meet a night attack. Such was the apprehension that Darius entertained of it that he formed his troops at evening in order of battle, and kept them under arms all night. The effect of this was that the morning found them jaded and dispirited, while it brought their adversaries all fresh and vigorous against them.

The written order of battle, which Darius himself caused to be drawn up, fell into the hands of the Macedonians after the engagement, and Aristobulus copied it into his journal. We thus possess, through Arrian, unusually authentic information as to the composition and arrangement of the Persian army. On the extreme left were the Bactrian, Daan, and Archosian cavalry. Next to these Darius placed the troops from Persia proper, both horse and foot. Then came the Susians, and next to these the Cadusians. These forces made up the left wing.

Darius's own station was in the centre. This was composed of the Indians, the Carians, the Mardian archers, and the division of Persians who were distinguished by the golden apples that formed knobs of their spears. Here also were stationed the body-guard of the Persian nobility. Besides these, there were in the centre, formed in deep order, the Uxian and Babylonian troops, and the soldiers from the Red Sea. The brigade of Greek mercenaries, whom Darius had in his service, and who were alone considered fit to stand in the charge of the Macedonian phalanx, was drawn up on either side of the royal chariot. The right wing was composed of the Cœlosyrians, and Mesopotamians, the Medes, the Parthians, the Sacians, the Tapurians, Hyrcanians, Albanians, and Sacesinæ. In advance of the line on the left wing were placed the Scythian cavalry, with a thousand of the Bactrian horse, and a hundred scythe-armed chariots. The elephants and fifty scythe-armed chariots were ranged in front of the centre; and fifty more chariots, with the Armenian and Cappadocian cavalry, were drawn up in advance of the right wing.

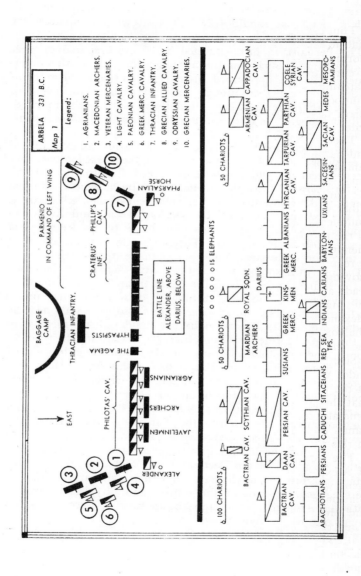

ARBELA 331 B.C.
Map 1

Legend:

1. AGRIANIANS.
2. MACEDONIAN ARCHERS.
3. VETERAN MERCENARIES.
4. LIGHT CAVALRY.
5. PAEONIAN CAVALRY.
6. GREEK MERC. CAVALRY.
7. THRACIAN INFANTRY.
8. GRECIAN ALLIED CAVALRY.
9. ODRYSSIAN CAVALRY.
10. GRECIAN MERCENARIES.

BATTLE LINE
ALEXANDER, ABOVE
DARIUS, BELOW

VI

Thus arrayed, the great host of King Darius passed the night, that to many of them was the last of their existence. The morning of the first of October, two thousand two hundred seventy-three years ago (1850), dawned slowly to their wearied watching, and they could hear the note of the Macedonian trumpet sounding to arms, and could see King Alexander's forces descend from their tents on the heights, and form in order of battle on the plain.

There was deep need of skill, as well as of valour, on Alexander's side; and few battlefields have witnessed more consummate generalship than was now displayed by the Macedonian king. There were no natural barriers by which he could protect his flanks; and not only was he certain to be overlapped on either wing by the vast lines of the Persian army, but there was imminent risk of their circling round him and charging him in the rear, while he advanced against their centre. He formed, therefore, a second or reserve line, which was to wheel round, if required, or to detach troops to either flank, as the enemy's movements might necessitate. And thus, with their whole army ready at any moment to be thrown into one vast hollow square, the Macedonians advanced in two lines against the enemy, Alexander himself leading on the right wing, and the renowned phalanx forming the centre, while Parmenio commanded on the left.

Such was the general nature of the disposition which Alexander made of his army. But we have in Arrian the details of the position of each brigade and regiment; and as we know that these details were taken from the journals of Macedonian generals, it is interesting to examine them, and to read the names and stations of King Alexander's generals and colonels in this the greatest of his battles.

The eight troops of the royal horse-guards formed the right of Alexander's line. Their captains were Cleitus (whose regiment was on the extreme right, the post of peculiar danger), Glaucias, Ariston, Sopolis, Heracleides, Demetrias, Meleager, and Hegelochus. Philotas was general of the whole division. Then came the shield-bearing infantry; Nicanor was their general. Then came the phalanx, in six brigades. Cœnus's brigade was on the right and nearest in this part of his army, Menidas's squadron of cavalry, and Aretes's and Ariston's light horse.

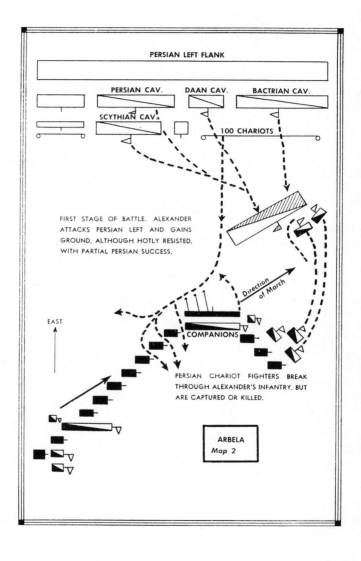

PERSIAN LEFT FLANK

PERSIAN CAV.   DAAN CAV.   BACTRIAN CAV.

SCYTHIAN CAV.

100 CHARIOTS

FIRST STAGE OF BATTLE. ALEXANDER
ATTACKS PERSIAN LEFT AND GAINS
GROUND, ALTHOUGH HOTLY RESISTED,
WITH PARTIAL PERSIAN SUCCESS.

Direction
of March

EAST

COMPANIONS

PERSIAN CHARIOT FIGHTERS BREAK
THROUGH ALEXANDER'S INFANTRY, BUT
ARE CAPTURED OR KILLED.

ARBELA
Map 2

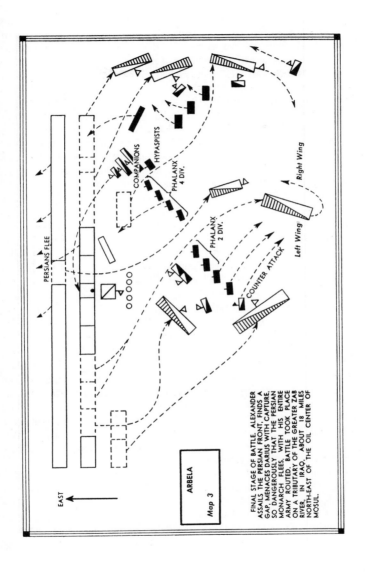

EAST

PERSIANS FLEE

COMPANIONS

HYPASPISTS

PHALANX 4 DIV.

Right Wing

PHALANX 2 DIV.

Left Wing

COUNTER ATTACK

ARBELA

Map 3

FINAL STAGE OF BATTLE. ALEXANDER ASSAILS THE PERSIAN FRONT, FINDS A GAP, MENACES DARIUS WITH CAPTURE, SO DANGEROUSLY THAT THE PERSIAN MONARCH FLEES, WITH HIS ENTIRE ARMY ROUTED. BATTLE TOOK PLACE ON A TRIBUTARY OF THE GREATER ZAB RIVER, IN IRAQ, ABOUT 18 MILES NORTH-EAST OF THE OIL CENTER OF MOSUL.

Menindas was ordered to watch if the enemy's cavalry tried to turn the flank, and, if they did so, to charge them before they wheeled completely round, and so take them in flank themselves. A similar force was arranged on the left of the second line for the same purpose. The Thracian infantry of Sitalces was placed there, and Cœranus's regiment of the cavalry of the Greek allies, and Agathon's troops of the Odrysian irregular horse. The extreme left of the second line in this quarter was held by Andromachus's cavalry. A division of Thracian infantry was left in guard of the camp. In advance of the right wing and centre was scattered a number of light-armed troops, of javelin-men and bow-men, with the intention of warding off the charge of the armed chariots. Kléber's arrangement of his troops at the battle of Heliopolis, where, with ten thousand Europeans, he had to encounter eighty thousand Asiatics in an open plain, is worth comparing with Alexander's tactics at Arbela. (Heliopolis, near Cairo; battle in 1799).

Conspicuous by the brilliancy of his armour, and by the chosen band of officers who were round his person, Alexander took his own station, as his custom was, in the right wing at the head of his cavalry; and when all the arrangements for the battle were complete, and his generals were fully instructed how to act in each probable emergency, he began to lead his men towards the enemy.

It was ever his custom to expose his life freely in battle, and to emulate the personal prowess of his great ancestor, Achilles. Perhaps in the bold enterprise of conquering Persia, it was politic for Alexander to raise his army's daring to the utmost by the example of his own heroic valour; and, in his subsequent campaigns, the love of the excitement, of "the rapture of the strife," may have made him, like Murat, continue from choice a custom which he commenced from duty. But he never suffered the ardour of the soldier to make him lose the coolness of the general.

Great reliance had been placed by the Persian king on the effects of the scythe-bearing·chariots. It was designed to launch these against the Macedonian phalanx, and to follow them up by a heavy charge of cavalry, which it was hoped would find the ranks of the spearmen disordered by the rush of the chariots, and easily destroy this most formidable part of Alexander's force.

In front, therefore, of the Persian centre, where Darius took his station, and which it was supposed the phalanx would attack, the ground had been carefully levelled and smoothed, so as to allow the chariots to charge over it with their full sweep and speed. As the Macedonian army approached the Persian, Alexander found that the front of his whole line barely equalled the front of the Persian centre, so that he was out-flanked on his right by the entire left wing of the enemy, and by their entire right wing on his left. His tactics were to assail some one point of the hostile army, and gain a decisive advantage; while he refused, as far as possible, the encounter along the rest of the line. He therefore inclined his order of march to the right, so as to enable his right wing and centre to come into collision with the enemy on as favourable terms as possible through the manœuvre might in some respect compromise his left.

The effect of this oblique movement was to bring the phalanx and his own wing nearly beyond the limits of the ground which the Persians had prepared for the operations of the chariots. Darius, fearing to lose the benefit of this arm against the most important parts of the Macedonian force, ordered the Scythian and Bactrian cavalry, who were drawn up in advance on his extreme left, to charge round upon Alexander's right wing, and check its further lateral progress. Against these assailants Alexander sent, from his second line, Menidas's cavalry. As these proved too few to make head against the enemy, he ordered Ariston also from the second line with his light horse, and Cleander with his foot, in support of Menidas. The Bactrians and Scythians now began to give way, but Darius reinforced them by the mass of Bactrian cavalry from his main line, and an obstinate cavalry fight now took place. The Bactrians and Scythians were numerous, and were better armed than the horsemen under Menidas and Ariston; and the loss at first was heaviest on the Macedonian side. But still the European cavalry stood the charge of the Asiatics and at last, by their superior discipline, and by acting in squadrons that supported each other, instead of fighting in a confused mass like the barbarians, the Macedonians broke their adversaries and drove them off the field.

The best explanation of this may be found in Napoleon's account of the cavalry fights between the French and the

Mamelukes; "Two Mamelukes were able to make head against
three Frenchmen, because they were better armed, better
mounted, and better trained; they had two pair of pistols, a
blunderbuss, a carbine, a helmet with a vizor, and a coat of
mail; they had several horses, and several attendants on foot.
One hundred cuirassiers, however, were not afraid of one hundred Mamelukes; three hundred could beat an equal number,
and one thousand could easily put to the route fifteen hundred,
so great is the influence of tactics, order, and evolutions! Leclerc
and Lasalle presented their men to the Mamelukes in several
lines. When the Arabs were on the point of overwhelming the
first, the second came to its assistance on the right and left; the
Mamelukes then halted and wheeled, in order to turn the wings
of this new line; this moment was always seized upon to charge
them, and they were uniformly broken."

(Originally slaves trained as soldiers, the Mamelukes through
their leaders, rose to great power in Egypt. Some of them became sultans there. Napoleon defeated them when he invaded
Egypt in 1798, and soon afterward they were virtually exterminated by the Turkish viceroy).

Darius directed the scythe-armed chariots to be driven against
Alexander's horse-guards and the phalanx; and these formidable
vehicles were accordingly sent rattling across the plain, against
the Macedonian line. When we remember the alarm which the
war-chariots of the Britons created among Cæsar's legions, we
shall not be prone to deride this arm of ancient warfare as always
useless. The object of the chariots was to create unsteadiness in
the ranks against which they were driven, and squadrons of cavalry followed close upon them, to profit by such disorder. But
the Asiatic chariots were rendered ineffective at Arbela by the
light-armed troops whom Alexander had specially appointed
for the service, and who, wounding the horses and drivers with
their missile weapons, and running alongside so as to cut the
traces or seize the reins, marred the intended charge. The few
chariots that reached the phalanx, passed harmlessly through
the intervals which the spearmen opened for them, and were
easily captured in the rear.

A mass of the Asiatic cavalry was now, for the second time,
collected against Alexander's extreme right, and moved round
it, with the view of gaining the flank of his army. At the
critical moment, Aretes, with his horsemen from Alexander's

second line, dashed on the Persian squadrons when their own
flanks were exposed by this evolution. While Alexander thus
met and baffled all the flanking attacks of the enemy with troops
brought up from his second line, he kept his own horse-guards
and the rest of the front line of his wing fresh, and ready to
take advantage of the first opportunity for striking a decisive
blow. This soon came. A large body of horse, who were posted
on the Persian left wing nearest to the centre, quitted their station, and rode off to help their comrades in the cavalry fight
that still was going on at the extreme right of Alexander's wing
against the detachments from his second line. This made a huge
gap in the Persian array, and into this space Alexander instantly
dashed with his guard; and then pressing towards his left, he
soon began to make havoc in the left flank of the Persian centre.
The shield-bearing infantry now charged also among the reeling
masses of the Asiatics. Five of the brigades of the phalanx,
with the irresistible might of their sarissas, bore down the
Greek mercenaries of Darius, and dug their way through the
Persian centre.

In the early part of the battle, Darius had showed skill and
energy; and he now for some time encouraged his men, by voice
and example, to keep firm. But the lances of Alexander's cavalry
and the pikes of the phalanx now gleamed nearer and nearer
to him. His charioteer was struck down by a javelin at his side;
and at last Darius's nerve failed him; and, descending from his
chariot, he mounted on a fleet horse and galloped from the
plain, regardless of the state of the battle in other parts of the
field, where matters were going on much more favourably for
his cause, and where his presence might have done much towards
gaining a victory.

VII

Alexander's operations with his right and centre had exposed
his left to an immensely preponderating force of the enemy.
Parmenio kept out of action as long as possible; but Mazæus,
who commanded the Persian right wing, advanced against him,
completely outflanked him, and pressed him severely with
reiterated charges by superior numbers. Seeing the distress of
Parmenio's wing, Simmias, who commanded the sixth brigade
of the phalanx, which was next to the left wing, did not advance
with the other brigades in the great charge upon the Persian

centre, but kept back to cover Parmenio's troops on *their* right
flank. Otherwise they would have been completely surrounded
and cut off from the rest of the Macedonian army. By so doing,
Simmias had unavoidably opened a gap in the Macedonian
left centre and a large column of Indian and Persian horse,
from the Persian right centre, had galloped forward through
this interval, and right through the troops of the Macedonian
second line.

Instead of then wheeling round upon Parmenio, or upon
the rear of Alexander's conquering wing, the Indian and Persian
cavalry rode straight on to the Macedonian camp, overpowered
the Thracians who were left in charge of it, and began to
plunder. This was stopped by the phalangite troops of the second line, who, after the enemy's horsemen had rushed by them,
faced about, countermarched upon the camp, killed many of the
Indians and Persians in the act of plundering, and forced the
rest to ride off again. Just at this crisis, Alexander had been
recalled from his pursuit of Darius, by tidings of the distress
of Parmenio, and of his inability to bear up any longer against
the hot attacks of Mazæus. Taking his horse-guards with him,
Alexander rode towards the part of the field where his left wing
was fighting; but on his way thither he encountered the
Persian and Indian cavalry, on their return from his camp.

These men now saw that their only chance of safety was
to cut their way through and in one huge column they charged
desperately upon the Macedonians. There was here a close
hand-to-hand fight, which lasted some time, and sixty of the
royal horse-guards fell, and three generals, who fought close
to Alexander's side, were wounded. At length the Macedonian
discipline and valour again prevailed, and a large number of
the Persian and Indian horsemen were cut down, some few
only succeeded in breaking through and riding away. Relieved
of these obstinate enemies, Alexander again formed his horse-
guards, and led them towards Parmenio; but by this time that
general also was victorious. Probably the news of Darius's
flight had reached Mazæus, and had damped the ardour of the
Persian right wing; while the tidings of their comrades' success
must have proportionally encouraged the Macedonian forces
under Parmenio. His Thessalian cavalry particularly distinguished themselves by their gallantry and persevering good conduct: and by the time that Alexander had ridden up to Par

menio, the whole Persian army was in full flight from the field.

It was of the deepest importance to Alexander to secure the person of Darius, and he now urged on the pursuit. The river Lycus was between the field of battle and the city of Arbela, whither the fugitives directed their course, and the passage of this river was even more destructive to the Persians than the swords and spears of the Macedonians had been in the engagement. The narrow bridge was soon choked up by the flying thousands who rushed towards it, and vast numbers of the *Persians threw themselves, or were *forced by others, into the rapid stream and perished in its waters. Darius had crossed it, and had ridden on through Arbela without halting. Alexander reached that city on the next day, and made himself master of all Darius's treasure and stores; but the Persian king, unfortunately for himself, had fled too fast for his conqueror; he had only escaped to perish by the treachery of his Bactrian satrap, Bessus. (A year later).

A few days after the battle, Alexander entered Babylon, "the oldest seat of earthly empire" then in existence, as its acknowledged lord and master. There were yet some campaigns of his brief and bright career to be accomplished. Central Asia was yet to witness the march of his phalanx. He was yet to effect that conquest of Afghanistan in which England later failed. His generalship, as well as his valour, were yet to be signalised on the banks of the Hydaspes, and the field of Chillianwallah; and he was yet to precede the Queen of England in annexing the Punjab to the dominions of a European sovereign. But the crisis of his career was reached; the great object of his mission was accomplished; and the ancient Persian empire, which once menaced all the nations of the earth with subjection, was irreparably crushed, when Alexander had won his crowning victory at Arbela.

SYNOPSIS OF EVENTS BETWEEN THE BATTLE OF ARBELA AND THE BATTLE OF THE METAURUS.

330 B.C. The Lacedæmonians endeavour to create a rising in Greece against the Macedonian power; they are defeated by Antipater, Alexander's viceroy; and their king, Agis, falls in the battle.

330 to 327. Alexander's campaigns in Upper Asia. "Having conquered Darius, Alexander pursued his way, encountering difficulties which would have appalled almost any other general, through Bactriana, and taking Bactra, or Zariaspa (now Balkh), the chief city of that province, where he spent the winter. Crossing the Oxus, he advanced in the

following spring to Maracanda (Samarkand) to replace the loss of horses which he had sustained in crossing the Caucasus, to obtain supplies from the rich valley of Sogd (the Mohammedan paradise of Mader-al-Nahr), and to enforce the submission of Transoxiana. The northern limit of his march is probably represented by the modern Uskand, or Aderkand, a village on the Iaxartes, near the end of the Fergánah district. In Margiana he founded another Alexandria. Returning from the north, he led on his army in the hope of conquering India, till at length, marching in a line apparently nearly parallel with the Kâbul river, he arrived at the celebrated rock Aornos, the position of which must have been on the right bank of the Indus, at some distance from Attock; and it may perhaps be represented by the modern Akora."— VAUX.

327, 326.   Alexander marches through Afghanistan to the Punjab. He defeats Porus. His troops refuse to march towards the Ganges, and he commences the descent of the Indus. On his march he attacks and subdues several Indian tribes, among others the Malli; in the storming of whose capital (Multan), he is severely wounded. He directs his admiral, Nearchus, to sail round from the Indus to the Persian Gulf; and leads the army back across Sind and Beluchistan.

324.   Alexander returns to Babylon. "In the tenth year after he had crossed the Hellespont, Alexander, having won his vast dominion, entered Babylon; and resting from his career in that oldest seat of earthly empire, he steadily surveyed the mass of various nations which owned his sovereignty, and revolved in his mind the great work of breathing into this huge but inert body the living spirit of Greek civilisation. In the bloom of youthful manhood, at the age of thirty-two, he paused from the fiery speed of his earlier course; and for the first time gave the nations an opportunity of offering their homage before his throne. They came from all the extremities of the earth to propitiate his anger, to celebrate his greatness, or to solicit his protection. . . . History may allow us to think that Alexander and a Roman ambassador did meet at Babylon, that the greatest man of the ancient world saw and spoke with a citizen of that great nation, which was destined to succeed him in his appointed work, and to found a wider and still more enduring empire. They met, too, in Babylon, almost beneath the shadow of the temple of Bel, perhaps the earliest monument ever raised by human pride and power, in a city, stricken, as it were, by the word of God's heaviest judgment, as the symbol of greatness apart from and opposed to goodness."—ARNOLD.

323.   Alexander dies at Babylon. On his death being known at Greece, the Athenians, and others of the southern states, take up arms to shake off the domination of Macedon. They are at first successful; but the return of some of Alexander's veterans from Asia enables Antipater to prevail over them.

317 to 289. Agathocles is tyrant of Syracuse; and carries on repeated wars with the Carthaginians; in the course of which (311) he invades Africa, and reduces the Carthaginians to great distress.

306.   After a long series of wars with each other, and after all the heirs of Alexander had been murdered, his principal surviving generals assume the title of king, each over the provinces which he has occupied. The four chief among them were Antigonus, Ptolemy, Lysimachus, and

Seleucus. Antipater was now dead, but his son Cassander succeeded to his power in Macedonia and Greece.

301. **Seleucus and Lysimachus defeat Antigonus at Ipsus.** Antigonus is killed in the battle.

290. **Rome had now thoroughly subdued the Samnites and the Etruscans,** and had gained numerous victories over the Cisalpine Gauls. Wishing to confirm her dominion in Lower Italy, she became entangled in a war with Pyrrhus, fourth king of Epirus, who was called over by the Tarentines to aid them. Pyrrhus was at first victorious, but in the year 275 was defeated by the Roman legions in a pitched battle. Rome becomes mistress of all Italy from the ·Rubicon to the Straits of Messina.

280. **Seleucus, the last of Alexander's captains, is assassinated.** Of all Alexander's successors, Seleucus had formed the most powerful empire. He had acquired all the provinces between Phrygia and the Indus. He extended his dominion in India beyond the limits reached by Alexander. Seleucus had some sparks of his great master's genius in promoting civilisation and commerce, as well as in gaining victories. Under his successors, the Seleucidæ, this vast empire rapidly diminished; Bactria became independent, and a separate dynasty of Greek kings ruled there in the year 125, when it was overthrown by the Scythian tribes. Parthia threw off its allegiance to the Seleucidæ in 250 B.C., and the powerful Parthian kingdom, which afterwards proved so formidable a foe to Rome, absorbed nearly all the provinces west of the Euphrates, that had obeyed the first Seleucus. Before the battle of Ipsus, Mithridates, a Persian prince of the blood-royal of the Achæmenidæ, had escaped to Pontus, and founded there the kingdom of that name.

Besides the kingdom of Seleucus, which, when limited to Syria, Palestine, and parts of Asia Minor, long survived, the most **important** kingdom formed by a general of Alexander, was that of the Ptolemies in Egypt. The throne of Macedonia was long and obstinately contended for by Cassander, Polysperchon, Lysimachus, Pyrrhus, Antigonus, and others; but at last was secured by the dynasty of Antigonus Gonatas. The old republics of southern Greece suffered severely during these tumults, and the only Greek states that showed any strength and spirit, were the cities of the Achæan league, the Ætolians, and the islanders of Rhodes.

264. **The first Punic war begins.** Its primary cause was the desire of both the Romans and the Carthaginians to possess themselves of Sicily. The Romans form a fleet, and successfully compete with the marine of Carthage. During the latter half of the war, the military genius of Hamilcar Barca sustains the Carthaginian cause in Sicily. At the end of twenty-four years, the Carthaginians sue for peace, though their aggregate loss in ships and men had been less than that sustained by the Romans since the beginning of the war. Sicily becomes a Roman province.

240 to 218. **The Carthaginian mercenaries who had been brought back from** Sicily to Africa, mutiny against Carthage, and nearly succeed in destroying her. After a sanguinary and desperate struggle, Hamilcar Barca crushes them. During this season of weakness to Carthage, Rome takes from her the island of Sardinia. Hamilcar Barca forms the proj-

ect of obtaining compensation by conquests in Spain, and thus enabling
Carthage to renew the struggle with Rome. He takes Hannibal (then
a child) to Spain with him. He and, after his death, his brother, win
great part of southern Spain to the Carthaginian interest. Hannibal
obtains the command of the Carthaginian armies in Spain, 221 B.C.,
being then twenty-six years old. He attacks Saguntum, a city on the
Ebro in alliance with Rome, which is the immediate pretext for the
second Punic war.

During this interval Rome had to sustain a storm from the north.
The Cisalpine Gauls, in 226, formed an alliance with one of the fiercest
tribes of their brethren north of the Alps, and began a furious war
against the Romans, which lasted six years. The Romans gave them
several severe defeats, and took from them part of their territories near
the Po. It was on this occasion that the Roman colonies of Cremona
and Placentia were founded, the latter of which did such essential
service to Rome in the second Punic war, by the resistance which it
made to the army of Hasdrubal. A muster-roll was made in this war
of the effective military force of the Romans themselves, and of those
Italian states that were subject to them. The return showed a force of
seven hundred thousand foot, and seventy thousand horse.

218. Hannibal crosses the Alps and invades Italy.

-⟦ FOUR ⟧-

The Metaurus, 207 B. C.

WHY DECISIVE: *"The battle of the Metaurus . . . not only determined the event of the strife between Rome and Carthage, but it ensured to Rome two centuries more of almost un-changed conquest. . . . After Hannibal's downfall the great military republic of the ancient world met in her career of conquest no other worthy competitor."* [Creasy.]

I

ABOUT midway between Rimini and Ancona a little river falls into the Adriatic. That stream is still called the Metauro and wakens by its name recollections of the reso-lute daring of ancient Rome, and of the slaughter that stained its current two thousand, one hundred and fifty years ago (1850), when the combined consular armies of Livius and Nero (Caius Claudius Nero, not to be mistaken for the last of the Cæsars, 37-68 A.D.), encountered and crushed near its banks the varied host which Hannibal's brother was leading from the Pyrenees, the Rhone, the Alps, and the Po, to aid the great Carthaginian in his stern struggle to annihilate the growing might of the Roman Republic, and make the Punic (Carthaginian) power supreme over all the nations of the world.

The Roman historian, who termed that struggle the most memorable of all wars that ever were carried on, wrote in no spirit of exaggeration. For it is not in ancient, but in modern history, that parallels for its incidents and its heroes are to be found. The similitude between the contest which Rome main-tained against Hannibal, and that which England was for many years engaged in against Napoleon, has not passed un-observed by recent historians. "Twice," says Arnold, "has there been witnessed the struggle of the highest individual genius against the resources and institutions of a great nation; and in both cases the nation has been victorious.

"For seventeen years Hannibal strove against Rome; for sixteen years Napoleon Bonaparte strove against England; the efforts of the first ended in Zama,—those of the second in Waterloo." One point, however, of the similitude between the two wars has scarcely been adequately dwelt on. That is, the remarkable parallel between the Roman general who finally defeated the great Carthaginian, and the English general who gave the last deadly overthrow to the French emperor. Scipio and Wellington both held for many years commands of high importance, but distant from the main theatres of warfare. The same country was the scene of the principal military career of each. It was in Spain that Scipio, like Wellington, successively encountered and overthrew nearly all the subordinate generals of the enemy, before being opposed to the chief champion and conqueror himself. Both Scipio and Wellington restored their country-men's confidence in arms, when shaken by a series of reverses. And each of them closed a long and perilous war by a complete and overwhelming defeat of the chosen leader and the chosen veterans of the foe.

Nor is the parallel between them limited to their military characters and exploits. Scipio, like Wellington, became an important leader of the aristocratic party among his countrymen, and was exposed to the unmeasured invectives of the violent section of his political antagonists. When an infuriated mob assaulted the Duke of Wellington in the streets of the English capital on the anniversary of Waterloo, England was even more disgraced by that outrage than Rome was by the factious accusations which demagogues brought against Scipio, but which he proudly repelled on the day of trial, by reminding the assembled people that it was the anniversary of the battle of Zama. (In North Africa, 202 B.C., which ended the second Punic war. "Puntic" is the Latin derivative of the Greek "Phoenica").

Scipio at Zama trampled in the dust the power of Carthage; but that power had been already irreparably shattered in another field, where neither Scipio nor Hannibal commanded. When the Metaurus witnessed the defeat and death of Hasdrubal, it witnessed the ruin of the scheme by which alone Carthage could hope to organise decisive success,—the scheme of enveloping Rome at once from the north and the south of Italy by chosen armies, led by two sons of Hamilcar. That battle was the determining crisis of the contest, not merely between Rome and Carthage, but between the two great families of the world, which then made Italy the arena of their oft-renewed contest for pre-eminence.

The French historian Michelet, whose *Histoire Romaine*

would have been invaluable, if the general industry and accuracy of the writer had in any degree equalled his originality and brilliancy, eloquently remarks, "It is not without reason that so universal and vivid a remembrance of the Punic wars has dwelt in the memories of men. They formed no mere struggle to determine the lot of two cities or two empires; but it was a strife, on the event of which depended the fate of two races of mankind, whether the dominion of the world should belong to the Indo-Germanic or to the Semitic family of nations. Bear in mind, that the first of these comprises, besides the Indians and the Persians, the Greeks, the Romans, and the Germans. In the other are ranked the Jews and the Arabs, the Phœnicians and the Carthaginians. On the one side is the genius of heroism, of art, and legislation: on the other, is the spirit of industry, of commerce, of navigation. The two opposite races have everywhere come into contact, everywhere into hostility. In the primitive history of Persia and Chaldea, the heroes are perpetually engaged in combat with their industrious and perfidious neighbours.

"The struggle is renewed between the Phœnicians and the Greeks on every coast of the Mediterranean. The Greek supplants the Phœnician in all his factories, all his colonies in the East: soon will the Roman come, and do likewise in the West. Alexander did far more against Tyre than Salmanasar or Nabuchodonosor had done. Not content with crushing her, he took care that she never should revive, for he founded Alexandria as her substitute, and changed for ever the track of the commerce of the world. There remained Carthage—the great Carthage, and her mighty empire,—mighty in a far different degree than Phœnicia's had been. Rome annihilated it. Then occurred that which has no parallel in history,—an entire civilisation perished at one blow—vanished, like a falling star. The *Periplus* of Hanno, a few coins, a score of lines in Plautus, and, lo, all that remains of the Carthaginian world! (Hanno, a Carthaginian navigator of the 5th Century. B.C., who explored the western coast of Africa as far as Sierra Leone, and founded towns. His *Periplus* is an account of his voyage.)

"Many generations must need pass away before the struggle between the two races could be renewed; and the Arabs, that formidable rear-guard of the Semitic world, dashed forth from their deserts. The conflict between the two races then became

the conflict of two religions. Fortunate was it that those daring
Saracenic cavaliers encountered in the East the impregnable
walls of Constantinople, in the West the chivalrous valour of
Charles Martel (in France), and the sword of the Cid (Rodrigo
Diaz de Bivar, of Spain, d. 1099). The crusades were the natural
reprisals for the Arab invasions, and form the last epoch of
that great struggle between the two principal families of the
human race."

II

It is difficult amid the glimmering light supplied by the al-
lusions of the classical writers to gain a full idea of the character and institutions of Rome's great rival. But we can perceive how inferior Carthage was to her competitor in military
resources; and how far less fitted than Rome she was to become
the founder of centralised and centralising dominion, that should
endure for centuries, and fuse into imperial unity the narrow
nationalities of the ancient races, that dwelt around and near
the shores of the Mediterranean sea.

Carthage was originally neither the most ancient nor the most
powerful of the numerous colonies, which the Phœnicians
planted on the coast of northern Africa. But her advantageous
position, the excellence of her constitution (of which, though
ill-informed as to its details, we know that it commanded the
admiration of Aristotle), and the commercial and political
energy of her citizens gave her the ascendancy over Hippo, Utica,
Leptis, and her other sister Phœnician cities in those regions;
and she finally reduced them to a condition of dependency,
similar to that which the subject allies of Athens occupied relatively to that once imperial city.

When Tyre and Sidon, and the other cities of Phœnicia itself
sank from independent republics into mere vassal states of the
great Asiatic monarchies, and obeyed by turns a Babylonian, a
Persian, and a Macedonian master, their power and their traffic
rapidly declined; and Carthage succeeded to the important
maritime and commercial character which they had previously
maintained. The Carthaginians did not seek to compete with
the Greeks on the northeastern shores of the Mediterranean, or
in the three inland seas which are connected with it; but they
maintained an active intercourse with the Phœnicians, and
through them with lower and central Asia; and they, and they

alone, after the decline and fall of Tyre, navigated the waters of the Atlantic. They had the monopoly of all the commerce of the world that was carried on beyond the Straits of Gibraltar.

We have yet extant (in a Greek translation) the narrative of the voyage of Hanno, one of their admirals, along the western coast of Africa as far as Sierra Leone. And in the Latin poem of Festus Avienus, frequent references are made to the records of the voyages of another celebrated Carthaginian admiral, Himilco, who had explored the north-western coast of Europe. The British islands are mentioned by Himilco as the lands of the Hiberni and the Albioni. It is indeed certain that the Carthaginians frequented the Cornish coast (as the Phœnicians had done before them) for the purpose of procuring tin; and there is every reason to believe that they sailed as far as the coasts of the Baltic for amber. When it is remembered that the mariner's compass was unknown in those ages, the boldness and skill of the seamen of Carthage, and the enterprise of her merchants, may be paralleled with any achievements that the history of modern navigation and commerce can supply.

In their Atlantic voyages along the African shores, the Carthaginians followed the double object of traffic and colonisation. The numerous settlements that were planted by them on the coast from Morocco to Senegal provided for the needy members of the constantly increasing population of a great commercial capital; and also strengthened the influence which Carthage exercised among the tribes of the African coast. Besides her fleets, her caravans gave her a large and lucrative trade with the native Africans; nor must we limit our belief of the extent of the Carthaginian trade with the tribes of central and western Africa, by the narrowness of the commercial intercourse which civilised nations of modern times have been able to create in those regions.

Although essentially a mercantile and seafaring people, the Carthaginians by no means neglected agriculture. On the contrary, the whole of their territory was cultivated like a garden. The fertility of the soil repaid the skill and toil bestowed on it; and every invader from Agathocles to Scipio Æmilianus, was struck with admiration at the rich pasture-lands carefully irrigated, the abundant harvests, the luxuriant vineyards, the plantations of fig and olive trees, the thriving villages, the populous towns, and the splendid villas of the wealthy Carthaginians through which his march lay, as long as he was on Carthaginian ground.

The Carthaginians abandoned the Ægean and the Pontus to the Greeks, but they were by no means disposed to relinquish to those rivals the commerce and the dominion of the coasts of the Mediterranean westward of Italy. For centuries the Carthaginians strove to make themselves masters of the islands that lie between Italy and Spain. They acquired the Balearic Islands, where the principal harbour, Port Mahon, still bears the name of the Carthaginian admiral. They succeeded in reducing the greater part of Sardinia, but Sicily could never be brought into their power. They repeatedly invaded that island, and nearly overran it, but the resistance which was opposed to them by the Syracusans under Gelon, Dionysius, Timoleon, and Agathocles, preserved the island from becoming Punic, though many of its cities remained under the Carthaginian rule, until Rome finally settled the question to whom Sicily was to belong, by conquering it for herself.

With so many elements of success, with almost unbounded wealth, with commercial and maritime activity, with a fertile territory, with a capital city of almost impregnable strength, with a constitution that ensured for centuries the blessings of social order, with an aristocracy singularly fertile in men of the highest genius, Carthage yet failed signally and calamitously in her contest for power with Rome. One of the immediate causes of this may seem to have been the want of firmness among her citizens, which made them terminate the first Punic war by begging peace, sooner than endure any longer the hardships and burdens caused by a state of warfare, although their antagonists had suffered far more severely than themselves. Another cause was the spirit of faction among their leading men, which prevented Hannibal in the second war from being properly reinforced and supported. But there were also more general causes why Carthage proved inferior to Rome. These were her position relative to the mass of the inhabitants of the country which she ruled, and her habit of trusting to mercenary armies in her wars.

Our clearest information as to the different races of men in and about Carthage, is derived from Diodorus Siculus. That historian enumerates four different races: first, he mentions the Phœnicians who dwelt in Carthage: next, he speaks of the Liby-

Phœnicians; these, he tells us, dwelt in many of the maritime cities, and were connected by intermarriages with the Phœnicians, which was the cause of their compound name: thirdly, he mentions the Libyans, the bulk and the most ancient part of the population, hating the Carthaginians intensely, on account of the oppressiveness of their domination: lastly, he names the Numidians, the nomad tribes of the frontier.

It is evident, from this description, that the native Libyans were a subject class, without franchise or political rights; and, accordingly, we find no instance specified in history of a Libyan holding political office or military command. The half-castes, the Liby-Phœnicians, seem to have been sometimes sent out as colonists; but it may be inferred, from what Diodorus says of their residence, that they had not the right of the citizenship of Carthage. Only a solitary case occurs of one of this race being entrusted with authority, and that, too, not emanating from the home government. This is the instance of the officer sent by Hannibal to Sicily, after the fall of Syracuse, whom Polybius calls Myttinus the Libyan, but whom, from the fuller account in Livy, we find to have been a Liby-Phœnician; and it is expressly mentioned what indignation was felt by the Carthaginian commanders in the island that this half-caste should control their operations.

With respect to the composition of their armies, it is observable that, though thirsting for extended empire, and though some of their leading men became generals of the highest order, the Carthaginians, as a people, were anything but personally warlike. So long as they could hire mercenaries to fight for them, they had little appetite for the irksome training, and they grudged the loss of valuable time which military service would have entailed on themselves.

As Michelet remarks, "The life of an industrious merchant, of a Carthaginian, was too precious to be risked, as long as it was possible to substitute advantageously for it that of a barbarian from Spain or Gaul. Carthage knew, and could tell to a drachma, what the life of a man of each nation came to. A Greek was worth more than a Campanian, a Campanian worth more than a Gaul or a Spaniard. When once this tariff of blood was correctly made out, Carthage began a war as a mercantile speculation. She tried to make conquests in the hope of getting new mines to work, or to open fresh markets

for her exports. In one venture she could afford to spend fifty
thousand mercenaries, in another rather more. If the returns
were good, there was no regret felt for the capital that had
been lavished in the investment: more money got more men,
and all went on well."

Armies composed of foreign mercenaries have, in all ages,
been as formidable to their employers as to the enemy against
whom they were directed. We know of one occasion (between
the first and second Punic wars) when Carthage was brought
to the very brink of destruction by a revolt of her foreign troops.
Other mutinies of the same kind must from time to time have
occurred. Probably one of these was the cause of the comparative weakness of Carthage at the time of the Athenian expedition against Syracuse; so different from the energy with
which she attacked Gelon half a century earlier, and Dionysius
half a century later. And even when we consider her armies
with reference only to their efficiency in warfare, we perceive
at once the inferiority of such bands of *condottieri*, brought
together without any common bond of origin, tactics, or cause,
to the legions of Rome, which at the time of the Punic wars
were raised from the very flower of a hardy agricultural population, trained in the strictest discipline, habituated to victory
and animated by the most resolute patriotism.

III

And this shows also the transcendency of the genius of Hannibal, which could form such discordant materials into a compact organised force, and inspire them with the spirit of patient
discipline and loyalty to their chief; so that they were true to
him in his adverse as well as in his prosperous fortunes. Also
throughout the chequered series of his campaigns no panic rout
ever disgraced a division under his command; no mutiny, or
even attempt at mutiny, was ever known in his camp; and,
finally, after fifteen years of Italian warfare, his men followed
their old leader to Zama, "with no fear and little hope;" and
there, on that disastrous field, stood firm around him, his Old
Guard, till Scipio's Numidian allies came up on their flank;
when at last, surrounded and overpowered, the veteran battalions
sealed their devotion to their general with their blood! To quote
Thomas Arnold:

"But if Hannibal's genius may be likened to the Homeric god, who, in his hatred to the Trojans, rises from the deep to rally the fainting Greeks, and to lead them against the enemy, so the calm courage with which Hector met his more than human adversary in his country's cause, is no unworthy image of the unyielding magnanimity displayed by the aristocracy of Rome. As Hannibal utterly eclipses Carthage, so, on the contrary, Fabius, Marcellus, Claudius, Nero, even Scipio himself, are as nothing when compared to the spirit, and wisdom, and power of Rome. The senate, which voted its thanks to its political enemy, Varro, after his disastrous defeat, 'because he had not despaired of the commonwealth,' and which disdained either to solicit, or to reprove, or to threaten, or in any way to notice the twelve colonies which had refused their customary supplies of men for the army, is far more to be honoured than the conqueror of Zama.

"This we should the more carefully bear in mind, because our tendency is to admire individual greatness far more than national; and, as no single Roman will bear comparison to Hannibal, we are apt to murmur at the event of the contest, and to think that the victory was awarded to the least worthy of the combatants. On the contrary, never was the wisdom of God's Providence more manifest than in the issue of the struggle between Rome and Carthage. It was clearly for the good of mankind that Hannibal should be conquered. His triumph would have stopped the progress of the world. For great men can only act permanently by forming great nations; and no one man, even though it were Hannibal himself, can in one generation effect such a work. But where the nation has been merely enkindled for a while by a great man's spirit, the light passes away with him who communicated it; and the nation, when he is gone, is like a dead body, to which magic power had, for a moment, given unnatural life: when the charm has ceased, the body is cold and stiff as before.

"He who grieves over the battle of Zama, should carry on his thoughts to a period thirty years later, when Hannibal must, in the course of nature have been dead, and consider how the isolated Phœnician city of Carthage was fitted to receive and so consolidate the civilisation of Greece, or by its laws and institutions to bind together barbarians of every race and language into an organised empire, and prepare them for becoming,

when that empire was dissolved, the free members of the commonwealth of Christian Europe."

IV

It was in the spring of 207 B.C. that Hasdrubal, after skilfully
disentangling himself from the Roman forces in Spain, and,
after a march conducted with great judgment and little loss
through the interior of Gaul and the passes of the Alps, appeared in the country that now is the north of Lombardy, at
the head of troops which he had partly brought out of Spain,
and partly levied among the Gauls and Ligurians on his way.
At this time Hannibal, with his unconquered, and seemingly
unconquerable army, had been eleven years in Italy, executing
with strenuous ferocity the vow of hatred to Rome, which had
been sworn by him while yet a child at the bidding of his father,
Hamilcar; who, as he boasted, had trained up his three sons,
Hannibal, Hasdrubal, and Mago, like three lion's whelps, to
prey upon the Romans.

But Hannibal's latter campaigns had not been signalised by
any such great victories as marked the first years of his invasion of Italy. The stern spirit of Roman resolution, ever
highest in disaster and danger, had neither bent nor despaired
beneath the merciless blows which "the dire African" dealt
her in rapid succession at Trebia, at Trasimene,. and at
Cannæ. Her population was thinned by repeated slaughter in
the field; poverty and actual scarcity wore down the survivors,
through the fearful ravages which Hannibal's cavalry spread
through their cornfields, their pasture-lands, and their vineyards; many of her allies went over to the invader's side and
new clouds of foreign war threatened her from Macedonia and
Gaul.

But Rome receded not. Rich and poor among her citizens
vied with each other in devotion to their country. The wealthy
placed their stores, and all placed their lives at the state's disposal. And though Hannibal could not be driven out of Italy,
though every year brought its sufferings and sacrifices, Rome
felt that her constancy had not been exerted in vain. If she
was weakened by the continued strife, so was Hannibal also;
and it was clear that the unaided resources of his army were
unequal to the task of her destruction. The single deerhound

could not pull down the quarry which he had so furiously assailed. Rome not only stood fiercely at bay, but had pressed back and gored her antagonist, that still, however, watched her in act to spring. She was weary, and bleeding at every pore; and there seemed to be little hope of her escape, if the other hound of old Hamilcar's race should come up in time to aid his brother in the death-grapple.

Hasdrubal had commanded the Carthaginian armies in Spain for some time with varying, but generally unpropitious fortune. He had not the full authority over the Punic forces in that country, which his brother and his father had previously exercised. The faction at Carthage, which was at feud with his family, succeeded in fettering and interfering with his power; and other generals were from time to time sent into Spain, whose errors and misconduct caused the reverses that Hasdrubal met with. This is expressly attested by the Greek historian, Polybius, who was the intimate friend of the younger Africanus, and drew his information respecting the second Punic war from the best possible authorities. Livy gives a long narrative of campaigns between the Roman commanders in Spain and Hasdrubal, which is so palpably deformed by fictions and exaggerations as to be hardly deserving of attention.

It is clear that, in the year 208 B.C., at least, Hasdrubal outmanœuvred Publius Scipio, who held the command of the Roman forces in Spain and whose object was to prevent him from passing the Pyrenees and marching upon Italy. Scipio expected that Hasdrubal would attempt the nearest route along the coast of the Mediterranean; and he therefore carefully fortified and guarded the passes of the eastern Pyrenees. But Hasdrubal passed these mountains near their western extremity; and then, with a considerable force of Spanish infantry, with a small number of African troops, with some elephants and much treasure, he marched, not directly towards the coast of the Mediterranean, but in a north-eastern line towards the centre of Gaul. He halted for the winter in the territory of the Arverni, the modern Auvergne; and conciliated or purchased the good-will of the Gauls in that region so far that he not only found friendly winter-quarters among them, but great numbers of them enlisted under him and on the approach of spring, marched with him to invade Italy.

By thus entering Gaul at the south-west, and avoiding its

southern maritime districts, **Hasdrubal** kept the Romans in complete ignorance of his precise operations and movements in that country; all that they knew was that Hasdrubal had baffled Scipio's attempts to detain him in Spain; that he had crossed the Pyrenees with soldiers, elephants, and money, and that he was raising fresh forces among the Gauls. The spring was sure to bring him into Italy; and then would come the real tempest of the war, when from the north and from the south the two Carthaginian armies, each under a son of the Thunderbolt (Hamilcar's surname), were to gather together around the seven hills of Rome.

V

In this emergency the Romans looked among themselves earnestly and anxiously for leaders fit to meet the perils of the coming campaign.

The senate recommended the people to elect, as one of their consuls, Caius Claudius Nero, a patrician of one of the families of the great Claudian house (not the Emperor, 54-68). Nero had served during the preceding years of the war, both against Hannibal in Italy and against Hasdrubal in Spain; but it is remarkable that the histories, which we possess, record no successes as having been achieved by him either before or after his great campaign of the Metaurus. It proves much for the sagacity of the leading men of the senate, that they recognized in Nero the energy and spirit which were required at this crisis, and it is equally creditable to the patriotism of the people that they followed the advice of the senate by electing a general who had no showy exploits to recommend him to their choice.

It was a matter of greater difficulty to find a second consul; the laws required that one consul should be a plebeian; and the plebeian nobility had been fearfully thinned by the events of the war. While the senators anxiously deliberated among themselves what fit colleague for Nero could be nominated at the coming comitia, and sorrowfully recalled the names of Marcellus, Gracchus, and other plebeian generals who were no more—one taciturn and moody old man sat in sullen apathy among the conscript fathers.

This was Marcus Livius, who had been consul in the year before the beginning of this war, and had then gained a vic-

tory over the Illyrians. After his consulship he had been im-
peached before the people on a charge of peculation and unfair division of the spoils among his soldiers; the verdict was
unjustly given against him, and the sense of this wrong, and
of the indignity thus put upon him, had rankled unceasingly
in the bosom of Livius, so that for eight years after his trial
he had lived in seclusion at his country seat, taking no part in
any affairs of state. Latterly the censors had compelled him
to come to Rome and resume his place in the senate, where he
used to sit gloomily apart, giving only a silent vote.

At last an unjust accusation against one of his near kinsmen
made him break silence; and he harangued the house in words
of weight and sense, which drew attention to him, and taught
the senators that a strong spirit dwelt beneath that unimposing
exterior. Now, while they were debating on what noble of a
plebeian house was fit to assume the perilous honours of the
consulate, some of the elder of them looked on Marcus Livius,
and remembered that in the very last triumph, which had
been celebrated in the streets of Rome, this grim old man had
sat in the car of victory; and that he had offered the last grand
thanksgiving sacrifice for the success of the Roman arms that
had bled before Capitoline Jove.

There had been no triumphs since Hannibal came into Italy.
The Illyrian campaign of Livius was the last that had been so
honoured; perhaps it might be destined for him now to renew
the long-interrupted series. The senators resolved that Livius
should be put in nomination as consul with Nero; the people
were willing to elect him; the only opposition came from himself. He taunted them with their inconsistency in honouring a
man they had convicted of a base crime. "If I am innocent,"
said he, "why did you place such a stain on me? If I am guilty,
why am I mcre fit for a second consulship than I was for my
first one?" The other senators remonstrated with him, urging
the example of the great Camillus, who, after an unjust con-
demnation on a similar charge, both served and saved his
country. At last Livius ceased to object, and Caius Claudius
Nero and Marcus Livius were chosen consuls of Rome.

A quarrel had long existed between the two consuls, and the
senators strove to effect a reconciliation between them before
the campaign. Here again Livius for a long time obstinately
resisted the wish of his fellow-senators. He said it was best for

the state that he and Nero should continue to hate one another. Each would do his duty better, when he knew that he was watched by an enemy in the person of his own colleague. At last the entreaties of the senators prevailed, and Livius consented to forego the feud, and to co-operate with Nero in preparing for the coming struggle.

VI

As soon as the winter snows were thawed, Hasdrubal commenced his march from Auvergne to the Alps. He experienced none of the difficulties which his brother had met with from the mountain tribes. Hannibal's army had been the first body of regular troops that had ever traversed their regions; and, as wild animals assail a traveller, the natives rose against it instinctively, in imagined defence of their own habitations, which they supposed to be the objects of Carthaginian ambition.

But the fame of the war, with which Italy had now been convulsed for eleven years, had penetrated into the Alpine passes and the mountaineers understood that a mighty city, southward of the Alps, was to be attacked by the troops whom they saw marching among them. They not only opposed no resistance to the passage of Hasdrubal, but many of them, out of the love of enterprise and plunder, or allured by the high pay that he offered, took service with him; and thus he advanced upon Italy with an army that gathered strength at every league. It is said, also, that some of the most important engineering works, which Hannibal had constructed, were found by Hasdrubal still in existence, and materially favoured the speed of his advance. He thus emerged into Italy from the Alpine valleys much sooner than had been anticipated. Many warriors of the Ligurian tribes joined him and, crossing the river Po, he marched down its southern bank to the city of Placentia, which he wished to secure as a base for his future operations. Placentia resisted him as bravely as it had resisted Hannibal eleven years before and for some time Hasdrubal was occupied with a fruitless siege before its walls.

Six armies were levied for the defence of Italy when the long-dreaded approach of Hasdrubal was announced. Seventy thousand Romans served in the fifteen legions, of which, with an equal number of Italians allies, those armies and the garrisons were composed. Upwards of thirty thousand more Romans were serving in Sicily, Sardinia, and Spain. The whole number of Roman citizens of an age fit for military duty, scarcely exceeded a hundred and thirty thousand. The census taken before the commencement of the war had shown a total of two hundred and seventy thousand, which had been diminished by more than half during twelve years. These numbers are fearfully emphatic of the extremity to which Rome was reduced, and of her gigantic efforts in that great agony of her fate.

Not merely men, but money and military stores were drained to the utmost; and if the armies of that year should be swept off by a repetition of the slaughters of Trasimene and Cannæ, all felt that Rome would cease to exist. Even if the campaign were to be marked by no decisive success on either side, her ruin seemed certain. In South Italy Hannibal had either detached Rome's allies from her, or had impoverished them by the ravages of his army. If Hasdrubal could have done the same in upper Italy; if Etruria, Umbria, and northern Latium had either revolted or been laid waste, Rome must have sunk beneath sheer starvation; for the hostile or desolated territory would have yielded no supplies of corn for her population and money, to purchase it from abroad, there was none. Instant victory was a matter of life or death. Three of her six armies were ordered to the north, but the first of these was required to overawe the disaffected Etruscans. The second army of the north was pushed forward, under Porcius, the prætor, to meet and keep in check the advanced troops of Hasdrubal; while the third, the grand army of the north, which was to be under the immediate command of the consul Livius, who had the chief command in all north Italy, advanced more slowly in its support. There were similarly three armies in the south, under the orders of the other consul, Claudius Nero.

VII

The lot had decided that Livius was to be opposed to Hasdrubal, and that Nero should face Hannibal. And as Sir Walter Raleigh wrote, "when all was ordered as themselves thought best, the two consuls went forth of the city; each his several way. The people of Rome were now quite otherwise affected, than they had been, when L. Æmilius Paulus and C. Terentius Varro were sent against Hannibal. They did no longer take upon them to direct their generals, or bid them despatch and win the victory betimes; but rather they stood in fear, lest all diligence, wisdom, and valour, should prove too little. For since, few years had passed, wherein some one of their generals had not been slain; and since it was manifest that if either of these present consuls were defeated, or put to the worst, the two Carthaginians would forthwith join, and make short work with the other: it seemed a greater happiness than could be expected, that each of them should return home victor and come off with honour from such mighty opposition as he was like to find.

"With extreme difficulty had Rome held up her head ever since the battle of Cannæ (where nine years before, in 216 B.C., Hannibal had beaten the Romans badly); though it were so, that Hannibal alone, with little help from Carthage, had continued the war in Italy. But there was now arrived another son of Hamilcar; and one that, in his present expedition, had seemed a man of more sufficiency than Hannibal himself. For, whereas in that long and dangerous march through barbarous nations, over great rivers and mountains, that were thought unpassable, Hannibal had lost a great part of his army, this Hasdrubal, in the same places, had multiplied his numbers and gathering the people that he found in the way, descended from the Alps like a rolling snowball, far greater than he came over the Pyrenees at his first setting out of Spain. These considerations, and the like, of which fear presented many unto them, caused the people of Rome to wait upon their consuls out of the town, like a pensive train of mourners, thinking upon Marcellus and Crispinus, upon whom, in the like sort, they had given attendance the last year, but saw neither of them return alive from a less dangerous war. Particularly old Q. Fabius gave his accustomed advice to M. Livius, that he should abstain from giving or taking battle, until he well understood the enemies' condition. But the consul made him a froward answer, and said that he would fight the very first day, for that he thought it long till he should either recover his honour by victory, or by seeing the overthrow of his own unjust citizens satisfy himself with the joy of a great, though not an honest revenge. But his meaning was better than his words."

Hannibal at this period occupied, with his veteran but much reduced forces, the extreme south of Italy. It had not been expected either by friend or foe, that Hasdrubal would effect his passage of the Alps so early in the year as actually occurred. And even when Hannibal learned that his brother was in Italy, and had advanced as far as Placentia, he was obliged to pause for further intelligence, before he himself commenced active operations, as he could not tell whether his brother might not be invited into Etruria, to aid the party there that was disaffected to Rome, or whether he would march down by the Adriatic sea.

Hannibal led his troops out of their winter quarters in Bruttium, and marched northward as far as Canusium. Nero had his headquarters near Venusia, with an army which he had increased to forty thousand foot and two thousand five hundred horse, by incorporating under his own command some of the legions which had been intended to act under other generals in the south. There was another Roman army twenty thousand strong, south of Hannibal, at Tarentum. The strength of that city secured this Roman force from any attack by Hannibal, and it was a serious matter to march northward and leave it in his rear, free to act against all his depots and allies in the friendly part of Italy, which for the two or three last campaigns had served him for a base of his operations.

Moreover, Nero's army was so strong that Hannibal could not concentrate troops enough to assume the offensive against it without weakening his garrisons, and relinquishing, at least for a time, his grasp upon the southern provinces. To do this before he was certainly informed of his brother's operations would have been an useless sacrifice, as Nero could retreat before him upon the other Roman armies near the capital, and Hannibal knew by experience that a mere advance of his army upon the walls of Rome would have no effect on the fortunes of the war. In the hope, probably, of inducing Nero to follow him, and of gaining an opportunity of outmanœuvring the Roman consul and attacking him on his march, Hannibal moved into Lucania and then back into Apulia; he again marched down into Bruttium, and strengthened his army by a levy of recruits in that district. Nero followed him, but gave him no chance of assailing him at a disadvantage.

Some partial encounters seem to have taken place, but the consul could not prevent Hannibal's junction with his Bruttian levies, nor could Hannibal gain an opportunity of surprising and crushing the consul.

The annalists whom Livy copied, spoke of Nero gaining repeated victories over Hannibal, and killing and taking his men by tens of thousands. The falsehood of all this is self-evident. If Nero could thus always beat Hannibal, the Romans would not have been in such an agony of dread about Hasdrubal, as all writers describe. Indeed, we have the express testimony of Polybius that such statements as we read in Livy of Marcellus, Nero, and others gaining victories over Hannibal in Italy, must be all fabrications of Roman vanity. Polybius states that Hannibal was never defeated before the battle of Zama; and in another passage he mentions that after the defeats which Hannibal inflicted on the Romans in the early years of the war, they no longer dared face his army in a pitched battle on a fair field, and yet they resolutely maintained the war. He rightly explains this by referring to the superiority of Hannibal's cavalry, the arm which gained him all his victories. By keeping within fortified lines, or close to the sides of the mountains when Hannibal approached them, the Romans rendered his cavalry ineffective, and a glance at the geography of Italy will show how an army can traverse the greater part of that country without venturing far from the high grounds.

Hannibal returned to his former headquarters at Canusium, and halted there in expectation of further tidings of his brother's movements. Nero also resumed his former position in observation of the Carthaginian army.

Meanwhile, Hasdrubal had raised the siege of Placentia, and was advancing towards Ariminum on the Adriatic, and driving before him the Roman army under Porcius. Nor when the consul Livius had come up, and united the second and third armies of the north, could he make head against the invaders. The Romans still fell back before Hasdrubal, beyond Ariminum, beyond the Metaurus, and as far as the little town of Sena, to the south-east of that river. Hasdrubal was not unmindful of the necessity of acting in concert with his brother. He sent messengers to Hannibal to announce his own line of march, and to propose that they should unite their armies in south Umbria, and then wheel round against

Rome. Those messengers traversed the greater part of Italy in safety; but, when close to the object of their mission, were captured by a Roman detachment and Hasdrubal's letter detailing his whole plan of the campaign, was laid, not in his brother's hands, but in those of the commander of the Roman armies of the south.

VIII

Nero saw at once the full importance of the crisis. The two sons of Hamilcar were now within two hundred miles of each other, and if Rome were to be saved, the brothers must never meet alive. Nero instantly ordered seven thousand picked men, a thousand being cavalry, to hold themselves in readiness for a secret expedition against one of Hannibal's garrisons; and as soon as night had set in, he hurried forward on his bold enterprise: but he quickly left the southern road towards Lucania, and wheeling round, pressed northward with the utmost rapidity towards Picenum. He had during the preceding afternoon sent messengers to Rome, who were to lay Hasdrubal's letters before the senate.

There was a law forbidding a consul to make war or to march his army beyond the limits of the province assigned to him, but in such an emergency, Nero did not wait for the permission of the senate to execute his project, but informed them that he was already on his march to join Livius against Hasdrubal. He advised them to send the two legions, which formed the home garrison, on to Narnia, so as to defend that pass of the Flaminian road against Hasdrubal in case he should march upon Rome before the consular armies could attack him. They were to supply the place of these two legions at Rome by a levy *en masse* in the city, and by ordering up the reserve legion from Capua. These were his communications to the senate. He also sent horsemen forward along his line of march, with orders to the local authorities to bring stores of provisions and refreshments of every kind to the roadside and to have relays of vehicles ready for the conveyance of the wearied soldiers.

Such were the precautions which he took for accelerating his march; and when he had advanced some little distance from his camp, he briefly informed his soldiers of the real object

of their expedition. He told them that there never was a design
more seemingly audacious, and more really safe. He said
he was leading them to a certain victory, for his colleague
had an army large enough to balance the enemy already, so
that *their* swords would decisively turn the scale. The very
rumour that a fresh consul and a fresh army had come up,
when heard on the battle-field (and he would take care that
they should not be heard of before they were seen and felt)
would settle the campaign. They would have all the credit
of the victory, and of having dealt the final decisive blow.
He appealed to the enthusiastic reception which they already
met with on their line of march as a proof and an omen
of their good fortune. And, indeed, their whole path was
amidst the vows and prayers and praises of their countrymen.

The entire population of the districts through which they
passed, flocked to the roadside to see and bless the deliverers
of their country. Food, drink, and refreshments of every kind
were eagerly pressed on their acceptance. Each peasant thought a
favour was conferred on him, if one of Nero's chosen band
would accept aught at his hands. The soldiers caught the full
spirit of their leader. Night and day they marched forward
taking their hurried meals in the ranks, and resting by relays
in the waggons which the zeal of the country people provided
and which followed in the rear of the column.

IX

Meanwhile, at Rome, the news of Nero's expedition had
caused the greatest excitement and alarm. All men felt the
full audacity of the enterprise, but hesitated what epithet to
apply to it. It was evident that Nero's conduct would be
judged of by the event, that most unfair criterion, as the
Roman historian truly terms it. People reasoned on the perilous
state in which Nero had left the rest of his army, without a
general, and deprived of the core of its strength, in the vicinity
of the terrible Hannibal. They speculated on how long it would
take Hannibal to pursue and overtake Nero himself, and his
expeditionary force. They talked over the former disasters
of the war, and the fall of both the consuls of the last year.
All these calamities had come on them while they had only
one Carthaginian general and army to deal with in Italy.

Now they had two Punic wars at a time. They had two **Carth-aginian** armies; they had almost two Hannibals in Italy. Hasdrubal was sprung from the same father, trained up in the same hostility to Rome, equally practised in battle against their legions, and, if the comparative speed and success with which he had crossed the Alps was a fair test, he was even a better general than his brother. With fear for their interpreter of every rumour, they exaggerated the strength of their enemy's forces in every quarter, and criticised and distrusted their own.

Fortunately for Rome, while she was thus a prey to terror and anxiety, her consul's nerves were strong, and he resolutely urged on his march towards Sena, where his colleague, Livius, and the prætor Porcius were encamped; Hasdrubal's army being in position about half a mile to their north. Nero had sent couriers forward to apprise his colleague of his project and of his approach; and by the advice of Livius, Nero so timed his final march as to reach the camp at Sena by night. According to a previous arrangement, Nero's men were received silently into the tents of their comrades, each according to his rank. By these means, there was no enlargement of the camp that could betray to Hasdrubal the accession of force which the Romans had received. This was considerable as Nero's numbers had been increased on the march by the volunteers, who offered themselves in crowds, and from whom he selected the most promising men, and especially the veterans of former campaigns. A council of war was held on the morning after his arrival, in which some advised that time should be given for Nero's men to refresh themselves, after the fatigue of such a march.

But Nero vehemently opposed all delay. "The officer," said he, "who is for giving time to my men here to rest themselves, is for giving time to Hannibal to attack my men, whom I have left in the camp in Apulia. He is for giving time to Hannibal and Hasdrubal to discover my march, and to manœuvre for a junction with each other in Cisalpine Gaul at their leisure. We must fight instantly, while both the foe here and the foe in the south are ignorant of our movements. We must destroy this Hasdrubal, and I must be back in Apulia before Hannibal awakes from his torpor."

Nero's advice prevailed. It was resolved to fight directly; and before the consuls and prætor left the tent of Livius, the red ensign, which was the signal to prepare for immediate action, was hoisted, and the Romans forthwith drew up in battle array outside the camp.

Hasdrubal had been anxious to bring Livius and Porcius to battle, though he had not judged it expedient to attack them in their lines. And now, on hearing that the Romans offered battle, he also drew up his men, and advanced towards them. No spy or deserter had informed him of Nero's arrival nor had he received any direct information that he had more than his old enemies to deal with. But as he rode forward to reconnoitre the Roman line, he thought that their numbers seemed to have increased, and that the armour of some of them was unusually dull and stained. He noticed also that the horses of some of the cavalry appeared to be rough and out of condition, as if they had just come from a succession of forced marches.

So also, though owing to the precaution of Livius the Roman camp showed no change of size, it had not escaped the quick ear of the Carthaginian general that the trumpet which gave the signal to the Roman legions sounded that morning once oftener than usual, as if directing the troops of some additional superior officer. Hasdrubal, from his Spanish campaigns, was well acquainted with all the sounds and signals of Roman war and from all that he heard and saw, he felt convinced that both the Roman consuls were before him. In doubt and difficulty as to what might have taken place between the armies of the south, and probably hoping that Hannibal also was approaching, Hasdrubal determined to avoid an encounter with the combined Roman forces, and to endeavor to retreat upon Insubrian Gaul, where he would be in a friendly country, and could endeavour to reopen his communications with his brother. He therefore led his troops back into their camp; and, as the Romans did not venture on an assault upon his entrenchments, and Hasdrubal did not choose to commence his retreat in their sight, the day passed away in inaction.

At the first watch of the night, Hasdrubal led his men silently out of their camp, and moved northwards towards the Metaurus, in the hope of placing that river between himself and the Romans before his retreat was discovered. His guides betrayed him; and having purposely led him away from the part of the river that was fordable, they made their escape in the dark

and left Hasdrubal and his army wandering in confusion along
the steep bank, and seeking in vain for a spot where the
stream could be safely crossed. At last they halted; and when
day dawned on them, Hasdrubal found that great numbers of
his men, in their fatigue and impatience, had lost all discipline
and subordination, and that many of the Gallic auxiliaries had
got drunk and were lying helpless in their quarters.   The
Roman cavalry was soon seen coming up in pursuit, followed
at no great distance by the legions, which marched in readiness
for an instant engagement. It was hopeless for Hasdrubal to
think of continuing his retreat before them.   The prospect
of immediate battle might recall the disordered part of his
troops to a sense of duty, and revive the instinct of discipline.
He therefore ordered his men to prepare for action instantly,
and made the best arrangement of them that the nature of
the ground would permit.

X

Heeren has well described the general appearance of a
Carthaginian army. He says, "It was an assemblage of the·
most opposite races of the human species from the farthest
parts of the globe. Hordes of half-naked Gauls were ranged
next to companies of white-clothed Iberians and savage Ligurians next to the far-travelled Nasamones and Lotophagi.
Carthaginians and Phœnici-Africans formed the centre; while
innumerable troops of Numidian horsemen, taken from all the
tribes of the desert, swarmed about on unsaddled horses, and
formed the wings; the van was composed of Balearic slingers
and a line of colossal elephants, with their Ethiopian guides,
formed, as it were, a chain of moving fortresses before the whole
army."

Such were the usual materials and arrangements of the hosts
that fought for Carthage; but the troops under Hasdrubal were
not in all respects thus constituted or thus stationed. He seems
to have been especially deficient in cavalry, and he had few
African troops, though some Carthaginians of high rank were
with him.   His veteran Spanish infantry armed with helmets
and shields, and short cut-and-thrust swords, were the best
part of his army. These, and his few Africans, he drew up on
his right wing, under his own personal command. In the centre,
he placed his Ligurian infantry, and on the left wing he placed

or retained the Gauls, who were armed with long javelins and with huge broadswords and targets. The rugged nature of the ground in front and on the flank of this part of his line made him hope that the Roman right wing would be unable to come to close quarters with these unserviceable barbarians, before he could make some impression with his Spanish veterans on the Roman left. This was the only chance that he had of victory or safety, and he seems to have done everything that good generalship could do to secure it.

He placed his elephants in advance of his centre and right wing. He had caused the driver of each of them to be provided with a sharp iron spike and a mallet; and had given orders that every beast that became unmanageable, and ran back upon his own ranks, should be instantly killed, by driving the spike into the vertebra at the junction of the head and the spine. Hasdrubal's elephants were ten in number. We have no trustworthy information as to the amount of his infantry, but it is quite clear that he was greatly outnumbered by the combined Roman forces.

The tactic of the Roman legions had not yet acquired the perfection which it received from the military genius of Marius, (seven times a consul and renowned as a successful general, 155-86 B.C.) and which we read of in the first chapter of Gibbon. We possess in that great work an account of the Roman legions at the end of the commonwealth, and during the early ages of the empire, which those alone can adequately admire who have attempted a similar description. We have also, in the sixth and seventeenth books of Polybius (a Greek historian) an elaborate discussion on the military system of the Romans in his time, which was not far distant from the time of the battle of the Metaurus. But the subject is beset with difficulties and instead of entering into minute, but inconclusive details, I would refer to Gibbon's first chapter, as serving for a general description of the Roman army in its period of perfection and remark that the training and armour which the whole legion received in the time of Augustus, was, two centuries earlier, only partially introduced.

Two divisions of troops, called hastati and principes, formed the bulk of each Roman legion in the second Punic war. Each of these divisions was twelve hundred strong. The hastatus and the princeps legionary bore a breast-plate or coat of mail, brazen greaves, and a brazen helmet, with a•lofty, upright crest of scarlet or black feathers. He had a large oblong shield and, as weapons of offence, two javelins, one of which was light and slender, but the other was a strong and massive weapon, with a shaft about four feet long, and an iron head of equal length. The sword was carried on the right thigh and was a short cut-and-thrust weapon, like that which was used by the Spaniards. Thus armed, the hastati formed the front division of the legion, and the principes the second.

Each division was drawn up about ten deep; a space of three feet being allowed between the files as well as the ranks, so as to give each legionary ample room for the use of his javelins, and of his sword and shield. The men in the second rank did not stand immediately behind those in the first rank, but the files were alternate, like the position of the men on a draught-board. This was termed the quincunx order. Niebuhr (German historian, 1776-1831) considers that this arrangement enabled the legion to keep up a shower of javelins on the enemy for some considerable time. He says, "When the first line had hurled its pila, it probably stept back between those who stood behind it, who with two steps forward restored the front nearly to its first position; a movement which, on account of the arrangement of the quincunx, could be executed without losing a moment. Thus one line succeeded the other in the front till it was time to draw the swords; nay, when it was found expedient, the lines which had already been in the front, might repeat this change, since the stores of pila were surely not confined to the two which each soldier took with him into battle.

"The same change must have taken place in fighting with the sword; which, when the same tactic was adopted on both sides, was anything but a confused *mêlée;* on the contrary, it was a series of single combats." He adds, that a military man of experience had been consulted by him on the subject, and had given it as his opinion, "that the change of the lines as described above was by no means impracticable; and in the absence of the deafening noise of gunpowder, it cannot have had even any difficulty with trained troops."

The third division of the legion was six hundred strong, and acted as a reserve. It was always composed of veteran soldiers, who were called the triarii. Their arms were the same as those of the principes and hastati; except that each

triarian carried a spear instead of javelins. The rest of the
legion consisted of light-armed troops, who acted as skirmishers.
The cavalry of each legion was at this period about three
hundred strong. The Italian allies, who were attached to the
legion, seem to have been similarly armed and equipped, but
their numerical proportion of cavalry was much larger.

XI

Such was the nature of the forces that advanced on the
Roman side to the battle of the Metaurus. Nero commanded
the right wing, Livius the left, and the prætor Porcius had
the command of the centre. "Both Romans and Carthaginians
well understood how much depended upon the fortune of this
day, and how little hope of safety there was for the vanquished,"
wrote Sir Walter Raleigh. "Only the Romans herein seemed to
have had the better in conceit and opinion, that they were to
fight with men desirous to have fled from them. And according
to this presumption came Livius the consul, with a proud
bravery, to give charge on the Spaniards and Africans, by whom
he was so sharply entertained, that victory seemed very doubtful. The Africans and Spaniards were stout soldiers, and well
acquainted with the manner of the Roman fight. The Ligurians, also, were a hardy nation, and not accustomed to give
ground; which they needed the less, or were able now to do,
being placed in the midst. Livius, therefore, and Porcius found
great opposition; and, with great slaughter on both sides, prevailed little or nothing.

"Besides other difficulties, they were exceedingly troubled by
the elephants, that brake their first ranks, and put them in
such disorder, as the Roman ensigns were driven to fall back.
All this while Claudius Nero, labouring in vain against a
steep hill, was unable to come to blows with the Gauls that
stood opposite him, but out of danger. This made Hasdrubal
the more confident, who, seeing his own left wing safe, did
the more boldly and fiercely make impression on the other
side upon the left wing of the Romans."

But at last Nero, who found that Hasdrubal refused his
left wing, and who could not overcome the difficulties of the
ground in the quarter assigned to him, decided the battle by
another stroke of that military genius which had inspired his

march. Wheeling a brigade of his best men round the rear
of the rest of the Roman army, Nero fiercely charged the
flank of the Spaniards and Africans. The charge was as successful as it was sudden. Rolled back in disorder upon each
other, and overwhelmed by numbers, the Spaniards and Ligurians died, fighting gallantly to the last. The Gauls, who had
taken little or no part in the strife of the day, were then
surrounded, and butchered almost without resistance. Hasdrubal, after having, by the confession of his enemies, done
all that a general could do, when he saw that the victory was
irreparably lost, scorning to survive the gallant host which
he had led and to gratify as a captive Roman cruelty and
pride, spurred his horse into the midst of a Roman cohort
where, sword in hand, he met the death that was worthy of
the son of Hamilcar and the brother of Hannibal.

Success the most complete had crowned Nero's enterprise.
Returning as rapidly as he had advanced, he was again facing
the inactive enemies in the south, before they even knew of
his march. But he brought with him a ghastly trophy of
what he had done. In the true spirit of that savage brutality
which deformed the Roman national character, Nero ordered
Hasdrubal's head to be flung into his brother's camp. Eleven
years had passed since Hannibal had last gazed on those
features. The sons of Hamilcar had then planned their system
of warfare against Rome, which they had so nearly brought
to successful accomplishment. Year after year had Hannibal
been struggling in Italy, in the hope of one day hailing the
arrival of him whom he had left in Spain and of seeing his
brother's eye flash with affection and pride at the junction
of their irresistible hosts. He now saw that eye glazed in
death, and, in the agony of his heart, the great Carthaginian
groaned aloud that he recognised his country's destiny.

XII

Rome was almost delirious with joy. So agonising had been
the suspense with which the battle's verdict on that great
issue of a nation's life and death had been awaited; so overpowering was the sudden reaction to the consciousness of security, and to the full glow of glory and success. From the
time when it had been known at Rome that the armies were

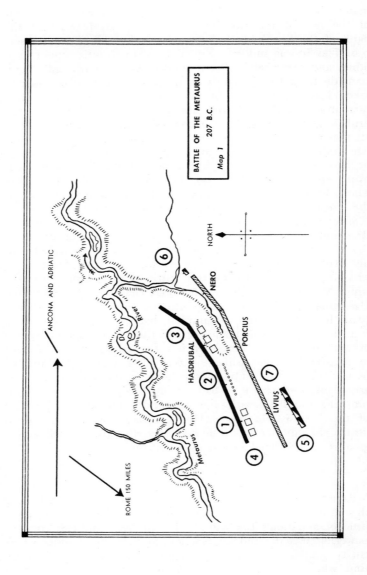

BATTLE OF THE METAURUS
207 B.C.
Map 1

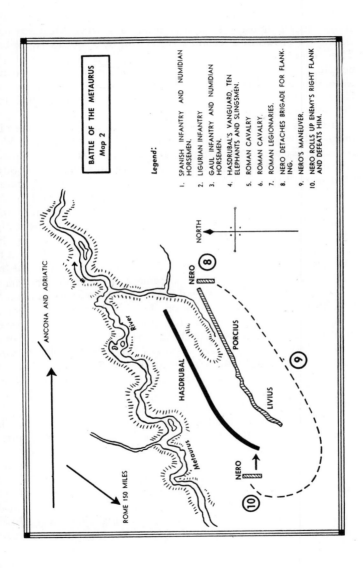

BATTLE OF THE METAURUS
Map 2

Legend:

1. SPANISH INFANTRY AND NUMIDIAN HORSEMEN.
2. LIGURIAN INFANTRY
3. GAUL INFANTRY AND NUMIDIAN HORSEMEN.
4. HASDRUBAL'S VANGUARD, TEN ELEPHANTS AND SLINGSMEN.
5. ROMAN CAVALRY
6. ROMAN CAVALRY.
7. ROMAN LEGIONARIES.
8. NERO DETACHES BRIGADE FOR FLANKING.
9. NERO'S MANEUVER.
10. NERO ROLLS UP ENEMY'S RIGHT FLANK AND DEFEATS HIM.

in presence of each other, the people had never ceased to throng the forum, the conscript fathers had been in permanent sitting at the senate house. Ever and anon a fearful whisper crept among the crowd of a second Cannæ won by a second Hannibal. Then came truer rumours that the day was Rome's; but the people was sick at heart, and heeded them not. The shrines were thronged with trembling women, who seemed to weary Heaven with prayers to shield them from the brutal Gaul and the savage African.

Presently the reports of good fortune assumed a more definite form. It was said that two Narnian horsemen had ridden from the East into the Roman camp of observation in Umbria, and had brought tidings of the utter slaughter of the foe. Such news seemed too good to be true. Men tortured their neighbours and themselves by demonstrating its improbability and by ingeniously criticising its evidence. Soon, however, a letter came from Lucius Manlius Acidinus, who commanded in Umbria, and who announced the arrival of the Narnian horsemen in his camp, and the intelligence which they brought thither. The letter was first laid before the senate, and then before the assembly of the people. The excitement grew more and more vehement. The letter was read and re-read aloud to thousands. It confirmed the previous rumour. But even this was insufficient to allay the feverish anxiety that thrilled through every breast in Rome. The letter might be a forgery; the Narnian horsemen might be traitors or impostors. "We must see officers from the army that fought, or hear despatches from the consuls themselves, and then only will we believe." Such was the public sentiment, though some of more hopeful nature already permitted themselves a foretaste of joy.

At length came news that officers who really had been in the battle were near at hand. Forthwith the whole city poured forth to meet them, each person coveting to be the first to receive with his own eyes and ears convincing proofs of the reality of such a deliverance. One vast throng of human beings filled the road from Rome to the Milvian bridge. The three officers, Lucius Veturius Pollio, Publius Licinius Varus, and Quintus Cæcilius Metellus came riding on, making their way slowly through the living sea around them. As they advanced, each told the successive waves of eager questioners that Rome was victorious. "We have destroyed Hasdrubal and his army;

our legions are safe, and our consuls are unhurt." Each happy listener, who caught the welcome sounds from their lips, retired to communicate his own joy to others, and became himself the centre of an anxious and inquiring group.

When the officers had, with much difficulty, reached the senate house, and the crowd was with still greater difficulty put back from entering and mingling with the conscript fathers, the despatches of Livius and Nero were produced and read aloud. From the senate house the officers proceeded to the public assembly, where the despatches were read again; and then the senior officer, Lucius Veturius, gave in his own words a fuller detail of how went the fight. When he had done speaking to the people, an universal shout of rapture rent the air. The vast assembly then separated: some hastening to the temples to find in devotion a vent for the overflowing excitement of their hearts; others seeking their homes to gladden their wives and children with the good news, and to feast their own eyes with the sight of the loved ones, who now, at last, were safe from outrage and slaughter. The senate ordained a thanksgiving of three days for the great deliverance which had been vouchsafed to Rome; and throughout that period the temples were incessantly crowded with exulting worshippers; and the matrons, with their children round them, in their gayest attire, and with joyous aspects and voices, offered grateful praises to the immortal gods, as if all apprehension of evil were over, and the war were already ended.

With the revival of confidence came also the revival of activity in traffic and commerce, and in all the busy intercourse of daily life. A numbing load was taken off each heart and brain, and once more men bought and sold, and formed their plans freely, as had been done before the dire Carthaginians came into Italy. Hannibal was, certainly, still in the land; but all felt that his power to destroy was broken, and that the crisis of the war-fever was past.

The battle of the Metaurus, indeed, had not only determined the event of the strife between Rome and Carthage, but it had ensured to Rome two centuries more of almost unchanged conquest. Hannibal did actually, with almost superhuman skill, retain his hold on Southern Italy for a few years longer, but the imperial city, and her allies, were no longer in danger from his arms; and, after Hannibal's downfall, the great military

Republic of the ancient world met in her career of conquest no
other worthy competitor. Byron has termed Nero's march "unequalled," and, in the magnitude of its consequences, it is so.
Viewed only as a military exploit, it remains unparalleled, save
by Marlborough's bold march from Flanders to the Danube, in
the campaign of Blenheim, and, perhaps, also, by the Archduke Charles's lateral march in 1796, by which he overwhelmed
the French under Jourdain, and then, driving Moreau through
the Black Forest and across the Rhine, for a while freed Germany from her invaders.

SYNOPSIS OF EVENTS BETWEEN THE BATTLE OF THE METAU-
   RUS, 207 B.C., AND ARMINIUS' VICTORY OVER THE ROMAN
   LEGIONS UNDER VARUS, A.D. 9.

205 to 201 B.C. Scipio is made consul, and carries the war into Africa. He
   gains several victories there, and the Carthaginians recall Hannibal
   from Italy to oppose him. Battle of Zama in 201. Hannibal is defeated, and Carthage sues for peace. End of the second Punic war,
   leaving Rome confirmed in the dominion of Italy, Sicily, Sardinia, and
   Corsica, and also mistress of great part of Spain, and virtually predominant in North Africa.

200. Rome makes war upon Philip, king of Macedonia. She pretends to
   take the Greek cities of the Achæan league and the Ætolians under
   her protection as allies. Philip is defeated by the proconsul Flaminius
   at Cynocephalæ, 198; and begs for peace. The Macedonian influence
   is now completely destroyed in Greece, and the Roman established
   in its stead, though Rome nominally acknowledged the independence
   of the Greek cities.

194. Rome makes war upon Antiochus, king of Syria. He is completely
   defeated at the battle of Magnesia, 192, and is glad to accept peace
   on conditions which leave him dependent upon Rome.

190. "Thus, within the short space of ten years, was laid the foundation of the Roman authority in the East, and the general state of
   affairs entirely changed. If Rome was not yet the ruler, she was at
   least the arbitress of the world from the Atlantic to the Euphrates.
   The power of the three principal states was so completely humbled,
   that they durst not, without the permission of Rome, begin any
   new war; the fourth, Egypt, had already, in the year 201, placed
   herself under the guardianship of Rome; and the lesser powers
   followed of themselves: esteeming it an honour to be called the allies
   of Rome. With this name the nations were lulled into security, and
   brought under the Roman yoke; the new political system of Rome was
   founded and strengthened, partly by exciting and supporting the
   weaker states against the stronger, however unjust the cause of the
   former might be, and partly by factions which she found means to
   raise in every state, even the smallest."—HEEREN.

172 War renewed between Macedonia and Rome. Decisive defeat of Perses,
   the Macedonian king, by Paulus Æmilius at Pydna, 168. Destruction
   of the Macedonian monarchy.

150. Rome oppresses the Carthaginians till they are driven to take up arms, and the third Punic war begins. Carthage is taken and destroyed by Scipio Æmilianus, 146, and the Carthaginian territory is made a Roman province.

146. In the same year in which Carthage falls, Corinth is stormed by the Roman army under Mummius. The Achæan league had been goaded into hostilities with Rome, by means similar to those employed against Carthage. The greater part of southern Greece is made a Roman province, under the name of Achaia.˙

134. Commencement of the revolutionary century at Rome, *i.e.* from the time of the excitement produced by the attempts made by the Cracchi to reform the commonwealth, to the battle of Actium (31 B.C.), which established Octavianus Cæsar as sole master of the Roman world. Throughout this period Rome was engaged in important foreign wars, most of which procured large accessions to her territory.

133. Numantium is destroyed by Scipio Æmilianus. "The war against the Spaniards, who, of all the nations subdued by the Romans, defended their liberty with the greatest obstinacy, began in the year 200, six years after the total expulsion of the Carthaginians from their country. It was exceedingly obstinate, partly from the natural state of the country, which was thickly populated, and where every place became a fortress; partly from the courage of the inhabitants; but at last all, owing to the peculiar policy of the Romans, who yielded to employ their allies to subdue other nations. This war continued, almost without interruption, from the year 200 to 133, and was for the most part carried on at the same time in Hispania Citerior, where the Celtiberi were the most formidable adversaries, and in Hispania Ulterior, where the Lusitani were equally powerful. Hostilities were at the highest pitch in 195, under Cato, who reduced Hispania Citerior to a state of tranquility in 185-179, when the Celtiberi were attacked in the native territory; and 155-150, when the Romans in both provinces were so often beaten, that nothing was more dreaded by the soldiers at home than to be sent there. The extortions and perfidy of Servius Calba placed Viriathus, in the year 146, at the head of his nation, the Lusitani: the war, however, soon extended itself to Hispania Citerior, where many nations, particularly the Numantines, took up arms against Rome, 143. Viriathus, sometimes victorious and sometimes defeated, was never more formidable than in the moment of defeat; because he knew how to take advantage of his knowledge of the country and of the dispositions of his countrymen. After his murder, caused by the treachery of Scipio, 140, Lusitania was subdued; but the Numantine war became still more violent, and the Numantines compelled the consul Mancinus to a disadvantageous treaty, 137. When Scipio, in the year 133, put an end to this war, Spain was certainly tranquil; the northern parts, however, were still unsubdued, though the Romans penetrated as far as Galata."—HEEREN.

118-106. The Jugurthine war. Numidia is conquered, and made a Roman province.

113-101. The great and terrible war of the Cimbri and Teutones against Rome. These nations of northern warriors slaughter several Roman armies in Gaul, and in 102, attempt to penetrate into Italy. The military genius of Marius here saves his country; he defeats the Teutones near Aix, in Provence; and in the following year he destroys the army of the Cimbri, who had passed the Alps, near Vercellæ.

91-88. The war of the Italian allies against Rome. This was caused by the refusal of Rome to concede to them the rights of Roman citizenship. After a sanguinary struggle, Rome gradually grants it.

89-85. First war of the Romans against Mithridates the Great, king of Pontus, who had overrun Asia Minor, Macedonia, and Greece. Sylla defeats his armies, and forces him to withdraw his forces from Europe. Sylla return to Rome to carry on the civil war against the son and partisans of Marius. He makes himself dictator.

74-64. The last Mithridatic wars. Lucullus, and after him Pompeius, command against the great king of Pontus, who at last is poisoned by his son, while designing to raise the warlike tribes of the Danube against Rome, and to invade Italy from the north-east. Great Asiatic conquests of the Romans. Besides the ancient province of Pergamus, the maritime countries of Bithynia, and nearly all Paphlagonio and Pontus, are formed into a Roman province, under the name of Bithynia; while on the southern coast Cilicia and Pamphylia form another, under the name of Cilicia; Phœnicia and Syria compose a third, under the name of Syria. On the other hand, Great Armenia is left to Tigranes; Cappadocia to Ariobarzanes; the Bosphorus to Pharnaces; Judæa to Hyrcanus; and some other small states are also given to petty princes, all of whom remain dependent on Rome.

58-50. Cæsar conquers Gaul.

54. Crassus attacks the Parthians with a Roman army, but is overthrown and killed at Carrhæ in Mesopotamia. His lieutenant Cassius collects the wrecks of the army, and prevents the Parthians from conquering Syria.

49.-45. The civil war between Cæsar and the Pompeian party. Cæsar drives Pompeius out of Italy, conquers his enemy's forces in Spain, and then passes into Greece, where Pompeius and the other aristocratic chiefs had assembled a large army. Cæsar gives them a decisive defeat at the great battle of Pharsalia. Pompeius flies for refuge to Alexandria, where he is assassinated. Cæsar, who had followed him thither, is involved in a war with the Egyptians, in which he is finally victorious. Cleopatra is made Queen of Egypt. Cæsar next marches into Pontus, and defeats the son of Mithridates, who had taken part in the war against him. He then proceeds to the Roman province of Africa, where some of the Pompeian chiefs had established themselves, aided by Juba, a native prince. He overthrows them at the battle of Thapsus. He is again obliged to lead an army into Spain, where the sons of Pompeius had collected the wrecks of their father's party. He crushes the last of his enemies at the battle of Munda. Under the title of dictator, he is sole master of the Roman world.

44. Cæsar is killed in the senate house; the civil wars are soon renewed, Brutus and Cassius being at the head of the aristocratic party, and the party of Cæsar being led by Mark Anthony and Octavianus Cæsar, afterward Augustus.

42. Defeat and death of Brutus and Cassius at Philippi. Dissensions soon break out between Octavianus Cæsar and Anthony.

31. Anthony is completely defeated by Octavianus Cæsar at Actium. He flies to Egypt with Cleopatra. Octavianus pursues him. Anthony and Cleopatra kill themselves. Egypt becomes a Roman province, and Octavianus Cæsar is left undisputed master of Rome, and all that is Rome's.

The 44th year of the reign of Augustus, and the 1st year of the 195th Olympiad, is commonly assigned as the date of THE NATIVITY OF OUR LORD. There is much of the beauty of holiness in the remarks with which the American historian, Eliot, closes his survey of the conquering career and civil downfall of the Roman Commonwealth:—

"So far as humility amongst men was necessary for the preparation of a truer freedom than could ever be known under heathenism, the part of Rome, however dreadful, was yet sublime. It was not to unite, to discipline, or to fortify humanity, but to enervate, to loosen, and to scatter its forces, that the people whose history we have read were allowed to conquer the earth, and were then themselves reduced to deep submission. Every good labour of theirs that failed was, by reason of what we esteem its failure, a step gained nearer to the end of the well-nigh universal evil that prevailed; while every bad achievement that may seem to us to have succeeded, temporarily or lastingly, with them was equally, by reason of its success, a progress toward the good of which the coming would have been longer and prayed for, could it have been comprehended. Alike in the virtues and in the vices of antiquity, we may read the progress towards its humiliation. Yet, on the other hand, it must not seem, at the last, that the disposition of the Romans or of mankind to submission was secured solely through the errors and the apparently ineffectual toils which we have traced back to these times of old. Desires too true to have been wasted, and strivings too humane to have been unproductive, though all were overshadowed by passing wrongs, still gleam as if in anticipation or in preparation of the advancing day.

"At length, when it had been proved by ages of conflict and loss, that no lasting joy and no abiding truth could be procured through the power, the freedom, or the faith of mankind, the angels sang their song in which the glory of God and the good-will of men were together blended. The universe was wrapped in momentary tranquillity, and 'peaceful was the night,' above the manger at Bethlehem. We may believe, that when the morning came, the ignorance, the confusion, and the servitude of humanity, had left their darkest forms amongst the midnight clouds. It was still, indeed, beyond the power of man to lay hold securely of the charity and the regeneration that were henceforth to be his law; and the indefinable terrors of the future, whether seen from the West or from the East, were not at once to be dispelled. But before the death of the Emperor Augustus, in the midst of his fallen subjects, the business of THE FATHER had already been begun in the Temple at Jerusalem; and near by, THE SON was increasing in wisdom and in stature, and in favour with God and man."—*Eliot's "Liberty of Rome."*

⊰[FIVE]⊱

Arminius Defeats Roman Legions, 9

WHY DECISIVE: *"Had Arminius been supine or unsuccessful, our Germanic ancestors would have been enslaved or exterminated in their original seats along the Eyder and the Elbe. This island never would have borne the name of England and as Thomas Arnold expresses it 'we this great English nation, whose race and language are now overrunning the earth, from one end of it to the other,' would have been entirely cut off from existence."* [Creasy.]

I

To a truly illustrious Frenchman, whose reverses as a minister can never obscure his achievements in the world of letters, we are indebted for the most profound and most eloquent estimate that we possess of the importance of the Germanic element in European civilisation, and of the extent to which the human race is indebted to those brave warriors, who long were the unconquered antagonists, and finally became the conquerors, of Imperial Rome.

Twenty-three eventful years (1850) have passed away since M. Guizot delivered from the chair of modern history at Paris his course of lectures on the History of Civilisation in Europe. During those years the spirit of earnest inquiry into the germs and early developments of existing institutions has become more and more active and universal; and the merited celebrity of M. Guizot's work has proportionally increased. Its admirable analysis of the complex political and social organisations, of which the modern civilised world is made up, must have led thousands to trace with keener interest the great crises of times past, by which the characteristics of the present were determined.

The narrative of one of these great crises, of the epoch A.D. 9, when Germany took up arms for her independence against Roman invasion, has for us this special attraction—that it forms part of our (British) own national history. Had Arminius been supine or unsuccessful, our Germanic ancestors would have been enslaved or exterminated in their original seats along the Eyder and the Elbe. This island would never have borne the name of

England, and in the phraseology or Thomas Arnold, "we, this great English nation, whose race and language are now overrunning the earth, from one end of it to the other," would have been utterly cut off from existence.

Arnold may, indeed, go too far in holding that we are wholly unconnected in race with the Romans and Britons who inhabited this country before the coming-over of the Saxons; that, "nationally speaking, the history of Cæsar's invasion has no more to do with us than the natural history of the animals which then inhabited our forests." There seems ample evidence to prove that the Romanised Celts, whom our Teutonic forefathers found here, influenced materially the character of our nation. But the main stream of our people was and is Germanic. Our language alone decisively proves this. Arminius is far more truly one of our national heroes than Caractacus (a British chief who resisted the Romans under Claudius, 50): and it was our own primeval fatherland that the brave German rescued, when, he slaughtered the Roman legions eighteen centuries ago, in the marshy glens between the Lippe and the Ems.

Dark and disheartening, even to heroic spirits, must have seemed the prospects of Germany, when Arminius planned the general rising of his countrymen against Rome. Half the land was occupied by Roman garrisons; and what was worse, many Germans seemed patiently acquiescent in their state of bondage. The braver portion, whose patriotism could be relied on, was ill-armed and undisciplined while the enemy's troops consisted of veterans in the highest state of equipment and training, familiarised with victory, and commanded by officers of proved skill and valour. The resources of Rome seemed boundless; her tenacity of purpose was believed to be invincible. There was no hope of foreign sympathy or aid, for "the self-governing powers, that had filled the old world, had bent one after another before the rising power of Rome, and had vanished. The earth seemed left void of independent nations." (Leopold V. Rancke, German historian 1795-1886)

The German chieftain knew well the gigantic power of the oppressor. Arminius was not a rude savage, fighting out of mere animal instinct, or in ignorance of the might of his adversary. He was familiar with the Roman language and civilisation; he had served in the Roman armies; he had been admitted to the Roman citizenship, and raised to the dignity of the equestrian order. It was part of the subtle policy of Rome to confer rank and privileges on the youth of the leading families in the nations which she wished to enslave. Among other young German chieftains, Arminius and his brother, who were the heads of the noblest house in the tribe of the Cherusci, had been selected as fit objects for the exercise of this insidious system. Roman refinements and dignities succeeded in denationalising the brother, who assumed the Roman name of Flavius, and adhered to Rome throughout all her wars against his country. Arminius remained unbought by honours or wealth, uncorrupted by refinement or luxury. He aspired to and obtained from Roman enmity a higher title than ever could have been given him by Roman favour. It is in the page of Rome's greatest historian, (Tacitus) that his name has come down to us with the proud addition of "Liberator of Germany".

Often must the young chieftain, while meditating the exploit which has thus immortalised him, have anxiously revolved in his mind the fate of the many great men, who had been crushed in the attempt which he was about to renew—the attempt to stay the chariot-wheels of triumphant Rome. Could he hope to succeed where Hannibal and Mithridates had perished? What had been the doom of Viriathus and what warning against vain valour was written on the desolate site where Numantia once had flourished? Nor was a caution wanting in scenes nearer home and in more recent times. The Gauls had fruitlessly struggled for eight years against Cæsar; and the gallant Vercingetorix, who in the last year of the war had roused all his countrymen to insurrection, who had cut off Roman detachments, and brought Cæsar himself to the extreme of peril at Alesia—he, too, had finally succumbed, had been led captive in Cæsar's triumph, and had then been butchered in cold blood in a Roman dungeon. (46 B.C. after he had for years led the most serious revolt against the Romans in Gaul).

II

It was true that Rome was no longer the great military republic which for many ages had shattered the kingdoms of the world. Her system of government was changed; and after a century of revolution and civil war, she had placed herself under the despotism of a single ruler. But the discipline of her troops was yet unimpaired, and her warlike spirit seemed unabated. The first years of the empire had been signalised by conquests as valuable as any gained by the republic in a corresponding period. It is a great fallacy, though apparently sanctioned by great authorities, to suppose that the foreign policy pursued by Augustus was pacific. He certainly recommended such a policy to his successors, either from timidity, or from jealousy of their fame outshining his own; but he himself, until Arminius broke his spirit, had followed a very different course. Besides his Spanish wars, his generals, in a series of principally aggressive campaigns, had extended the Roman frontier from the Alps to the Danube; and had reduced into subjection the large and important countries that now form the territories of all Austria south of that river, and of East Switzerland, Lower Wirtemberg, Bavaria, the Valteline, and the Tyrol.

While the progress of the Roman arms thus pressed the Germans from the south, still more formidable inroads had been made by the Imperial legions in the west. Roman armies, moving from the province of Gaul, established a chain of fortresses along the right as well as the left bank of the Rhine, and, in a series of victorious campaigns advanced their eagles as far as the Elbe; which now seemed added to the list of vassal rivers, to the Nile, the Rhine, the Rhone, the Danube, the Tagus, the Seine, and many more, that acknowledged the supremacy of the Tiber. Roman fleets also, sailing from the harbours of Gaul along the German coasts and up the estuaries, cooperated with the land-forces of the empire and seemed to display, even more decisively than her armies, her overwhelming superiority over the rude Germanic tribes. Throughout the territory thus invaded the Romans had, with their usual military skill, established chains of fortified posts; and a powerful army of occupation was kept on foot, ready to move instantly on any spot where a popular outbreak might be attempted.

Vast, however, and admirably organized as the fabric of Roman power appeared on the frontiers and in the provinces, there was rottenness at the core. In Rome's unceasing hostilities with foreign foes, and still more, in her long series of desolating civil wars, the free middle classes of Italy had almost wholly disappeared. Above the position which they had occupied, an oligarchy of wealth had reared itself: beneath that position a degraded mass of poverty and misery was fermenting. Slaves, the chance sweepings of every conquered country, shoals of Africans, Sardinians, Asiatics, Illyrians, and others, made up the bulk of the population of the Italian Peninsula. The foulest profligacy of manners was general in all ranks. In universal weariness of revolution and civil war, and in consciousness of being too debased for self-government, the nation had submitted itself to the absolute authority of Augustus. Adulation was now the chief function of the senate: and the gifts of genius and accomplishments of art were devoted to the elaboration of eloquently false panegyrics upon the prince and his favorite courtiers.

With bitter indignation must the German chieftain have beheld all this, and contrasted with it the rough worth of his own countrymen—their bravery, their fidelity to their word, their manly independence of spirit, their love of their national free institutions, and their loathing of every pollution and meanness. Above all, he must have thought of the domestic virtues that hallowed a German home; of the respect there shown to the female character, and of the pure affection by which that respect was repaid. His soul must have burned within him at the contemplation of such a race yielding to these debased Italians.

III

Still, to persuade the Germans to combine, in spite of their frequent feuds among themselves, in one sudden outbreak against Rome; to keep the scheme concealed from the Romans until the hour for action arrived; and then, without possessing a single walled town, without military stores, without training, to teach his insurgent countrymen to defeat veteran armies, and storm fortifications, seemed so perilous an enterprise, that probably Arminius would have receded from it, had not a stronger feeling even than patriotism urged him on.

Among the Germans of high rank who had most readily submitted to the invaders, and become zealous partisans of Roman authority, was a chieftain named Segestes. His daughter, Thusnelda, was pre-eminent among the noble maidens of Germany. Arminius had sought her hand in marriage; but Segestes, who probably discerned the young chief's disaffection to Rome, forbade his suit, and strove to preclude all communication between him and his daughter. Thusnelda, however, sympathised far more with the heroic spirit of her lover, than with the time-serving policy of her father. An elopment baffled the precautions of Segestes; who, disappointed in his hope of preventing the marriage, accused Arminius, before the Roman governor, of having carried off his daughter, and of planning treason against Rome. Thus assailed, and dreading to see his bride torn from him by the officials of the foreign oppressor, Arminius delayed no longer, but bent all his energies to organise and execute a general insurrection of the great mass of his countrymen, who hitherto had submitted in sullen inertness to the Roman dominion.

A change of governors had recently taken place, which, while it materially favoured the ultimate success of the insurgents, served by the immediate aggravation of the Roman oppressions which it produced, to make the native population more universally eager to take arms. Tiberius, who was afterwards emperor, had lately been recalled from the command in Germany, and sent into Pannonia to put down a dangerous revolt which had broken out against the Romans in that province. The German patriots were thus delivered from the stern supervision of one of the most suspicious of mankind, and were also relieved from having to contend against the high military talents of a veteran commander, who thoroughly understood their national character, and the nature of the country, which he himself had principally subdued.

In the room of Tiberius, Augustus sent into Germany Quintilius Varus, who had lately returned from the proconsulate of Syria. Varus was a true representative of the higher classes of the Romans; among whom a general taste for literature, a keen susceptibility to all intellectual gratifications, a minute acquaintance with the principles and practice of their own national jurisprudence, a careful training in the schools of the rhetoricians, and a fondness for either partaking in or watching the intellectual strife of forensic oratory, had become generally diffused; without, however, having humanised the old Roman spirit of cruel indifference for human feelings and human sufferings, and without acting as the least check on unprincipled avarice and ambition, or on habitual and gross profligacy.

Accustomed to govern the depraved and debased natives of

Syria, a country where courage in man, and virtue in woman, had for centuries been unknown, Varus thought that he might gratify his licentious and rapacious passions with equal impunity among the high-minded sons and pure-spirited daughters of Germany. When the general of an army sets the example of outrages of this description, he is soon faithfully imitated by his officers, and surpassed by his still more brutal soldiery. The Romans now habitually indulged in those violations of the sanctity of the domestic shrine, and those insults upon honour and modesty, by which far less gallant spirits than those of our Teutonic ancestors have often been maddened into insurrection.

Arminius found among the other German chiefs many who sympathised with him in his indignation at their country's debasement, and many whom private wrongs had stung yet more deeply. There was little difficulty in collecting bold leaders for an attack on the oppressors, and little fear of the population not rising readily at those leaders' call. But to declare open war against Rome, and to encounter Varus's army in a pitched battle, would have been merely rushing upon certain destruction. Varus had three legions under him, a force which, after allowing for detachments cannot be estimated at less than fourteen thousand Roman infantry. He had also eight or nine hundred Roman cavalry, and at least an equal number of horse and foot sent from the allied states, or raised among those provincials who had not received the Roman franchise.

It was not merely the number, but the quality of this force that made it formidable; and however contemptible Varus might be as a general, Arminius well knew how admirably the Roman armies were organised and officered, and how perfectly the legionaries understood every manœuvre and every duty which the varying emergencies of a stricken field might require. Stratagem was, therefore, indispensable; and it was necessary to blind Varus to his schemes until a favourable opportunity should arrive for striking a decisive blow.

IV

For this purpose, the German confederates frequented the headquarters of Varus, which seem to have been near the centre of modern Westphalia, where the Roman general conducted himself with all the arrogant security of the governor of a perfectly submissive province. There Varus gratified at once his vanity, his rhetorical taste, and his avarice, by holding courts, to which he summoned the Germans for the settlement of all their disputes, while a bar of Roman advocates attended to argue the cases before the tribunal of the Proconsul who did not omit the opportunity of exacting court-fees and accepting bribes. Varus trusted implicitly to the respect which the Germans pretended to pay to his abilities as a judge, and to the interest which they affected to take in the forensic eloquence of their conquerors.

Meanwhile a succession of heavy rains rendered the country more difficult for the operations of regular troops; and Arminius, seeing that the infatuation of Varus was complete, secretly directed the tribes, near the Weser and the Ems, to take up arms in open revolt against the Romans. This was represented to Varus as an occasion which required his prompt attendance at the spot; but he was kept in studied ignorance of its being part of a concerted national rising and he still looked on Arminius as his submissive vassal, whose aid he might rely on in facilitating the march of his troops against the rebels, and in extinguishing the local disturbance. He therefore set his army in motion, and marched eastward in a line parallel to the course of the Lippe. For some distance his route lay along a level plain; but on arriving at the tract between the curve of the upper part of that stream and the sources of the Ems, the country assumes a very different character; and here, in the territory of the modern little principality of Lippe, it was that Arminius had fixed the scene of his enterprise.

A woody and hilly region intervenes between the heads of the two rivers, and forms the watershed of their streams. This region still retains the name (Teutobergerwald) which it bore in the days of Arminius. The nature of the ground has probably also remained unaltered. The eastern part of it, around Detmoldt, the present capital of the principality of Lippe, is described by a modern German scholar, Dr. Plate, as being "a table-land intersected by numerous deep and narrow valleys, which in some places form small plains, surrounded by steep mountains and rocks and accessible only by narrow defiles. All the valleys are traversed by rapid streams, shallow in the dry season, but subject to sudden swellings in autumn and winter. The vast forests which cover the summits and slopes of the hills consist chiefly of oak; there is little underwood, and both men and horse would move with ease in the forests if the ground were not broken by gullies, or rendered impracticable by fallen trees." This is the district to which Varus is supposed to have marched; and Dr. Plate adds, that "the names of several localities on and near that spot seem to indicate that a great battle had once been fought there. We find the names 'das Winnefeld' (the field of victory), 'die Knochenbahn' (the bone-lane), 'die Knochenleke (the bone-brook), 'der Mordkessel' (the kettle of slaughter), and others."

Contrary to the usual strict principles of Roman discipline, Varus had suffered his army to be accompanied and impeded by an immense train of baggage-waggons, and by a rabble of camp followers, as if his troops had been merely changing their quarters in a friendly country. When the long array quitted the firm level ground, and began to wind its way among the woods, the marshes, and the ravines, the difficulties of the march, even without the intervention of an armed foe, became fearfully apparent. In many places the soil, sodden with rain, was impracticable for cavalry and even for infantry until trees had been felled, and a rude causeway formed through the morass.

The duties of the engineer were familiar to all who served in the Roman armies. But the crowd and confusion of the columns embarrassed the working parties of the soldiery, and in the midst of their toil and disorder the word was suddenly passed through their ranks that the rearguard was attacked by the barbarians. Varus resolved on pressing forward; but a heavy discharge of missiles from the woods on either flank taught him how serious was the peril, and he saw his best men falling round him without the opportunity of retaliation; for his light-armed auxiliaries, who were principally of Germanic race, now rapidly deserted, and it was impossible to deploy the legionaries on such broken ground for a charge against the enemy.

Choosing one of the most open and firm spots which they could force their way to, the Romans halted for the night; and, faithful to their national discipline and tactics, formed their camp amid the harassing attacks of the rapidly thronging foes, with the elaborate toil and systematic skill, the traces of which are impressed permanently on the soil of so many European countries, attesting the presence of the imperial eagles.

V

On the morrow the Romans renewed their march; the veteran officers, who served under Varus, now probably directing the operations, and hoping to find the Germans drawn up to meet them; in which case they relied on their own superior discipline and tactics for such a victory as should reassure the supremacy of Rome. But Arminius was far too sage a commander to lead on his followers with their unwieldy broad-swords and inefficient defensive armour, against the Roman legionaries, fully armed with helmet, cuirass, greaves, and shield; who were skilled to commence the conflict with a murderous volley of heavy javelins, hurled upon the foe when a few yards distant, and then, with their short cut-and-thrust swords, to hew their way through all opposition, preserving the utmost steadiness and coolness, and obeying each word of command in the midst of strife and slaughter, with the same precision and alertness as if upon parade.

Arminius suffered the Romans to march out from their camp, to form first in line for action, and then in column for marching, without the show of opposition. For some distance Varus was allowed to move on, only harassed by slight skirmishes, but struggling with difficulty through the broken ground, the toil and distress of his men being aggravated by heavy torrents of rain, which burst upon the devoted legions, as if the angry gods of Germany were pouring out the vials of their wrath upon the invaders. After some little time their van approached a ridge of high woody ground, which is one of the offshoots of the great Hercynian forest, and is situated between the modern villages of Driburg and Bielefeld. Arminius had caused barricades of hewn trees to be formed here, so as to add to the natural difficulties of the passage.

Fatigue and discouragement now began to betray themselves in the Roman ranks. Their line became less steady; baggage-waggons were abandoned from the impossibility of forcing them along; and, as this happened, many soldiers left their ranks and crowded round the waggons to secure the most valuable portions of their property; each was busy about his own affairs, and purposely slow in hearing the word of command from his officers. Arminius now gave the signal for a general attack. The fierce shouts of the Germans pealed through the gloom of the forests, and in thronging multitudes they assailed the flank of the invaders, pouring in clouds of darts on the encumbered legionaries, as they struggled up the glens or floundered in the morasses, and watching every opportunity of charging through the intervals of the disjoined column, and so cutting off the communication between its several brigades.

Arminius, with a chosen band of personal retainers round him, cheered on his countrymen by voice and example. He and his men aimed their weapons particularly at the horses of the Roman cavalry. The wounded animals, slipping about in the mire and their own blood, threw their riders, and plunged among the ranks of the legions, disordering all round them. Varus now ordered the troops to be countermarched, in the hope of reaching the nearest Roman garrison on the Lippe. But retreat now was as impracticable as advance; and the falling back of the Romans only augmented the courage of their assailants, and caused fiercer and more frequent charges on the flanks of the disheartened army. The Roman officer who commanded the cavalry, Numonius Vala, rode off with his squadrons, in the vain hope of escaping by thus abandoning his comrades. Unable to keep together, or force their way across the woods and swamps, the horsemen were overpowered in detail and slaughtered to the last man. The Roman infantry still held together and resisted, but more through the instinct of discipline and bravery than from any hope of success or escape.

Varus, after being severely wounded in a charge of the Germans against his part of the column, committed suicide to avoid falling into the hands of those whom he had exasperated by his oppressions. One of the lieutenant-generals of the army fell fighting; the other surrendered to the enemy. But mercy to a fallen foe had never been a Roman virtue, and those among her legions who now laid down their arms in hope of quarter drank deep of the cup of suffering, which Rome had held to the lips of many a brave, but unfortunate enemy. The infuriated Germans slaughtered their oppressors with deliberate ferocity and those prisoners who were not hewn to pieces on the spot were only preserved to perish by a more cruel death in cold blood.

The bulk of the Roman army fought steadily and stubbornly, frequently repelling the masses of the assailants, but gradually losing the compactness of their array, and becoming weaker

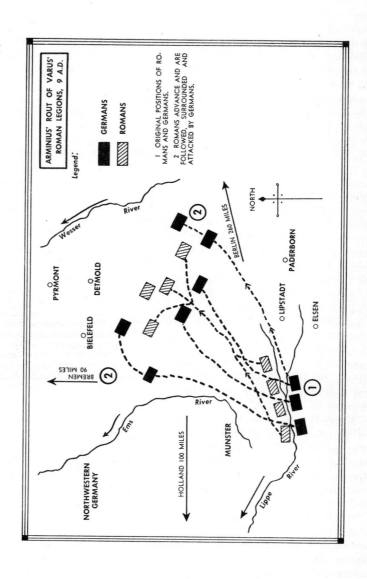

ARMINIUS' ROUT OF VARUS'
ROMAN LEGIONS, 9 A.D.

Legend:

GERMANS

ROMANS

1 ORIGINAL POSITIONS OF RO-
MANS AND GERMANS.

2 ROMANS ADVANCE AND ARE
FOLLOWED, SURROUNDED AND
ATTACKED BY GERMANS.

NORTH

Wesser River

PYRMONT

DETMOLD

BIELEFELD

BREMEN 90 MILES

BERLIN 260 MILES

LIPSTADT

PADERBORN

ELSEN

Ems River

River

Lippe River

MUNSTER

HOLLAND 100 MILES

NORTHWESTERN
GERMANY

and weaker beneath the incessant shower of darts and the re-iterated assaults of the vigorous and unencumbered Germans. At last, in a series of desperate attacks the column was pierced through and through, two of the eagles captured, and the Roman host, which on the yester morning had marched forth in such pride and might, now broken up into confused fragments, either fell fighting beneath the overpowering numbers of the enemy, or perished in the swamps and woods in unavailing efforts at flight.

Few, very few, ever saw again the left bank of the Rhine. One body of brave veterans, arraying themselves in a ring on a little mound, beat off every charge of the Germans, and prolonged their honourable resistance to the close of that dreadful day. The traces of a feeble attempt at forming a ditch and mound attested in after years the spot where the last of the Romans passed their night of suffering and despair. But on the morrow, thus remnant also, worn out with hunger, wounds and toil, was charged by the victorious Germans, and either massacred on the spot, or offered up in fearful rites at the altars of the deities of the old mythology of the North.

A gorge in the mountain ridge, through which runs the modern road between Paderborn and Pyrmont, leads from the spot where the heat of the battle raged, to the Exterstein, a cluster of bold and grotesque rocks of sandstone; near which is a small sheet of water, overshadowed by a grove of aged trees. According to local tradition, this was one of the sacred groves of the ancient Germans, and it was here that the Roman captives were slain in sacrifice by the victorious warriors of Arminius.

Never was victory more decisive, never was the liberation of an oppressed people more instantaneous and complete. Throughout Germany the Roman garrisons were assailed and cut off; and, within a few weeks after Varus had fallen, the German soil was freed from the foot of an invader.

VI

At Rome, the tidings of the battle were received with an agony of terror, the description of which we should deem exaggerated, did they not come from Roman historians themselves. These passages in the Roman writers not only tell em-

phatically how great was the awe which the Romans felt of the
prowess of the Germans, if their various tribes could be brought
to reunite for a common purpose, but also they reveal how
weakened and debased the population of Italy had become.
Dion Cassius says,

"Then Augustus, when he heard the calamity of Varus, rent
his garments, and was in great affliction for the troops he had
lost, and for terror respecting the Germans and the Gauls. And
his chief alarm was, that he expected them to push on against
Italy and Rome: and there remained no Roman youth fit for
military duty, who were worth speaking of, and the allied populations that were at all serviceable, had been wasted away. Yet
he prepared for the emergency as well as his means allowed;
and when none of the citizens of military age were willing to
enlist, he made them cast lots, and punished by confiscation of
goods and disfranchisement every fifth man among those under
thirty-five, and every tenth man of those above that age. At
last, when he found that not even thus could he make many
come forward, he put some of them to death. So he made a
conscription of discharged veterans and emancipated slaves and
collecting as large a force as he could, sent it, under Tiberius,
with all speed into Germany."

Dion mentions, also, a number of terrific portents that were
believed to have occurred at the time; and the narration of
which is not immaterial, as it shows the state of the public mind,
when such things were so believed in, and so interpreted. The
summits of the Alps were said to have fallen, and three columns
of fire to have blazed up from them. In the Campus Martius,
the temple of the War-God, from whom the founder of Rome
had sprung, was struck by a thunderbolt. The nightly heavens
glowed several times, as if on fire. Many comets blazed forth
together; and fiery meteors, shaped like spears, had shot from
the northern quarter of the sky, down into the Roman camps.
It was said, too, that a statue of Victory, which had stood at a
place on the frontier, pointing the way towards Germany, had,
of its own accord, turned round, and now pointed to Italy.
These and other prodigies were believed by the multitude to
accompany the slaughter of Varus's legions, and to manifest
the anger of the gods against Rome.

Augustus himself was not free from superstition; but on this
occasion no supernatural terrors were needed to increase the

alarm and grief that he felt; and which made him, even for months after the news of the battle had arrived, often beat his head against the wall, and exclaim, "Quintilius Varus, give me back my legions!" We learn this from his biographer, Suetonius; and, indeed, every ancient writer who alludes to the overthrow of Varus, attests the importance of the blow against the Roman power, and the bitterness with which it was felt.

The Germans did not pursue their victory beyond their own territory. But that victory secured at once and for ever the independence of the Teutonic race. Rome sent, indeed, her legions again into Germany, to parade a temporary superiority; but all hopes of permanent conquest were abandoned by Augustus and his successors.

The blow which Arminius had struck never was forgotten. Roman fear disguised itself under the specious title of moderation; and the Rhine became the acknowledged boundary of the two nations, until the fifth century of our era, when the Germans became the assailants, and carved with their conquering swords the provinces of Imperial Rome into the kingdoms of modern Europe.

VII

It seems probable that the jealousy with which **Maraboduus**, the king of the Suevi and Marcomanni, regarded **Arminius**, and which ultimately broke out into open hostilities between those German tribes and the Cherusci, prevented Arminius from leading the confederate Germans to attack Italy after his first victory. Perhaps he may have had the rare moderation of being content with the liberation of his country, without seeking to retaliate on her former oppressors. When Tiberius marched into Germany in the year 10, Arminius was too cautious to attack him on ground favorable to the legions, and Tiberius was too skilful to entangle his troops in the difficult parts of the country. His march and counter-march were as unresisted as they were unproductive.

A few years later, when a dangerous revolt of the Roman legions near the frontier caused their generals to find them active employment by leading them into the interior of Germany, we find Arminius again energetic in his country's defence. The old quarrel between him and his father-in-law, Segestes, had broken out afresh. Segestes now called in the aid of the Roman general, Germanicus, to whom he surrendered himself; and by his contrivance, his daughter Thusnelda, the wife of Arminius, also came into the hands of the Romans, being far advanced in pregnancy. She showed, as Tacitus re-relates, more of the spirit of her husband than of her father, a spirit that could not be subdued into tears or supplications. She was sent to Ravenna, and there gave birth to a son, whose life we find, from an allusion in Tacitus, to have been eventful and unhappy; but the part of the great historian's work which narrated his fate has perished, and we only know from another quarter that the son of Arminius was, at the age of four years, led captive in a triumphal pageant along the streets of Rome.

The high spirit of Arminius was goaded almost into frenzy by these bereavements. The fate of his wife, thus torn from him, and of his babe doomed to bondage even before its birth, inflamed the eloquent invectives with which he roused his countrymen against home traitors, and against their invaders, who thus made war upon women and children. Germanicus had marched his army to the place where Varus had perished, and had there paid funeral honours to the ghastly relics of his predecessor's legions that he found heaped around him. Arminius lured him to advance a little further into the country, and then assailed him, and fought a battle, which, by the Roman accounts, was a drawn one. The effect of it was to make Germanicus resolve on retreating to the Rhine. He himself with part of his troops, embarked in some vessels on the Ems, and returned by that river, and then by sea; but part of his forces were entrusted to a Roman general, named Cæcina, to lead them back by land to the Rhine.

Arminius followed this division on its march, and fought several battles with it, in which he inflicted heavy loss on the Romans, captured the greater part of their baggage, and would have destroyed them completely, had not his skilful system of operations been finally thwarted by the haste of Inguiomerus, a confederate German chief, who insisted on assaulting the Romans in their camp, instead of waiting till they were entangled in the difficulties of the country, and assailing their columns on the march.

In the following year the Romans were inactive, but in the year afterwards, Germanicus led a fresh invasion. He placed his army on ship-board, and sailed to the mouth of the Ems, where he disembarked, and marched to the Weser, where he encamped, probably in the neighbourhood of Minden. Arminius had collected his army on the other side of the river; and a scene occurred, which is powerfully told by Tacitus, and which is the subject of a beautiful poem by Praed.

It has been already mentioned that the brother of Arminius, like himself, had been trained up, while young, to serve in the Roman armies; but, unlike Arminius, he not only refused to quit the Roman service for that of his country, but fought against his country with the legions of Germanicus. He had assumed the Roman name of Flavius, and had gained considerable distinction in the Roman service, in which he had lost an eye from a wound in battle. When the Roman outposts approached the river Weser, Arminius called out to them from the opposite bank, and expressed a wish to see his brother. Flavius stepped forward, and Arminius ordered his own followers to retire, and requested that the archers should be removed from the Roman bank of the river.

This was done: and the brothers, who apparently had not seen each other for some years, began a conversation from the opposite sides of the stream, in which Arminius questioned his brother respecting the loss of his eye, and what battle it had been lost in, and what reward he had received for his wound. Flavius told him how the eye was destroyed, and mentioned the increased pay that he had on account of its loss, and showed the collar and other military decorations that had been given him. Arminius mocked at these as badges of slavery; and then each began to try to win the other over, Flavius boasting the power of Rome, and her generosity to the submissive; Arminius appealing to him in the name of their country's gods, of the mother that had borne them, and by the holy names of fatherland and freedom, not to prefer being the betrayer to being the champion of his country. They soon proceeded to mutual taunts and menaces, and Flavius called aloud for his horse and his arms, that he might dash across the river and attack his brother; nor would he have been checked from doing so, had not the Roman general, Stertinius, run up to him, and forcibly detained him. Arminius stood on the other bank, threatening the renegade, and defying him to battle.

On the day after the Romans had reached the Weser,

Germanicus led his army across that river, and a partial encounter took place, in which Arminius was successful. But on the succeeding day a general action was fought, in which Arminius was severely wounded, and the German infantry routed with heavy loss. The horsemen of the two armies encountered without either party gaining the advantage. But the Roman army remained master of the ground, and claimed a complete victory. Germanicus erected a trophy in the field, with a vaunting inscription, that the nations between the Rhine and the Elbe had been thoroughly conquered by his army. But that army speedily made a final retreat to the left bank of the Rhine; nor was the effect of their campaign more durable than their trophy. The sarcasm with which Tacitus speaks of certain other triumphs of Roman generals over Germans may apply to the pageant which Germanicus celebrated on his return to Rome from his command of the Roman army of the Rhine.

After the Romans had abandoned their attempts on Germany, we find Arminius engaged in hostilities with Maroboduus, the king of the Suevi and Marcomanni, who was endeavoring to bring the other German tribes into a state of dependency on him. Arminius was at the head of the Germans who took up arms against this home invader of their liberties. After some minor engagements, a pitched battle was fought between the two confederacies, A.D. 16, in which the loss on each side was equal; but Maroboduus confessed the ascendancy of his antagonist by avoiding a renewal of the engagement, and by imploring the intervention of the Romans in his defence. The younger Drusus then commanded the Roman legions in the province of Illyricum, and by his mediation a peace was concluded between Arminius and Maroboduus, by the terms of which it is evident that the latter must have renounced his ambitious schemes against the freedom of the other German tribes.

VIII

Arminius did not long survive this second war of independence, which he successfully waged for his country. He was assassinated in the thirty-seventh year of his age, by some of his own kinsmen, who conspired against him. Tacitus says that this happened while he was engaged in a civil war, which had been caused by his attempts to make himself king over his countrymen. It is far more probable (as one of the best biographers of Arminius has observed), that Tacitus misunderstood an attempt of Arminius to extend his influence as elective war-chieftain of the Cherusci, and other tribes, for an attempt to obtain the royal dignity. When we remember that his father-in-law and his brother were renegades, we can well understand that a party among his kinsmen may have been bitterly hostile to him, and have opposed his authority with the tribe by open violence, and when that seemed ineffectual, by secret assassination.

Arminius left a name which the historians of the nation against which he combated so long and so gloriously have delighted to honour. It is from the most indisputable source, from the lips of enemies, that we know his exploits. His countrymen made history, but did not write it. But his memory lived among them in the lays of their bards, who recorded—

> "The deeds he did, the fields he won,
> The freedom he restored."

As time passed on, the gratitude of ancient Germany to her great deliverer grew into adoration, and divine honours were paid for centuries to Arminius by every tribe of the Low Germanic division of the Teutonic races. The Irmin-sul, or the column of Herman, near Eresburg, the modern Stadtberg, was the chosen object of worship to the descendants of the Cherusci, the old Saxons, and defence of which they fought most desperately against Charlemagne and his Christianised Franks. "Irmin, in the cloudy Olympus of Teutonic belief, appears as a king and a warrior; and the pillar, the 'Irmin-sul,' bearing the statue, and considered as the symbol of the deity, was the palladium of the Saxon nation, until the temple of Eresburg was destroyed by Charlemagne, and the column itself transferred to the monastery of Corbey, where, perhaps, a portion of the rude rock idol yet remains, covered by the ornaments of the Gothic era." (Palegrave on *"The English Commonwealth."*)

Traces of the worship of Arminius are to be found among our Anglo-Saxon ancestors, after their settlement in this island. One of the four great highways was held to be under the protection of the deity, and was called the "Irmin-street." The name Arminius is, of course, the mere Latinised form of "Herman," the name by which the hero and the deity were known by every man of Low German blood, on either side of the German sea. It means, etymologically, the "War-man," the "man of hosts."

About ten centuries and a half after the demolition of the Irmin-sul, and nearly eighteen after the death of Arminius, the modern Germans conceived the idea of rendering tardy homage to their great hero; and, accordingly in the first half of the 19th century a general subscription was organized in Germany, for the purpose of erecting on the Osning—a conical mountain, which forms the highest summit of the Teutoberger Wald, and is eighteen hundred feet above the level of the sea —a colossal bronze statue of Arminius. The statue was designed by Bandel. The hero was to stand uplifting a sword in his right hand, and looking towards the Rhine. The height of the statue was to be eighty feet from the base to the point of the sword, and was to stand on a circular Gothic temple, ninety feet high, and supported by oak trees as columns. The mountain, where it was to be erected, is wild and stern, and overlooks the scene of the battle. It was calculated that the statue would be clearly visible at a distance of sixty miles. The temple nearly finished, and the statue itself cast at the copper works at Lemgo. But there, through want of funds to set it up, it laid for some years, in disjointed fragments, exposed to the mutilating homage of relic-seeking travellers.

SYNOPSIS OF EVENTS BETWEEN ARMINIUS'S VICTORY OVER VARUS, AND THE BATTLE OF CHALONS.

A.D. 43. The Romans commence the conquest of Britain, Claudius being then the emperor of Rome. The population of this island was then Celtic. In about forty years all the tribes south of the Clyde were subdued, and their land made a Roman province.

58-60. Successful campaigns of the Roman general Corbulo against the Parthians.

64. First persecution of the Christians at Rome under Nero.

68-70. Civil wars in the Roman world. The emperors Nero, Galba, Otho, and Vitellius, cut off successively by violent deaths. Vespasian becomes emperor.

70. Jerusalem destroyed by the Romans under Titus.

83. Futile attack of Domitian on the Germans.

86. Beginning of the wars between the Romans and the Dacians.

98-117. Trajan emperor of Rome. Under him the empire acquires its greatest territorial extent by his conquests in Dacia and in the East. His successor, Hadrian, abandons the provinces beyond the Euphrates, which Trajan had conquered.

138-180. Era of the Antonines.

167-176. A long and desperate war between Rome, and a great confederacy of the German nations. Marcus Antoninus at last succeeds in repelling them.

192-197. Civil wars throughout the Roman world. Severus becomes emperor. He relaxes the discipline of the soldiers. After his death in 211, the series of military insurrections, civil wars, and murders of emperors recommences.

226. Artaxerxes (Ardisheer) overthrows the Parthian, and restores the Persian kingdom in Asia. He attacks the Roman possessions in the East.

250. The Goths invade the Roman provinces. The emperor Decius is defeated and slain by them.

253-260. The Franks and Alemanni invade Gaul, Spain, and Africa. The Goths attack Asia Minor and Greece. The Persians conquer Armenia. Their king, Sapor, defeats the Roman emperor Valerian, and takes him prisoner. General distress of the Roman empire.

268-283. The emperors Claudius, Aurelian, Tacitus, Probus, and Carus defeat the various enemies of Rome, and restore order in the Roman state.

285. Diocletian divides and reorganizes the Roman Empire. After his abdication in 305 a fresh series of civil wars and confusion ensues. Constantine, the first Christian emperor, reunites the empire in 324.

330. Constantine makes Constantinople the seat of empire instead of Rome.

363. The emperor Julian is killed in action against the Persians.

364-375. The empire is again divided, Valentinian being emperor of the West, and Valens of the East. Valentinian repulses the Alemanni, and other German invaders from Gaul. Splendour of the Gothic kingdom under Hermanric, north of the Danube.

375-395. The Huns attack the Goths, who implore the protection of the Roman emperor of the East. The Goths are allowed to pass the Danube, and to settle in the Roman provinces. A war soon breaks out between them and the Romans, and the emperor Valens and his army are destroyed by them. They ravage the Roman territories. The emperor Theodosius reduces them to submission. They retain settlements in Thrace and Asia Minor.

395. Final division of the Roman empire between Arcadius and Honorius, the two sons of Theodosius. The Goths revolt, and under Alaric attack various parts of both the Roman empires.

410. Alaric takes the city of Rome.

412. The Goths march into Gaul, and in 414 into Spain, which had been already invaded by hosts of Vandals, Suevi, Alani, and other Germanic

nations. Britain is formally abandoned by the Roman emperor of the West.

428. Genseric, king of the Vandals, conquers the Roman province of North Africa.

441. The Huns attack the Eastern empire.

-⟦ SIX ⟧-

Chalons, 451

WHY DECISIVE: "[the battle] not only rescued for a time from destruction the old age of Rome, but preserved for centuries of power and glory the Germanic element in the civilization of modern Europe. . . . And on his [Attila's] death, two years after the battle, the vast empire which his genius had founded was soon dissevered. . . . The name of the Huns ceased for some centuries to inspire terror in western Europe and their ascendancy passed away with the life of the great king by which it had been so fearfully augmented." [Creasy.]

I

A BROAD expanse of plains, the Campi Catalaunici of the ancients, spreads far and wide around the city of Chalons, in the north-east of France. The long rows of poplars, through which the river Marne winds its way, and a few thinly-scattered villages are almost the only objects that vary the monotonous aspect of the greater part of this region. But about five miles from Chalons, near the little hamlets of Chape and Cuperly, the ground is indented and heaped up in ranges and grassy mounds and trenches, which attest the work of man's hand in ages past; and which, to the practised eye, demonstrate that this quiet spot had once been the fortified position of a huge military host.

Local tradition gives to these ancient earth-works the name of Attila's Camp. Nor is there any reason to question the correctness of the title, or to doubt that behind these very ramparts it was that, over 1500 years ago, the most powerful heathen king that ever ruled in Europe mustered the remnants of his vast army, which had striven on these plains against the Christian soldiery of Thoulouse and Rome. Here it was that Attila prepared to resist to the death his victors in the field; and here he heaped up the treasures of his camp in one vast pile, which was to be his funeral pyre should his camp be stormed. It was here that the Gothic and Italian forces watched, but dared not assail, their enemy in his despair, after that great and terrible day of battle.

The victory which the Roman general Aetius, with his Gothic allies, had then gained over the Huns, was the last victory of Imperial Rome. But among the long list of her triumphs, few can be found that, for their importance and ultimate benefit to mankind, are comparable with this expiring effort of her arms. It did not, indeed, open to her any new career of conquest —it did not consolidate the relics of her power—it did not turn the rapid ebb of her fortunes.

The mission of Imperial Rome was, in truth, already accomplished. She had received and transmitted through her once ample dominion the civilisation of Greece. She had broken up the barriers of narrow nationalities among the various states and tribes that dwelt around the coasts of the Mediterranean. She had fused these and many other races into one organised empire, bound together by a community of laws, of government, and institutions. Under the shelter of her full power the True Faith had arisen in the earth, and during the years of her decline it had been nourished to maturity, and had overspread all the provinces that ever obeyed her sway.

For no beneficial purpose to mankind could the dominion of the seven-hilled city have been restored or prolonged. But it was all-important to mankind what nations should divide among them Rome's rich inheritance of empire: whether the Germanic and Gothic warriors should form states and kingdoms out of the fragments of her dominions, and become the free members of the commonwealth of Christian Europe; or whether pagan savages from the wilds of Central Asia should crush the relics of classic civilisation, and the early institutions of the Christianised Germans in one hopeless chaos of barbaric conquest. The Christian Visigoths of King Theodoric fought and triumphed at Chalons, side by side with the legions of Aetius. Their joint victory over the Hunnish host not only rescued for a time from destruction the old age of Rome, but preserved for centuries of power and glory the Germanic element in the civilisation of modern Europe.

II

In order to estimate the full importance to mankind of the battle of Chalons, we must keep steadily in mind who and what the Germans were and the important distinctions between them and the numerous other races that assailed the Roman Empire: and it is to be understood that the Gothic and Scandinavian nations are included in the German race. Now, as Prichard points out, "in two remarkable traits the Germans differed from the Sarmatic, as well as from the Slavic nations, and indeed, from all those other races to whom the Greeks and Romans gave the designation of barbarians. I allude to their personal freedom and regards for the rights of men; secondly, to the respect paid by them to the female sex, and the chastity for which the latter were celebrated among the people of the North. These were the foundations of that probity of character, self-respect, and purity of manners which may be traced among the Germans and Goths even during pagan times, and which, when their sentiments were enlightened by Christianity, brought out those splendid traits of character which distinguished the age of chivalry and romance." What the intermixture of the German stock with the classic, at the fall of the Western Empire, has done for mankind, may be best felt by watching, with Thomas Arnold, over how large a portion of the earth the influence of the German element is now extended.

"It affects, more or less, the whole west of Europe, from the head of the Gulf of Bothnia to the most southern promontory of Sicily, from the Oder and the Adriatic to the Hebrides and to Lisbon. It is true that the language spoken over a large portion of this space is not predominantly German; but even in France and Italy and Spain, the influence of the Franks, Burgundians, Visigoths, Ostrogoths, and Lombards, while it has coloured even the language, has in blood and institutions left its mark legibly and indelibly.

"Germany, the Low Countries, Switzerland for the most part, Denmark, Norway, and Sweden, and our own islands, are all in language, in blood and in institutions, German most decidedly. But all South America is peopled with Spaniards and Portuguese; all North America, and all Australia, with Englishmen. I say nothing of the prospects and influence of the German race in Africa and in India: it is enough to say that half of Europe, and all America and Australia, are German, more or less completely, in race, in language, or in institutions, or in all."

By the middle of the fifth century, Germanic nations had settled themselves in many of the fairest regions of the Roman Empire, had imposed their yoke on the provincials, and had undergone, to a considerable extent, that moral conquest which the arts and refinements of the vanquished in arms have so often achieved over the rough victor. The Visigoths held the north of Spain, and Gaul south of the Loire. Franks, Alemanni, Alans, and Burgundians, had established themselves in other Gallic provinces, and the Suevi were masters of a large southern portion of the Spanish peninsula. A king of the Vandals reigned in North Africa, and the Ostrogoths had firmly planted themselves in the provinces north of Italy. Of these powers and principalities, that of the Visigoths, under their king Theodoric, son of Alaric, was by far the first in power and in civilisation.

The pressure of the Huns upon Europe had first been felt in the fourth century of our era. They had long been formidable to the Chinese empire; but the ascendancy in arms which another nomadic tribe of Central Asia, the Sienpi, gained over them, drove the Huns from their Chinese conquests westward; and this movement once being communicated to the whole chain of barbaric nations that dwelt northward of the Black Sea and the Roman Empire, tribe after tribe of savage warriors broke in upon the barriers of civilised Europe.

The Huns crossed the Tanais into Europe in 375, and rapidly reduced to subjection the Alans, the Ostrogoths, and other tribes that were then dwelling along the course of the Danube. The armies of the Roman emperor that tried to check their progress, were cut to pieces by them; and Pannonia and other provinces south of the Danube were speedily occupied by the victorious cavalry of these new invaders. Not merely the degenerate Romans, but the bold and hardy warriors of Germany and Scandinavia were appalled at the numbers, the ferocity, the ghastly appearance, and the lightning-like rapidity of the Huns. Strange and loathsome legends were coined and credited, which attributed their origin to the union of

"Secret, black, and midnight hags

with the evil spirits of the wilderness.

Tribe after tribe, and city after city, fell before them. Then came a pause in their career of conquest in south-western

Europe, caused probably bv dissensions among their chiefs, and also by their arms being employed in attacks upon the Scandinavian nations. But when Attila (or Atzel, as he is called in the Hungarian language) became their ruler, the torrent of their arms was directed with augmented terrors upon the west and the south; and their myriads marched beneath the guidance of one master-mind to the overthrow both of the new and the old powers of the earth.

III

Recent events have thrown such a strong interest over everything connected with the Hungarian name that even the terrible name of Attila now impresses us the more vividly through our sympathising admiration of the exploits of those who claim to be descended from his warriors, and "ambitiously insert the name of Attila among their native kings." The authenticity of this martial genealogy is denied by some writers, and questioned by more. But it is at least certain that the Magyars of Arpad, who are the immediate ancestors of the bulk of the modern Hungarians, and who conquered the country which bears the name of Hungary in A.D. 889, were of the same stock of mankind as were the Huns of Attila, even if they did not belong to the same subdivision of that stock. Nor is there any improbability in the tradition that after Attila's death many of his warriors remained in Hungary, and that their descendants afterwards joined the Huns of Arpad in their career of conquest. It is certain that Attila made Hungary the seat of his empire. It seems also susceptible of clear proof that the territory was then called Hungvar and Attila's soldiers Hungvari.

Both the Huns of Attila and those of Arpad came from the family of nomadic nations, whose primitive regions were those of the vast wilderness of high Asia, which are included between the Altaic and the Himalayan mountain-chains. The inroads of these tribes upon the lower regions of Asia, and into Europe, have caused many of the most remarkable revolutions in the history of the world. There is every reason to believe that swarms of these nations made their way into distant parts of the earth, at periods long before the date of the Scythian invasion of Asia, which is the earliest inroad of the nomadic race that history records. The first, as far as we can conjecture, in respect to the time of their descent, were the Finnish and Ugrian tribes, who appear to have come down from the Altaic border of high Asia towards the north-west, in which direction they advanced to the Uralian Mountains. There they established themselves: and that mountain-chain, with its valleys and pasture lands, became to them a new country, whence they sent out colonies on every side; but the Ugrian colony, which, under Arpad, occupied Hungary, and became the ancestors of the bulk of the present Hungarian nation did not quit their settlements on the Uralian Mountains till a very late period, not until four centuries after the time when Attila led from the primary seats of the nomadic races in high Asia the host with which he advanced into the heart of France. That host was Turkish; but closely allied in origin, language, and habits with the Finno-Ugrian settlers on the Ural.

Attila's fame has not come down to us through the partial and suspicious medium of chroniclers and poets of his own race. It is not from Hunnish authorities that we learn the extent of his might: it is from his enemies, from the literature and the legends of the nations whom he afflicted with his arms that we draw the unquestionable evidence of his greatness. Besides the express narratives of Byzantine, Latin, and Gothic writers, we have the strongest proof of the stern reality of Attila's conquests, in the extent to which he and his Huns have been the themes of the earliest German and Scandinavian lays.

Wild as many of these legends are, they bear concurrent and certain testimony to the awe with which the memory of Attila was regarded by the bold warriors who composed and delighted in them. Attila's exploits, and the wonders of his unearthly steed and magic sword, repeatedly occur in the sagas of Norway and Iceland; and the celebrated "Niebelungen Lied," ("Song of the Niebelungen," they being in German legend an evil family possessing a magic hoard of gold, which is obtained by the warrior, Siegfried. Wagner partly used elements from the myth in an operatic tetralogy.) the most ancient of Germanic poetry, is full of them. There Etsel, or Attila, is described as the wearer of twelve mighty crowns, and as promising to his bride the lands of thirty kings, whom his irresistible sword had subdued. As hero of the poem, it is at his capital, Etselenburgh, corresponding to modern Buda, that much of its action takes place.

When we turn from the legendary to the historic Attila, we see clearly that he was not one of the vulgar herd of barbaric conquerors. Consummate military skill may be traced in his campaigns; and he relied far less on the brute force of armies for the aggrandisement of his empire, than on the unbounded influence over the affections of friends and the fears of foes, which his genius enabled him to acquire. Austerely sober in his private life—severely just on the judgment-seat—conspicuous among a nation of warriors for hardihood, strength, and skill in every martial exercise—grave and deliberate in counsel, but rapid and remorseless in execution—he gave safety and security to all who were under his dominion, while he waged a warfare of extermination against all who opposed or sought to escape from it.

He watched the national passions, the prejudices, the creeds, and the superstitions of the varied nations over which he ruled, and of those which he sought to reduce beneath his sway: all these feelings he had the skill to turn to his own account. His own warriors believed him to be the inspired favourite of their deities, and followed him with fanatic zeal: his enemies looked on him as the preappointed minister of Heaven's wrath against themselves; and, though they believed not in his creed, their own made them tremble before him.

In one of his early campaigns he appeared before his troops with an ancient iron sword in his grasp, which he told them was the god of war whom their ancestors had worshipped. It is certain that the nomadic tribes of northern Asia, whom Herodotus described under the name of Scythians, from the earliest times worshipped as their god a bare sword. That sword-god was supposed, in Attila's time, to have disappeared from earth, but the Hunnish king now claimed to have received it by special revelation.

It was said that a herdsman, who was tracking in the desert a wounded heifer by the drops of blood, found the mysterious sword standing fixed in the ground, as if it had been darted down from heaven. The herdsman bore it to Attila, who thenceforth was believed by the Huns to wield the Spirit of Death in battle; and the seers prophesied that that sword was to destroy the world. A Roman, who was on an embassy to the Hunnish camp, recorded in his memoirs Attila's acquisition of this supernatural weapon, and the immense influence over the minds of the barbaric tribes which its possession gave him. In the title which he assumed, we shall see the skill with which he availed himself of the legends and creeds of other nations as well as of his own. He designated himself "Attila, Descendant of the Great Nimrod. Nurtured in Engaddi. By the Grace of God, King of the Huns, the Goths, the Danes, and the Medes. The Dread of the World."

Herbert states that Attila is represented on an old medallion with a teraphim, or a head, on his breast; and the same writer adds: "We know, from the *Hamartigenea* of Prudentius, that Nimrod, (the son of Cush, described in Genesis 10:8 as a mighty hunter and ruler) with a snaky-haired head, was the object of adoration to the heretical followers of Marcion; and the same head was the palladium set up by Antiochus Epiphanes over the gates of Antioch, though it has been called the visage of Charon. The memory of Nimrod was certainly regarded with mystic veneration by many; and by asserting himself to be the heir of that mighty hunter before the Lord, he vindicated himself to at least the whole Babylonian kingdom."

It is obvious enough why he styled himself "By the Grace of God, King of the Huns and Goths;" and it seems far from difficult to see why he added the names of the Medes and the Danes. His armies had been engaged in warfare against the Persian kingdom of the Sassanidæ; and it is certain that he meditated the attack and overthrow of the Medo-Persian power. Probably some of the northern provinces of that kingdom had been compelled to pay him tribute, and this would account for his styling himself King of the Medes, they being his remotest subjects to the south. From a similar cause he may have called himself King of the Danes, as his power may well have extended northwards as far as the nearest of the Scandinavian nations; and this mention of Medes and Danes as his subjects, would serve at once to indicate the vast extent of his dominion. In the "Niebelungen Lied," the old poet who describes the reception of the heroine Kriemhild by Attila [Etsel], says that Attila's dominions were so vast, that among his subject-warriors there were Russian, Greek, Wallachian, Polish, and even Danish knights.

The extensive territory north of the Danube and Black
Sea, and eastward of Caucasus, over which Attila ruled, first
in conjunction with his brother Bleda and afterwards alone,
cannot be very accurately defined, but it must have comprised within it, besides the Huns, many nations of Slavic,
Gothic, Teutonic, and Finnish origin. South also of the
Danube, the country, from the river Sau as far as Novi in
Thrace, was a Hunnish province. Such was the empire of
the Huns in A.D. 445; a memorable year, in which Attila founded
Buda on the Danube, as his capital city; and ridded himself
of his brother by a crime, which seems to have been prompted
not only by selfish ambition, but also by a desire of turning to his
purpose the legends and forebodings, which then were universally spread ,throughout the Roman Empire, and must have
been well known to the watchful and ruthless Hun.

IV

The year 445 of our era completed the twelfth century
from the foundation of Rome, according to the best chro-
nologers. It had always been believed among the Romans,
that the twelve vultures, which were said to have appeared
to Romulus when he founded the city, signified the time during
which the Roman power should endure. The twelve vultures
denoted twelve centuries. This interpretation of the vision of
the birds of destiny was current among learned Romans, even
where there were yet many of the twelve centuries to run, and
while the imperial city was at the zenith of its power.

But as the allotted time drew nearer and nearer to its con-
clusion, and as Rome grew weaker and weaker beneath the
blows of barbaric invaders, the terrible omen was more and
more talked and thought of; and in Attila's time, men watched
for the momentary extinction of the Roman State with the last
beat of the last vulture's wing. Moreover, among the numerous
legends connected with the foundation of the city, and the
fratricidal death of Remus, there was one most terrible one,
which told that Romulus did not put his brother to death in
accident, or in hasty quarrel, but that

> "He slew his gallant twin
> With inexpiable sin,"

deliberately, and in compliance with the warnings of supernatural powers. The shedding of a brother's blood was believed to have been the price at which the founder of Rome had purchased from destiny her twelve centuries of existence.

We may imagine, therefore, with what terror in this, the twelve-hundredth year after the foundation of Rome, the inhabitants of the Roman Empire must have heard the tidings that the royal breathren, Attila and Bleda, had founded a new capitol on the Danube, which was designed to rule over the ancient capitol on the Tiber; and that Attila, like Romulus, had consecrated the foundations of his new city by murdering his brother; so that for the new cycle of centuries then about to commence, dominion had been bought from the gloomy spirits of destiny in favour of the Hun, by a sacrifice of equal awe and value with that which had formerly obtained it for the Roman.

An attempt to assassinate Attila, made, or supposed to have been made, at the instigation of Theodosius the younger, the Emperor of Constantinople, drew the Hunnish armies, in 445, upon the Eastern Empire, and delayed for a time the destined blow against Rome. Probably a more important cause of delay was the revolt of some of the Hunnish tribes to the north of the Black Sea against Attila, which broke out about this period, and is cursorily mentioned by the Byzantine writers. Attila quelled this revolt; and having thus consolidated his power, and having punished the presumption of the Eastern Roman Emperor by fearful ravages of his fairest provinces, Attila, in 450 A.D., prepared to set his vast forces in motion for the conquest of Western Europe. He sought unsuccessfully by diplomatic intrigues to detach the king of the Visigoths from his alliance with Rome, and he resolved first to crush the power of Theodoric, and then to advance with overwhelming power to trample out the last sparks of the doomed Roman Empire.

A strange invitation from a Roman princess gave him a pretext for the war, and threw an air of chivalric enterprise over his invasion. Honoria, sister of Valentinian III, the Emperor of the West, had sent to Attila to offer him her hand, and her supposed right to share in the imperial power. This had been discovered by the Romans, and Honoria had been forthwith closely imprisoned.

Attila now pretended to take up arms in behalf of his self-

promised bride, and proclaimed that he was about to march
to Rome to redress Honoria's wrongs. Ambition and spite
against her brother must have been the sole motives that led
the lady to woo the royal Hun, for Attila's face and person had
all the national ugliness of his race.

V

Two chiefs of the Franks, who were then settled on the
lower Rhine, were at this period engaged in a feud with
each other; and while one of them appealed to the Romans
for aid, the other invoked the assistance and protection of
the Huns. Attila thus obtained an ally, whose co-operation
secured for him the passage of the Rhine; and it was this
circumstance which caused him to take a northward route
from Hungary for his attack upon Gaul. The muster of the
Hunnish hosts was swollen by warriors of every tribe that
they had subjugated; nor is there any reason to suspect the
old chroniclers of wilful exaggeration in estimating Attila's
army at seven hundred thousand strong. Having crossed the
Rhine, probably a little below Coblentz, he defeated the king
of the Burgundians, who endeavoured to bar his progress. He
then divided his vast forces into two armies, one of which
marched north-west upon Tongres and Arras and the other
cities of that part of France; while the main body, under Attila
himself, marched up the Moselle, and destroyed Besançon, and
other towns in the country of the Burgundians. One of the
latest and best biographers of Attila well observes, that, "having
thus conquered the eastern part of France, Attila prepared for
an invasion of the west Gothic territories beyond the Loire.
He marched upon Orleans, where he intended to force the
passage of that river, and only a little attention is requisite to
enable us to perceive that he proceeded on a systematic plan:
he had his right wing on the north, for the protection of his
Frank allies; his left wing on the south, for the purpose of preventing the Burgundians from rallying and of menacing the
passes of the Alps from Italy; and he led his centre towards
the chief object of the campaign—the conquest of Orleans, and
an easy passage into the West Gothic dominion. The whole
plan is very like that of the allied powers in 1814, with this
difference, that their left wing entered France through the de-

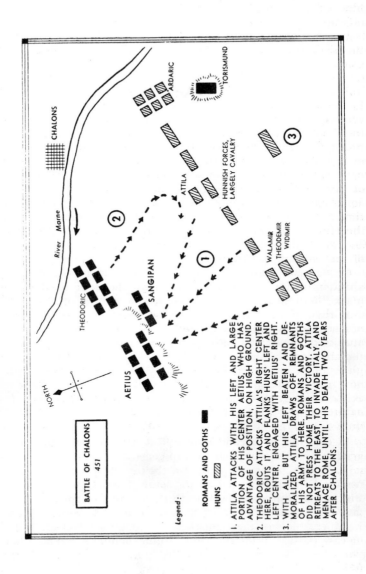

Legend:

BATTLE OF CHALONS
451

ROMANS AND GOTHS ▨
HUNS ▨

1. ATTILA ATTACKS WITH HIS LEFT AND LARGER PORTION OF HIS CENTER. AETIUS, WHO HAS ADVANTAGE OF POSITION, ON HIGH GROUND.

2. THEODORIC ATTACKS ATTILA'S RIGHT CENTER HERE, ROUTS IT AND FLANKS HUNS' LEFT AND LEFT CENTER, ENGAGED WITH AETIUS' RIGHT.

3. WITH ALL BUT HIS LEFT BEATEN, AND DE-MORALIZED, ATTILA DRAWS OFF REMNANTS OF HIS ARMY TO HERE. ROMANS AND GOTHS DID NOT PRESS HOME THEIR VICTORY. ATTILA RETREATS TO THE EAST, TO INVADE ITALY, AND MENACE ROME, UNTIL HIS DEATH TWO YEARS AFTER CHALONS.

NORTH

CHALONS

River Marne

THEODORIC

AETIUS

SANGIPAN

ATTILA

WALAMIR
THEODEMIR
WIDIMIR

HUNNISH FORCES, LARGELY CAVALRY

ARDARIC

TORISMUND

files of the Jura, in the direction of Lyons, and that the military object of the campaign was the capture of Paris."

It was not until the year 451 that the Huns commenced the siege of Orleans; and during their campaign in eastern Gaul, the Roman general Aetius had strenuously exerted himself in collecting and organizing such an army as might, when united to the soldiery of the Visigoths, be fit to face the Huns in the field. He enlisted every subject of the Roman Empire, whom patriotism, courage, or compulsion could collect beneath the standards; and round these troops, which assumed the once proud title of the legions of Rome, he arrayed the large forces of barbaric auxiliaries, whom pay, persuasion, or the general hate and dread of the Huns, brought to the camp of the last of the Roman generals. King Theodoric exerted himself with equal energy. Orleans resisted her besiegers bravely as in after times. The passage of the Loire was skilfully defended against the Huns; and Aetius and Theodoric, after much manœuvring and difficulty, effected a junction of their armies to the south of that important river.

On the advance of the allies upon Orleans, Attila instantly abandoned the siege of that city, and retreated towards the Marne. He did not choose to risk a decisive battle with only the central corps of his army against the combined power of his enemies; and he therefore fell back upon his base of operations; calling in his wings from Arras and Besançon, and concentrating the whole of the Hunnish forces on the vast plains of Chalons-sur-Marne. A glance at the map will show how scientifically this place was chosen by the Hunnish general, as the point for his scattered forces to converge upon; and the nature of the ground was eminently favourable for the operations of cavalry, the arm in which Attila's strength peculiarly lay.

It was during the retreat from Orleans that a Christian hermit is reported to have approached the Hunnish king, and said to him, "Thou art the Scourge of God for the chastisement of Christians." Attila instantly assumed this new title of terror, which thenceforth became the appellation by which he was most widely and most fearfully known.

The confederate armies of Romans and Visigoths at last met their great adversary, face to face, on the ample battle-ground of the Chalons plains. Aetius commanded on the right of the allies; King Theodoric on the left; and Sangipan, king

of the Alans, whose fidelity was suspected, was placed purposely
in the centre, and in the very front of the battle. Attila commanded his centre in person, at the head of his own countrymen, while the Ostrogoths, the Gepidæ, and the other subject
allies of the Huns, were drawn up on the wings.

Some manœuvring appears to have occurred before the engagement, in which Aetius had the advantage, inasmuch as he
succeeded in occupying a sloping hill, which commanded the
left flank of the Huns. Attila saw the importance of the
position taken by Aetius on the high ground, and commenced
the battle by a furious attack on this part of the Roman lines,
in which he seems to have detached some of his best troops
from his centre to aid his left. The Romans, having the
advantage of the ground, repulsed the Huns, and while the
allies gained this advantage on their right, their left, under
King Theodoric, assailed the Ostrogoths, who formed the
right of Attila's army. The gallant king was himself struck
down by a javelin, as he rode onward at the head of his men,
and his own cavalry charging over him trampled him to death
in the confusion. But the Visigoths, infuriated, not dispirited,
by their monarch's fall, routed the enemies opposed to them,
and then wheeled upon the flank of the Hunnish centre,
which had been engaged in a sanguinary and indecisive contest
with the Alans.

In this peril Attila made his centre fall back upon his
camp; and when the shelter of its intrenchments and waggons
had once been gained, the Hunnish archers repulsed, without
difficulty, the charges of the vengeful Gothic cavalry. Aetius
had not pressed the advantage which he gained on his side of the
field, and when night fell over the wild scene of havoc, Attila's
left was still unbroken, but his right had been routed, and
his centre forced back upon his camp.

Expecting an assault on the morrow, Attila stationed his
best archers in front of the cars and waggons, which were
drawn up as a fortification along his lines, and made every
preparation for a desperate resistance. But the "Scourge of
God" resolved that no man should boast of the honour of
having either captured or slain him; and he caused to be
raised in the centre of his encampment a huge pyramid of
the wooden saddles of his cavalry: round it he heaped the
spoils and the wealth that he had won; on it he stationed

his wives who had accompanied him in the campaign and on the summit Attila placed himself, ready to perish in the flames, and baulk the victorious foe of their choicest booty, should they succeed in storming his defences.

But when the morning broke and revealed the extent of the carnage, with which the plains were heaped for miles, the successful allies saw also and respected the resolute attitude of their antagonist. Neither were any measures taken to block-ade him in his camp, and so to extort by famine that sub-mission which it was too plainly perilous to enforce with the sword. Attila was allowed to march back the remnants of his army without molestation, and even with the semblance of success.

It is probable that the crafty Aetius was unwilling to be too victorious. He dreaded the glory which his allies the Visigoths had acquired; and feared that Rome might find a second Alaric in Prince Thorismund, who had signalised himself in the battle, and had been chosen on the field to succeed his father Theodoric. He persuaded the young king to return at once to his capital and thus relieved himself at the same time of the presence of a dangerous friend, as well as of a formidable though beaten foe.

Attila's attacks on the Western Empire were soon renewed, but never with such peril to the civilised world as had menaced it before his defeat at Chalons. And on his death, two years after that battle, the vast empire, which his genius had founded, was soon dissevered by the successful revolts of the subject na-tions. The name of the Huns ceased for some centuries to in-spire terror in Western Europe, and their ascendancy passed away with the life of the great king, by whom it had been so fearfully augmented.

SYNOPSIS OF EVENTS BETWEEN THE BATTLE OF CHALONS, 451, AND THE BATTLE OF TOURS, 732.

476. The Roman Empire of the West extinguished by Odoacer.

481. Establishment of the French monarchy in Gaul by Clovis.

455-582. The Saxons, Angles, and Frisians conquer Britain, except the northern parts, and the districts along the west coast. The German conquerors found eight independent kingdoms.

533-568. The generals of Justinian, the Emperor of Constantinople, conquer Italy and North Africa; and these countries are for a short time annexed to the Roman Empire of the East.

568-570. The Lombards conquer a great part of Italy.

570-627. The wars between the Emperors of Constantinople and the Kings of Persia are actively continued.

622. The Mohammedan area of the Hegira. Mohammed is driven from Mecca and is received as prince of Medina.

629-632. Mohammed conquers Arabia.

632-651. Mohammedan Arabs invade and conquer Persia.

632-709. They attack the Roman Empire of the East. They conquer Syria, Egypt, and Africa.

709-713. They cross the Straits of Gibraltar, and invade and conquer Spain.
   "At the death of Mohammed, in 632, his temporal and religious sovereignty embraced and was limited by the Arabian peninsula. The Roman and Persian empires, engaged in tedious and indecisive hostility upon the rivers of Mesopotamia and the Armenian mountains, were viewed by the ambitious fanatics of his creed as their quarry. In the very first year of Mohammed's immediate successor, Abubeker, each of these mighty empires was invaded. The crumbling fabric of Eastern despotism is never secure against rapid and total subversion; a few victories, a few sieges, carried the Arabian arms from the Tigris to the Oxus, and overthrew, with the Sassanian dynasty, the ancient and famous religion they had professed. Seven years of active and unceasing warfare sufficed to subjugate the rich province of Syria, though defended by numerous armies and fortified cities; and the Khalif Omar had scarcely returned thanks for the accomplishment of this conquest, when Amrou, his lieutenant, announced to him the entire reduction of Egypt. After some interval, the Saracens won their way along the coast of Africa, as far as the pillars of Hercules, and a third province was irretrievably torn from the Greek Empire. These Western conquests introduced them to fresh enemies, and ushered in more splendid successes. Encouraged by the disunion of the Visigoths, and invited by treachery, Musa, the general of a master who sat beyond the opposite extremity of the Mediterranean Sea, passed over into Spain, and within about two years the name of Mohammed was invoked under the Pyrenees."—HALLAM.

-⊰[SEVEN]⊱-

Tours, 732

WHY DECISIVE: *"The great victory won by Charles Martel over the Saracens . . . gave a decisive check to the career of Arab conquest in western Europe, rescued Christendom from Islam, preserved the relics of ancient and the germs of modern civilization and reestablished the old superiority of the Indo-European over the Semitic family of mankind."* [Creasy] *"'The event that rescued our ancestors of Britain and our neighbors of Gaul from the civil and religious yoke of the Koran.'"* [Gibbon.]

I

THE broad tract of flat, open country which intervenes between the French cities of Poictiers and Tours is principally composed of a succession of rich pasture-lands, which are traversed and fertilised by the Cher, the Creuse, the Vienne, the Claine, the Indre and other tributaries of the river Loire. Here and there the ground swells into picturesque eminences and occasionally a belt of forest-land, a brown heath, or a clustering series of vineyards, breaks the monotony of the widespread meadows; but the general character of the land is that of a grassy plain, and it seems naturally adapted for the evolutions of numerous armies, especially of those vast bodies of cavalry, which principally decided the fate of nations during the centuries that followed the downfall of Rome, and preceded the consolidation of the modern European powers.

This region has been signalised by more than one memorable conflict; but it is principally interesting to the historian by having been the scene of the great victory won by Charles Martel over the Saracens, A.D. 732, which gave a decisive check to the career of Arab conquest in western Europe, rescued Christendom from Islam, preserved the relics of ancient and the germs of modern civilisation, and reestablished the old superiority of the Indo-European over the Semitic family of mankind.

Some French writers have underrated the enduring interest of this great appeal of battle between the champions of the Crescent and the Cross. But if they have slighted the exploits of their national hero, the Saracenic trophies of Charles Martel have had full justice done to them by English and German historians. Gibbon (1737-1794) devotes several pages of his great work to the narrative of the battle of Tours, and to the consideration of the consequences which probably would have resulted, if Abderrahman's enterprise had not been crushed by the Frankish chief. Schlegel (Frederick, 1772-1845) speaks of this "mighty victory" in terms of fervent gratitude; and tells how "the arms of Charles Martel saved and delivered the Christian nations of the West from the deadly grasp of all-destroying Islam;" and Ranke (Leopold 1795-1886) points out, as "one of the most important epochs in the history of the world, the commencement of the eighth century; when, on the one side, Mahommedanism threatened to overspread Italy and Gaul, and on the other, the ancient idolatry of Saxony and Friesland once more forced its way across the Rhine. In this peril of Christian institutions, a youthful prince of Germanic race, Karl Martel, arose as their champion; maintained them with all the energy which the necessity for self-defence calls forth, and finally extended them into new regions."

Arnold ranks the victory of Charles Martel even higher than the victory of Arminius, "among those signal deliverances which have affected for centuries the happiness of mankind." In fact, the more we test its importance, the higher we shall be led to estimate it; and, though the authentic details which we possess of its circumstances and its heroes are but meagre, we can trace enough of its general character to make us watch with deep interest this encounter between the rival conquerors of the decaying Roman Empire.

That old classic world, the history of which occupies so large a portion of our early studies, lay in the eighth century of our era utterly exanimate and overthrown. On the north the German, on the south of Arab, were rending away its provinces. At last the spoilers encountered one another, each striving for the full mastery of the prey. Their conflict brought back to the memory of Gibbon the old Homeric simile, where the strife of Hector and Patroclus over the dead body of Cebriones is compared to the combat of two lions, that in their hate and hunger fight together on the mountain-tops over the carcass of a slaughtered stag: and the reluctant yielding of the Saracen power to the superior might of the Northern warriors might not in-

aptly recall those other lines of the same book of the Iliad,
where the downfall of Patroclus beneath Hector is likened to
the forced yielding of the panting and exhausted wild-boar,
that had long and furiously fought with a superior beast of
prey for the possession of the fountain among the rocks, at
which each burned to drink.

II

Although three centuries had passed away since the Germanic
conquerors of Rome had crossed the Rhine, never to repass
that frontier stream, no settled system of institutions or government, no amalgamation of the various races into one people,
no uniformity of language or habits, had been established in
the country, at the time when Charles Martel was called on to
repel the menacing tide of Saracenic invasion from the South.

Gaul was not yet France. In that, as in other provinces of
the Roman Empire of the West, the dominion of the Cæsars
had been shattered as early as the fifth century, and barbaric
kingdoms and principalities had promptly arisen on the ruins
of the Roman power. But few of these had any permanency;
and none of them consolidated the rest, or any considerable
number of the rest, into one coherent and organised civil and
political society. The great bulk of the population still consisted of the conquered provincials, that is to say, of Romanised
Celts, of a Gallic race which had long been under the dominion
of the Cæsars, and had acquired, together with no slight in-
fusion of Roman blood, the language, the literature, the laws,
and the civilisation of Latium.

Among these, and dominant over them, roved or dwelt the
German victors: some retaining nearly all the rude independence
of their primitive national character; others, softened and disciplined by the aspect and contact of the manners and institutions of civilised life. For it is to be borne in mind that the
Roman Empire in the West was not crushed by any sudden
avalanche of barbaric invasion. The German conquerors came
across the Rhine, not in enormous hosts, but in bands of a few
thousand warriors at a time. The conquest of a province was
the result of an infinite series of partial local invasions, carried
on by little armies of this description. The victorious warriors
either retired with their booty, or fixed themselves in the invaded district, taking care to keep sufficiently concentrated for

military purposes, and ever ready for some fresh foray, either against a rival Teutonic band, or some hitherto unassailed city of the provincials.

Gradually, however, the conquerors acquired a desire for permanent landed possessions. They lost somewhat of the restless thirst for novelty and adventure, which had first made them throng beneath the banner of the boldest captains of their tribe, and leave their native forests for a roving military life on the left bank of the Rhine. They were converted to the Christian faith; and gave up with their old creed much of the coarse ferocity which must have been fostered in the spirits of the ancient warriors of the North by a mythology which promised, as the reward of the brave on earth, an eternal cycle of fighting and drunkenness in a heaven as they conceived it.

But although their conversion and other civilising influences operated powerfully upon the Germans in Gaul; and although the Franks (who were originally a confederation of the Teutonic tribes that dwelt between the Rhine, the Maine, and the Weser) established a decisive superiority over the other conquerors of the province, as well as over the conquered provincials, the country long remained a chaos of uncombined and shifting elements. The early princes of the Merovingian dynasty (the first of Frankish origin in France, *circ.* 500-752) were generally occupied in wars against other princes of their house, occasioned by the frequent subdivisions of the Frank monarchy: and the ablest and best of them had found all their energies tasked to the utmost to defend the barrier of the Rhine against the pagan Germans, who strove to pass that river and gather their share of the spoils of the empire.

III

The conquests, which the Saracens effected over the southern and eastern provinces of Rome, were far more rapid than those achieved by the Germans in the north; and the new organisations of society which the Moslems introduced were summarily and uniformly enforced. Exactly a century passed between the death of Mohammed and the date of the battle of Tours. During that century the followers of the Prophet had torn away half the Roman Empire; and, besides their conquests over Persia, the Saracens had overrun Syria, Egypt, Africa, and Spain, in an unchequered, and apparently irresistible career of victory.

Nor, at the commencement of the eighth century of our era, was the Mohammedan world divided against itself, as it subsequently became. All these vast regions obeyed the Caliph; throughout them all, from the Pyrenees to the Oxus, the name of Mohammed was invoked in prayer, and the Koran revered as the book of the law.

It was under one of their ablest and most renowned commanders, with a veteran army, and with every apparent advantage of time, place, and circumstance, that the Arabs made their great effort at the conquest of Europe north of the Pyrenees. The victorious Moslem soldiery in Spain,

> "A countless multitude;
> Syrian, Moor, Saracen, Greek renegade,
> Persian, and Copt, and Tartar, in one bond
> Of erring faith conjoined—strong in the youth
> And heat of zeal—a dreadful brotherhood,"

were eager for the plunder of more Christian cities and shrines, and full of fanatic confidence in the invincibility of their arms.

> "Nor were the chiefs
> Of victory less assured, by long success
> Elate, and proud of that o'erwhelming strength
> Which, surely they believed, as it had rolled
> Thus far uncheck'd, would roll victorious on,
> Till, like the Orient, the subjected West
> Should bow in reverence at Mahommed's name;
> And pilgrims from remotest Arctic shores
> Tread with religious feet the burning sands
> Of Araby and Mecca's stony soil."
>
> SOUTHEY'S *Roderick.*

It is not only by the modern Christian poet, but by the old Arabian chroniclers also that these feelings of ambition and arrogance are attributed to the Moslems, who had overthrown the Visigoth (Teutons of the west who early in the Christian era overran the greater part of the Roman Empire) power in Spain. And their eager expectations of new wars were excited to the utmost on the reappointment by the caliph of Abderrahman Ibn Abdillah Alghafeki to the government of that country, A.D. 729, which restored them a general who had signalised his skill and prowess during the conquests of Africa and Spain, whose ready valour and generosity had made him the idol of the troops, who had already been engaged in several expeditions into Gaul, so as to be well acquainted with the national character and tactics of the Franks, and who was known to thirst, like a good Moslem, for revenge for the slaughter of some detachments of the true believers, which had been cut off on the north of the Pyrenees.

In addition to his cardinal military virtues, Abderrahman is described by the Arab writers as a model of integrity and justice. The first two years of his second administration in Spain were occupied in severe reforms of the abuses which under· his predecessors had crept into the system of government, and in extensive preparations for his intended conquest of Gaul. Besides the troops which he collected from his province, he obtained from Africa a large body of chosen Berber cavalry, officered by Arabs of proved skill and valour: and in the summer of 732, he crossed the Pyrenees (between Spain and France) at the head of an army, which some Arab writers rate at eighty thousand strong, while some of the Christian chroniclers swell its numbers to many hundreds of thousands more. Probably the Arab account diminishes, but of the two keeps nearer to the truth.

It was from this formidable host, after Eudes, the Count of Acquitaine, had vainly striven to check it, after many strong cities had fallen before it, and half the land had been overrun, that Gaul and Christendom were at last rescued by the strong arm of Prince Charles, who acquired a surname (Martel, hammer, which in Scandinavian mythology was given as the favorite weapon of Thor, the god of thunder) like that of the war-god of his forefathers' creed, from the might with which he broke and shattered his enemies in the battle.

IV

The Merovingian kings had sunk into absolute insignificance, and had become mere puppets of royalty before the eighth century. Charles Martel, like his father, Pepin Heristal, was duke of the Austrasian Franks (from between the Meuse and the Rhine), the bravest and most thoroughly Germanic part of the nation and exercised, in the name of the titular king what little paramount authority the turbulent minor rulers of districts and towns could be persuaded or compelled to acknowledge. Engaged with his national competitors in perpetual conflicts for power, engaged also in more serious struggles for safety against the fierce tribes of the unconverted Frisians, Bavarians,

Saxons, and Thuringians, who at that epoch assailed with peculiar ferocity the Christianised Germans on the left bank of the Rhine, Charles Martel added experienced skill to his natural courage, and he had also formed a militia of veterans among the Franks.

Hallam (Henry, English historian, 1777-1859) has thrown out a doubt whether, in our admiration of his victory at Tours we do not judge a little too much by the event, and whether there was not rashness in his risking the fate of France on the result of a general battle with the invaders. But, when we remember that Charles had no standing army, and the independent spirit of the Frank warriors who followed his standard, it seems most probable that it was not in his power to adopt the cautious policy of watching the invaders, and wearing out their strength by delay. So dreadful and so widespread were the ravages of the Saracenic light cavalry throughout Gaul that it must have been impossible to restrain for any length of time the indignant ardour of the Franks. And, even if Charles could have persuaded his men to look tamely on while the Arabs stormed more towns and desolated more districts, he could not have kept an army together when the usual period of a military expedition had expired. If, indeed, the Arab account of the disorganisation of the Moslem forces be correct, the battle was as well-timed on the part of Charles, as it was, beyond all question, well-fought.

The monkish chroniclers, from whom we are obliged to glean a narrative of this memorable campaign, bear full evidence to the terror which the Saracen invasion inspired, and to the agony of that great struggle. The Saracens, say they, and their king, who was called Abdirames, came out of Spain, with all their wives, and their children, and their substance, in such great multitudes that no man could reckon or estimate them. They brought with them all their armour, and whatever they had, as if they were thenceforth always to dwell in France.

"Then Abderrahman, seeing the land filled with the multitude of his army, pierces through the mountains, tramples over rough and level ground, plunders far into the country of the Franks, and smites all with the sword, insomuch that when Eudo came to battle with him at the river Garonne, and fled before him, God alone knows the number of the slain. Then Abderrahman pursued after Count Eudo, and while he strives to spoil and burn the holy shrine at Tours, he encounters the chief of the Austrasian Franks, Charles, a man of war from his youth up, to whom Eudo had sent warning. There, for nearly seven days they strive intensely, and at last they set themselves in battle array; and the nations of the north standing firm as a wall, and impenetrable as a zone of ice, utterly slay the Arabs with the edge of the sword."

The European writers all concur in speaking of the fall of Abderrahman as one of the principal causes of the defeat of the Arabs; who, according to one writer, after finding that their leader was slain, dispersed in the night, to the agreeable surprise of the Christians, who expected the next morning to see them issue from their tents, and renew the combat. One monkish chronicler puts the loss of the Arabs at 375,000 men, while he says that only 1007 Christians fell—a disparity of loss which he feels bound to account for by a special interposition of Providence.

V

Though, however, we may have cause to regret the meagerness and doubtful character of these narratives, we have the great advantage of being able to compare the accounts given by Abderrahman's expedition by the national writers of each side. This is a benefit which the inquirer into antiquity so seldom can obtain that the fact of possessing it, in the instance of the battle of Tours, makes us think the historical testimony respecting that great battle is even more certain and satisfactory than is the case in many other instances where we possess abundant details respecting military exploits, but where those details come to us from the annalist of one nation only; and where we have, consequently, no safeguard against the exaggerations, the distortions, and the fictions, which national vanity has so often put forth in the garb and under the title of history. The Arabian writers who recorded the conquests and wars of their countrymen in Spain, have narrated also the expedition into Gaul of their great Emir, and his defeat and death near Tours in battle with the host of the Franks under King Caldus, the name into which they metamorphose Charles. The Arabian chronicles were compiled and translated into Spanish by Don Jose Antonio Conde, in his *"Historia de la Dominacion de los Arabes en España,"* published at Madrid in 1820. **Conde's** plan, which I have endeavoured to follow, was to preserve both the style and spirit of his Oriental authorities, so that we find in his pages a genuine Saracenic narrative of the wars in Western Europe between the Mohammedans and the Christians.

They tell us how there was war between the count of the Frankish frontier and the Moslems, and how the count gathered together all his people, and fought for a time with doubtful success. "But," say the Arabian chroniclers, "Abderrahman drove them back; and the men of Abderrahman were puffed up in spirit by their repeated successes, and they were full of trust in the valour and the practice in war of their Emir. So the Moslems smote their enemies, and passed the river Garonne, and laid waste the country and took captives without number. And that army went through all places like a desolating storm.

"Prosperity made those warriors insatiable. At the passage of the river, Abderrahman overthrew the count, and the count retired into his stronghold, but the Moslems fought against it, and entered it by force, and slew the count; for everything gave way to their scimitars, which were the robbers of lives. All the nations of the Franks trembled at that terrible army, and they betook them to their king Caldus, and told him of the havoc made by the Moslem horsemen, and how they rode at their will through all the land of Narbonne, Toulouse, and Bordeaux, and they told the king of the death of their count. Then the king bade them be of good cheer, and offered to aid them.

"And in the 114th year (of the Hegira, or flight of Mohammed from Mecca to Medina, 622) he mounted his horse, and he took with him a host that could not be numbered, and went against the Moslems. And he came upon them at the great city of Tours. And Abderrahmen and other prudent cavaliers saw the disorder of the Moslem troops, who were loaded with spoil; but they did not venture to displease the soldiers by ordering them to abandon everything except their arms and war-horses. And Abderrahman trusted in the valour of his soldiers, and in the good fortune which had ever attended him. But such defect of discipline always is fatal to armies. So Abderrahman and his host attacked Tours to gain still more spoil, and they fought against it so fiercely that they stormed the city almost before the eyes of the army that came to save it; and the fury and the cruelty of the Moslems towards the inhabitants of the city were like the fury and cruelty of raging tigers. It

was manifest that God's chastisement was sure to follow such
excesses; and fortune thereupon turned her back upon the
Moslems.

"Near the river Owar (probably the Loire), the two great
hosts of the two languages and the two creeds were set in array
against each other. The hearts of Abderrahman, his captains,
and his men were filled with wrath and pride, and they were the
first to begin to fight. The Moslem horsemen dashed fierce and
frequent forward against the battalions of the Franks, who resisted manfully, and many fell dead on either side, until the
going down of the sun. Night parted the two armies: but in
the grey of the morning the Moslems returned to the battle.
Their cavaliers had soon hewn their way into the centre of
the Christian host.

"But many of the Moslems were fearful for the safety of the
spoil which they had stored in their tents, and a false cry arose
in their ranks that some of the enemy were plundering the
camp; whereupon several squadrons of the Moslem horsemen
rode off to protect their tents. But it seemed as if they fled
and all the host was troubled. And while Abderrahman strove
to check their tumult, and to lead them back to battle, the
warriors of the Franks came around him, and he was pierced
through with many spears so that he died. Then all the host
fled before the enemy, and many died in the flight. This deadly
defeat of the Moslems, and the loss of the great leader and good
cavalier, Abderrahman, took place in the hundred and fifteenth
year."

It would be difficult to expect from an adversary a more ex-
plicit confession of having been thoroughly vanquished than
the Arabs here accord to the Europeans. The points on which
their narrative differs from those of the Christians—as to how
many days the conflict lasted, whether the assailed city was
actually rescued or not, and the like—are of little moment compared with the admitted great fact that there was a decisive trial
of strength between Frank and Saracen, in which the former con
quered. The enduring importance of the battle of Tours in
the eyes of the Moslems, is attested not only by the expressions
of "the deadly battle," and "the disgraceful overthrow," which
their writers constantly employ when referring to it, but also
by the fact that no further serious attempts at conquest beyond
the Pyrenees were made by the Saracens.

Charles Martel, and his son and grandson, were left at leisure to consolidate and extend their power. The new Christian Roman Empire of the West, which the genius of Charlemagne founded, and throughout which his iron will imposed peace on the old anarchy of creeds and races, did not indeed retain its integrity after its great ruler's death. Fresh troubles came over Europe; but Christendom, though disunited, was safe. The progress of civilisation, and the development of the nationalities and governments of modern Europe, from that time forth, went forward in not uninterrupted, but ultimately, certain career.

(The final conquest of the Moors in Spain did not come until more than eight centuries later, in 1492. The "contributions of the Moslems to Spain and through Spain to Europe were incalculably great; art, architecture, science, learning—the Moors developed all these to a high degree"—The Columbia Encyclopedia).

SYNOPSIS OF EVENTS BETWEEN THE BATTLE OF TOURS, 732, AND THE BATTLE OF HASTINGS, 1066

768-814. Reign of Charlemagne. This monarch has justly been termed the principal regenerator of Western Europe, after the destruction of the Roman Empire. The early death of his brother, Carloman, left him sole master of the dominions of the Franks, which, by a succession of victorious wars, he enlarged into the new Empire of the West. He conquered the Lombards, and re-established the pope at Rome, who, in return, acknowledged Charles as suzerain of Italy. And in the year 800, Leo III., in the name of the Roman people, solemnly crowned Charlemagne at Rome, as Emperor of the Roman Empire of the West. In Spain, Charlemagne ruled the country between the Pyrenees and the Ebro; but his most important conquests were affected on the eastern side of his original kingdom, over the Sclavonians of Bohemia, the Avars of Pannonia, and over the previously uncivilized German tribes, who had remained in their fatherland. The old Saxons were his most obstinate antagonists, and his wars with them lasted for thirty years. Under him the greater part of Germany was compulsorily civilized, and converted from Paganism to Christianity. His empire extended eastward as far as the Elbe, the Saal, the Bohemian mountains, and a line drawn from thence crossing the Danube above Vienna, and prolonged to the Gulf of Istria.

Throughout this vast assemblage of provinces, Charlemagne established an organized and firm government. But it is not as a mere conqueror that he demands admiration. "In a life restlessly active, we see him reforming the coinage, and establishing the legal divisions of money, gathering about him the learned of every country; founding schools and collecting libraries; interfering, with the air of a king, in religious controversies; attempting, for the sake of commerce, the magnificent enterprise of uniting the Rhine and the Danube, and meditating to mould the discordant code of Roman and barbarian laws into an uniform system." [Hallam]

814-888. Repeated partitions of the empire and civil wars between Charlemagne's descendants. Ultimately the kingdom of France is finally separated from Germany and Italy. In 962, Otho the Great of Germany revives the imperial dignity.

827. Egbert, King of Wessex, acquires the supremacy over the other Anglo-Saxon kingdoms.

832. The first Danish squadron attacks part of the English coast. The Danes, or Northmen, had begun their ravages in France a few years earlier. For two centuries Scandinavia sends out fleet after fleet of sea-rovers, who desolate all the western kingdoms of Europe, and in many cases effect permanent conquests.

871-900. Reign of Alfred in England. After a long and varied struggle, he rescues England from the Danish invaders.

911. The French king cedes Neustria to Hrolf the Northman. Hrolf (or Duke Rollo, as he thenceforth was termed) and his army of Scandinavian warriors, become the ruling class of the population of the province, which is called after them Normandy.

1016. Four knights from Normandy, who had been on a pilgrimage to the Holy Land, while returning through Italy, help the people of Salerno in repelling an attack of a band of Saracen corsairs. In the next year many adventurers from Normandy settle in Italy, where they conquer Apulia (1040), and afterward (1060) Sicily.

1017. Canute, King of Denmark, becomes King of England. On the death of the last of his sons, in 1041, the Saxon line is restored, and Edward the Confessor (who had been bred in the court of the Duke of Normandy) is called by the English to the throne as the representative of the House of Cerdic.

1035. Duke Robert of Normandy dies on his return from a pilgrimage to the Holy Land, and his son William (afterwards the conqueror of England) succeeds to the dukedom of Normandy.

-◄[EIGHT]►-

Hastings, 1066

WHY DECISIVE: *"No one who appreciates the influence of England and her empire upon the destinies of the world will ever rank that victory* [Hastings] *as one of secondary importance. . . . Small indeed had been the figure which England made in the world before the coming of the Normans, and without them she never would have emerged from insignificance. . . . And we may proudly accept the comment of the Frenchman, Rapin, who writing of the battle of Hastings more than a century ago . . . speaks of the revolution effected by it as 'the first step by which England has arrived to that height of grandeur and glory which we behold in it at present . . . .'"* [Creasy.]

I

ARLETTA'S pretty feet twinkling in the brook gained her a Duke's love, and gave us William the Conqueror. Had she not thus fascinated Duke Robert the Liberal of Normandy, Harold would not have fallen at Hastings, no Anglo-Norman dynasty could have arisen, no British empire. The reflection is Sir Francis Palgrave's (in his History of Normandy and England): and it is emphatically true. If any one should write a history of "Decisive loves that have materially influenced the drama of the world in all its subsequent scenes," the daughter of the tanner of Falaise would deserve a conspicuous place in his pages. But it is her son, the victor of Hastings, who is now the object of our attention; and no one, who appreciates the influence of England and her empire upon the destinies of the world, will ever rank that victory as one of secondary importance.

It is true that in the last century some writers of eminence on our history and laws mentioned the Norman conquest in terms from which it might be supposed that the battle of Hastings led to little more than the substitution of one royal family for another on the throne of this country, and to the garbling and changing of some of our laws through the "cunning of the Norman lawyers." But, at least since the appearance of the work of Augustin Thierry on the Norman conquest, these forensic fallacies have been exploded.

Thierry made his readers keenly appreciate the magnitude of that political and social catastrophe. He depicted in vivid colours the atrocious cruelties of the conquerors, and the sweeping and enduring innovations that they wrought, involving the overthrow of the ancient constitution, as well as of the last of the Saxon kings. In his pages we see new tribunals and tenures superceding the old ones, new divisions of race and class introduced, whole districts devastated to gratify the vengeance or the caprice of the new tyrant, the greater part of the lands of the English confiscated, and divided among aliens, the very name of Englishmen turned into a reproach, the English language rejected as servile and barbarous, and all the high places in church and state for upwards of a century filled exclusively by men of foreign race.

No less true than eloquent is Thierry's summing up of the social effects of the Norman conquest on the generation that witnessed it, and on many of their successors. He tells his reader that "if he would form a just idea of England conquered by William of Normandy, he must figure to himself—not a mere change of political rule—not the triumph of one candidate over another candidate—of the man of one party over the man of another party, but the intrusion of one people into the bosom of another people—the violent placing of one society over another society, which it came to destroy, and the scattered fragments of which it retained only as personal property, or (to use the words of an old act) as 'the clothing of the soil;' he must not picture to himself, on the one hand, William, a king and a despot—on the other, subjects of William's high and low, rich and poor, all inhabiting England, and consequently all English: but he must imagine two nations, of one of which William is a member and the chief—two nations which (if the term must be used) were both *subject* to William; but as applied to which the word has quite different senses, meaning in the one case, *subordinate*—in the other subjugated.

"He must consider that there are two countries, two soils, included in the same geographical circumference; that of the Normans rich and free; that of the Saxons poor and serving, vexed by *rent* and *taillage* (feudal imposts); the former full of spacious mansions, and walled and moated castles—the latter scattered over with huts and straw, and ruined hovels; that peopled with the happy and the idle—with men of the army and of the court—with knights and nobles—this with men of pain and labour—with farmers and artisans: on the one side, luxury and insolence—on the other, misery and envy—not the envy of the poor at the sight of opulence they cannot reach, but the envy of the despoiled when in presence of the despoilers."

Perhaps the effect of Thierry's work has been to cast into the shade the ultimate good effects on England of the Norman conquest. Yet these are as undeniable as are the miseries which that conquest inflicted on our Saxon ancestors from the time of the battle of Hastings to the time of the signing of the Great Charter at Runnymede (in 1215). That last is the true epoch of English nationality; it is the epoch when Anglo-Norman and Anglo-Saxon ceased to keep aloof from each other, the one in haughty scorn, the other in sullen abhorrence; and when all the free men of the land, whether barons, knights, yeomen, or burghers, combined to lay the foundations of English freedom.

Our Norman barons were the chiefs of that primary constitutional movement; those "iron barons," whom Chatham has so nobly eulogised. This alone should make England remember her obligations to the Norman conquest, which planted far and wide, as a dominant class in her land, a martial nobility of the bravest and most energetic race that ever existed.

It may sound paradoxical, but it is in reality no exaggeration to say, with Guizot, that England owes her liberties to her having been conquered by the Normans. It is true that the Saxon institutions were the primitive cradle of English liberty, but by their own intrinsic force they could never have founded the enduring free English constitution. It was the Conquest that infused into them a new virtue; and the political liberties of England arose from the situation in which the Anglo-Saxon and the Anglo-Norman populations and laws found themselves placed relatively to each other in this island.

The state of England under her last Anglo-Saxon kings, closely resembled the state of France under the last Carlovingian, and the first Capetian princes. The crown was feeble, the great nobles were strong and turbulent. And although there was more national unity in Saxon England than in France; although the English local free institutions had more reality and energy than was the case with anything analogous to them on the Continent in the eleventh century, still, the probability is that the Saxon system of polity, if left to itself, would have

fallen into utter confusion, out of which would have arisen
first, an aristocratic hierarchy, like that which rose in France;
next, an absolute monarchy; and finally a series of anarchical
revolutions, such as we now behold around, but not among us.

The latest conquerors of this island were also the bravest and
the best. I do not except even the Romans. And, in spite of
our sympathies with Harold and Hereward, and our abhorrence of the founder of the New Forest, and the desolator of
Yorkshire, we must confess the superiority of the Normans to
the Anglo-Saxons and Anglo-Danes, whom they met here in
1066, as well as to the degenerate Frank noblesse and the
crushed and servile Romanesque provincials, from whom, in
912, they had wrested the district in the north of Gaul, which
still bears the name of Normandy.

It was not merely by extreme valour and ready subordination
or military discipline that the Normans were pre-eminent among
all the conquering races of the Gothic stock, but also by their
instinctive faculty of appreciating and adopting the superior
civilisations which they encountered. Thus Duke Rollo and
his Scandinavian warriors readily embraced the creed, the
language, the laws and the arts, which France, in those troubled
and evil times with which the Capetian dynasty commenced,
still inherited from imperial Rome and imperial Charlemagne.

"They adopted the customs, the duties, the obedience that
the capitularies of emperors and kings had established; but that
which they brought to the application of those laws was the
spirit of life, the spirit of liberty—the habits also of military
subordination, and the aptness for a state politic, which could
reconcile the security of all with the independence of each."
(Jean Sismondi, Swiss historian, 1773-1842.)

So also in all chivalric feelings, in enthusiastic religious zeal,
in almost idolatrous respect to females of gentle birth, in
generous fondness for the nascent poetry of the time, in a
keen intellectual relish for subtle thought and disputation, in
a taste for architectural magnificence, and all courtly refinement
and pageantry, the Normans were the Paladins of the world.
Their brilliant qualities were sullied by many darker traits of
pride, of merciless cruelty, and of brutal contempt for the industry, the rights and the feelings of all whom they considered
the lower classes of mankind.

Their gradual blending with the Saxons softened these harsh

and evil points of their national character, and in return they fired the duller Saxon mass with a new spirit of animation and power. As Campbell boldly expressed it, "They high-mettled the blood of our veins." Small had been the figure which England made in the world before the coming over of the Normans; and without them she never would have emerged from insignificance. The authority of Gibbon may be taken as decisive, when he pronounces that, "Assuredly England was a gainer by the Conquest." And we may proudly adopt the comment of the Frenchman, Rapin, who, writing of the battle of Hastings more than a century ago, speaks of the revolution effected by it as "the first step by which England has arrived to that height of grandeur and glory we behold it in at present."

II

The interest of this eventful struggle, by which William of Normandy became king of England, is materially enhanced by the high personal characters of the competitors for our crown. They were three in number. One was a foreign prince from the North. One was a foreign prince from the South: and one was a native hero of the land. Harald Hardrada, the strongest and the most chivalric of the kings of Norway, was the first; Duke William of Normandy was the second; and the Saxon Harold, the son of Earl Godwin, was the third. Never was a nobler prize sought by nobler champions, or striven for more gallantly. The Saxon triumphed over the Norwegian, and the Norman triumphed over the Saxon; but Norse valour was never more conspicuous than when Harald Hardrada and his host fought and fell at Stamford Bridge: nor did Saxons ever face their foes more bravely than our Harold and his men on the fatal day of Hastings.

During the reign of King Edward the Confessor over this land, the claims of the Norwegian king to our crown were little thought of; and though Hardrada's predecessor, King Magnus of Norway, had on one occasion asserted that, by virtue of a compact with our former king, Hardicanute, he was entitled to the English throne, no serious attempt had been made to enforce his pretensions. But the rivalry of the Saxon Harold and the Norman William was foreseen and bewailed by the Confessor, who was believed to have predicted on his deathbed the calamities that were pending over England. Duke William was King Edward's kinsman. Harold was the head of the most powerful noble house, next to the royal blood, in England; and personally, he was the bravest and most popular chieftain in the land. King Edward was childless, and the nearest collateral heir was a puny unpromising boy. England had suffered too severely during royal minorities, to make the accession of Edgar Atheling desirable; and long before King Edward's death Earl Harold was the destined king of the nation's choice, though the favour of the Confessor was believed to lean towards the Norman duke.

A little time before the death of King Edward, Harold was in Normandy. The causes of the voyage of the Saxon Earl to the continent are doubtful; but the fact of his having been, in 1065, at the ducal court, and in the power of his rival, is indisputable. William made skilful and unscrupulous use of the opportunity. Though Harold was treated with outward courtesy and friendship, he was made fully aware that his liberty and life depended on his compliance with the duke's requests. William said to him, in apparent confidence and cordiality, "When King Edward and I once lived like brothers under the same roof, he promised that if ever he became king of England, he would make me heir to his throne. Harold, I wish that thou wouldst assist me to realise this promise."

Harold replied with expressions of assent and further agreed, at William's request, to marry William's daughter, Adela, and to send over his own sister to be married to one of William's barons. The crafty Norman was not content with this extorted promise; he determined to bind Harold by a more solemn pledge, which, if broken, would be a weight on the spirit of the gallant Saxon, and a discouragement to others from adopting his cause. Before a full assembly of the Norman barons, Harold was required to do homage to Duke William, as the heir-apparent of the English crown. Kneeling down, Harold placed his hands between those of the duke, and repeated the solemn form, by which he acknowledged the duke as his lord, and promised to him fealty and true service.

But William exacted more. He had caused all the bones and relics of saints, that were preserved in the Norman monasteries and churches, to be collected into a chest, which was placed in the council-room, covered over with a cloth of gold. On the chest of relics, which were thus concealed, was laid a missal.

The duke then solemnly addressed his titular guest and real captive, and said to him, "Harold, I require thee, before this noble assembly, to confirm by oath the promises which thou hast made me, to assist me in obtaining the crown of England after King Edward's death, to marry my daughter Adela, and to send me thy sister, that I may give her in marriage to one of my barons." Harold, once more taken by surprise, and not able to deny his former words, approached the missal, and laid his hand on it, not knowing that the chest of relics was beneath.

The old Norman chronicler, who describes the scene most minutely, says, when Harold placed his hand on it, the hand trembled, and the flesh quivered; but he swore, and promised upon his oath, to take Ele (Adela) to wife, and to deliver up England to the duke, and thereunto to do all in his power, according to his might and wit, after the death of Edward, if he himself should live: so help him God. Many cried, "God grant it!" and when Harold rose from his knees, the duke made him stand close to the chest, and took off the pall that had covered it, and showed Harold upon what holy relics he had sworn; and Harold was sorely alarmed at the sight.

III

Harold soon after this was permitted to return to England; and, after a short interval, during which he distinguished himself by the wisdom and humanity with which he pacified some formidable tumults of the Anglo-Danes in Northumbria, he found himself called on to decide whether he would keep the oath which the Norman had obtained from him, or mount the vacant throne of England in compliance with the nation's choice. King Edward the Confessor died on the 5th of January, 1066, and on the following day an assembly of the thanes and prelates present in London, and of the citizens of the metropolis, declared that Harold should be their king. It was reported that the dying Edward had nominated him as his successor. But the sense which his countrymen entertained of his pre-eminent merit was the true foundation of his title to the crown. Harold resolved to disregard the oath which he made in Normandy, as violent and void, and on the 7th day of that January he was anointed King of England, and received from the archbishop's hands the golden crown and sceptre of England, and also an

ancient national symbol, a weighty battle-axe. He had deep
and speedy need of this significant part of the insignia of Saxon
royalty.

A messenger from Normandy soon arrived to remind Harold
of the oath which he had sworn to the duke "with his mouth,
and his hand upon good and holy relics." "It is true," replied
the Saxon king, "that I took an oath to William; but I took it
under constraint: I promised what did not belong to me—what
I could not in any way hold: my royalty is not my own; I
could not lay it down against the will of the country, nor can
I against the will of the country take a foreign wife. As for
my sister, whom the duke claims that he may marry her to
one of his chiefs, she has died within the year. Would he have
me send her corpse?"

William sent another message which met with a similar
answer; and then the duke published far and wide through
Christendom what he termed the perjury and bad faith of his
rival; and proclaimed his intention of asserting his rights by
the sword before the year should expire, and of pursuing and
punishing the perjurer even in those places where he thought
he stood most strongly and most securely.

Before, however, he commenced hostilities, William, with deep-
laid policy, submitted his claims to the decision of the pope.
Harold refused to acknowledge this tribunal, or to answer before an Italian priest for his title as an English king. After a
formal examination of William's complaints by the pope and
the cardinals, it was solemnly adjudged at Rome that England
belonged to the Norman duke; and a banner was sent to William from the holy see, which the pope himself had consecrated
and blessed for the invasion of this island. The clergy throughout the Continent were now assiduous and energetic in preaching William's enterprise as undertaken in the cause of God.

Besides these spiritual arms (the effect of which in the
eleventh century must not be measured by the philosophy or
the indifferentism of the nineteenth), the Norman duke applied
all the energies of his mind and body, all the resources of his
duchy, and all the influence he possessed among vassals or allies,
to the collection of "the most remarkable and formidable armament which the western nations had witnessed." All the adventurous spirits of Christendom flocked to the holy banner, under
which Duke William, the most renowned knight and sagest gen-

eral of the age, promised to lead them to glory and wealth in the fair domains of England. His army was filled with the chivalry of continental Europe, all eager to save their souls by fighting at the pope's bidding, ardent to signalise their valour in so great an enterprise, and longing also for the pay and the plunder which William liberally promised. But the Normans themselves were the pith and the flower of the army; and William himself was the strongest, the sagest, and fiercest spirit of them all.

IV

Throughout the spring and summer of 1066, all the sea-ports of Normandy, Picardy, and Brittany rang with the busy sound of preparation. On the opposite side of the Channel King Harold collected the army and the fleet, with which he hoped to crush the southern invaders. But the unexpected attack of King Harald Hardrada of Norway upon another part of England, disconcerted the skilful measures which the Saxon had taken against the menacing armada of Duke William.

Harold's renegade brother, Earl Tostig, had excited the Norse king to this enterprise, the importance of which has naturally been eclipsed by the superior interest attached to the victorious expedition of Duke William, but which was on a scale of grandeur which the Scandinavian ports had rarely, if ever, before witnessed. Hardrada's fleet consisted of two hundred war-ships and three hundred other vessels, and all the best warriors of Norway were in his host. He sailed first to the Orkneys, where many of the islanders joined him, and then to Yorkshire. After a severe conflict near York, he completely routed Earls Edwin and Morcar, the governors of Northumbria. The city of York opened its gates, and all the country, from the Tyne to the Humber, submitted to him.

The tidings of the defeat of Edwin and Morcar compelled Harold to leave his position on the southern coast, and move instantly against the Norwegians. By a remarkably rapid march he reached Yorkshire in four days, and took the Norse king and his confederates by surprise. Nevertheless, the battle which ensued, and which was fought near Stamford Bridge, was desperate and was long doubtful. Unable to break the ranks of the Norwegian phalanx by force, Harold at length tempted them to quit their close order by a pretended flight. Then the

English columns burst in among them and a carnage ensued, the extent of which may be judged of by the exhaustion and inactivity of Norway for a quarter of a century afterwards. King Harald Hardrada and all the flower of his nobility, perished on the 25th of September 1066, at Stamford Bridge; a battle which was a Flodden (a hill in Northumberland, scene of battle in which the English defeated and killed James IV of Scotland, 1513) to Norway.

Harold's victory was splendid; but he had bought it dearly by the fall of many of his best officers and men; and still more dearly by the opportunity which Duke William had gained of effecting an unopposed landing on the Sussex coast. The whole of William's shipping had assembled at the mouth of the Dive, a little river between the Seine and the Orme, as early as the middle of August. The army which he had collected, amounted to fifty thousand knights, and ten thousand soldiers of inferior degree. Many of the knights were mounted, but many must have served on foot; as it is hardly possible to believe that William could have found transports for the conveyance of fifty thousand warhorses across the Channel.

For a long time the winds were adverse and the duke employed the interval that passed before he could set sail in completing the organisation, and in improving the discipline, of his army which he seems to have brought into the same state of perfection as was seven centuries and a half afterwards the boast of another army assembled on the same coast, and which Napoleon designed (but providentially in vain) for a similar descent upon England.

It was not till the approach of the equinox that the wind veered from the north-east to the west, and gave the Normans an opportunity of quitting the weary shores of the Dive. They eagerly embarked, and set sail; but the wind soon freshened to a gale, and drove them along the French coast to St. Valery, where the greater part of them found shelter, but many of their vessels were wrecked, and the whole coast of Normandy was strewn with the bodies of the drowned.

William's army began to grow discouraged and averse to the enterprise, which the very elements thus seemed to fight against, though in reality the north-east wind which had cooped them so long at the mouth of the Dive, and the western gale which had forced them into St. Valery, were the best possible friends to the invaders. They prevented the Normans from crossing the Channel until the Saxon king and his army of defence had been called away from the Sussex coast to encounter Harald Hardrada in Yorkshire: and also until a formidable English fleet, which by King Harold's orders had been cruising in the Channel to intercept the Normans, had been obliged to disperse temporarily for the purpose of refitting and taking in fresh stores of provisions.

Duke William used every expedient to reanimate the drooping spirits of his men at St. Valery; and at last he caused the body of the patron saint of the place to be exhumed and carried in solemn procession, while the whole assemblage of soldiers, mariners and appurtenant priests implored the saint's intercession for a change of wind. That very night the wind veered, and with full sails and a following southern breeze the Norman Armada left the French shores, and steered for England. The invaders crossed an undefended sea, and found an undefended coast. It was in Pevensey Bay in Sussex, at Bulverhithe, between the castle of Pevensey and Hastings, that the last conquerors of this island landed on the 29th of September, 1066.

V

Harold was at York, rejoicing over his recent victory, which had delivered England from her ancient Scandinavian foes, and resettling the government of the counties which Harald Hardrada had overrun, when the tidings reached him that Duke William of Normandy and his host had landed on the Sussex shore. Harold instantly hurried southward to meet this long-expected enemy. The severe loss which his army had sustained in the battle with the Norwegians must have made it impossible for any large number of veteran troops to accompany him in his forced march to London, and thence to Sussex. He halted at the capital only six days; and during that time gave orders for collecting forces from his southern and midland counties, and also directed his fleet to reassemble off the Sussex coast.

Harold was well received in London and his summons to arms was promptly obeyed by citizen, by knight, serving man and churl, for he had shown himself during his brief reign a just and wise king, affable to all men, active for the good of his country, and (in the words of the old historian) sparing himself from no fatigue by land or sea. He might have gathered a much more numerous force than that of William, but his recent victory had made him overconfident, and he was irritated by the reports of the country being ravaged by the invaders. As soon, therefore, as he had collected a small army in London, he marched off towards the coast, pressing forward as rapidly as his men could traverse Surrey and Sussex in the hope of taking the Normans unawares, as he had recently by a similar forced march succeeded in surprising the Norwegians. But he had now to deal with a foe equally brave with Harald Hardrada, and far more skilful and wary.

The old Norman chroniclers describe the preparations of William on his landing, with a graphic vigour, which would be wholly lost by transfusing their racy Norman couplets and terse Latin prose into the current style of modern history. It is best to follow them closely, though at the expense of much quaintness and occasional uncouthness of expression. They tell us how Duke William's own ship was the first of the Norman fleet.

"It was called the *Mora,* and was the gift of his duchess, Matilda. On the head of the ship in the front which mariners call the prow there was a brazen child bearing an arrow with a bended bow. His face was turned towards England, and thither he looked, as though he was about to shoot. The breeze became soft and sweet, and the sea was smooth for their landing. The ships ran on dry land and each ranged by the other's side. There you might see the good sailors, the sergeants, and squires sally forth and unload the ships; cast the anchors, haul the ropes, bear out shields and saddles, and land the war-horses and palfreys. The archers came forth, and touched land the first, each with his bow strung and with his quiver full of arrows, slung at his side. All were shaven and shorn; and all clad in short garments, ready to attack, to shoot, to wheel about and skirmish. All stood well equipped, and of good courage for the fight; and they scoured the whole shore, but found not an armed man there.

"After the archers had thus gone forth, the knights landed all armed, with their hauberks on, their shields slung at their necks, and their helmets laced. They formed together on the shore, each armed and mounted on his war-horse: all had their swords girded on, and rode forward into the country with their lances raised. Then the carpenters landed, who had great axes in their hands, and planes and adzes hung at their sides. They took counsel together, and sought for a good spot to place a castle on. They had brought with them in the fleet three wooden castles from Normandy, in pieces, all ready for framing together, and they took the materials of one of these out of the ships, all shaped and pierced to receive the pins which they had brought cut and ready in large barrels; and before evening had set in, they had finished a good fort on the English ground, and there they placed their stores. All then ate and drank enough, and were right glad that they were ashore.

"When Duke William himself landed, as he stepped on the shore, he slipped and fell forward upon his two hands. Forthwith all raised a loud cry of distress. 'An evil sign,' said they, 'is here.' But he cried out lustily, 'See! my lord! By the splendour of God, I have taken possession of England with both my hands. It is now mine, and what is mine is yours.'

"The next day they marched along the sea-shore to Hastings. Near that place the Duke fortified a camp, and set up the two other wooden castles. The foragers, and those who looked out for booty, seized all the clothing and provisions they could find, lest what had been brought by the ships should fail them. And the English were to be seen fleeing before them, driving off their cattle, and quitting their houses. Many took shelter in burying-places, and even there they were in grievous alarm."

VI

Besides the marauders from the Norman camp, strong bodies of cavalry were detached by William into the country, and these, when Harold and his army made their rapid march from London southward, fell back in good order upon the main body of the Normans, and reported that the Saxon king was rushing on like a madman. But Harold, when he found that his hopes of surprising his adversary were vain, changed his tactics, and halted about seven miles from the Norman lines. He sent some spies, who spoke the French language, to examine the number and preparations of the enemy, who, on their return, related with astonishment that there were more priests in William's camp than there were fighting men in the English army. They had mistaken for priests all the Norman soldiers who had short hair and shaven chins; for the English laymen were then accustomed to wear long hair and mustachios. Harold, who knew the Norman usages, smiled at their words and said, "Those whom you have seen in such numbers are not priests, but stout soldiers, as they will soon make us feel."

Harold's army was far inferior in number to that of the Normans, and some of his captains advised him to retreat upon London and lay waste the country, so as to starve down the strength of the invaders. The policy thus recommended was unquestionably the wisest; for the Saxon fleet had now re-assembled and intercepted all William's communications with Normandy, so that as soon as his stores of provisions were exhausted he must have moved forward upon London, where Harold, at the head of the full military strength of the kingdom, could have defied his assault, and probably might have witnessed his rival's destruction by famine and disease, without having to strike a single blow. But Harold's bold blood was up and his kindly heart could not endure to inflict on his South Saxon subjects even the temporary misery of wasting the country. "He would not burn houses and villages, neither would be take away the substance of his people."

Harold's brothers, Gurth and Leofwine, were with him in the camp, and Gurth endeavoured to persuade him to absent himself from the battle. The incident shows how well devised had been William's scheme of binding Harold by the oath on the holy relics. "My brother," said the young Saxon prince, "thou canst not deny that either by force or free-will thou hast made Duke William an oath on the bodies of saints. Why then risk thyself in the battle with a perjury upon thee? To us, who have sworn nothing, this is a holy and a just war, for we are fighting for our country. Leave us, then, alone to fight this battle, and he who has the right will win."

Harold replied that he would not look on while others risked their lives for him. Men would hold him a coward, and blame him for sending his best friends where he dared not go himself. He resolved, therefore, to fight, and to fight in person: but he was still too good a general to be the assailant in the action. He strengthened his position on the hill where he had halted by a palisade of stakes interlaced with osier hurdles, and there, he said, he would defend himself against whoever should seek him.

The ruins of Battle Abbey at this hour attest the place where Harold's army was posted. The high altar of the abbey stood on the very spot where Harold's own standard was planted during the fight, and where the carnage was the thickest. Immediately after his victory William vowed to build an abbey on the site; and a fair and stately pile soon rose there, where for many ages the monks prayed and said masses for the souls of those who were slain in the battle, whence the abbey took its name. Before that time the place was called Senlac. Little of the ancient edifice now remains, but it is easy to trace among its relics and in the neighbourhood the scenes of the chief incidents in the action and it is impossible to deny the generalship shown by Harold in stationing his men, especially when we bear in mind that he was deficient in cavalry, the arm in which his adversary's main strength consisted.

A neck of hills trends inward for nearly seven miles from the high ground immediately to the north-east of Hastings. The line of this neck of hills is from south-east to north-west, and the usual route from Hastings to London must, in ancient as in modern times, have been along its summits. At the distance from Hastings which has been mentioned, the continuous chain of hills ceases. A valley must be crossed, and on the other side of it, opposite to the last of the neck of hills, rises a high ground of some extent, facing to the south-east. This high ground, then termed Senlac, was occupied by Harold's army. It could not be attacked in front without considerable disadvantage to the assailants, and could hardly be turned without those engaged in the manœuvre exposing themselves to a fatal charge in flank, while they wound round the base of the height, and underneath the ridges which project from it on either side.

There was a rough and thickly-wooded district in the rear, which seemed to offer Harold great facilities for rallying his men, and checking the progress of the enemy, if they should succeed in forcing him back from his post. And it seemed scarcely possible that the Normans, if they met with any repulse, could save themselves from utter destruction. With such hopes and expectations, which cannot be termed unreasonable, King Harold bade his standard be set up a little way down the slope of Senlac Hill, where the ascent was least steep, and the fiercest attacks sure to be directed.

The foundation stones of the high altar of Battle Abbey have been discovered; and we may place our feet on the very spot where Harold stood with England's banner waving over him; where, when the battle was joined, he defended himself to the utmost; where the fatal arrow came down on him; where he "leaned in agony on his shield,"—and where at last he was beaten to the earth, and with him the Saxon banner was beaten down, like him never to rise again. The ruins of the altar are a little to the west of the high-road, which leads from Hastings along the neck of hills already described, across the valley, and through the modern town of Battle, towards London. Before a railway was made along this valley, some of the old local features were more easy than now to recognise. The eye then at once saw that the ascent from the valley was least steep at the point which Harold selected for his own post in the engagement. But this is still sufficiently discernible and we can fix the spot a little lower down the slope, immediately in front of the high altar, where the brave Kentish men stood, "whose right it was to strike first whenever the king went to battle," and who, therefore, were placed where the Normans would be most likely to make their first charge.

Round Harold himself, and where the plantations wave which now surround the high altar's ruins, stood the men of London, "whose privilege it was to guard the king's body, to place themselves around it, and to guard his standard." On the right and left were ranged the other warriors of central and southern England, whose shires the old Norman chronicler distorts in his French nomenclature. Looking thence in the direction of Hastings, we can distinguish the "ridge of the rising ground over which the Normans appeared advancing." It is the nearest of the neck of hills. It is along that hill that Harold and his brothers saw approach in succession the three divisions of the Norman army. The Normans came down that slope, and then formed in the valley so as to assault the whole front of the English position. Duke William's own division, with "the best men and greatest strength of the army," made the Norman centre, and charged the English immediately in front of Harold's banner, as the nature of the ground had led the Saxon king to anticipate.

There are few battles, the localities of which can be more completely traced and the whole scene is fraught with associations of deep interest, but the spot which, most of all, awakens our sympathy and excites our feelings is that where Harold himself fought and fell. The crumbling fragments of the grey altar stones, with the wild flowers that cling around their base, seem fitting memorial of the brave Saxon who there bowed his head in death; while the laurel trees, that are planted near, and wave over the ruins, remind us of the Conqueror, who there, at the close of that dreadful day, reared his victorious standard high over the trampled banner of the Saxon, and held his triumphant carousal amid the corses of the slain, with his Norman chivalry exulting around him.

When it was known in the invaders' camp at Hastings that King Harold had marched southward with his power, only a brief interval ensued before the two hosts met in decisive encounter.

VII

William's only chance of safety lay in bringing on a general engagement and he joyfully advanced his army from their camp on the hill over Hastings, nearer to the Saxon position. But he neglected no means of weakening his opponent, and renewed his summonses and demands on Harold with an ostentatious air of sanctity and moderation. To quote from Thierry's narrative:

"A monk named Hugues Maigrot, came in William's name to call upon the Saxon king to do one of three things—either to resign his royalty in favour of William, or to refer it to the arbitration of the pope to decide which of the two ought to be king, or to let it be determined by the issue of a single combat. Harold abruptly replied, 'I will not resign my title, I will not refer it to the pope, nor will I accept the single combat.' He was far from being deficient in bravery; but he was no more at liberty to stake the crown which he had received from a whole people on the chance of a duel, than to deposit it in the hands of an Italian priest.

"William was not at all ruffled by the Saxon's refusal, but steadily pursuing the course of his calculated measures, sent the Norman monk again, after giving him these instructions: 'Go and tell Harold, that if he will keep his former compact with me, I will leave to him all the country which is beyond the Humber, and will give his brother Gurth all the lands which

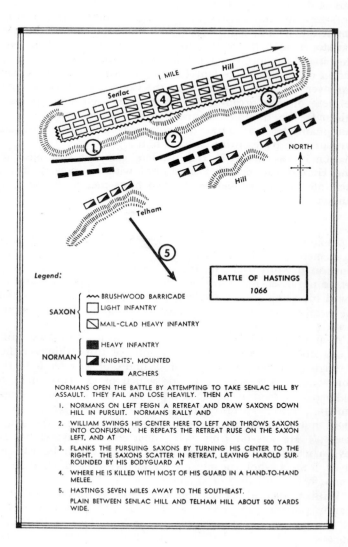

Legend:

SAXON
- 〰〰 BRUSHWOOD BARRICADE
- ☐ LIGHT INFANTRY
- ◹ MAIL-CLAD HEAVY INFANTRY

NORMAN
- ▰ HEAVY INFANTRY
- ◪ KNIGHTS', MOUNTED
- ▬ ARCHERS

**BATTLE OF HASTINGS
1066**

NORMANS OPEN THE BATTLE BY ATTEMPTING TO TAKE SENLAC HILL BY ASSAULT. THEY FAIL AND LOSE HEAVILY. THEN AT

1. NORMANS ON LEFT FEIGN A RETREAT AND DRAW SAXONS DOWN HILL IN PURSUIT. NORMANS RALLY AND

2. WILLIAM SWINGS HIS CENTER HERE TO LEFT AND THROWS SAXONS INTO CONFUSION. HE REPEATS THE RETREAT RUSE ON THE SAXON LEFT, AND AT

3. FLANKS THE PURSUING SAXONS BY TURNING HIS CENTER TO THE RIGHT. THE SAXONS SCATTER IN RETREAT, LEAVING HAROLD SURROUNDED BY HIS BODYGUARD AT

4. WHERE HE IS KILLED WITH MOST OF HIS GUARD IN A HAND-TO-HAND MELEE.

5. HASTINGS SEVEN MILES AWAY TO THE SOUTHEAST.

PLAIN BETWEEN SENLAC HILL AND TELHAM HILL ABOUT 500 YARDS WIDE.

Godwin held.   If he still persist in refusing my offers, then thou shalt tell him, before all his people, that he is a perjurer and a liar, that he and all who shall support him, are excommunicated by the mouth of the pope; and that the bull to that effect is in my hands.'

"Hugues Maigrot delivered this message in a solemn tone; and the Norman chronicle says that at the word *excommunication,* the English chiefs looked at one another as if some great danger were impending.   One of them then spoke as follows: 'We must fight, whatever may be the danger to us; for what we have to consider is not whether we shall accept and receive a new lord as if our king were dead; the case is quite otherwise. The Norman has given our lands to his captains, to his knights, to all his people, the greater part of whom have already done homage to him for them; they will all look for their gift, if their duke become our king; and he himself is bound to deliver up to them our goods, our wives, and our daughters: all is promised to them beforehand.   They come, not only to ruin us, but to ruin our descendants also, and to take from us the country of our ancestors.   And what shall we do—whither shall we go—when we have no longer a country?'   The English promised, by a unanimous oath, to make neither peace, nor truce, nor treaty with the invader, but to die, or drive away the Normans."

The 13th of October was occupied in these negotiations; and at night the duke announced to his men that the next day would be the day of battle.   That night is said to have been passed by the two armies in very different manners.   The Saxon soldiers spent it in joviality, singing their national songs, and draining huge horns of ale and wine round their camp fires. The Normans, when they had looked to their arms and horses, confessed themselves to the priests, with whom their camp was thronged, and received the sacrament by thousands at a time.

VIII

On Saturday the 14th of October was fought the great battle. It is not difficult to compose a narrative in its principal incidents, from the historical information which we possess, especially if aided by an examination of the ground.   But it is far better to adopt the spirit-stirring words of the old chroniclers, who wrote while the recollections of the battle were yet fresh, and while the feelings and prejudices of the combatants yet glowed in the bosoms of their near descendants. Robert Wace, the Norman poet, is the most picturesque and animated of the old writers; and from him we can obtain a more vivid and full description of the conflict, than even the most brilliant romance-writer of the present time can supply.

We have also an antique memorial of the battle, more to be relied on than either chronicler or poet (and which confirms Wace's narrative remarkably), in the celebrated Bayeux tapestry, which represents the principal scenes of Duke William's expedition, and of the circumstances connected with it, in minute though occasionally grotesque details, and which was undoubtedly the production of the same age in which the battle took place, whether we admit or reject the legend that Queen Matilda and the ladies of her court wrought it with their own hands in honour of the royal conqueror.

Let us therefore suffer the old Norman chronicler to transport our imaginations to the fair Sussex scenery, north-west of Hastings, with its breezy uplands, its grassy slopes, and ridges of open down swelling inland from the sparkling sea, its scattered copses, and its denser glades of intervening forests, clad in all the varied tints of autumn, as they appeared on the morning of the fourteenth of October, 877 years ago (1850). The Norman host is pouring forth from its tents; and each troop, and each company, is forming fast under the banner of its leader. The masses have been sung, which were finished betimes in the morning; the barons have all assembled round Duke William and the duke has ordered that the army shall be formed in three divisions, so as to make the attack upon the Saxon position in three places. The duke stood on a hill where he could best see his men; the barons surrounded him, and he spake to them proudly. He told them how he trusted them, and how all that he gained should be theirs; and how sure he felt of conquest, for in all the world there was not so brave an army, or such good men and true as were then forming around him. Then they cheered him in turn and cried out, to follow from here on Robert Wace's story of the battle:

" 'You will not see one coward; none here will fear to die for love of you, if need be.' And he answered them, 'I thank you well. For God's sake spare not; strike hard at the beginning;

stay not to take spoil; all the booty shall be in common, and there will be plenty for every one. There will be no safety in asking quarter or in flight: the English will never love or spare a Norman. Felons they were, and felons they are; false they were, and false they will be. Show no weakness towards them, for they will have no pity on you. Neither the coward for running well, nor the bold man for smiting well, will be the better liked by the English, nor will any be the more spared on either account.

" 'You may fly to the sea, but you can fly no further; you will find neither ships nor bridge there; there will be no sailors to receive you; and the English will overtake you there and slay you in your shame. More of you will die in flight than in the battle. Then, as flight will not secure you, fight, and you will conquer. I have no doubt of the victory: we are come for glory, the victory is in our hands, and we may make sure of obtaining it if we so please.' As the duke was speaking thus, and would yet have spoken more, William Fitz Osbert rode up with his horse all coated with iron; 'Sire,' said he, 'we tarry here too long, let us all arm ourselves. *Allons! Allons!*'

"Then all went to their tents, and armed themselves as they best might; and the duke was very busy, giving every one his orders; and he was courteous to all the vassals, giving away many arms and horses to them. When he prepared to arm himself, he called first for his good hauberk, and a man brought it on his arm, and placed it before him, but in putting his head in, to get it on, he unawares turned it the wrong way, with the back part in front. He soon changed it, but when he saw that those who stood by were sorely alarmed, he said, 'I have seen many a man who, if such a thing had happened to him, would not have borne arms, or entered the field the same day; but I never believed in omens, and I never will. I trust in God, for he does in all things his pleasure, and ordains what is to come to pass, according to his will. I have never liked fortune-tellers, nor believed in diviners: but I commend myself to Our Lady. Let not this mischance give you trouble. The hauberk which was turned wrong, and then set right by me, signifies that a change will arise out of the matter which we are now stirring. You shall see the name of duke changed into king. Yea, a king shall I be, who hitherto have been but duke.'

"Then he crossed himself, and straightway took his hauberk,

stooped his head, and put it on aright, and laced his helmet, and girt on his sword, which a varlet brought him. Then the duke called for his good horse—a better could not be found. It had been sent him by a King of Spain, out of very great friendship. Neither arms nor the press of fighting men did it fear, if its lord spurred it on. Walter Giffard brought it. The duke stretched out his hand, took the reins, put foot in stirrup, and mounted; and the good horse pawed, pranced, reared himself up, and curvetted. The Viscount of Toarz saw how the duke bore himself in arms, and said to his people that were around him, 'Never have I seen a man so fairly armed, nor one who rode so gallantly, or bore his arms, or became his hauberk so well; neither any one who bore his lance so gracefully, or sat his horse and managed him so nobly. There is no such knight under heaven! a fair count he is, and fair king he will be. Let him fight, and he shall overcome; shame be to the man who shall fail him.'

IX

"Then the duke called for the standard which the pope had sent him, and he who bore it having unfolded it, the duke took it, and called to Raol de Conches. 'Bear my standard,' said he, 'for I would not but do you right; by right and by ancestry your line are standard-bearers of Normandy, and very good knights have they all been.' But Raol said that he would serve the duke that day in other guise, and would fight the English with his hand as long as life should last. Then the duke bade Galtier Giffart bear the standard. But he was old and white-headed, and bade the duke give the standard to some younger and stronger man to carry. Then the duke said fiercely. 'By the splendour of God, my lords, I think you mean to betray and fail me in this great need.' 'Sire,' said Giffart, 'not so! we have done no treason, nor do I refuse from any felony towards you; but I have to lead a great chivalry, both hired men and the men of my fief. Never had I such good means of serving you as I now have; and, if God please, I will serve you: if need be, I will die for you, and will give my own heart for yours.'

" 'By my faith,' quoth the duke, 'I have always loved thee, and now I love thee more; if I survive this day, thou shalt be the better for it all thy days.' Then he called out a knight, whom he had heard much praised, Tosteins Fitz-Rou le Blanc by name,

whose abode was at Bec-en-Caux. To him he delivered the
standard; and Tosteins took it right cheerfully, and bowed low
to him in thanks, and bore it gallantly, and with good heart.
His kindred still have quittance of all service for their inheritance on that account, and their heirs are entitled so to
hold their inheritance for ever.

"William sat on his war-horse, and called on Rogier, whom
they call de Montgomeri. 'I rely much upon you,' said he,
'lead your men thitherward, and attack them from that side.
William, the son of Osbert, the seneschal, a right good vassal,
shall go with you and help in the attack, and you shall have
the men of Boulogne and Poix, and all my soldiers. Alain
Fergert and Ameri shall attack on the other side; they shall
lead the Poitevins and the Bretons, and all the Barons of
Maine; and I, with my own great men, my friends and kindred,
will fight in the middle throng, where the battle shall be the
hottest.'

"The barons, and knights, and men-at-arms were all now
armed; the foot-soldiers were well-equipped, each bearing bow
and sword; on their heads were caps, and to their feet were
bound buskins. Some had good hides which they had bound
round their bodies; and many were clad in frocks, and had
quivers and bows hung to their girdles. The knights had
hauberks and swords, boots of steel and shining·helmets; shields
at their necks, and in their hands lances. And all had their
cognizances, so that each might know his fellow, and Norman
might not strike Norman, nor Frenchman kill his countryman
by mistake. Those on foot led the way, with serried ranks,
bearing their bows. The knights rode next, supporting the
archers from behind. Thus both horse and foot kept their
course and order of march as they began; in close ranks at a
gentle pace, that the one might not pass or separate from the
other. All went firmly and compactly, bearing themselves
gallantly.

X

"Harold had summoned his men, earls, barons, and vavas-
sours, from the castles and the cities; from the ports, the villages,
and boroughs. The peasants were also called together from
the villages, bearing such arms as they found; clubs and great
picks, iron forks and stakes. The English had enclosed the

place where Harold was with his friends and the barons of the country whom he had summoned and called together.

"Those of London had come at once, and those of Kent, Hertfort, and of Essesse; those of Surée and Susesse, of St. Edmund and Sufoc; of Norwis and Norfoc; of Cantorbierre and Stanfort; Bedefort and Hundetone. The men of Northanton also came; and those of Eurowic and Bokinkeham, of Bed and Notinkeham, Lindesie and Nichole. There came also from the west all who heard the summons; and very many were to be seen coming from Salebiere and Dorset, from Bat and from Somerset. Many came, too, from about Glocestre, and many from Wirecestre, from Wincestre, Hontesire, and Brichesire; and many more from other counties that we have not named, and cannot, indeed, recount. All who could bear arms, and had learnt the news of the duke's arrival, came to defend the land. But none came from beyond Humbre, for they had other business upon their hands; the Danes and Tosti having much damaged and weakened them.

"Harold knew that the Normans would come and attack him hand to hand; so he had early enclosed the field in which he placed his men. He made them arm early, and range themselves for the battle; he himself having put on arms and equipments that became such a lord. The duke, he said, ought to seek him, as he wanted to conquer England; and it became him to abide the attack, who had to defend the land. He commanded the people, and counselled his barons, to keep themselves altogether, and defend themselves in a body; for if they once separated, they would with difficulty recover themselves. 'The Normans,' he said, 'are good vassals, valiant on foot and on horseback; good knights are they on horseback, and well used to battle; all is lost if they once penetrate our ranks. They have brought long lances and swords, but you have pointed lances and keen-edged bills; and I do not expect that their arms can stand against yours. Cleave wherever you can; it will be ill done if you spare aught.'

"The English had built up a fence before them with their shields, and with ash and other wood; and had well joined and wattled in the whole work, so as not to leave even a crevice; and thus they had a barricade in their front, through which any Norman who would attack them must first pass. Being covered in this way by their shields and barricades, their aim was to defend themselves: and if they had remained steady for that purpose, they would not have been conquered that day; for every Norman who made his way in, lost his life, either by hatchet or bill, by club, or other weapon.   They wore short and close hauberks, and helmets that hung over their garments.

"King Harold issued orders and made proclamation round, that all should be ranged with their faces towards the enemy; and that no one should move from where he was; so that, whoever came, might find them ready; and that whatever any one, be he Norman or other, should do, each should do his best to defend his own place. Then he ordered the men of Kent to go where the Normans were likely to make the attack; for they say that the men of Kent are entitled to strike first; and that whenever the king goes to battle, the first blow belongs to them. The right of the men of London is to guard the king's body, to place themselves around him, and to guard his standard; and they were accordingly placed by the standard to watch and defend it.

"When Harold had made his reply, and given his orders, he came into the midst of the English, and dismounted by the side of the standard. Leofwin and Gurth, his brothers, were with him, and around him he had barons enough, as he stood by his standard, which was in truth a noble one, sparkling with gold and precious stones. After the victory William sent it to the pope, to prove and commemorate his great conquest and glory. The English stood in close ranks, ready and eager for the fight; and they moreover made a fosse, which went across the field, guarding one side of their army.

XI

"Meanwhile the Normans appeared advancing over the ridge of a rising ground; and the first division of their troops moved onwards along the hill and across a valley. And presently another division, still larger, came in sight, close following upon the first, and they were led towards another part of the field, forming together as the first body had done.

"And while Harold saw and examined them, and was pointing them out to Gurth, a fresh company came in sight, covering all the plain; and in the midst of them was raised the standard that came from Rome. Near it was the duke, and the best men and greatest strength of the army were there. The good knights, the good vassals, and brave warriors were there; and there were gathered together the gentle barons, the good archers, and the men-at-arms, whose duty it was to guard the duke, and range themselves around him. The youths and common herd of the camp, whose business was not to join in the battle, but to take care of the harness and stores, moved off towards a rising ground. The priests and the clerks also ascended a hill, there to offer up prayers to God, and watch the event of the battle.

"The English stood firm on foot in close ranks, and carried themselves right boldly. Each man had his hauberk on, with his sword girt, and his shield at his neck. Great hatchets were also slung at their necks, with which they expected to strike heavy blows.

"The Normans brought on the three divisions of their army to attack at different places. They set out in three companies, and in three companies did they fight. The first and second had come up, and then advanced the third, which was the greatest; with that came the duke with his own men, and all moved boldly forward.

"As soon as the two armies were in full view of each other, great noise and tumult arose. You might hear the sound of many trumpets, of bugles, and of horns; and then you might see men ranging themselves in line, lifting their shields, raising their lances, bending their bows, handling their arrows, ready for assault and defence.

"The English stood steady to their post, the Normans still moved on; and when they drew near, the English were to be seen stirring to and fro; were going and coming; troops ranging themselves in order; some with their colour rising, others turning pale; some making ready their arms; others raising their shields; the brave man rousing himself to fight, the coward trembling at the approach of danger.

"Then Taillefer, who sang right well, rode mounted on a swift horse, before the duke, singing of Charlemagne, and of Roland, of Oliver, and the peers who died in Roncesvalles. And when they drew nigh to the English, 'A boon, sire!' cried Taillefer; 'I have long served you, and you owe me for all such service. To-day, so please you, you shall repay it. I ask as my guerdon and beseech you for it earnestly, that you will allow me to strike the first blow in the battle!'

And the duke answered, 'I grant it.' Then Taillefer put his horse to a gallop, charging before all the rest, and struck an Englishman dead, driving his lance below the breast into his body, and stretching him upon the ground. Then he drew his sword, and struck another, crying out, 'Come on, come on! What do ye, sirs? lay on, lay on!' At the second blow he struck, the English pushed forward, and surrounded and slew him. Forthwith arose the noise and cry of war, and on either side the people put themselves in motion.

XII

"The Normans moved on to the assault, and the English defended themselves well. Some were striking, others urging onwards; all were bold, and cast aside fear. And now, behold, that battle was gathered, whereof the fame is yet mighty.

"Loud and far resounded the bray of the horns; and the shocks of the lances, the mighty strokes of maces, and the quick clashing of swords. One while the Englishmen rushed on, another while they fell back; one while the men from over sea charged onwards, and again at other times retreated. Then came the cunning manœuvres, the rude shocks and strokes of the lance and blows of the swords, among the serjeants and soldiers, both English and Norman.

"When the English fall, the Normans shout. Each side taunts and defies the other, yet neither knoweth what the other saith; and the Normans say the English bark, because they understand not their speech.

"Some wax strong, others weak: the brave exult, but the cowards tremble, as men who are sore dismayed. The Normans press on the assault, and the English defend their post well: they pierce the hauberks, and cleave the shields, receive and return mighty blows. Again, some press forwards; others yield, and thus in various ways the struggle proceeds. In the plain was a fosse, which the Normans had now behind them, having passed it in the fight without regarding it. But the English charged and drove the Normans before them till they made them fall back upon their fosse, overthrowing into it horses and men. Many were to be seen falling therein, rolling one over the other, with their faces to the earth, and unable to rise. Many of the English, also, whom the Normans drew

down along with them, died there. At no time during the
day's battle did so many Normans die as perished in that
fosse. So those said who saw the dead.

"The varlets who were set to guard the harness began to
abandon it as they saw the loss of the Frenchmen, when
thrown back upon the fosse without power to recover themselves. Being greatly alarmed at seeing the difficulty in restoring
order, they began to quit the harness, and sought around, not
knowing where to find shelter. Then Duke William's brother,
Odo, the good priest, the bishop of Bayeux, galloped up, and
said to them, 'Stand fast! stand fast! be quiet and move not!
fear nothing, for if God please, we shall conquer yet.' So they
took courage, and rested where they were; and Odo returned
galloping back to where the battle was most fierce, and was
of great service on that day. He had put a hauberk on, over
a white aube; wide in the body, with the sleeve tight; and sat
on a white horse, so that all might recognize him. In his
hand he held a mace, and wherever he saw most need he held
up and stationed the knights, and often urged them on to
assault and strike the enemy.

"From nine o'clock in the morning, when the combat began
till three o'clock came, the battle was up and down, this way
and that, and no one knew who would conquer and win the
land. Both sides stood so firm and fought so well, that no one
could guess which would prevail. The Norman archers with
their bows shot thickly upon the English; but they covered
themselves with their shields, so that the arrows could not
reach their bodies, nor do any mischief, how true soever was
their aim, or however well they shot. Then the Normans
determined to shoot their arrows upwards into the air, so that
they might fall on their enemies' heads, and strike their faces.
The archers adopted this scheme, and shot up into the air
towards the English; and the arrows in falling struck their
heads and faces, and put out the eyes of many; and all feared
to open their eyes, or leave their faces unguarded.

XIII

"The arrows now flew thicker than rain before the wind;
fast sped the shafts that the English called 'wibetes.' Then
it was that an arrow, that had thus been shot upwards, struck

Harold above his right eye, and put it out. In his agony he drew the arrow and threw it away, breaking it with his hands: and the pain to his head was so great, that he leaned upon his shield. So the English were wont to say, and still say to the French, that the arrow was well shot which was so sent up against their king; and that the archer won them great glory, who thus put out Harold's eye.

"The Normans saw that the English defended themselves well, and were so strong in their position that they could do little against them. So they consulted together privily, and arranged to draw off, and pretend to flee, till the English should pursue and scatter themselves over the field; for they saw that if they could once get their enemies to break their ranks, they might be attacked and discomfited much more easily. As they had said, so they did. The Normans by little and little fled, the English following them. As the one fell back, the other pressed after; and when the Frenchmen retreated, the English thought and cried out, that the men of France fled, and would never return.

"Thus they were deceived by the pretended flight, and great mischief thereby befell them; for if they had not moved from their position, it is not likely that they would have been conquered at all; but like fools they broke their lines and pursued.

"The Normans were to be seen following up their stratagem, retreating slowly so as to draw the English further on. As they still flee, the English pursue; they push out their lances and stretch forth their hatchets: following the Normans, as they go rejoicing in the success of their scheme, and scattering themselves over the plain. And the English meantime jeered and insulted their foes with words. 'Cowards,' they cried, 'you came hither in an evil hour, wanting our lands, and seeking to seize our property, fools that ye were to come! Normandy is too far off, and you will not easily reach it. It is of little use to run back; unless you can cross the sea at a leap, or can drink it dry, your sons and daughters are lost to you.'

"The Normans bore it all, but in fact they knew not what the English said; their language seemed like the baying of dogs, which they could not understand. At length they stopped and turned round, determined to recover their ranks; and the barons might be heard crying for a halt. Then the Normans

resumed their former position, turning their faces towards the
enemy; and their men were to be seen facing round and rushing
onwards to a fresh *mêlée;* the one party assaulting the other;
this man striking, another pressing onwards. One hits, another
misses; one flies, another pursues: one is aiming a stroke, while
another discharges his blow. Norman strives with Englishman
again, and aims his blows afresh. One flies, another pursues
swiftly: the combatants are many, the plain wide, the battle
and the *mêlée* fierce. On every hand they fight hard, the blows
are heavy, and the struggle becomes fierce.

XIV

"The Normans were playing their part well, when an English
knight came rushing up, having in his company a hundred
men, furnished with various arms. He wielded a northern
hatchet, with the blade a full foot long; and was well armed
after his manner, being tall, bold, and of noble carriage. In
the front of the battle where the Normans thronged most, he
came bounding on swifter than the stag, many Normans falling
before him and his company. He rushed straight upon a Norman who was armed and riding on a war-horse, and tried with
his hatchet of steel to cleave his helmet; but the blow mis-
carried, and the sharp blade glanced down before the saddle-
bow, driving through the horse's neck down to the ground, so
that both horse and master fell together to the earth.

"I know not whether the Englishman struck another blow;
but the Normans who saw the stroke were astonished, and
about to abandon the assault, when Roger de Montgomeri
came galloping up, with his lance set, and heeding not the
long-handled axe, which the Englishman wielded aloft, struck
him down, and left him stretched upon the ground. Then
Roger cried out, 'Frenchmen, strike! the day is ours!' And again
a fierce *mêlée* was to be seen, with many a blow of lance and
sword; the English still defending themselves, killing the horses
and cleaving the shields.

"There was a French soldier of noble mien, who sat his
horse gallantly. He spied two Englishmen who were also
carrying themselves boldly. They were both men of great
worth, and had become companions in arms and fought together, the one protecting the other. They bore two long and

broad bills, and did great mischief to the Normans, killing both horses and men. The French soldier looked at them and their bills, and was sore alarmed, for he was afraid of losing his good horse, the best that he had; and would willingly have turned to some other quarter, if it would not have looked like cowardice. He soon, however, recovered his courage, and spurring his horse gave him the bridle, and galloped swiftly forward. Fearing the two bills, he raised his shield, and struck one of the Englishmen with his lance on the breast, so that the iron passed out at his back. At the moment that he fell, the lance broke, and the Frenchman seized the mace that hung at his right side, and struck the other Englishman a blow that completely broke his skull.

"On the other side was an Englishman who much annoyed the French, continually assaulting them with a keen-edged hatchet. He had a helmet made of wood, which he had fastened down to his coat, and laced round his neck, so that no blows could reach his head. The ravage he was making was seen by a gallant Norman knight, who rode a horse that neither fire nor water could stop in its career, when its master urged it on. The knight spurred, and his horse carried him on well till he charged the Englishman, striking him over the helmet, so that it fell down over his eyes; and as he stretched out his hand to raise it and uncover the face, the Norman cut off his right hand, so that his hatchet fell to the ground.

"Another Norman sprang forward and eagerly seized the prize with both his hands, but he kept it little space, and paid dearly for it, for as he stooped to pick up the hatchet, an Englishman with his long-handled axe struck him over the back, breaking all his bones, so that his entrails and lungs gushed forth. The knight of the good horse meantime returned without injury; but on his way he met another Englishman, and bore him down under his horse, wounding him grievously and trampling him altogether under foot.

"And now might be heard the loud clang and cry of battle, and the clashing of lances. The English stood firm in their barricades, and shivered the lances, beating them into pieces with their bills and maces. The Normans drew their swords, and hewed down the barricades, and the English in great trouble fell back upon their standard, where were collected the maimed and wounded.

"There were many knights of Chauz, who jousted and made attacks. The English knew not how to joust, or bear arms on horseback, but fought with hatchets and bills. A man, when he wanted to strike with one of their hatchets, was obliged to hold it with both his hands, and could not at the same time, as it seems to me, both cover himself and strike with any freedom.

"The English fell back towards the standard which was upon a rising ground, and the Normans followed them across the valley, attacking them on foot and horseback. Then Hue de Mortemer, with the sires D'Auviler, D'Onebac, and St. Cler, rode up and charged, overthrowing many.

"Robert Fitz Erneis fixed his lance, took his shield, and, galloping towards the standard, with his keen-edged sword struck an Englishman who was in front, killed him, and then drawing back his sword, attacked many others, and pushed straight for the standard, trying to beat it down, but the English surrounded it, and killed him with their bills. He was found on the spot, when they afterwards sought for him, dead, and lying at the standard's foot.

"Duke William pressed close upon the English with his lance; striving hard to reach the standard with the great troop he led; and seeking earnestly for Harold, on whose account the whole war was. The Normans follow their lord, and press around him; they ply their blows upon the English; and these defend themselves stoutly, striving hard with their enemies, returning blow for blow.

"One of them was a man of great strength, a wrestler, who did great mischief to the Normans with his hatchet; all feared him, for he struck down a great many Normans. The duke spurred on his horse, and aimed a blow at him, but he stooped, and so escaped the stroke; then jumping on one side, he lifted his hatchet aloft, and as the duke bent to avoid the blow, the Englishman boldly struck him on the head, and beat in his helmet, though without doing much injury. He was very near falling, however, but bearing on his stirrups he recovered himself immediately; and when he thought to have revenged himself upon the churl by killing him, he had escaped, dreading the duke's blow. He ran back in among the English, but he was not safe even there; for the Normans seeing him, pursued and caught him; and having pierced him through and through with their lances, left him dead on the ground.

XV

"Where the throng of the battle was greatest, the men of Kent and Essex fought wondrously well, and made the Normans again retreat, but without doing them much injury. And when the duke saw his men fall back, and the English triumphing over them, his spirit rose high, and he seized his shield and his lance, which a vassal handed to him, and took his post by his standard.

"Then those who kept close guard by him and rode where he rode, being about a thousand armed men, came and rushed with closed ranks upon the English; and with the weight of their good horses, and the blows the knights gave, broke the press of the enemy, and scattered the crowd before them, the good duke leading them on in front. Many pursued and many fled; many were the Englishmen who fell around, and were trampled under the horses, crawling upon the earth, and not able to rise. Many of the richest and noblest men fell in that rout, but the English still rallied in places; smote down those whom they reached, and maintained the combat the best they could; beating down the men and killing the horses. One Englishman watched the duke, and plotted to kill him; he would have struck him with his lance, but he could not, for the duke struck him first, and felled him to the earth.

"Loud was now the clamour, and great the slaughter; many a soul then quitted the body it inhabited. The living marched over the heaps of dead, and each side was weary of striking. He charged on who could, and he who could no longer strike still pushed forward. The strong struggled with the strong; some failed, others triumphed; the cowards fell back, the brave pressed on; and sad was his fate who fell in the midst, for he had little chance of rising again; and many in truth fell, who never rose at all, being crushed under the throng.

"And now the Normans pressed on so far, that at last they had reached the standard. There Harold had remained, defending himself to the utmost; but he was sorely wounded in his eye by the arrow, and suffered grievous pain from the blow. An armed man came in the throng of the battle, and

struck him on the ventaille of his helmet, and beat him to the
ground; and as he sought to recover himself, a knight beat
him down again, striking him on the thick of his thigh down
to the bone.

"Gurth saw the English falling around, and that there
was no remedy. He saw his race hastening to ruin, and
despaired of any aid; he would have fled, but could not,
for the throng continually increased. And the duke pushed
on till he reached him, and struck him with great force.
Whether he died of that blow I know not, but it was said
that he fell under it, and rose no more.

"The standard was beaten down, the golden standard was
taken, and Harold and the best of his friends were slain;
but there was so much eagerness, and throng of so many
around, seeking to kill him, that I know not who it was that
slew him.

"The English were in great trouble at having lost their
king, and at the duke having conquered and beat down the
standard; but they still fought on, and defended themselves
long, and in fact till the day drew to a close. Then it
clearly appeared to all that the standard was lost, and the
news had spread throughout the army that Harold for certain
was dead; and all saw that there was no longer any hope,
so they left the field, and those fled who could.

"William fought well; many an assault did he lead, many
a blow did he give, and many receive, and many fell dead
under his hand. Two horses were killed under him, and he
took a third at time of need, so that he fell not to the ground;
and he lost not a drop of blood. But whatever any one did,
and whoever lived or died, this is certain, that William conquered, and that many of the English fled from the field, and
many died on the spot. Then he returned thanks to God,
and in his pride ordered his standard to be brought and set
up on high, where the English standard had stood; and that
was the signal of his having conquered, and beaten down the
foe. And he ordered his tent to be raised on the spot among
the dead, and had his meat brought thither, and his supper
prepared there.

"Then he took off his armour; and the barons and knights,
pages and squires, came, when he had unstrung his shield;
and they took the helmet from his head, and the hauberk from

his back, and saw the heavy blows upon his shield, and how his helmet was dinted in. And all greatly wondered, and said, 'Such a baron never bestrode war-horse, or dealt such blows, or did such feats of arms; neither has there been on earth such a knight since Rollant and Olivier.'

"Thus they lauded and extolled him greatly, and rejoiced in what they saw; but grieving also for their friends who were slain in the battle. And the duke stood meanwhile among them of noble stature and mien; and rendered thanks to the King of Glory, through whom he had the victory; and thanked the knights around him, mourning also frequently for the dead. And he ate and drank among the dead, and made his bed that night upon the field.

"The morrow was Sunday; and those who had slept upon the field of battle, keeping watch around, and suffering great fatigue, bestirred themselves at break of day, and sought out and buried such of the bodies of their dead friends as they might find. The noble ladies of the land also came, some to seek their husbands, and others their fathers, sons, or brothers. They bore the bodies to their villages, and interred them at the churches; and the clerks and priests of the country were ready, and at the request of their friends, took the bodies that were found, and prepared graves and laid them therein.

"King Harold was carried and buried at Varham; but I know not who it was that bore him thither, neither do I know who buried him. Many remained on the field, and many had fled in the night."

XVI

Such is a Norman account of the Battle of Hastings, which does full justice to the valour of the Saxons, as well as to the skill and bravery of the victors. It is indeed evident that the loss of the battle to the English was owing to the wound which Harold received in the afternoon, and which must have incapacitated him from effective command. When we remember that he had himself just won the battle of Stamford Bridge over Harald Hardrada by the manœuvre of a feigned flight, it is impossible to suppose that he could be deceived by the same stratagem on the part of the Normans at Hastings. But his men, when deprived of his control, would very naturally be led by their inconsiderate ardour into the pursuit that proved so fatal to them.

All the narratives of the battle, however much they may vary
as to the precise time and manner of Harold's fall, eulogise
the generalship and the personal prowess which he displayed,
until the fatal arrow struck him. The skill with which he
had posted his army was proved, both by the slaughter which
it cost the Normans to force the position and also by the
desperate rally which some of the Saxons made after the battle
in the forest in the rear, in which they cut off a large number
of the pursuing Normans. This circumstance is particularly
mentioned by William of Poictiers, the Conqueror's own chaplain. Indeed, if Harold, or either of his brothers, had survived, the remains of the English army might have formed
again in the wood, and could at least have effected an orderly
retreat, and prolonged the war.

But both Gurth and Leofwine, and all the bravest thanes of
Southern England, lay dead on Senlac, around their fallen
king and the fallen standard of their country. The exact
number of the slain on the Saxon side is unknown; but we
read that on the side of the victors, out of sixty thousand
men who had been engaged, no less than a fourth perished.
So well had the English bill-men "plied the ghastly blow," and
so sternly had the Saxon battle-axe cloven Norman casque
and mail. The old historian Daniel, justly as well as forcibly
remarks, "Thus was tried, by the great assize of God's judgment in battle, the right of power between the English and
Norman nations; a battle the most memorable of all others;
and, however miserably lost, yet most nobly fought on the part
of England."

Many a pathetic legend was told in after years respecting
the discovery and the burial of the corpse of our last Saxon
king. The main circumstances, though they seem to vary,
are perhaps reconcilable. Two of the monks of Walthem
Abbey, which Harold had founded a little time before his
election to the throne, had accompanied him to the battle.
On the morning after the slaughter they begged and gained
permission of the Conqueror to search for the body of their
benefactor. The Norman soldiery and camp-followers had
stripped and gashed the slain; and the two monks vainly strove
to recognize from among the mutilated and gory heaps around
them the features of their former king. They sent for Harold's
mistress, Edith, surnamed "The Fair" and the "Swan-necked,"

to aid them. The eye of love proved keener than the eye of gratitude, and the Saxon lady, even in that Aceldama, (from the Greek, "Field of Blood") knew her Harold.

The king's mother now sought the victorious Norman and begged the dead body of her son. But William at first answered in his wrath, and in the hardness of his heart, that a man who had been false to his word and his religion, should have no other sepulchre than the sand of the shore. He added, with a sneer, "Harold mounted guard on the coast while he was alive; he may continue his guard now he is dead." The taunt was an unintentional eulogy; and a grave washed by the spray of the Sussex waves would have been the noblest burial-place for the martyr of Saxon freedom. But Harold's mother was urgent in her lamentations and her prayers: the Conqueror relented: gave up the dead body of his fallen foe to a parent's supplications and the remains of King Harold were deposited with regal honours in Waltham Abbey.

On Christmas-day of the same year, William the Conqueror was crowned king of England, at London.

SYNOPSIS OF EVENTS BETWEEN THE BATTLE OF HASTINGS, A.D. 1066, AND JOAN OF ARC'S VICTORY AT ORLEANS, A.D. 1429.

A.D. 1066-1087. Reign of William the Conqueror. Frequent risings of the English against him, which are quelled with merciless rigour.

1096. The first Crusade.

1112. Commencement of the disputes about investitures between the emperors and the popes.

1140. Foundation of the city of Lubeck, whence originated the Hanseatic League. Commencement of the feuds in Italy between the Guelphs and Ghibellines.

1146. The second Crusade.

1154. Henry II, becomes King of England. Under him Thomas à Becket is made Archbishop of Canterbury: the first instance of any man of the Saxon race being raised to high office in Church or State since the Conquest.

1170. Strongbow, Earl of Pembroke, lands with an English army in Ireland.

1189. Richard Cœur de Lion becomes King of England. He and King Philip Augustus of France join in the third Crusade.

1199-1204. On the death of King Richard, his brother John claims and makes himself master of England and Normandy and the other large continental possessions of the early Plantagenet princes. Philip Augustus asserts the cause of Prince Arthur, John's nephew, against him. Arthur is murdered, but the French king continues the war against John, and conquers from him Normandy, Brittany, Anjou, Maine, Touraine, and Poictiers.

1215. The barons, the freeholders, the citizens, and the yeomen of England rise against the tyranny of John and his foreign favourites. They compel him to sign the Magna Charta. This is the commencement of our nationality: for our history from this time forth is the history of a national life, then complete, and still in being. All English history before this period is a mere history of elements, of their collisions, and of the processes of their fusion. For upwards of a century after the Conquest, Anglo-Norman and Anglo-Saxon had kept aloof from each other: the one in haughty scorn, the other in sullen abhorrence. They were two peoples, though living in the same land. It is not until the thirteenth century, the period of the reigns of John and his son and grandson, that we can perceive the existence of any feeling of common patriotism among them. But in studying the history of these reigns, we read of the old dissensions no longer. The Saxon no more appears in civil war against the Norman; the Norman no longer scorns the language of the Saxon, or refuses to bear together with him the name of Englishman. No part of the community think themselves foreigners to another part. They feel that they are all one people, and they have learned to unite their efforts for the common purpose of protecting the rights and promoting the welfare of all. The fortunate loss of the Duchy of Normandy in John's reign, greatly promoted these new feelings. Thenceforth our barons' only homes were in England. One language had, in the reign of Henry III., become the language of the land; and that, also, had then assumed the form in which we still possess it. One law, in the eye of which all freemen are equal without distinction of race was modelled, and steadily enforced, and still continues to form the groundwork of our judicial system.

1273. Rodolph of Hapsburg chosen emperor of Germany.

1283. Edward I. conquers Wales.

1346. Edward III. invades France, and gains the battle of Crecy.

1356. Battle of Poictiers.

1360. Treaty of Bretigny between England and France. By it Edward III. renounces his pretensions to the French crown. The treaty is ill kept, and indecisive hostilities continue between the forces of the two countries.

1414. Henry V. of England claims the crown of France, and resolves to invade and conquer that kingdom. At this time France was in the most deplorable state of weakness and suffering, from the factions that raged among her nobility, and from the cruel oppressions which the rival nobles practised on the mass of the community. "The people were exhausted by taxes, civil wars, and military executions; and they had fallen into that worst of all states of mind, when the independence of one's country is thought no longer a paramount and sacred object. 'What can the English do to us worse than the thing we suffer at the hands of our own princes?' was a common exclamation among the poor people of France."

1415. Henry invades France, takes Harfleur, and wins the great battle of Agincourt.

1417-1419. Henry conquers Normandy. The French dauphin assassinates the Duke of Burgundy, the most powerful of the French nobles, at Montereau. The successor of the murdered duke becomes the active ally of the English.

1420. The Treaty of Troyes is concluded between Henry V. of England and Charles VI. of France, and Philip, Duke of Burgundy. By this treaty it was stipulated that Henry should marry the Princess Catherine of France; that King Charles, during his lifetime, should keep the title and dignity of King of France, but that Henry should succeed him, and should at once be entrusted with the administration of the government, and that the French crown should descend to Henry's heirs; that France and England should for ever be united under one king, but should still retain their several usages, customs, and privileges; that all the princes, peers, vassals, and communities of France should swear allegiance to Henry as their future king, and should pay him present obedience as regent; that Henry should unite his arms to those of King Charles and the Duke of Burgundy, in order to subdue the adherents of Charles, the pretended dauphin; and that these three princes should make no peace or truce with the dauphin, but by the common consent of all three.

1421. Henry V. gains several victories over the French, who refuse to acknowledge the Treaty of Troyes. His son, afterwards Henry VI., is born.

1422. Henry V. and Charles VI. of France die. Henry VI. is proclaimed at Paris, King of England and France. The followers of the French dauphin proclaim him Charles VII., King of France. The Duke of Bedford, the English Regent in France, defeats the army of the dauphin at Crevant.

1424. The Duke of Bedford gains the great victory of Verneuil, over the French partisans of the dauphin, and their Scotch auxiliaries.

1428. The English begin the siege of Orleans.

NINE

Orleans; Joan of Arc's Victory Over the English, 1429

WHY DECISIVE: *"The eyes of all Europe were turned toward this scene, where . . . the French were to make their last stand for maintaining the independence of their monarchy and the rights of their sovereign."* [Hume] *"It may be asserted without exaggeration that the future career of every nation was involved in the result of the struggle, by which the unconscious heroine of France . . . rescued her country from becoming a second Ireland under the yoke of the triumphant English."* [Creasy.]

I

WHEN, after their victory at Salamis, the generals of the various Greek states voted the prizes for distinguished individual merit, each assigned the first place of excellence to himself, but they all concurred in giving their second votes to Themistocles. This was looked on as a decisive proof that Themistocles ought to be ranked first of all. If we were to endeavour, by a similar test, to ascertain which European nation has contributed the most to the progress of European civilisation, we should find Italy, Germany, England, and Spain, each claiming the first degree, but each also naming France as clearly next in merit.

It is impossible to deny her paramount importance in history. Besides the formidable part that for more than three centuries she played, as the Bellona of the European commonwealth of states, her influence during all this period over the arts, the literature, the manners and the feelings of mankind, has been such as to make the crisis of her earlier fortunes a point of worldwide interest; and it may be asserted without exaggeration, that the future career of every nation was involved in the result of the struggle, by which the unconscious heroine of France, in the beginning of the fifteenth century, rescued her country from becoming a second Ireland under the yoke of the triumphant English.

Seldom has the extinction of a nation's independence appeared more inevitable than was the case in France, when

the English invaders completed their lines round Orleans, five
hundred fourteen years ago (1850). A series of dreadful defeats
had thinned the chivalry of France, and daunted the spirits of
her soldiers. A foreign king had been proclaimed in her capital
and foreign armies of the bravest veterans, and led by the ablest
captains then known in the world, occupied the fairest portions of her territory. Worse to her, even than the fierceness
and strength of her foes, were the factions, the vices, and the
crimes of her own children. Her native prince was a dissolute
trifler, stained with the assassination of the most powerful
noble of the land, whose son, in revenge, had leagued himself
with the enemy. Many more of her nobility, many of her
prelates, her magistrates, and rulers, had sworn fealty to the
English king. The condition of the peasantry amid the general
prevalence of anarchy and brigandage, which were added to
the customary devastations of contending armies, was wretched
beyond the power of language to describe. The sense of terror
and suffering seemed to have extended itself even to the brute
creation, for according to de Serres:

"In sooth, the estate of France was then most miserable.
There appeared nothing but a horrible face, confusion, poverty,
desolation, solitarinesse, and feare. The lean and bare labourers
in the country did terrifie even theeves themselves, who had
nothing left them to spoile but the carkasses of these poore
miserable creatures, wandering up and down like ghostes drawne
out of their graves. The least farmes and hamlets were fortified
by these robbers, English, Bourguegnons, and French, every
one striving to do his worst; all men-of-war were well agreed
to spoile the countryman and merchant. Even the cattell, accustomed to the larume bell, the signe of the enemy's approach,
would run home of themselves without any guide, by this accustomed misery."

In the autumn of 1428, the English, who were already masters of all France north of the Loire, prepared their forces
for the conquest of the southern provinces, which yet adhered to
the cause of the dauphin. The city of Orleans, on the banks
of that river, was looked upon as the last stronghold of the
French national party. If the English could once obtain possession of it, their victorious progress through the residue of
the kingdom seemed free from any serious obstacle. Accordingly, the Earl of Salisbury, one of the bravest and most ex-

perienced of the English generals, who had been trained under
Henry V., marched to the attack of the all-important city; and,
after reducing several places of inferior consequence in the
neighbourhood, appeared with his army before its walls on the
12th of October, 1428.

II

The city of Orleans itself was on the north side of the
Loire, but its suburbs extended far on the southern side, and
a strong bridge connected them with the town. A fortification which in modern military phrase would be termed a
tête-de-pont, defended the bridge-head on the southern side,
and two towers, called the Tourelles, were built on the bridge
itself, where it rested on an island at a little distance from
the *tête-de-pont*. Indeed, the solid masonry of the bridge
terminated at the Tourelles; and the communication thence
with the *tête-de-pont* on the southern shore was by means of
a drawbridge. The Tourelles and the *tête-de-pont* formed together a strong fortified post, capable of containing a garrison
of considerable strength and so long as this was in possession
of the Orleannais, they could communicate freely with the
southern provinces, the inhabitants of which, like the Orleannais
themselves, supported the cause of their dauphin against the
foreigners.

Lord Salisbury rightly judged the capture of the Tourelles to
be the most material step towards the reduction of the city
itself. Accordingly he directed his principal operations against
this post, and after some severe repulses, he carried the Tourelles
by storm, on the 23rd of October. The French, however, broke
down the part of the bridge which was nearest to the north
bank, and thus rendered a direct assault from the Tourelles upon
the city impossible. But the possession of this post enabled
the English to distress the town greatly by a battery of cannon
which they planted there, and which commanded some of the
principal streets.

It has been observed by Hume, that this is the first siege
in which any important use appears to have been made of
artillery. And even at Orleans both besiegers and besieged
seem to have employed their cannons more as instruments
of destruction against their enemy's *men* than as engines of
demolition against their enemy's walls and works. The efficacy

of cannon in breaching solid masonry was taught Europe by the Turks, a few years afterwards, at the memorable siege of Constantinople.

In our French wars, as in the wars of the classic nations, famine was looked on as the surest weapon to compel the submission of a well-walled town; and the great object of the besiegers was to effect a complete circumvallation. The great ambit of the walls of Orleans, and the facilities which the river gave for obtaining succour and supplies, rendered the capture of the place by this process a matter of great difficulty. Nevertheless, Lord Salisbury, and Lord Suffolk, who succeeded him in command of the English after his death by a cannon-ball, carried on the necessary works with great skill and resolution. Six strongly-fortified posts, called bastilles, were formed at certain intervals round the town; and the purpose of the English engineers was to draw strong lines between them. During the winter little progress was made with the entrenchments, but when the spring of 1429 came, the English resumed their works with activity; the communications between the city and the country became more difficult, and the approach of want began already to be felt in Orleans.

The besieging force also fared hardly for stores and provisions, until relieved by the effects of a brilliant victory which Sir John Fastolfe, one of the best English generals, gained at Rouvrai, near Orleans, a few days after Ash Wednesday, 1429. With only sixteen hundred fighting men, Sir John completely defeated an army of French and Scots, four thousand strong, which had been collected for the purpose of aiding the Orleannais, and harassing the besiegers. After this encounter, which seemed decisively to confirm the superiority of the English in battle over their adversaries, Fastolfe escorted large supplies of stores and food to Suffolk's camp, and the spirits of the English rose to the highest pitch at the prospect of the speedy capture of the city before them; and the consequent subjection of all France beneath their arms.

The Orleannais now in their distress offered to surrender the city into the hands of the Duke of Burgundy, who, though the ally of the English, was yet one of their native princes. The Duke of Bedford, the English regent in France, refused these terms, and the speedy submission of the city to the English seemed inevitable. The dauphin (title of heir presumptive to the French throne) Charles, who was now at Chinon with his remnant of a court, despaired of maintaining any longer the struggle for his crown; and was only prevented from abandoning the country by the more masculine spirits of his mistress and his queen. Yet neither they, nor the boldest of Charles's captains, could have shown him where to find resources for prolonging the war; and least of all, could any human skill have predicted the quarter whence rescue was to come to Orleans and to France.

III

In the village of Domremy, on the borders of Lorraine, there was a poor peasant of the name of Jacques d'Arc, respected in his station of life, and who had reared a family in virtuous habits and in the practice of the strictest devotion. His eldest daughter was named by her parents Jeannette, but she was called Jeanne by the French, which was Latinised into Johanna, and Anglicised into Joan.

At the time when Joan first attracted attention, she was about eighteen years of age. She was naturally of a susceptible disposition, which diligent attention to the legends of saints and tales of fairies, aided by the dreamy loneliness of her life while tending her father's flocks, had made peculiarly prone to enthusiastic fervour.

Southey, in one of the speeches which he puts in the mouth of his Joan of Arc, has made her beautifully describe the effect on her mind of the scenery in which she dwelt.

> "Here in solitude and peace
> My soul was nurst, amid the loveliest scenes
> Of unpolluted nature. Sweet it was
> As the white mists of morning rolled away,
> To see the mountain's wooded heights appear
> Dark in the early dawn, and mark its slope
> With gorse-flowers glowing, as the rising sun
> On the golden ripeness pour'd a deepening light.
> Pleasant at noon beside the vocal brook
>
> To lay me down, and watch the floating clouds,
> And shape to Fancy's wild similitudes
> Their ever-varying forms; and oh, how sweet,
> To drive my flock at evening to the fold,
> And hasten to our little hut, and hear
> The voice of kindness bid me welcome home!"

At the same time she was eminent for piety and purity of soul, and for her compassionate gentleness to the sick and the distressed.

The district where she dwelt had escaped comparatively free from the ravages of war, but the approach of roving bands of Burgundian or English troops frequently spread terror through Domremy. Once the village had been plundered by some of these marauders, and Joan and her family had been driven from their home, and forced to seek refuge for a time at Neufchâteau. The peasantry in Domremy were principally attached to the house of Orleans and the dauphin; and all the miseries which France endured, were there imputed to the Burgundian faction and their allies, the English, who were seeking to enslave unhappy France.

Thus from infancy to girlhood, Joan had heard continually of the woes of the war, and she had herself witnessed some of the wretchedness that it caused. A feeling of intense patriotism grew in her with her growth. The deliverance of France from the English was the subject of her reveries by day and her dreams by night. Blended with these aspirations were recollections of the miraculous interpositions of Heaven in favour of the oppressed, which she had learned from the legends of her church. Her faith was undoubting; her prayers were fervent. "She feared no danger, for she felt no sin" and at length she believed herself to have received the supernatural inspiration which she sought.

According to her own narrative, delivered by her to her merciless inquisitors, in the time of her captivity and approaching death, she was about thirteen years old when her revelations commenced. As the record set down says: "At the age of thirteen, a voice from God came near to her to help her in ruling herself, and that voice came to her about the hour of noon, in summer time, while she was in her father's garden. And she had fasted the day before. And she heard the voice on her right, in the direction of the church; and when she heard the voice she also saw a bright light. Afterwards, St. Michael and St. Margaret and St. Catherine appeared to her. They were always in a halo of glory; she could see that their heads were crowned with jewels: and she heard their voices, which were sweet and mild. She did not distinguish their arms or limbs. She heard them more frequently than she saw them;

and the usual time when she heard them was when the church bells were sounding for prayer. And if she was in the woods when she heard them, she could plainly distinguish their voices drawing near to her. When she thought that she discerned the Heavenly Voices, she knelt down, and bowed herself to the ground. Their presence gladdened her even to tears; and after they departed she wept because they had not taken her with them back to Paradise. They always spoke soothingly to her. They told her that France would be saved, and that she was to save it."

Such were the visions and the voices that moved the spirit of the girl of thirteen and as she grew older they became more frequent and more clear. At last the tidings of the siege of Orleans reached Domremy. Joan heard her parents and neighbours talk of the sufferings of its population, of the ruin which its capture would bring on their lawful sovereign, and of the distress of the dauphin and his court. Joan's heart was sorely troubled at the thought of the fate of Orleans; and her voices now ordered her to leave her home and warned her that she was the instrument chosen by Heaven for driving away the English from that city, and for taking the dauphin to be anointed king at Rheims.

At length she informed her parents of her divine mission, and told them that she must go to the Sire de Baudricourt, who commanded at Vaucouleurs, and who was the appointed person to bring her into the presence of the king, whom she was to save. Neither the anger nor the grief of her parents, who said that they would rather see her drowned than exposed to the contamination of the camp, could move her from her purpose. One of her uncles consented to take her to Vaucouleurs, where de Baudricourt at first thought her mad, and derided her; but by degrees was led to believe, if not in her inspiration, at least in her enthusiasm, and in its possible utility to the dauphin's cause.

The inhabitants of Vaucouleurs were completely won over to her side, by the piety and devoutness which she displayed, and by her firm assurance in the truth of her mission. She told them that it was God's will that she should go to the king, and that no one but her could save the kingdom of France. She said that she herself would rather remain with her poor mother and spin, but the Lord had ordered her forth. The fame of "The Maid," as she was termed, the renown of her holiness and of her mission, spread far and wide. Baudricourt sent her with an escort to Chinon, where the Dauphin Charles was dallying away his time. Her voices had bidden her assume the arms and the apparel of a knight and the wealthiest inhabitants of Vaucouleurs had vied with each other in equipping her with war-horse, armour, and sword. On reaching Chinon, she was, after some delay, admitted into the presence of the dauphin.

Charles designedly dressed himself far less richly than many of his courtiers were apparelled, and mingled with them, when Joan was introduced, in order to see if the Holy Maid would address her exhortations to the wrong person. But she instantly singled him out, and kneeling before him, said, "Most noble dauphin, the King of Heaven announces to you by me, that you shall be anointed and crowned king in the city of Rheims, and that you shall be his viceregent in France." His features may probably have been seen by her previously in portraits or have been described to her by others, but she herself believed that her voices inspired her when she addressed the king and the report soon spread abroad that the Holy Maid had found the king by a miracle; and this, with many other similar rumours, augmented the renown and influence that she now rapidly acquired.

IV

The state of public feeling in France was now favourable to an enthusiastic belief in a Divine interposition in favour of the party that had hitherto been unsuccessful and oppressed. The humiliations which had befallen the French royal family and nobility, were looked on as the just judgments of God upon them for their vice and impiety. The misfortunes that had come upon France as a nation were believed to have been drawn down by national sins. The English, who had been the instruments of Heaven's wrath against France, seemed now by their pride and cruelty to be fitting objects of it themselves.

France in that age was a profoundly religious country. There was ignorance, there was superstition, there was bigotry but there was faith—a faith that itself worked true miracles, even while it believed in unreal ones. At this time, also, one of those devotional movements began among the clergy in France which from time to time occur in national churches, without it being possible for the historian to assign any adequate human cause for their immediate date or extension. Numberless friars and priests traversed the rural districts and towns of France, preaching to the people that they must seek from Heaven a deliverance from the pillages of the soldiery, and the insolence of the foreign oppressors.

The idea of a Providence that works only by general laws was wholly alien to the feelings of the age. Every political event, as well as every natural phenomenon, was believed to be the immediate result of a special mandate of God. This led to the belief that His holy angels and saints were constantly employed in executing his commands and mingling in the affairs of men. The church encouraged these feelings and at the same time sanctioned the concurrent popular belief that hosts of evil spirits were also ever actively interposing in the current of earthly events, with whom sorcerers and wizards could league themselves, and thereby obtain the exercise of supernatural power.

Thus all things favoured the influence which Joan obtained both over friends and foes. The French nation, as well as the English and the Burgundians, readily admitted that superhuman beings inspired her: the only question was, whether these things were good or evil angels; whether she brought with her "airs from heaven, or blasts from hell." This question seemed to her countrymen to be decisively settled in her favour by the austere sanctity of her life, by the holiness of her conversation, but still more by her exemplary attention to all the services and rites of the church. The dauphin at first feared the injury that might be done to his cause if he had laid himself open to the charge of having leagued himself with a sorceress. Every imaginable test, therefore, was resorted to in order to set Joan's orthodoxy and purity beyond suspicion. At last, Charles and his advisers felt safe in accepting her services as those of a true and virtuous Christian daughter of the Holy Church.

It is indeed probable that Charles himself and some of his counsellors may have suspected Joan of being a mere enthusiast; and it is certain that Dunois, and others of the best generals, took considerable latitude in obeying or deviating from the military orders that she gave. But over the mass of the people and the soldiery, her influence was unbounded. While Charles

and his doctors of theology, and court ladies, had been de-
liberating as to recognising or dismissing the Maid, a considerable period had passed away, during which a small army,
the last gleanings, as it seemed, of the English sword, had been
assembled at Blois, under Dunois, La Hire, Xaintrailles, and
other chiefs, who to their natural valour were now beginning
to unite the wisdom that is taught by misfortune. It was resolved to send Joan with this force and a convoy of provisions
to Orleans. The distress of that city had now become urgent.
But the communication with the open country was not entirely
cut off: the Orleannais had heard of the Holy Maid whom
Providence had raised up for their deliverance, and their messengers urgently implored the dauphin to send her to them without delay.

V

Joan appeared at the camp at Blois, clad in a new suit of
brilliant white armour, mounted on a stately black war-horse
and with a lance in her right hand, which she had learned to
wield with skill and grace. Her head was unhelmeted so that
all could behold her fair and expressive features, her deep-set
and earnest eyes, and her long black hair, which was parted
across her forehead and bound by a ribbon behind her back.
She wore at her side a small battle-axe and the consecrated
sword, marked on the blade with five crosses, which had at her
bidding been taken for her from the shrine of St. Catherine at
Fierbois. A page carried her banner, which she had caused to
be made and embroidered as her voices enjoined. It was white
satin, strewn with *fleurs-de-lis;* and on it were the words "JHESUS
MARIA," and the representation of the Saviour in His glory.
Joan afterwards generally bore her banner herself in battle;
she said that though she loved her sword much, she loved her
banner forty times as much and she loved to carry it because it
could not kill any one.

Thus accoutred, she came to lead the troops of France, who
looked with soldierly admiration on her well-proportioned and
upright figure, the skill with which she managed her war-horse,
and the easy grace with which she handled her weapons. Her
military education had been short, but she had availed herself
of it well. She had also the good sense to interfere little with
the manœuvres of the troops; leaving those things to Dunois

and others whom she had the discernment to recognise as the best officers in the camp. Her tactics in action were simple enough. As she herself described it: "I used to say to them, 'Go boldly in among the English,' and then I used to go in boldly myself." Such, as she told her inquisitors, was the only spell she used; and it was one of power.

But while interfering little with the military discipline of the troops, in all matters of moral discipline she was inflexibly strict. All the abandoned followers of the camp were driven away. She compelled both generals and soldiers to attend regularly at confessional. Her chaplain and other priests marched with the army under her orders and at every halt an altar was set up and the sacrament administered. No oath or foul language passed without punishment or censure. Even the roughest and most hardened veterans obeyed her. They put off for a time the bestial coarseness which had grown on them during a life of bloodshed and rapine; they felt that they must go forth in a new spirit to a new career, and acknowledged the beauty of the holiness in which the Heaven-sent Maid was leading them to certain victory.

Joan marched from Blois on the 25th of April with a convoy of provisions for Orleans, accompanied by Dunois, La Hire, and the other chief captains of the French; and on the evening of the 28th they approached the town. In the words of the old chronicler, Hall: "The Englishmen, perceiving that they within could not long continue for faute of vitaile and pouder, kept not their watche so diligently as thei were accustomed, nor scoured now the countrey environed as their before had ordained. Whiche negligence the citizens shut in perceiving, sent worde thereof to the French captaines, which with Pucelle (the Maid) in the dedde tyme of the nighte, and in a greate rayne and thundere, with all their vitaile and artillery entered into the citie."

When it was day, the Maid rode in solemn procession through the city, clad in complete armour, and mounted on a white horse. Dunois was by her side, and all the bravest knights of her army and of the garrison followed in her train. The whole population thronged around her; and men, women, and children strove to touch her garments, or her banner, or her charger. They poured forth blessings on her, whom they already considered their deliverer. In the words used by two of them afterwards before the tribunal which reversed the sentence, but could not restore the life, of the Virgin-martyr of France, "the people of Orleans, when they first saw her in their city, thought that it was an angel from Heaven that had come down to save them."

Joan spoke gently in reply to their acclamations and addresses. She told them to fear God, and trust in Him for safety from the fury of their enemies. She first went to the principal church, where *Te Deum* was chanted; and then she took up her abode in the house of Jacques Bourgier, one of the principal citizens, and whose wife was a matron of good repute. She refused to attend a splendid banquet which had been provided for her, and passed nearly all her time in prayer.

When it was known by the English that the Maid was in Orleans, their minds were not less occupied about her than were the minds of those in the city, but it was in a very different spirit. The English believed in her supernatural mission as firmly as the French did; but they thought her a sorceress who had come to overthrow them by her enchantments. An old prophecy, which told that a damsel from Lorraine was to save France, had long been current and it was known and applied to Joan by foreigners as well as by the natives.

For months the English had heard of the coming Maid and the tales of miracles which she was said to have wrought, had been listened to by the rough yeomen of the English camp with anxious curiosity and secret awe. She had sent a herald to the English generals before she marched for Orleans; and he had summoned the English generals in the name of the Most High to give up to the Maid, who was sent by Heaven, the keys of the French cities which they had wrongfully taken; and he also solemnly adjured the English troops, whether archers, or men of the companies of war, or gentlemen or others, who were before the city of Orleans, to depart thence to their homes, under peril of being visited by the judgment of God. On her arrival in Orleans, Joan sent another similar message but the English scoffed at her from their towers, and threatened to burn her heralds. She determined before she shed the blood of the besiegers to repeat the warning with her own voice; and accordingly she mounted one of the boulevards of the town and thence she spoke to the English, and bade them depart, otherwise they would meet with shame and woe.

Sir William Gladsdale (whom the French call *Glacidas*) commanded the English post at the Tourelles, and he and another English officer replied by bidding her go home and keep her cows, and by ribald jests, that brought tears of shame and indignation into her eyes. But though the English leaders vaunted aloud, the effect produced on their army by Joan's presence in Orleans was proved four days after her arrival when, on the approach of reinforcements and stores to the town, Joan and La Hire marched out to meet them, and escorted the long train of provision wagons safely into Orleans, between the bastilles of the English, who cowered behind their walls, instead of charging fiercely and fearlessly, as had been their wont, on any French band that dared to show itself within reach.

VI

Thus far she had prevailed without striking a blow, but the time was now come to test her courage amid the horrors of actual slaughter. On the afternoon of the day on which she had escorted the reinforcements into the city, while she was resting fatigued at home, Dunois had seized an advantageous opportunity of attacking the English bastille of St. Loup, and a fierce assault of the Orleannais had been made on it, which the English garrison of the fort stubbornly resisted. Joan was roused by a sound which she believed to be that of her Heavenly Voices; she called for her arms and horse and quickly equipping herself she mounted to ride off to where the fight was raging. In her haste she had forgotten her banner; she rode back and without dismounting, had it given to her from the window, and then she galloped to the gate, whence the sally had been made.

On her way she met some of the wounded French who had been carried back from the fight. "Ha," she exclaimed, "I never can see French blood flow, without my hair standing on end." She rode out of the gate, and met the tide of her countrymen, who had been repulsed from the English fort and were flying back to Orleans in confusion. At the sight of the Holy Maid and her banner they rallied, and renewed the assault. Joan rode forward at their head, waving her banner and cheering them on. The English quailed at what they believed to be the charge of hell; St. Loup was stormed, and its

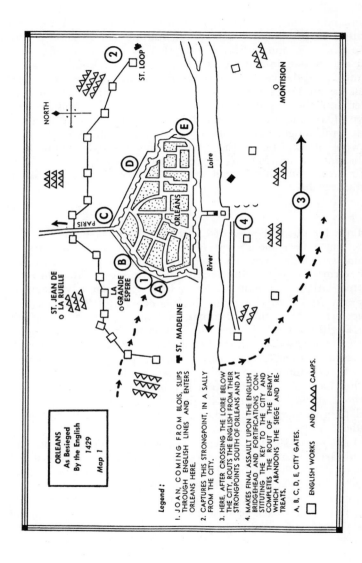

ORLEANS
As Besieged
By the English
1429
Map 1

NORTH

Legend:

1. JOAN, COMING FROM BLOIS, SLIPS THROUGH ENGLISH LINES AND ENTERS ORLEANS HERE.

2. CAPTURES THIS STRONGPOINT, IN A SALLY FROM THE CITY.

3. HERE, AFTER CROSSING THE LOIRE BELOW THE CITY, ROUTS THE ENGLISH FROM THEIR STRONGPOINTS SOUTH OF ORLEANS AND AT

4. MAKES FINAL ASSAULT UPON THE ENGLISH BRIDGEHEAD AND FORTIFICATIONS CONSTITUTING THE KEY TO THE CITY AND COMPLETES THE ROUT OF THE ENEMY, WHICH ABANDONS THE SIEGE AND RETREATS.

A, B, C, D, E, CITY GATES.

☐ ENGLISH WORKS   AND △△△△ CAMPS.

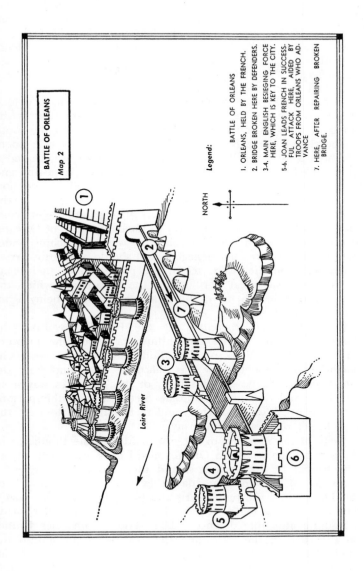

BATTLE OF ORLEANS
Map 2

Loire River

NORTH

Legend:

BATTLE OF ORLEANS

1. ORLEANS, HELD BY THE FRENCH.

2. BRIDGE BROKEN HERE BY DEFENDERS.

3-4. MAIN ENGLISH BESIEGING FORCE HERE, WHICH IS KEY TO THE CITY.

5-6. JOAN LEADS FRENCH IN SUCCESSFUL ATTACK HERE, AIDED BY TROOPS FROM ORLEANS WHO ADVANCE

7. HERE, AFTER REPAIRING BROKEN BRIDGE.

defenders put to the sword, except some few whom Joan succeeded in saving. All her woman's gentleness returned when the combat was over. It was the first time that she had ever seen a battle-field. She wept at the sight of so many blood-stained and mangled corpses; and her tears flowed doubly when she reflected that they were the bodies of Christian men who had died without confession.

The next day was Ascension-day, and it was passed by Joan in prayer. But on the following morrow it was resolved by the chiefs of the garrison to attack the English forts on the south of the river. For this purpose they crossed the river in boats, and after some severe fighting, in which the Maid was wounded in the heel, both the English bastilles of the Augustins and St. Jean de Blanc were captured. The Tourelles were now the only post which the besiegers held on the south of the river. But that post was formidably strong, and by its command of the bridge it was the key to the deliverance of Orleans. It was known that a fresh English army was approaching under Fastolfe to reinforce the besiegers, and should that army arrive while the Tourelles were yet in the possession of their comrades, there was great peril of all the advantages which the French had gained being nullified, and of the siege being again actively carried on.

It was resolved, therefore, by the French, to assail the Tourelles at once, while the enthusiasm which the presence and the heroic valour of the Maid had created was at its height. But the enterprise was difficult. The rampart of the *tête-de-pont,* or landward bulwark, of the Tourelles was steep and high and Sir John Gladsdale occupied this all-important fort with five hundred archers and men-at-arms, who were the very flower of the English army.

Early in the morning of the 7th of May, some thousands of the best French troops in Orleans heard mass and attended the confessional by Joan's orders; and then crossing the river in boats, as on the preceding day, they assailed the bulwark of the Tourelles, "with light hearts and heavy hands." But Gladsdale's men, encouraged by their bold and skilful leader, made a resolute and able defence. The Maid planted her banner on the edge of the fosse, and then springing down into the ditch, she placed the first ladder against the wall, and began to mount. An English archer sent an arrow at her, which

pierced her corslet and wounded her severely between the neck
and shoulder. She fell bleeding from the ladder and the
English were leaping down from the wall to capture her, but
her followers bore her off. She was carried to the rear, and
laid upon the grass; her armour was taken off, and the anguish
of her wound and the sight of her blood, made her at first
tremble and weep.

But her confidence in her celestial mission soon returned;
her patron saints seemed to stand before her, and reassure her.
She sat up and drew the arrow out with her own hands.
Some of the soldiers who stood by wished to stanch the blood
by saying a charm over the wound, but she forbade them,
saying, that she did not wish to be cured by unhallowed means.
She had the wound dressed with a little oil, and then bidding
her confessor come to her, she betook herself to prayer.

In the meanwhile, the English in the bulwark of the Tourelles
had repulsed the oft-renewed efforts of the French to scale the
wall. Dunois, who commanded the assailants, was at last discouraged, and gave orders for a retreat to be sounded. Joan
sent for him and the other generals, and implored them not
to despair. "By my God," she said to them, "you shall soon
enter in there. Do not doubt it. When you see my banner
wave again up to the wall, to your arms again! The fort is yours.
For the present, rest a little, and take some food and drink."
"They did so," says the old chronicler of the siege, "for they
obeyed her marvellously."

The faintness caused by her wound had now passed off, and
she headed the French in another rush against the bulwark.
The English, who had thought her slain, were alarmed at her
reappearance, while the French pressed furiously and fanatically
forward. A Biscayan soldier was carrying Joan's banner. She
had told the troops that directly the banner touched the wall
they should enter. The Biscayan waved the banner forward
from the edge of the fosse, and touched the wall with it; and
then all the French host swarmed madly up the ladders that
now were raised in all directions against the English fort. At
this crisis, the efforts of the English garrison were distracted
by an attack from another quarter. The French troops who
had been left in Orleans, had placed some planks over the
broken part of the bridge, and advanced across them to the
assault of the Tourelles on the northern side. Gladsdale re-

solved to withdraw his men from the landward bulwark and concentrate his whole force in the Tourelles themselves. He was passing for this purpose across the drawbridge that connected the Tourelles and the *tête-de-pont,* when Joan, who by this time had scaled the wall of the bulwark, called out to him, "Surrender, surrender to the King of Heaven. Ah, Glacidas, you have foully wronged me with your words, but I have great pity on your soul and the souls of your men."

The Englishman, disdainful of her summons, was striding on across the drawbridge, when a cannon-shot from the town carried it away, and Gladsdale perished in the water that ran beneath. After his fall, the remnant of the English abandoned all further resistance. Three hundred of them had been killed in the battle, and two hundred were made prisoners.

The broken arch was speedily repaired by the exulting Orleannais; and Joan made her triumphal re-entry into the city by the bridge that had so long been closed. Every church in Orleans rang out its gratulating peal; and throughout the night the sounds of rejoicing echoed, and the bonfires blazed up from the city. But in the lines and forts which the besiegers yet retained on the northern shore there was anxious watching of the generals, and there was desponding gloom among the soldiery. Even Talbot now counselled retreat.

On the following morning, the Orleannais, from their walls, saw the great forts called "London" and "St. Lawrence" in flames; and witnessed their invaders busy in destroying the stores and munitions which had been relied on for the destruction of Orleans. Slowly and sullenly the English army retired, but not before it had drawn up in battle array opposite to the city, as if to challenge the garrison to an encounter. The French troops were eager to go out and attack, but Joan forbade it. The day was Sunday. "In the name of God," she said, "let them depart, and let us return thanks to God." She led the soldiers and citizens forth from Orleans, but not for the shedding of blood. They passed in solemn procession round the city walls; and then, while their retiring enemies were yet in sight, they knelt in thanksgiving to God for the deliverance which He had vouchsafed them.

VII

Within three months from the time of her first interview with the dauphin, Joan had fulfilled the first part of her promise, the raising of the siege of Orleans. Within three months more she fulfilled the second part also; and she stood with her banner in her hand by the high altar at Rheims, while he was anointed and crowned as King Charles VII of France. In the interval she had taken Jargeau, Troyes, and other strong places and she had defeated an English army in a fair field at Patay. The enthusiasm of her countrymen knew no bounds; but the importance of her services, and especially of her primary achievement at Orleans, may perhaps be best proved by the testimony of her enemies. There is extant a fragment of a letter from the Regent Bedford to his royal nephew, Henry VI, in which he bewails the turn that the war had taken, and especially attributes it to the raising of the siege of Orleans by Joan. Bedford's own words, are as follows:

"And alle thing there prospered for you til the tyme of the Siege of Orleans, taken in hand, God knoweth by what advis.

"At the whiche tyme, after the adventure fallen to the persone of my cousin of Salisbury, whom God assoille, there felle, by the hand of God as it seemeth, a great strook upon your peuple that was assembled there in grete nombre, caused in grete partie, as y trowe, of lakke of saddle believe, and of unlevefulle doubte, that thei hadde of a disciple and lyme of the Feende, called the Pucelle, that used fals enchantments and sorcerie.

"The whiche strooke and discomfiture not oonly lessed in grete parie the nombre of your peuple ther, but as well withdrewe the courage of the remenant in merveillous wyse, and couraiged your adverse partie and ennemys to assemble them forthwith in grete nombre."

When Charles had been anointed King of France, Joan believed that her mission was accomplished. And in truth the deliverance of France from the English, though not completed for many years afterwards, was then ensured. The ceremony of a royal coronation and anointment was not in those days regarded as a mere costly formality. It was believed to confer the sanction and the grace of Heaven upon the prince, who had previously ruled with mere human authority. Thenceforth he was the Lord's anointed. Moreover, one of the difficulties that had previously lain in the way of many Frenchmen when called on to support Charles VII, was now removed. He had been publicly stigmatised, even by his own parents, as no true son of the royal race of France. The queen-mother, the English, and the partisans of Burgundy, called him the "Pretender to the title of Dauphin;" but those who had been led to doubt his legitimacy, were cured of their scepticism by the victories of the Holy Maid, and by the fulfilment of her pledges. They thought that Heaven had now declared itself in favour of Charles as the true heir of the crown of St. Louis; and the tales about his being spurious were thenceforth regarded as mere English calumnies.

With this strong tide of national feeling in his favour, with victorious generals and soldiers round him, and a dispirited and divided enemy before him, he could not fail to conquer. Though his own imprudence and misconduct, and the stubborn valour which some of the English still displayed, prolonged the war in France nearly to the time when the civil war of the Roses broke out in England, and ensured for France peace and repose.

Joan knelt before the new-crowned king in the cathedral of Rheims, and shed tears of joy. She said that she had then fulfilled the work which the Lord had commanded her. The young girl now asked for her dismissal. She wished to return to her peasant home, to tend her parents' flocks again, and to live at her own will in her native village. She had always believed that her career would be a short one.

But Charles and his captains were loth to lose the presence of one who had such an influence upon the soldiery and the people. They persuaded her to stay with the army. She still showed the same bravery and zeal for the cause of France. She was as fervent as before in her prayers, and as exemplary in all religious duties. She still heard her Heavenly voices, but she now no longer thought herself the appointed minister of Heaven to lead her countrymen to certain victory. Our admiration for her courage and patriotism ought to be increased a hundred-fold by her conduct throughout the latter part of her career, amid dangers, against which she no longer believed herself to be divinely secured. Indeed she believed herself doomed to perish in little more than a year, but she still fought on as resolutely, if not as exultingly as ever.

As in the case of Arminius, the interest attached to individual heroism and virtue makes us trace the fate of Joan of Arc after she had saved her country. She served well with Charles's army in the capture of Laon, Soissons, Compeigne, Beauvais, and other strong places; but in a premature attack on Paris, in September, 1429, the French were repulsed, and Joan was severely wounded. In the winter she was again in the field with some of the French troops and in the following spring she threw herself into the fortress of Compeigne, which she had herself won for the French king in the preceding autumn, and which was now besieged by a strong Burgundian force.

She was taken prisoner in a sally from Compeigne, on the 24th of May, and was imprisoned by the Burgundians first at Arras, and then at a place called Crotoy, on the Flemish coast, until November, when for payment of a large sum of money she was given up to the English, and taken to Rouen, which was then their main stronghold in France.

> "Sorrow it were, and shame to tell,
> The butchery that there befell:"

The revolting details of the cruelties practised upon this young girl may be left to those whose duty, as avowed biographers, it is to describe them. She was tried before an ecclesiastical tribunal on the charge of witchcraft, and on the 30th of May 1431 she was burnt alive in the market-place at Rouen.

(This sentence was annulled, *pro forma,* in 1456, a quarter of a century after her death, following a rehabilitation trial ordered by Charles VII. Joan was beatified in 1909 and canonized in 1919.)

SYNOPSIS OF EVENTS BETWEEN JOAN OF ARC'S VICTORY AT ORLEANS, 1429, AND THE DEFEAT OF THE SPANISH ARMADA, 1588.

1452. Final expulsion of the English from France.

1453. Constantinople taken, and the Roman Empire of the East destroyed by the Turkish Sultan Mahomet II.

1455. Commencement of the civil wars in England between the houses of York and Lancaster.

1479. Union of the Christian kingdoms of Spain under Ferdinand and Isabella.

1492. Capture of Grenada by Ferdinand and Isabella, and end of the Moorish dominion in Spain.

1492. Columbus discovers the New World.

1494. Charles VIII. of France invades Italy.

1497. Expedition of Vasco di Gama to the East Indies round the Cape of Good Hope.

1503. Naples conquered from the French by the great Spanish general, Gonsalvo of Cordova.

1508. League of Cambray, by the Pope, the Emperor, and the King of France, against Venice.

1509. Albuquerque establishes the empire of the Portuguese in the East Indies.

1516. Death of Ferdinand of Spain; he is succeeded by his grandson Charles, afterwards the Emperor Charles V.

1517. Dispute between Luther and Tetzel respecting the sale of indulgences; which is the immediate cause of the Reformation.

1519. Charles V. is elected Emperor of Germany.

1519. Cortes begins his conquest of Mexico.

1525. Francis I. of France defeated and taken prisoner by the imperial army at Pavia.

1529. League of Smalcald formed by the Protestant princes of Germany.

1532. Pizarro begins his conquest of Peru.

1533. Henry VIII. renounces the Papal supremacy.

1547. Henry VIII. dies; Mary succeeds as Queen of England.

1556. Abdication of the Emperor Charles V. Philip II. becomes King of Spain, and Ferdinand I. Emperor of Germany.

1557. Mary dies and Elizabeth becomes Queen of England.

1557. The Spaniards defeat the French at the battle of St. Quentin.

1571. Don John of Austria at the head of the Spanish fleet, aided by the Venetian and the Papal squadrons, defeats the Turks at Lepanto.

1572. Massacre of the Protestants in France on St. Bartholomew's day.

1579. The Netherlands revolt against Spain.

1580. Philip II. conquers Portugal.

TEN

The Spanish Armada, 1588

WHY DECISIVE: *"One nation only had been his [Philip II's] active, his persevering, his successful foe. . . . Were she (England) once subdued . . . universal dominion seemed sure to be the result of the conquest , of that . . . nation."* [Creasy]. *"In that memorable year, when Europe stood by in fearful suspense to behold what should be the result of that great cast in the game of human politics, what the craft of Rome, the power of Philip, the genius of Farnese [Prince of Parma, captain-general of the Spanish armies, the greatest military leader of his age] could not achieve against the island-queen with her Drakes and Cecils—in that agony of the Protestant faith and the English name [the Armada was destroyed]."* [Hume.]

I

O N the afternoon of the 19th of July, A.D. 1588, a group of English captains was collected at the bowling green on the Hoe at Plymouth, whose equals have never before or since been brought together, even at that favourite mustering-place of the heroes of the British navy. There was Sir Francis Drake, the first English circumnavigator of the globe, the terror of every Spanish coast in the Old World and the New; there was Sir John Hawkins, the rough veteran of many a daring voyage on the African and American seas, and of many a desperate battle; there was Sir Martin Frobisher, one of the earliest explorers of the Arctic seas in search of that North-West Passage which long was the darling object of England's boldest mariners. There was the high-admiral of England, Lord Howard of Effingham, prodigal of all things in his country's cause, and who had recently had the noble daring to refuse to dismantle part of the fleet, though the queen had sent him orders to do so, in consequence of an exaggerated report that the enemy had been driven back and shattered by a storm. Lord Howard (whom contemporary writers describe as being of a wise and noble courage, skilful in sea matters, wary and provident, and of great esteem among the sailors) resolved to risk his sovereign's anger, and to keep the ships afloat at his own charge, rather than that England should run the peril of losing their protection.

Another of our Elizabethan sea-kings, Sir Walter Raleigh, was at that time commissioned to raise and equip the land-forces of Cornwall; but, as he was also commander of Plymouth, we may well believe that he must have availed himself of the opportunity of consulting with the lord-admiral and other high officers, which was offered by the English fleet putting into that port; and we may look on Raleigh as one of the group that was assembled at the bowling green on the Hoe. Many other brave men and skilful mariners, besides the chiefs whose names have been mentioned, were there, enjoying, with true sailor-like merriment their temporary relaxation from duty. In the harbour lay the English fleet with which they had just returned from a cruise to Corunna in search of information respecting the real condition and movements of the hostile armada. Lord Howard had ascertained that our enemies, though tempest-tost, were still formidably strong and fearing that part of their fleet might make for England in his absence, he had hurried back to the Devonshire coast. He resumed his station at Plymouth, and waited there for certain tidings of the Spaniard's approach.

A match at bowls was being played, in which Drake and other high officers of the fleet were engaged, when a small armed vessel was seen running before the wind into Plymouth harbour, with all sails set. Her commander landed in haste, and eagerly sought the place where the English lord-admiral and his captains were standing. His name was Fleming; he was the master of a Scotch privateer and he told the English officers that he had that morning seen the Spanish Armada off the Cornish coast.

At this exciting information the captains began to hurry down to the water, and there was a shouting for the ships' boats; but Drake coolly checked his comrades and insisted that the match should be played out. He said that there was plenty of time both to win the game and beat the Spaniards. The best and bravest match that ever was scored was resumed accordingly. Drake and his friends aimed their last bowls with the same steady calculating coolness with which they were about to point their guns. The winning cast was made; and then they went on board, and prepared for action, with their hearts as light and their nerves as firm as they had been on the Hoe bowling green.

Meanwhile the messengers and signals had been despatched fast and far through England, to warn each town and village that the enemy had come at last. In every seaport there was instant making ready by land and by sea; in every shire and every city there was instant mustering of horse and man. But England's best defence then, as ever, was her fleet; and after warping laboriously out of Plymouth harbour against the wind, the lord-admiral stood westward under easy sail, keeping an anxious look-out for the armada, the approach of which was soon announced by Cornish fisher-boats, and signals from the Cornish cliffs.

II

The England of our own days is so strong, and the Spain of our own days is so feeble, that it is not possible, without some reflection and care, to comprehend the full extent of the peril which England then ran from the power and the ambition of Spain, or to appreciate the importance of that crisis in the history of the world.

Queen Elizabeth had found at her accession (thirty years before) an encumbered revenue, a divided people, and an unsuccessful foreign war, in which the last remnant of our possessions in France had been lost; she had also a formidable pretender to her crown, whose interests were favoured by all the Roman Catholic powers; and even some of her subjects were warped by religious bigotry to deny her title, and to look on her as an heretical usurper. It is true that during the years of her reign which had passed away before the attempted invasion of 1588, she had revived the commercial prosperity, the national spirit, and the national loyalty of England. But her resources, to cope with the colossal power of Philip II, still seemed most scanty; and she had not a single foreign ally, except the Dutch, who were themselves struggling hard, and, as it seemed, hopelessly, to maintain their revolt against Spain.

On the other hand Philip II was absolute master of an empire so superior to the other states of the world in extent, in resources, and especially in military and naval forces, as to make the project of enlarging that empire into a universal monarchy seem a perfectly feasible scheme; and Philip had both the ambition to form that project, and the resolution to devote all his energies, and all his means, to its realisation. Since the downfall of the Roman Empire no such preponderating power had existed in the world.

During the medieval centuries the chief European kingdoms were slowly moulding themselves out of the feudal chaos. And, though their wars with each other were numerous and desperate, and several of their respective kings figured for a time as mighty conquerors, none of them in those times acquired the consistency and perfect organisation which are requisite for a long-sustained career of aggrandisement. After the consolidation of the great kingdoms, they for some time kept each other in mutual check. During the first half of the sixteenth century, the balancing system was successfully practised by European statesmen.

(This system became known in international relations as "the balance of power." It depended upon operation of the principle that, to quote the Columbia Encyclopedia, "the maintenance of peace depends on no nation's becoming powerful enough to menace the independence of any other. . . . Grotius (Dutch jurist and humanist, 1583-1645) in his codification of international law in the 17th century stated the principles of the balance of power; and the development of nationalism increased its importance." To it were due the various coalitions of Europe, such as the Holy Alliance (product of the religious zeal of Czar Alexander I. The Alliance was merely a vague agreement that the subscribing powers, which ultimately included all the countries of Europe excepting England and Turkey, besides the Vatican, would conduct themselves according to Christian principles) which became symbol and instrument of political reaction. The League of Nations was designed to replace the balance of power by keeping peace through community action and cooperation.)

But when Philip II reigned, France had become so miserably weak through her civil wars, that he had nothing to dread from the rival state, which had so long curbed his father the Emperor Charles V. In Germany, Italy, and Poland, he had either zealous friends and dependents, or weak and divided enemies. Against the Turks he had gained great and glorious successes; and he might look round the continent of Europe without discerning a single antagonist of whom he could stand in awe.

Spain, when he acceded to the throne, was at the zenith of

her power. The hardihood and spirit which the Arragonese, the Castilians, and the other nations of the peninsula had acquired during centuries of free institutions and successful war against the Moors, had not yet become obliterated. Charles V had, indeed, destroyed the liberties of Spain, but that had been done too recently for its full evil to be felt in Philip's time. A people cannot be debased in a single generation and the Spaniards under Charles V and Philip II proved the truth of the remark, that no nation is ever so formidable to its neighbours for a time as is a nation which, after being trained up in self-government, passes suddenly under a despotic ruler. The energy of democratic institutions survives for a few generations and to it are superadded the decision and certainty, which are the attributes of government, when all its powers are directed by a single mind. It is true that this preternatural vigour is short-lived; national corruption and debasement gradually follow the loss of the national liberties; but there is an interval before their workings are felt, and in that interval the most ambitious schemes of foreign conquest are often successfully undertaken.

Philip had also the advantage of finding himself at the head of a large standing army in a perfect state of discipline and equipment, in an age when, except some few insignificant corps, standing armies were unknown in Christendom. The renown of the Spanish troops was justly high, and the infantry in particular was considered the best in the world. His fleet, also, was far more numerous, and better appointed, than that of any other European power; and both his soldiers and his sailors had the confidence in themselves and their commanders which a long career of successful warfare alone can create.

Besides the Spanish crown, Philip succeeded to the kingdom of Naples and Sicily, the duchy of Milan, Franche-Conté, (an old province of eastern France) and the Netherlands. In Africa he possessed Tunis, Oran, the Cape Verde, and the Canary Islands; and in Asia, the Philippine and Sunda Islands, and a part of the Moluccas. Beyond the Atlantic he was lord of the most splendid portions of the New World which "Columbus found for Castile and Leon." The empires of Peru and Mexico, New Spain, and Chile, with their abundant mines of precious metals, Hispaniola and Cuba, and many other of the American islands, were provinces of the sovereign of Spain.

Philip had, indeed, experienced the mortification of seeing the inhabitants of the Netherlands revolt against his authority, nor could he succeed in bringing back beneath the Spanish sceptre all the possessions which his father had bequeathed to him. But he had reconquered a large number of the towns and districts that originally took up arms against him. Belgium was brought more thoroughly into implicit obedience to Spain than she had been before her insurrection, and it was only Holland and the six other Northern States that still held out against his arms. The contest had also formed a compact and veteran army on Philip's side, which, under his great general, the Prince of Parma, had been trained to act together under all difficulties and all vicissitudes of warfare; and on whose steadiness and loyalty perfect reliance might be placed throughout any enterprise, however difficult and tedious.

Alexander Farnese, Prince of Parma, captain-general of the Spanish armies, and governor of the Spanish possessions in the Netherlands, was beyond all comparison the greatest military genius of his age. He was also highly distinguished for political wisdom and sagacity, and for his great administrative talents. He was idolised by his troops, whose affections he knew how to win without relaxing their discipline or diminishing his own authority. Pre-eminently cool and circumspect in his plans, but swift and energetic when the moment arrived for striking a decisive blow, neglecting no risk that caution could provide against, conciliating even the populations of the districts which he attacked, by his scrupulous good faith, his moderation, and his address, Farnese was one of the most formidable generals that ever could be placed at the head of an army designed not only to win battles, but to effect conquests. Happy it is for England and the world that this island was saved from becoming an arena for the exhibition of his powers.

Whatever diminution the Spanish empire might have sustained in the Netherlands, seemed to be more than compensated by the acquisition of Portugal, which Philip had completely conquered in 1580. Not only that ancient kingdom itself, but all the fruits of the maritime enterprises of the Portuguese had fallen into Philip's hands. All the Portuguese colonies in America, Africa, and the East Indies, acknowledged the sovereignty of the King of Spain who thus not only united the whole Iberian peninsula under his single sceptre, but had acquired a transmarine empire, little inferior in wealth and extent to that which he had inherited at his accession.

The splendid victory which his fleet, in conjunction with the Papal and Venetian galleys, had gained at Lepanto over the Turks, had deservedly exalted the fame of the Spanish marine throughout Christendom; and when Philip had reigned thirty-five years, the vigour of his empire seemed unbroken, and the glory of the Spanish arms had increased, and was increasing throughout the world.

One nation only had been his active, his preserving, and his successful foe. England had encouraged his revolted subjects in Flanders against him, and given them the aid in men and money, without which they must soon have been humbled in the dust. English ships had plundered his colonies; had defied his supremacy in the New World, as well as the Old; they had inflicted ignominious defeats on his squadrons; they had captured his cities, and burned his arsenals on the very coasts of Spain. The English had made Philip himself the object of personal insult. He was held up to ridicule in their stage plays and masks, and these scoffs at the man had (as is not unusual in such cases) excited the anger of the absolute king even more vehemently than the injuries inflicted on his power. Personal as well as political revenge urged him to attack England. Were she once subdued, the Dutch must submit; France could not cope with him, the empire would not oppose him and universal dominion seemed sure to be the result of the conquest of that malignant island.

III

There was yet another and a stronger feeling which armed King Philip against England. He was one of the sincerest and sternest bigots of his age. He looked on himself, and was looked on by others, as the appointed champion to extirpate heresy and re-establish the Papal power throughout Europe. A powerful reaction against Protestantism had taken place since the commencement of the second half of the sixteenth century, and Philip believed that he was destined to complete it.

The Reform doctrines had been thoroughly rooted out from Italy and Spain. Belgium, which had previously been half Protestant, had been reconquered both in allegiance and creed

by Philip, and had become one of the most Catholic countries
in the world. Half of Germany had been won back to the old
faith. In Savoy, in Switzerland, and many other countries, the
progress of the counter-Reformation had been rapid and
decisive. The Catholic league seemed victorious in France. The
Papal Court itself had shaken off the supineness of recent
centuries and, at the head of the Jesuits and the other new
ecclesiastical orders, was displaying a vigour and a boldness
worthy of the days of Hildebrand or Innocent III.

Throughout continental Europe, the Protestants, discomfited
and dismayed, looked to England as their protector and refuge.
England was the acknowledged central point of Protestant
power and policy and to conquer England was to stab Protestantism to the very heart. Sixtus V., the then reigning pope,
earnestly exhorted Philip to this enterprise. And when the
tidings reached Italy and Spain that the Protestant Queen
of England had put to death her Catholic prisoner, Mary
Queen of Scots, the fury of the Vatican and the Escurial knew no
bounds.

The Prince of Parma, who was appointed military chief of
the expedition, collected on the coasts of Flanders a veteran
force that was planned to play a principal part in the conquest of England. Besides the troops who were in his garrisons,
or under his colours, five thousand infantry were sent to him
from northern and central Italy, four thousand from the kingdom of Naples, six thousand from Castile, three thousand from
Arragon, three thousand from Austria and Germany, together
with four squadrons of heavy-armed horse; besides which he
received forces from the Franche-Comté and the Walloon
country.

By his command, the forest of Waes was felled for the purpose
of building flat-bottomed boats, which, floating down the
rivers and canals to Meinport and Dunkerque, were to carry
this large army of chosen troops to the mouth of the Thames,
under the escort of the great Spanish fleet. Gun-carriages,
fascines, machines used in sieges, together with every material
requisite for building bridges, forming camps, and raising
fortresses, were to be placed on board the flotillas of the
Prince of Parma, who followed up the conquest of the Netherlands, whilst he was making preparations for the invasion of
this island.

Favoured by the dissensions between the insurgents of the United Provinces and Leicester, the Prince of Parma had recovered Deventer, as well as a fort before Zutphen, which the English commanders, Sir William Stanley and Sir Roland York, had surrendered to him, when with their troops they passed over to the service of Philip II, after the death of Mary Stuart, and he had also made himself master of the Sluys. His intention was to leave to the Count de Mansfeldt sufficient forces to follow up the war with the Dutch, which had now become a secondary object, whilst he himself went at the head of fifty thousand men of the armada and the flotilla, to accomplish the principal enterprise—that enterprise, which, in the highest degree, affected the interests of the pontifical authority. In a bull, intended to be kept secret until the day of landing, Sixtus V., renewing the anathema fulminated against Elizabeth by Pius V. and Gregory XIII., affected to depose her from our throne.

Elizabeth was denounced as a murderous heretic whose destruction was an instant duty. A formal treaty was concluded (in June, 1587), by which the pope bound himself to contribute a million scudi to the expenses of the war; the money to be paid as soon as the king had actual possession of an English port. Philip, on his part, strained the resources of his vast empire to the utmost. The French Catholic chiefs eagerly cooperated with him. In the seaports of the Mediterranean, and along almost the whole coast from Gibraltar to Jutland, the preparations for the great armament were urged forward with all the earnestness of religious zeal, as well as of angry ambition.

"Thus," says Ranke, the German historian of the popes, "thus did the united powers of Italy and Spain, from which such mighty influences had gone forth over the whole world, now rouse themselves for an attack upon England! The king had already compiled, from the archives of Simancas, a statement of the claims which he had to the throne of that country on the extinction of the Stuart line; the most brilliant prospects, especially that of an universal dominion of the seas, were associated in his mind with this enterprise.

"Everything seemed to conspire to such end; the predominance of Catholicism in Germany, the renewed attack upon the Huguenots in France, the attempt upon Geneva, and the

enterprise against England. At the same moment a thoroughly
Catholic prince, Sigismund III., ascended the throne of Pol⋅•.d,
with the prospect also of future succession to the throne of
Sweden. But whenever any principle or power, be it what
it may, aims at unlimited supremacy in Europe, some vigorous
resistance to it, having its origin in the deepest springs of
human nature, invariably arises.

"Philip II. had had to encounter newly-awakened powers,
braced by the vigour of youth, and elevated by a sense of their
future destiny. The intrepid corsairs, who had rendered every
sea insecure, now clustered round the coasts of their native
island. The Protestants in a body,—even the Puritans, although
they had been subjected to as severe oppressions as the Catholics,
—rallied round their queen, who now gave admirable proof of
her masculine courage, and her princely talent of winning the
affections, and leading the minds, and preserving the allegiance
of men."

Ranke should have added that the English Catholics at
this crisis proved themselves as loyal to their queen, and
true to their country, as were the most vehement anti-Catholic
zealots in the island. Some few traitors there were, but as a
body, the Englishmen who held the ancient faith stood the
trial of their patriotism nobly. The lord-admiral himself was
a Catholic, and (to adopt the words of Hallam) "then it was
that the Catholics in every county repaired to the standard
of the lord-lieutenant, imploring that they might not be suspected of bartering the national independence for their religion
itself." The Spaniard found few partisans in the country which
he assailed.

IV

For some time the destination of the enormous armament
of Philip was not publicly announced. Only Philip himself,
the Pope Sixtus, the Duke of Guise, and Philip's favourite
minister, Mendoza, at first knew its real object. Rumours
were sedulously spread that it was designed to proceed to
the Indies to realise vast projects of distant conquest. Sometimes hints were dropped by Philip's ambassadors in foreign
courts, that his master had resolved on a decisive effort to
crush his rebels in the Low Countries. But Elizabeth and
her statesmen could not view the gathering of such a storm

without feeling the probability of its bursting on their own shores.

As early as the spring of 1587, Elizabeth sent Sir Francis Drake to cruise off the Tagus. Drake sailed into the Bay of Cadiz and the Lisbon roads, and burnt much shipping and military stores, causing thereby an important delay in the progress of the Spanish preparations. Drake called this "singeing the King of Spain's beard." Elizabeth also increased her succours of troops to the Netherlands, to prevent the Prince of Parma from overwhelming them, and from thence being at full leisure to employ his army against her dominions.

Each party at this time thought it politic to try to amuse its adversary by pretending to treat for peace, and negotiations were opened at Ostend in the beginning of 1588, which were prolonged during the first six months of that year. Nothing real was effected, and probably nothing real had been intended to be effected by them. But, in the meantime, each party had been engaged in important communications with the chief powers in France, in which Elizabeth seemed at first to have secured a great advantage, but in which Philip ultimately prevailed. As Mignet explains: "Henry III. of France was alarmed at the negotiations that were going on at Ostend; and he especially dreaded any accommodation between Spain and England, in consequence of which Philip II. might be enabled to subdue the United Provinces, and make himself master of France. In order, therefore, to dissuade Elizabeth from any arrangement, he offered to support her, in case she were attacked by the Spaniards, with twice the number of troops, which he was bound by the treaty of 1574 to send to her assistance. He had a long conference with her ambassador, Stafford, upon this subject, and told him that the pope and the Catholic king had entered into a league against the queen, his mistress, and had invited himself and the Venetians to join them, but they had refused to do so. 'If the Queen of England,' he added, 'concludes a peace with the Catholic king, that peace will not last three months, because the Catholic king will aid the League with all his forces to overthrow her, and you may imagine what fate is reserved for your mistress after that.'

"On the other hand, in order most effectually to frustrate this negotiation, he proposed to Philip II. to form a still closer union between the two crowns of France and Spain and, at the same time, he secretly despatched a confidential envoy to Constantinople to warn the Sultan that if he did not again declare war against the Catholic king, that monarch, who already possessed the Netherlands, Portugal, Spain, the Indies, and nearly all Italy, would soon make himself master of England, and would then turn the forces of all Europe against the Turks."

But Philip had an ally in France, who was far more powerful than the French king. This was the Duke of Guisè, the chief of the League, and the idol of the fanatic partisans of the Romish faith. Philip prevailed on Guise openly to take up arms against Henry III. (who was reviled by the Leaguers as a traitor to the true Church, and a secret friend to the Huguenots) and thus prevent the French king from interfering in favour of Queen Elizabeth. "With this object, the commander, Juan Iniguez Moreo, was despatched by him in the early part of April to the Duke of Guise at Soissons," narrates Mignet. He met with complete success. He offered the Duke of Guise, as soon as he took the field against Henry III., three hundred thousands crowns, six thousand infantry, and twelve hundred pikemen, on behalf of the king his master, who would, in addition, withdraw his ambassador from the court of France, and accredit an envoy to the Catholic party. A treaty was concluded on these conditions, and the Duke of Guise entered Paris, where he was expected by the Leaguers, and whence he expelled Henry III. on the 12th of May, by the insurrection of the barricades. A fortnight after this insurrection, which reduced Henry III. to impotence, and, to use the language of the Prince of Parma, did not even 'permit him to assist the Queen of England with his tears, as he needed them all to weep over his own misfortunes,' the Spanish fleet left the Tagus and sailed towards the British Isles."

V*

Thirty years of peace were supposed abroad to have emasculated the once warlike English nation, and to have so enamoured the people of quiet that they had no longer energy to defend their own firesides. If their vigour was unimpaired it was held

*From here the story of the Armada is taken in part from James Anthony Froude's "The Reign of Queen Elizabeth." The reader may judge for himself as to the soundness of Froude's promise to, in effect, make his story of the Armada "as interesting as a novel." EDITOR.

certainly that they must want skill and experience. Their peculiar weapon the long bow, though it had not yet become a toy for the playground, could no longer decide a battle in the face of muskets and cannon; and ardent Catholic Europe expected confidently that in collision with the trained regiments of Spain or France, the English militia would break in pieces at the first encounter. On the sea they were acknowledged to be still dangerous. The English corsair was a name of terror wherever there were Catholic traders to be pillaged. English merchantmen in the Mediterranean defied, engaged, and defeated the royal galleys of Spain, though outmatched to twice their strength. The general impression, however, was that if the naval defences could be pierced, and a well-founded army be thrown on shore in any part of the kingdom, the power of England would collapse in ruins. London itself was undefended and there was not a fortress in the whole island which would delay an army for an hour.

It has been seen that the Prince of Parma knew better what the country was made of. Although the hundred Beef-eaters (palace guards, so nicknamed by the London populace because one of the prescribed staples of their rations was always beef, despite that it rarely was available to poorer folk) at court constituted the only permanently existing force in the service of the government, yet English and Spanish soldiers had encountered in many a hard fight on the Antwerp dykes or in the open field, and man to man the Spaniard could claim no superiority. Parma had experienced at Sluys that their engineering skill was not contemptible. He knew perhaps, to use the language of a writer, who after his own people respected the Spaniards above all other nations in the world, that "the English had always been, and at that present were, a free people, such as in few or no other realms were to be found the like, by which freedom was maintained a valiant courage in that people." Flanders, France, and Ireland had been training schools where many thousands of Englishmen of all ranks had learnt the art as well as the practice of war, while for the last eight years the militia had been carefully trained in the use of the modern weapons. Volunteer military schools had been established all over the country, gentlemen who had served abroad drilling the sons of the knights and squires. Three hundred London merchants who had seen service took charge of the city corps, and the example it is likely was imitated in the other towns; while along the coast the privateering trade had made lessons in fighting a part of the education of every high-spirited lad.

In this way for eight years all England had been in preparation for the day of trial. It had not been without danger, for the general military organisation had been made a shield behind which the Catholic families had been invited to make ready for rebellion. But the recusants were known and marked; though every able-bodied man was put in training, the custody of the arms was reserved for those who could be trusted; while the Protestants had the essential advantage that only they could furnish experienced soldiers. The Catholic English who made war their profession were serving abroad in the armies of Parma or Guise.

Thus it was that when the long-talked-of peril was at the doors, and the people were called on to take their harness to resist invasion, a hundred thousand men, well officered and appointed, were ready at a day's notice to fall into their companies, and move wherever they were wanted. In the uncertainty where the Spaniards would land they were left at their homes, but with their line of action accurately laid down. The musters of the midland counties, thirty thousand strong, were to form a separate army for the defence of the queen's person, and were directed to assemble on the first note of alarm between Windsor and Harrow. The rest were to gather to the point of danger. The coast companies had orders to fall back, wherever the enemy landed, removing the corn and cattle, and avoiding a battle till the force of the neighbouring counties joined them. Should the landing be, as was expected, in Suffolk, Kent, or Sussex, it was calculated that between thirty and forty thousand men could be thrown in their way before they could reach London, while twenty thousand would still remain to encounter Guise, should he attempt a diversion in Hampshire or Dorsetshire.

VI

It was not by land, however, either that the Spaniards most feared the English, or that English statesmen and officers most relied on the powers of the country to defend itself, if it was only allowed fair play. An Englishman writing from Lisbon in the heat of the preparations for the Armada, reported, "that he had talked to many of the people there. They confessed they feared England on the water, but not on the land. The English, they said, were better warriors than they on the seas. Their mariners and gunners were better, and they feared their fireworks." Their experience with Drake and Hawkins and their companions had made them modestly conscious of their own inferiority where numbers were in any way equal.

But a fleet was not like the militia, a thing which the country could extemporise out of its own resources. The sea towns and private adventurers could fit out merchantmen to fight effectively against an enemy of their own size and strength; but the largest ship in England at this time belonging to a private owner did not exceed four hundred tons, and of vessels of that size there were not more than two or three sailing from any port in the country. The armed cruisers which had won so distinguished a name in both hemispheres were of the dimensions of the present schooner yachts in the Cowes squadron. Philip, as a paternal governor, had encouraged shipbuilding in Spain by grants from the crown. Elizabeth had been advised to imitate the example. But she had preferred to leave her subjects to their own enterprise, nor had she cared herself to lead the way of improvement.

When her naval resources were all counted, including vessels which had been built by her father and sister, (Queen Mary) the entire English navy contained but thirteen ships above four hundred tons, and in the whole fleet, including fifteen small cutters and pinnaces, there were only thirty-eight vessels of all sorts and sizes carrying the queen's flag. She had extended to the dockyards the same hard thrift with which she had pared down her expenses everywhere. One precaution only she had taken on the other side, characteristic also of herself. She had placed at the head of her naval administration the fittest person in her dominions to manage it—Sir John Hawkins—who, sea robber, corsair, slave hunter, as he was, yet with scrupulous fidelity threw his mind and his fortune into his charge. When the moment of trial came, Hawkins sent her ships to sea in such condition, hull, rigging, spars, and running rope, that they had no match in the world either for speed, safety, or endurance. In the small *Swallow*, which had been built by King Henry, Lord Howard offered to sail to Rio Janeiro in the wildest storm that could blow.

A few words in detail may be spared to the constitution of the fleet which was about to accomplish so splendid a service. In ordinary times, one or two second class vessels alone were kept in commission, which discharged the duties very imperfectly of Channel police. The navy did not exist as a profession. It was the queen's policy to appear as little as possible in any work that had to be done, and to leave it to privateers. When officers were wanted, they were chosen from those who, like Sir Francis Drake, had distinguished themselves as adventurers. The crews were engaged by the week, by the month, or for some special service. A commission was appointed in 1583 to examine into the condition of ships and stores, and so to organize the yards at Portsmouth and Chatham that a squadron could be held ready for sea if suddenly called for.

The whole navy was then thoroughly overhauled and repaired. The charges for its future maintenance were divided into ordinary and extraordinary. The first covered repairs of all kinds, wages of shipwrights, carpenters, clerks, watchmen, and cost of timbers, ropes, anchors, mooring cables, and other necessary dockyard expenses. For all this the queen allowed four thousand pounds a year. She thought the sum excessive, but it could not be brought lower. The second, or extra-ordinary charges, covered special expeditions, for which in every instance a particular estimate was made by the council, with the lighter cordage, canvas, provisions, and other perishable stores of which the consumption varied with the nature and extent of the service. It included also the building of wharves, sheds, and storehouses, and also of new ships, of which it was then decided that one at least must every year be added to the fleet. Construction of this kind was done by contract. The ships were expected to last in good condition thirty years at least.

The *Bonaventura*, a vessel of six hundred tons, was built in 1560. She was with Drake in his expedition to the West Indies in 1586. She carried his flag at Cadiz in 1587. She had been engaged in every service of consequence which had been undertaken since the queen's accession. She was caught in a gale in the beginning of 1588 and ran on a sandbank at the mouth of the Scheldt, when, to use Lord Howard's words, "it was thought impossible, unless she had been made of iron, that she should not have been severely injured if not lost." She was got off "without a spoonful of water in her well;" and after a hard life of twenty-eight years, the admiral said "there was not in the world a stronger ship."

The cost at which vessels of this kind were constructed indicates that although contractors did their work well, they were contented with moderate profits. The *Rainbow,* a ship of five hundred tons, was set afloat fit at all points for sea for two thousand one hundred pounds; the *Vanguard,* also of five hundred tons, for two thousand six hundred pounds—or, allowing for the difference in the value of money, about thirteen thousand and sixteen thousand pounds respectively.

The wages of an able seaman under Henry VIII had been sixpence a day, or calculated in meat, drink, and clothing, according to the prices at the beginning of the sixteenth century, equal to six shillings of our money. Out of this he found his own living. As the value of money began to fall with the introduction of bullion from America, the government altered the mode of payment, themselves supplying the ships' rations. In 1585 the sixpence tried by the same standard was worth but three shillings, and the sailor received in money six and eightpence a month, while of food "of good and seasonable victuals" his allowance for every flesh day, *i.e.* for every Sunday, Monday, Tuesday, and Thursday, was a pound of biscuit or a pound and a half of bread, a gallon of beer, and two pounds of meat—salt beef, fresh beef or mutton, as the case might be. On the three other days he had the same quantity of beer and biscuit with half a ling or a cod, and half a pound of butter or a pound of cheese. The diet was occasionally varied by substituting bacon for beef and mutton, reducing the salt fish and increasing the butter and cheese; in all cases however the beer and bread remaining constant. These allowances were never altered whatever might be the variation of price; the cost of each man's three daily meals ranging from fourpence to sevenpence, at which it had permanently settled by 1588. The pay had been raised three years before at the intercession of Sir John Hawkins from six and eightpence a month to ten shillings. The increase however cost nothing to the crown, a smaller crew better paid being found to do more effective service. Hawkins said he had observed that with higher wages men became more healthy and self-respecting, "such as could make shift for themselves and keep themselves clean, without vermin."

The Spaniards, still more aware of the importance of change

of diet at sea, varied the rations more frequently. A pound and a half of bread and a pint of Andalusian wine was allowed daily. Meat, fish, and cheese alternated in rather smaller quantities than in England, but with the addition of peas, beans, and garlic, made into soup.

At the recommendation of the committee of 1583, five new ships had been added to the navy, larger than any which were already afloat; the *Ark* and the *Victory* of eight hundred tons, the *Bear* and the *Elizabeth Jonas* of nine hundred, and the *Triumph* of a thousand. The four last named had not been commissioned before 1588. They had been constructed upon a new principle introduced by Hawkins. The high sterns and forecastles were lowered, the keels lengthened, and the lines made finer and sharper. Old seamen shook their heads at the innovation, and foretold the usual disasters. They would be too crank, it was said, to carry sail. They were fit only for smooth water, and would founder in the heavy seas of the Atlantic. The queen having paid dear for them, shrunk from experiments which might show her to have countenanced an expensive folly, and had preferred so far to keep them safe at their moorings in the Medway.

This was the condition of the royal navy of England when called on to face the most powerful fleet which had existed from the beginning of time. The privateers promised to be useful as auxiliaries. The great merchants in every port armed the best of their ships. London provided thirty; Southampton, Poole, Dartmouth, Plymouth, Barnstaple, and Bristol contributed as they were able; and English brigs and barques of two hundred tons, which never went to sea without being prepared to encounter pirates, were no contemptible allies. Lord Howard of Effingham had also two ships of his own. Hawkins had four or five. Drake had a whole squadron, for the western privateers rallied of themselves to the flag of their chosen hero. But it was on the queen's ships that the brunt of the battle would have to fall, and above the largest of them the vast Spanish galleons and galleasses towered up like Flemish dray-horses by the side of the light Arabian coursers.

The *Bonaventura*, the *Golden Lion*, the *Rainbow,* and the *Dreadnought* had been with Drake at Cadiz, and on Drake's return, contrary to the advice of Burghley, had been paid off and dismantled. The dockyards had suffered like every other

department of the public service from the queen's determination
to make peace. The repairing work had fallen far into arrears;
and in September, 1587, when Philip sent orders to Santa Cruz
to sail, and bade Parma prepare for his immediate arrival, there
was not a vessel in the Channel carrying the queen's flag larger
than a pinnace. The ships were lying half-rigged at Chatham,
with neither crews nor officers, and requiring all of them to be
examined and refitted before they could be sent to sea for a
winter's cruise. Several weeks at least would be consumed
before men in sufficient numbers could be collected and arms
and stores taken on board. The queen, in Leicester's words,
"was treating for peace disarmed;" and had Santa Cruz been
able to use the opportunity he would have found his way to
Margate Roads without receiving or firing a shot. Burghley,
(Elizabeth's Lord High Treasurer) who had believed that, for
this year at least, the danger had passed over, was roused at
the beginning of October from his dangerous security. The
galleon which Drake had brought home with him in August
(from Cadiz) was sold with her cargo, and the money returned
to instant account. An embargo was laid on the merchant-ships
in the various ports, and their crews were impressed for the
queen's service. Hawkins was directed to put the whole navy
as rapidly as possible in condition for sea; and, on the 21st of
December, instructions were sent to Howard of Effingham "to
take the ships into the Channel to defend the realm against
the Spaniards."

VII

Just as in Spain the intended storming of the stronghold of
heresy had stirred the crusading spirit, and the Castilian nobles
had sent the best of their sons to the Armada, so when the call
was sounded at last for the defence of England, it rang like a
trumpet-note through manor-house and castle. The chief of
the house of Howard was in the Tower, praying for the success
of the servants of the pope; but the admiral, as if to wipe the
stain from the scutcheon, brought his son-in-law, Lord Sheffield,
and one at least of the Duke of Norfolk's sons, to serve at his
side. Lord Henry Seymour came too, and all the distinguished
seamen, Hawkins, Frobisher, Palmer, Townsend, and numbers
more, whose names were only less illustrious. Drake was
already at Plymouth with his own squadron of privateers and

the *Revenge,* a queen's ship which had been sent down to him. The common sailors who had volunteered "were as able a company as were ever seen"—ill found in apparel, and desiring, not unreasonably, a month's wages in advance to provide themselves, but otherwise the pride and flower of English mariners.

Lord Howard's first commission, drawn by Drake's advice, left him free to act at his discretion, "to invade the Spanish dominions," if it should be thought good, or to go wherever he saw a chance to strike a blow. The fleet was on fire with enthusiasm. Seamen and officers, honest Englishmen everywhere, had for years been longing to have done with privateering, false colours, lies, and pretences, and "to have a good severe open war with Spain, as the only road to an honourable settlement." Their wishes seemed likely to be gratified at last. Mid-winter as it was, the general desire was to follow up Drake's work at Cadiz, lie on the coast of Spain, and either dash into the Tagus and burn the fleet as it lay at anchor there, or else enrich England and ruin Philip by seizing the Indian treasures at the mouth of his own harbours.

But the vessel of the state was still far from open waters. To the disgust of every one it was announced, immediately after the issue of the commission, that the services of the fleet would be required only for six weeks, before the end of which the queen confidently hoped that peace would be established. The limitation itself made a distant enterprise impossible; but she could not wait till even this short period had elapsed. She had allowed herself to be persuaded that soldiers and sailors wished for war because it was their trade, and that Howard and Drake, if left at sea, would do some rash violent action which would make negotiations more difficult. A random story came up from Spain that the Armada was dissolving, and on the credit of it she directed the dismissal of half the crews which had been collected and engaged at so much expense. She ordered two-thirds of the fleet to stay in the Thames with reduced complements. She sent Drake to lie at Portsmouth with three small vessels, and Lord Henry Seymour to cruise shorthanded with the rest in the Channel, but with strict injunctions not to pass beyond it.

Her orders were obeyed. The men were dispersed, the fleet was made practically useless, and the sea was again open; and it was at this moment that Philip, as if he had divined what his sister-in-law would do, or as if he had received secret information from England, sent the Armada the second orders to sail, which were unfulfilled only through the death of Santa Cruz. (One of Philip's best soldiers and mariners) "Never," said Lord Howard, savage at his mistress's perversity, "never since England was England was there such a stratagem and mask made to deceive us withal as this treaty." "We are wasting money," said Sir John Hawkins, "Wasting strength, dishonouring and discrediting ourselves, by our uncertain dallying."

Nothing that could be said in the least availed. The merchant-ships were released, and the best of the crews rejoined them, and went their way upon other voyages beyond reach of recovery. "God send me to see such a company together again when need is," wrote the lord admiral. "If the power of Spain come before the middle of April there will be as much ado to have men to furnish us as ever was, and men we must have or the ships will do no good." "What did move her majesty," he continued, "to diminish our forces on the sudden I know not. If anything be attempted now upon the sudden, either for Scotland or to invade this coast, we shall do as much good for the service as the hoys which lie at Lyon quay. There is no master in England that will undertake with these men that are now in them to carry the ships back to Chatham. Our state is well known in Flanders, and as we were a terror to them at our first coming out, so now they make little reckoning of us. They know that we are like bears tied to stakes, and they may come as dogs to offend us, and we cannot hurt them."

VIII

It would have been easy now for Parma, if the weather would have allowed him, either to land a few thousand men on the coast of Fife, or to transport his entire army to England. Howard could not have fired a shot to interfere with him. The Scotch plan however had been given up for reasons best known to Philip. The weather was wild and boisterous beyond experience. Exposure and sickness had thinned the rolls of the prince's companies far below the number with which he believed that he could prudently make the venture; nor if his ranks had been as full as he could have wished to see them would he have risked his army upon the Channel in the wave-

swept hoys and barges of the Belgian ports till a more advanced
season brought smoother seas. The worst actual mischief was
the false economy of the changes of plan. A week after the
strength of the fleet had been reduced, the queen grew uneasy
at being defenceless. Orders were sent to restore Seymour's
squadron to its full numbers, while the ships in the Thames
were recalled to Chatham to be paid off. A fortnight later,
in a fresh panic, they were commanded again to sea; men had
to be collected wherever they could be found, and bounties
and allowances were made necessary, which doubled the cost
at which they could have kept in commission from the
beginning.

There had been the same "uncertain dallying" with Sir
Francis Drake. The order to Portsmouth was recalled, and,
at his earnest entreaty, he obtained leave to go down to the
coast of Spain with the *Revenge* and the privateer squadron.
But the permission was withdrawn as soon as given. Although
Parma had distinctly refused to grant a general armistice
which would guarantee England against attacks, the queen
discovered that if Drake showed himself off Lisbon "it would
be a hindrance to the peace; the King of Spain would take
it ill."

With the small progress made by her commissioners in
Flanders, and with the daily reports which came in from Spain
of the approach of the Armada, she could not refuse to allow
the fleet to remain at sea. But she permitted some miserable
scoundrel to lay a plan before her for saving expenses by cutting
down the seamen's diets, stopping the beef and mutton, and
setting them to defend their country and her throne on fish,
dried peas, and oil. Clinging to her hopes of peace, and afraid
probably of the navy endangering it, she tied the ships to harbour by supplying the stores in driblets. She allowed rations but
for a month at a time, and permitted no reserves to be provided
in the victualling offices. Drake had offended her by consuming
ammunition at target practice. She would not give him a
second opportunity. "The proportion of powder" in the
largest ships was "sufficient but for a day and a half's service
if it was begun and continued as the service might require;"
in the rest of the fleet "it was sufficient but for one day's
service." "Good my lords," expostulated Drake with the
council, "consider deeply of this, for it importeth the loss of

all." It was no fault of the council. The council would not have left Drake to ask for what was obviously necessary. The queen had taken upon herself the detailed management of everything. Lord Howard's letters prove that she and she only was responsible. As if every officer she possessed were in a conspiracy to ruin her, she appears to have kept all descriptions of supplies within her own reach in London or at Chatham, permitting nothing to be served out without an order from herself; and the ships at Plymouth, furnished from a distance with small quantities at a time, were often for many days without food of any kind.

"Such a thing was never heard of since there were ships in England," Lord Howard wrote to Burghley, "as no victuals in store. Her majesty's father (Henry VIII) never made a less supply than six weeks, and yet there was marvellous help upon extremity, for there were ever provisions at Portsmouth; and also at Dover store ever at hand upon necessity."

And again to Walsingham:—

"I am very sorry her majesty is so careless of this most dangerous time. I fear over much and with grief think it, her majesty relies upon a hope that will deceive her and greatly endanger her, and then it will not be her money nor her jewels that will help her; for as they will do good in time, so will they help nothing for the redeeming of time being lost. I dare say her majesty will look that men should fight for her, and I know they will; but I pray heartily for a peace, for I see that which should be the ground of an honourable war will never appear; for sparing and war have no affinity together."

The alterations of purpose had created so much confusion that the four largest ships, the *Triumph,* the *Victory,* the *Elizabeth Jonas,* and the *Bear,* were for many weeks left behind for want of hands to man them, "keeping Chatham church." The queen indeed had considered that they would not be wanted, and that it would be a waste of money to refit them. By the beginning of May, the hopes of peace having faded away, and certain information having arrived that the Armada was on the point of sailing. the council so far prevailed that they were put in order and allowed to join Howard in Margate Roads.

Supplies were issued to the entire fleet calculated to last to the middle of June; and leaving Lord Henry Seymour with the *Vanguard,* the *Rainbow,* the *Antelope,* and a squadron of privateers to watch Dunkirk, the admiral stood down Channel to join Drake and wait for the Spaniards' coming. Looking on his way, into Boulogne which the Duke of Aumale was vainly besieging, he was off Plymouth on the morning of the 23rd of May (June 2nd). Drake with forty sail, adventurers all of them except the *Revenge,* and sent to sea by himself and his friends, came out to meet him, and the united fleets, imposing at least in numbers, entered the Sound together. Spies had brought word that the Armada intended to sail in the middle of the month. In the condition of the English magazines, it could not come too soon; and the plan was to take in water and at once make for the mouth of the Channel and force an engagement in the open sea.

The weather however continued desperate: a wild winter had been followed by a wilder spring, and the lengthening days were still the only signs of approaching summer. A severe south-westerly gale set in. Plymouth roadstead, undefended by a breakwater, was a dangerous anchorage, and to put to sea was more dangerous still. Howard, with the great ships, took his chance, and lay rolling in the Sound, "dancing lustily as the gallantest dancer at court." Had he gone into the harbour, he could not have come out unless the weather moderated. The rest of the fleet, being smaller and more manageable, went for shelter into the mouth of the Tamar, and there lay chafing with impatience while their provisions wasted away. Fresh supplies had been promised, but the days passed and the victualling hoys did not arrive; on the 28th of May (June 7th), there was but food for eighteen days, and Devonshire, strange to say, could not furnish anything. If the eighteen days ran out, and the Spaniards came at the end of them, the sailors would have to go into action starving. They continued in good spirits, ready, "if well handled," to go through fire and water. They were put on short rations, but they caught fish to eke out their reduced mess-dinners. There was sickness, but they would not yield to it; one and all praying only either "for the speedy coming of the enemy," or the expected but lingering victuallers.

The impression left upon those who were at this time most about ·the queen, who saw her daily and transacted business with her, was that she would succeed this time in what she had often escaped doing by a narrow accident, and finally ruin both herself and the country. She now knew that in dancing after peace she had been pursuing a mirage, yet the knowledge made no difference. She was incapable of personal fear, and she skipped and joked and wrangled over her money-bags, as if the Spanish fleet was a dream and Philip fabulous as a wizard of romance. "I am sorry," wrote Walsingham from his bed to Burghley, (Walsingham was subject to epilepsy, and was lying, as he pathetically said, "waiting for my fit.") "to see so great a danger hanging over this realm so slightly regarded and so carelessly provided for. I would to God the enemy were no more careful to assail than we to defend, and there would be the less cause of fear. Seeing that we have neither recourse to prayer, nor to such effectual preparations as the danger importeth, I cannot but conclude according to man's judgment, *Salus ipsa non potest servare hanc rempublicam.*" ("The goddess of safety herself is not able to save this state." The quotation is slightly modified from Cicero's oration in defense of Marcus Fonteius.)

"For the love of Jesus Christ, madam," said Lord Howard to her, "awake and see the villainous treasons round about you, against your majesty and the realm." He was addressing ears closed by a levity and obstinacy which were alike incurable. The victuallers came to Plymouth at last, ten days beyond their time. They had brought provisions but for one additional month only, and a positive message that no more should be sent. So peremptory Elizabeth was about it that she forbade further preparations to be made, nor till the month was out could a consent be wrung from her for any further supply.

The contractors, when the order reached them, answered that they could not execute it within less than four weeks, and for those four weeks therefore, if a knowledge of their mistress's character had not prepared the officers for what might possibly happen, the entire fleet would have been without food. The one month's provisions which came on the 23rd of June were distributed to make them last for six weeks at least. Six men were placed at every four men's mess. They bore it without complaining. The beer which had been sent at the same time was sour and poisonous. They bore this too, or would have borne it, but that it brought dysentery, a more dreaded enemy than the Spaniard, which carried them off by scores. Unable to endure the sight of their patient suffering, Drake and Howard ordered wine and arrowroot at Plymouth on their own respons-

ibility for the sick beds. When all was over, the queen called
them to a sharp account for an extravagance which had saved
possibly a thousand brave men to fight for her. Howard disdained to defend himself, and paid the bill out of his own
purse.

Here for the present we leave the English fleet, the summer
as it deepened becoming only more and more stormy—gales
blowing from all quarters, now a hurricane of thirty hours from
the north, now shifting to east and south-east, and then to west.
The "wind and rain" was uniform in nothing but violence,
"so stormy and tempestuous as would not be credited." The
"oldest fisherman" on the coast could not remember "such
a summer season." One satisfaction only Lord Howard found,
and that a great one. Hawkins at least had done his share of
the work right excellently. The English ships were "in royal
and perfect estate, feeling the seas no more than if they had
been riding at Chatham." Through the whole fleet not a spar
was sprained, not a rope parted, timbers and cordage remained
staunch and sound within and without. The *Triumph* and her
four large consorts were grounded again and again "to tallow
and to wash." They suffered nothing from the strain, and they
were dry to the keel as Arabian sand. Their seaworthiness
however would serve them nothing if the enemy lingered till
their magazines were empty.

Drake's hopes were still to make for the coast of Spain, supply
his necessities from Philip's store-ships since his mistress failed
him, and fight the Spaniards in their own harbours. He feared
that Philip knew their condition and was waiting purposely till
want of food dissolved them. Once, at the beginning of July, with
a north wind the fleet stood across to Ushant. Then however
the wind shifted. They feared the enemy might pass them and,
afraid to venture further, ran back to the Sound, and there they
waited, in all twenty-nine queen's ships of all sizes, ten small
vessels belonging to Lord Howard and his family, and forty-
three privateers between forty tons and four hundred, under
Drake, the united crews amounting to something over nine
thousand men.

IX

Meanwhile the slow, lingering, long-expected Armada was
at last really approaching. Lisbon through the spring months

had been a scene of extraordinary confusion. Three nations, Spanish, Italian, and Portuguese, had furnished their several contingents. The Spaniards themselves not wholly moulded into unity—Gallicians, Andalusians, Catalans, Castilians—were divided into squadrons, imperfectly understanding each other, and separated by hereditary feuds. The hidalgos from Valladolid and Burgos, ardent and enthusiastic volunteers, lay in their tents surrounded by their servants. Portuguese and Castilian peasants, not so enthusiastic, and impressed from their farms to serve, were kept in gangs under guard lest they should run away. Six different languages were spoken among Philip's own free subjects, and besides these there was a motley company from every corner of the known world—galley slaves from Constantinople and Algiers, Jesuits from Rheims, exiled priests, Irish and English, gathering like ravens to the spoil of the heretics. Lord Baltinglass was there from the Wicklow hills; Lord Maxwell, turned now into Earl of Morton, from the Scotch borders; Caley O'Connor, a distinguished "murderer," "who could speak nothing but his own tongue;" and Maurice Fitzgerald dreaming of the Desmond coronet; with many a young Scotch and English gentleman besides, who had listened too ardently to the preaching of Campian and Holt (Catholic leaders). The faithful of all countries had rushed together, as at the call of an archangel, to take part in the great battle for the cause of God and the Church.

Among these elements Medina Sidonia kept such order as he could, his chief difficulty being to prevent Spaniards and Portuguese from breaking each other's heads upon the quays. At length the weary preparations were completed; the galleons were equipped for sea, the stores laid in, the soldiers, sailors, and volunteers all embarked. On the fleet itself the treasures of the Indian mines had for three years been freely lavished. In the six squadrons there were sixty-five large ships; the smallest of them was of seven hundred tons; seven were over a thousand, and the largest *La Regazona,* an Italian, was thirteen hundred. They were all "built high like castles," their upper works musket proof, their main timbers "four and five feet thick," of a strength which it was fondly supposed no English cannon could pierce.

As a symbol of the service on which they were going, and to secure the guardianship of heaven, they had been baptised

after the celestial hierarchy. The names on both sides, either
by accident or purpose, corresponded to the character of the
struggle; the *St. Matthew,* the *St. Philip,* the *St. James,* the *St.
John,* the *St. Martin,* and the *Lady of the Rosary* were coming
to encounter the *Victory,* the *Revenge,* the *Dreadnaught,* the
Bear, the *Lion,* and the *Bull:* dreams were ranged against
realities, fiction against fact, and imaginary supernatural patron-
age against mere human courage, strength, and determination.

Next to the galleons were four galleasses, gigantic galleys,
carrying each of them fifty guns, four hundred and fifty soldiers
and sailors, and rowed by three hundred slaves. In addition to
these were four large galleys, fifty-six armed merchant vessels,
the best that Spain possessed, and twenty caravels or pinnaces
attached to the larger ships.

The fighting fleet, or Armada proper, thus consisted of a
hundred and twenty-nine vessels, seven of them larger than
the *Triumph,* and the smallest of the sixty-five galleons of
larger tonnage than the finest ship in the English navy, except
the five which had been last added to it. The aggregate of
cannon was two thousand four hundred and thirty. They were
brass and iron of various sizes, the finest that the Spanish
foundries could produce. The weight of metal which they
were able to throw exceeded enormously the power of the
English broadsides. In compensation, however, and making up
fortunately for the imperfect provision allowed by Elizabeth,
the supply of cartridges was singularly small. The king probably calculated that a single action would decide the struggle,
and it amounted to but fifty rounds for each gun.

The store of provisions was enormous. It was intended for
the use of the army after it landed in England, and was sufficient
to feed forty thousand men for six months. The powder and
lead for small arms was also infinite. The complement of
sailors was moderate considering the size and number of the
ships—all told they amounted to no more than eight thousand.
The disposable space was probably required for the land force
which was going to Parma's assistance. Of soldiers, Castilian
and Portuguese, there were nineteen thousand; of gentlemen
volunteers a thousand; six hundred priests, servants, strangers,
and miscellaneous officers; and two thousand aliens besides, of
not sufficient importance to be described particularly in the
Spanish records, who rowed as slaves in the galleys and galleasses.

X

Medina Sidonia had been recommended to the command in chief by his rank, and by his connection with the Princess of Eboli; but immediately under him were the ablest officers in Philip's dominions. Martinez de Recalde, governor of Gallicia and vice-admiral, was said to be the best seaman that Spain possessed next to Santa Cruz. Pedro de Valdez, general of the squadron of Andalusia, had commanded the Spanish fleet on the coast of Holland when Don Juan (of Austria, illegitimate half brother of Philip) was in the Netherlands, and knew the English Channel well. Miguel de Oquendo, who had the squadron of Guipiscoa, was a Spanish Philip Sidney, a young chivalrous nobleman of distinguished promise, who, a month before the fleet sailed, had obtained from the king a reluctant permission to take part in the expedition.

Among the other names of interest in the list of officers was that of Hugo de Monçada, chief of the galleasses, made remarkable by the fate which overtook him; that of Diego de Pimentel, afterwards viceroy of Mexico; and more particularly that of the brillant Don Alonzo de Leyva who commanded the land forces. Born of a family who had for several generations been the terror of the Mediterranean corsairs, Don Alonzo had won his spurs as a boy in the last revolt of the Moors. Afterwards he had himself formed and led a company of Spanish lancers, who fought at Gemblours under Don Juan of Austria, and on Don Juan's death he was removed from the Netherlands and put at the head of the fleet which was permanently stationed at Sicily. He was so celebrated personally, and so many attractions combined in him of birth, bearing, and distinguished services, that the fathers of the high-born youths who had volunteered to accompany the Armada, most of them committed their sons to de Leyva's special charge.

The short supply of cannon cartridge was one serious deficiency. Masters of the art of war as the Spaniards believed themselves, and cheap as they held English inexperience, they had not yet comprehended the exigencies of a naval engagement. Another misfortune of even greater consequence to them was the incompetency of their pilots. The time had been when Spanish seamen knew the intricacies of the Channel as well as the English themselves; but since the capture of Flushing their ships of war had no longer any occupation left them there, and their commerce in those seas had been left to the Dutch, who, though in revolt, still traded with their ports, supplied them with salt herring for their fasting days, and had brought to Lisbon from the Baltic the hemp and tar with which the Armada itself had been fitted out.

But though willing in the ways of merchandise to supply the Spaniards with materials of war, they had declined to furnish them with pilots, and Parma, to whom Philip wrote in his difficulty, was obliged to reply that the best sailors were heretics, and that in all the Low Countries he was unable to find more than two or three competent men whom he could bribe or force to take service with the Armada. All else was going well. The pope would not indeed advance a ducat of his promised subsidy till the Spaniards were actually in England; but he had been more compliant about the succession, promising to leave it at Philip's disposition. The Duke of Mantua had relieved Philip's money difficulties, and Parma's hollowed ranks were filled again with fresh recruits. The prince had once more his thirty thousand Spaniards, Germans, Italians, and Walloons in his camp, and the treaty having exploded upon the cautionary towns, he no longer affected any kind of concealment. The quays of Nieuport and Dunkirk were thronged with hoys and barges. The cavalry horses were stabled in the towns ready to embark, the troops encamped in the immediate environs. Artillery stores, platforms, crates, pioneers' tools, were already on board. The fleet at Antwerp, though unable to pass Flushing, yet succeeded in keeping the Dutch in check. They ventured out occasionally in front of Dunkirk, but could not lie there. When the crisis actually came they had not a sail on the seas; but they were able to prevent Parma from making use of Sluys, which had cost him so dear to capture, and this after all was as much or more than Elizabeth had a right to expect.

The Armada was coming to execute the censures of the Church, and a spiritual demonstration was prepared to accompany it. In addition to his other dignities, the Archbishop-elect of Canterbury was named legate for England, and he had prepared a pastoral letter, which was printed in Flanders, to be carried over by Parma and issued at the moment of his arrival. The burden of it was an exhortation to the faithful to rise in arms and welcome their deliverer, and copies had **been** already smuggled across the Channel and distributed through the secret agencies of the Catholic missions.

The Spanish arms, the new legate said, were not directed against his countrymen. Their sins had been many, but the retribution was to fall only on the wicked queen, on the usurping heretic Elizabeth, the bane of Christendom, and the murderess of the souls of her subjects. Henry VIII., tyrant as he was, had fallen short in atrocity of his infamous daughter. Vengeance was falling upon her at last. Ruin was now to overwhelm her, and the just of the earth would say, "Lo, this is she who took not God for her strength, that trusted in the multitude of her riches and prevailed in her iniquities, but was struck down under the hand of the Most High." The Church, he said, in pity had chastised her offences by excommunication, but she had despised correction, and those who had been sent to bring her to repentance she had slain with the sword. Innocent, godly, and learned men, priests and bishops in England and Ireland, had been racked, torn, chained, famished, buffeted, and at last barbarously executed; and fulfilling the measure of her iniquities she had at length killed the anointed of God, the Lady Mary (Queen of Scots) her nearest kinswoman, and by law the right owner of her crown. The execution of the Church's judgment upon her had been long deferred, in part because she was too strong to be overthrown by her subjects alone, without danger to the lives of many noble and godly persons; in part through the long-suffering and sweet and fatherly forbearance of the chief shepherd of the Church, who had persevered in hoping that she might be converted from her evil ways. Seeing however that gentleness had availed nothing, the holy father had at length besought the princes of Christendom to assist him in the chastisement of so wicked a monster, the scourge of God and shame of womankind. The most Catholic king had accepted the glorious charge, and his legions were about to appear on the English shores.

All being thus in order, the Prince of Parma ready to embark, the paternal admonition to the English nation to commit treason prepared for circulation, and the last touches added to the completeness of the fleet in the Tagus, the Duke of Medina Sidonia sailed from Lisbon on the 19th of May. The northerly breeze which prevails on the coast of Portugal was unusually strong. The galleons standing high out of the water, and carrying small canvas in proportion to their size, worked badly to windward. They were three weeks in reaching Finisterre, where the wind having freshened to a gale, they were scattered, some standing out to sea, some into the Bay of Biscay. Their orders, in the event of such a casualty, had been to make for Ferrol. The wind shifting suddenly to the west, those that had gone into the bay could not immediately reach it, and were driven into Santander. The officers however were, on the whole, well satisfied with the qualities which the ships had displayed. A mast or two had been sprung, a few yards and bowsprits had been carried away; but beyond loss of time there had been no serious damage.

The weather moderating, the fleet was again collected in the Bay of Ferrol by the 6th of July. All repairs were completed by the 11th, and the next day, the 12th, the Armada took leave of Spain for the last time.

XI

The scene as the fleet passed out of the harbour must have been singularly beautiful. It was a treacherous interval of real summer. The early sun was lighting the long chain of the Gallician mountains, marking with shadows the cleft defiles and shining softly on the while walls and vineyards of Coruña. The wind was light and falling towards a calm; the great galleons drifted slowly with the tide on the purple water, the long streamers trailing from the trucks, the red crosses, the emblem of the crusade, showing bright upon the hanging sails. The fruit boats were bringing off the last fresh supplies, and the pinnaces hastening to the ships with the last loiterers on shore. Out of thirty thousand men who had that morning stood upon the decks of the proud Armada, twenty thousand and more were never again to see the hills of Spain. Of the remnant who in two short months crept back ragged and torn, all but a few hundreds returned only to die.

The Spaniards, though a great people, were usually over-conscious of their greatness, and boasted too loudly of their fame and prowess; but among the soldiers and sailors of the doomed expedition against England the national vainglory was singularly silent. They were the flower of the country, culled and chosen over the entire peninsula, and they were going with a modest nobility upon the service which they knew to be dangerous, but which they believed to be peculiarly sacred. Every one, seaman, officer, and soldier, had confessed and communicated before he went on board.

Gambling, swearing, profane language of all kinds had been peremptorily forbidden. Private quarrels and differences had been made up or suspended. The loose women who accompanied Spanish armies, and sometimes Spanish ships to sea, had been ordered away, and no unclean thing or person permitted to defile the Armada; and in every vessel, and in the whole fleet, the strictest order was prescribed and observed. Medina Sidonia led the way in the *San Martin,* showing lights at night, and firing guns when the weather was hazy. Mount's Bay was to be the next place of rendezvous if they were again separated.

On the first evening the wind dropped to a calm. The morning after, the 13th, a fair fresh breeze came up from the south and south-west; the ships ran flowingly before it; and in two days and nights they had crossed the bay and were off Ushant. The fastest of the pinnaces was dispatched from thence to Parma, with a letter bidding him expect the duke's immediate coming.

But they had now entered the latitude of the storms which through the whole season had raged round the English shore. The same night a south-west gale overtook them. They lay-to, not daring to run further. The four galleys unable to keep the sea were driven in upon the French coast and wrecked. The *Santa Ana,* a galleon of eight hundred tons, went down, carrying with her ninety seamen, three hundred soldiers, and fifty thousand ducats in gold. The weather was believed to be under the peculiar care of God, and this first misfortune was of evil omen for the future. The storm lasted two days, and then the sky cleared, and again gathering into order they proceeded on their way.

On the 19th they were in the mouth of the Channel. At daybreak on the morning of the 20th the Lizard was under their lee, and an English fishing-boat was hanging near them counting their numbers. They gave chase, but the boat shot away down wind and disappeared. They captured another an hour or two later, from which they learned the English fleet was in Plymouth, and Medina Sidonia called a council of war to consider whether they should go in and fall upon it while at anchor. Philip's orders however were peremptory that they should turn neither right nor left and make straight for Margate Roads and Parma. The duke was unenterprising and consciously unequal to his work; and already bending under his responsibilities he hesitated to add to them.

Had he decided otherwise it would have made no difference, for the opportunity was not allowed him. Long before the Spaniards saw the Lizard they had themselves been seen, and on the evening of the 19th, the beacons along the coast had told England that the hour of its trial was come.

To the ships at Plymouth the news was as a message of salvation. By thrift and short rations, by good management, contented care, and lavish use of private means, there was still one week's provisions in the magazines, with powder and shot for one day's sharp fighting, according to English notions of what fighting ought to be. They had to meet the enemy, as it were, with one arm bandaged by their own sovereign; but all wants, all difficulties, were forgotten in the knowledge that he was come, and that they could grapple with him before they were dissolved by starvation.

The warning light flew on to London, swift messengers galloping behind it. There was saddling and arming in village and town, and musters flocking to their posts. Loyal England forgot its difference of creeds and knew nothing but that the invader was at the door. One thing was wanting, a soldier to take the supreme command; but the queen found what she needed, found it in the person in whom in her eyes, notwithstanding his offences in the Low Countries, all excellencies were still combined—her own Leicester (Robert Dudley, Earl of Leicester, one of Elizabeth's favorites). Worse appointment could not possibly have been made; but even Leicester was lifted into a kind of hero by the excitement of the moment. He was not a coward, and not entirely a fool. Tilbury had been chosen as the place where the force was to assemble which was intended to cover London. It was the lowest spot where the Thames could be easily crossed, and it was impossible to say on which side of the river the enemy might choose to approach. Leicester flew at once to his post there, and so far he had fulfilled his duty that he had sixteen thousand men with him at Tilbury, with thirty thousand forming rapidly in his rear out of the musters of the midland counties, before Parma could have advanced, under the most favourable circumstances, within a day's march of London.

XII

The Armada reached Calais on Saturday, the 27th. Had all gone well Parma might, with very great exertion, have crossed on the following Wednesday, the 31st. His own letters prove that he could not have been ready sooner. His plan was to land at Margate, and even if he was unopposed three days at least would have been required to move his army within thirty miles of London. On the 26th of July, Leicester had ten thousand men with him at Tilbury. There were nine thousand on the same day in London, and the musters of the midland counties, even if they marched no more than fifteen miles a day, must have joined him at latest, had their presence been required, before the 4th of August. Provisions had been as little attended to for one service as the other. When four thousand Essex men came in on the 26th of July, after a hot march of twenty miles, "there was neither a barrel of beer nor a loaf of bread for them." London happily exerted itself and sent stores down the river; the spirit of the men deserved better treatment. Famished as they were, "they said they would abide more hunger than that to serve her majesty and the country."

Meanwhile, on the night of the 19th, while the Armada was still some leagues to the south of the Lizard, the wind blowing fresh into Plymouth Sound, the queen's ships and a few of the privateers were warped out behind the shelter of Mount Edgecombe. All hands went merrily to work; vessel after vessel was brought to moorings behind Ram Head, so placed that they could fetch clear to the sea and by Saturday morning, when the Spaniards were first sighting the coast of Cornwall, forty sail were lying ready for action under the headland.

The day wore on; noon passed and nothing had been seen. At length, towards three in the afternoon, the look-out men on the hill reported a line of sails on the western horizon, the centre being first visible, the two wings gradually rising and spreading along the rim of the sea. On they swept in a broad crescent, slowly, for the air was light; and as the hulls showed clear, it was seen that report had not exaggerated the numbers

Legend:

IN FAR INFERIOR FORCE, BOTH IN NUMBER OF VESSELS, THEIR SIZE AND ARMAMENT, THE ENGLISH FIRST SUCCESSFULLY ASSAILED THE SPANIARDS AT

1 AND LATER AT

2 WHERE THEY INFLICTED HEAVY LOSSES. FOUL WEATHER FORCED THE SPANIARDS TO FLEE INTO THE NORTH SEA, PURSUED FOR A SHORT DISTANCE BY THE ENGLISH

THE ARMADA CONSISTED OF 155 VESSELS, WITH A TONNAGE OF 60,000, BEARING 8000 SAILORS, 20,000 SOLDIERS, 2100 SLAVES AND ARMED WITH 2600 GUNS. AN ADDITIONAL SPANISH FORCE OF 300 CRAFT AND 30,000 SOLDIERS, GATHERED FOR AN INVASION OF ENGLAND, AWAITED THE ARMADA AT GRAVELINES AND OTHER SPANISH-DOMINATED CONTINENTAL PORTS. ONLY 53 VESSELS OF THE ARMADA SURVIVED TO RETURN TO SPAIN.

said to be coming. A hundred and fifty, large and small, were
counted and reported to Lord Howard; a few stray tenders
bound for Flanders having sought the company and the protection of the mighty escort.

The English ships at once weighed, but showed themselves
as little as they could. The evening was cloudy, with the wind
hanging to the land. It was growing dusk when the Armada
opened Plymouth, and then for the first time Medina Sidonia
perceived that Howard was prepared for him, and that if he
wished it he could not enter the Sound without an action.
There was not enough light for him to measure his enemy's
strength. He saw sails passing continually between his fleet
and the land, and vessels tacking and manœuvring; but confident in his own overpowering force he sent up signals to lie-to
for the night and to prepare for a general action at daybreak.

About two o'clock, the moon rose with a clear sky—a gibbous
moon, little more than a half circle, but by the light of it the
Spaniards perceived that sixty or seventy ships had glided out
behind them, and were hovering at their rear just out of cannon-
shot.

The dawn was still, but toward eight o'clock the breeze
freshened from the west. The Armada made sail, and attempted
to close. To Medina Sidonia's extreme astonishment, it seemed
at the pleasure of the English to leave him or allow him to
approach them as they chose. The high-towered, broad-bowed
galleons moved like Thames barges piled with hay while the
sharp, low English sailed at once two feet to the Spaniards' one
and shot away as if by magic in the eye of the wind. It was as
if a modern steam fleet was engaged with a squadron of the old-
fashioned three-deckers, choosing their own distance and fighting
or not fighting as suited their convenience.

The action opened with the *Ark,* carrying Howard's flag, and
three other English ships, whose names the Spaniards did not
know, running along their entire rear line, firing successively
into each galleon as they passed, then wearing round and
returning over the same course. The *San Matteo* luffed into
the wind as far as she could, inviting them to board, but they
gave her their broadsides a second time and passed on.

Astonished and confounded as well by the manœuvring as
by the rapidity of the fire, the Spanish officers could not refuse
their admiration. They knew that they were inferior at sea,

but how inferior they had not realised. The English were firing four shots to one, and with a fresh breeze even the galleasses could not touch them. Such artillery practice and ships so handled had never been seen. Alonzo de Leyva in the *Rata* attempted to cross the *Ark*. Howard kept away as if to meet him, but ran by, again fired into the *San Matteo*, which was lying head to wind unable to move, and swept on upon his way.

The rest of the English ships were now engaged on the same conditions. The action continued through the whole forenoon, the Spaniards making efforts to close and always failing. Conscious of their disadvantage, they still fought bravely. "So far as we see," wrote Drake, "they mean to sell their lives with blows." But they had been flurried and surprised. Being to leeward, and leaning over to the wind, their shots had flown high, and had scarcely touched the English ships at all, while they had themselves suffered considerably. The Biscayan flagship, the *San Juan,* had her mizzenmast shot through in two places, many spars carried away, the captain wounded, and fifteen men killed. Oquendo had specially distinguished himself, being present wherever the danger was greatest, driving back into action vessels which were inclined to flinch; but as the wind held neither he nor any one could change the fortunes of the day, or enable the Spaniards to hurt an enemy whom they could not touch; and the rest of the English fleet coming out of the harbour, Medina Sidonia signalled to make sail up Channel, Martinez de Recalde covering the rear with the squadron of Biscay.

The wind was now rising and promised a squally evening. A fast boat was sent on with letters to Lord Henry Seymour reporting progress so far, and bidding him prepare in the Downs. An express went to London, begging for an instant supply of ammunition and while Drake went in pursuit of a detachment which appeared to be parted from the main Spanish fleet, and proved only to be the Flemish traders, Howard hung upon Recalde, sparing his powder but firing an occasional shot to prevent the enemy from recovering from their confusion.

The misfortunes of the first day were not yet over.

Afraid to spread lest any of them should be cut off, the different squadrons huddled together. A rolling sea came up from the west, and as evening fell the *Capitana,* of the Andalusian division, a galleon of 1200 tons, carrying the flag of Pedro de

Valdez, fouled the *Santa Catalina* and broke her bowsprit. The forestays parted and the foremast fell overboard, and the ship, hampered by the wreck, dropped behind. Don Pedro fired a distress gun, and two of the galleasses came to his assistance and tried to take him in tow, but the waves were running so high that the cable broke.

Don Pedro was the only high officer in the fleet who was well acquainted with the Channel. He was himself of more importance than his ship, and the duke despatched boats to bring him off with his crew. But he would not leave his charge and he was left to his fate. It was almost dark. Howard, believing the wreck to be deserted, did not stay for her, and went on in pursuit. A London privateer hung behind at her side till midnight, exchanging occasional shots with her, and sometimes hearing voices calling, but "the wind and sea being very great," the words could not be distinguished. Drake, returning from his chase, came up with her in the morning. She struck her flag, and he took her with him to Torbay, where he left her to the care of the Brixham fishermen, and himself hastened after the admiral, carrying on with him de Valdez and the other officers. The prize proved of unexpected value. Many casks of reals were found in her, and, infinitely more important, some tons of gunpowder, with which the *Roebuck,* the swiftest trawler in the harbour, flew in pursuit of the fleet.

Two hours after the accident to the Andalusian *Capitana,* another disaster overtook the galleon of Oquendo. He was himself apparently not on board at the time. The officers impatient and irritated at the results of the action, were quarrelling with themselves and one another. The captain struck the master gunner with a stick. The master gunner, who was a German, went below in a rage, thrust a burning linstock into a powder-barrel, and sprang through a port-hole into the sea. The deck was blown off from stem to stern. Two hundred seamen and soldiers were sent into the air; some fell into the water and were drowned; some scorched or mutilated dropped back into the wreck. The ship, which was also one of the largest in the fleet, was built so strongly that she survived the shock and floated, and her masts still stood. The flash was seen. The duke sent boats to learn what had happened and to save the men. The officers and the few who were unhurt were taken off, but there were no means of removing the wounded. They too

were abandoned therefore, to be picked up at daylight by the
English and sent on shore, where the disabled were kindly
treated. The hull was still worth rifling. It contained money
like all the rest of the ships, and at the bottom of the hold there
were powder barrels which had escaped the explosion.

XIII

Lord Howard was supplying his worst deficiencies out of the
enemy's own resources, and wringing from themselves the
means of completing their destruction. After a wild night, the
morning broke fine and still. The wind had shifted with the
dawn and a light air was now coming up from the east. The
Armada was off Portland; the English three or four miles to the
west; both fleets lying motionless in the calm, and rising and
falling to the swell. Howard being now to leeward had lost
his advantage of the day before. Sidonia, had he wished it,
might have forced another engagement with fairer chances in
his favour, but he preferred to rest his shaken crews and
give them breathing-time to recover their confidence. He despatched a second letter to the Prince of Parma, describing
his position and relating his adventures. He made the best of
what had befallen him, and concluded, on the whole, that the
English were afraid of him, because they had declined to close
but he was evidently extremely anxious. He knew nothing
of the coast. He begged Parma most earnestly to send him
pilots and he confessed himself at an entire loss what to do or
where to go if he was overtaken by a storm.

In the Channel during fine summer weather the wind, as the
fishermen say, goes round with the sun. It blows sometimes
freshly from the north-east in the morning; it drops to the south
at noon; to south-west in the afternoon; and so, falling calm
at sunset, rises again at night from the north. Sidonia knew
nothing of these local peculiarities; the next morning the
relative positions of the fleets remaining unchanged, and finding
himself to windward, he bore down upon Howard, with a steady
easterly breeze, to offer battle.

The English headed out towards the sea. He supposed that
they were flying, and though he could not overtake them, was
tempted to give chase. The galleons, though bad sailers all,
were of unequal slowness. The *San Marcos* outsailed the rest
and was led far beyond her consorts in the pursuit. When

the breeze headed round as usual, Lord Howard was now to windward of her, while she was herself several miles to windward of her consorts and beyond reach of help from them.

The object of the English was to avoid a general engagement, and especially to avoid coming to close quarters, where the enemy would be on more equal terms with them; outnumbered as they were, and short of powder, their plan was to make the best of their superiority as sailors, and wound and injure as many of the galleons as possible with least damage to themselves. The *San Marcos* was instantly set upon. She defended herself with extreme courage and, as the Spaniards thought, with no less skill. She fought single-handed for an hour and a half, firing what they considered the unexampled number of eighty shots, and receiving five hundred.

Oquendo came at last to the rescue, and the action off Plymouth having almost exhausted his stock of powder, and the Brixham sloop not having yet overtaken him, Howard was obliged to draw off till he could be relieved from the shore. Sidonia, ignorant of the cause of his retreat, believed that he had been worsted by the *San Marcos* alone, and that if the galleasses had gone into the action, as they might and ought to have done, they would have won a signal victory.

A stray Venetian had been meanwhile taken by the privateers, with one or two other small vessels, and carried into Weymouth. The news that the Spaniards were in the Channel had by this time penetrated into every corner of the country, and the patriotic heart of England was on fire; and from Lyme, and Weymouth, and Poole, and the Isle of Wight, young lords and gentlemen came streaming out in every smack or sloop that they could lay hold of, to snatch their share of danger and glory at Howard's side. The strength which they were able to add was little or nothing; but they brought enthusiasm, they brought to the half-starved and neglected crews the sense that the heart of England was with them, and transformed every common seaman into a hero. On the Tuesday evening after the fight Medina Sidonia counted a hundred sail behind him, and observed, with some uneasiness, that the numbers were continually increasing.

Wednesday was again calm. Neither shot nor powder had yet arrived, though express after express had been sent for it. No risk might be ventured, and the English lay now six miles from the Armada, waiting till their magazines were refilled. The duke, supposing them to be afraid, sent Don Hugo de Moncada with the galleasses to engage. On that day there was not a breath of wind of any kind, and the galleasses had Howard at some advantage. There was no serious loss however; that night ammunition came sufficient for one more day's fighting, and Sir George Carey, who had run out from behind the Isle of Wight in a pinnace to see what was going on, found himself at five in the morning, "in the midst of round shot flying as thick as musket-balls in a skirmish on land." The night had been still and dark. With the first light, the Spaniards saw two of their store-vessels, loaded with provisions, being towed away by some English launches. The wind rising, Alonza de Leyva in the *Rata,* with two galleasses, which had taken Recalde's place in the rear, at once started in pursuit. The main body of the Armada lying open, and the *San Martin* with Sidonia's own flag being clearly distinguishable, Howard for the first time determined to try a close engagement.

It was a day of special distinction for the Howard family. He took his cousin Lord Thomas with him in the *Lion,* his two sons-in-law, Lord Sheffield and Sir R. Southwell, in the *Bear* and the *Elizabeth Jonas,* and with his own and one other ship, the *Victory,* under Captain Barker, he went straight into the centre of the Armada, steering direct for the *San Martin* herself, and exchanging broadsides at speaking distance with every galleon that he passed. Oquendo, sure to be found where hardest blows were going, threw himself across the *Ark's* course before she could reach the *San Martin.* The *Ark* ran into him, and two soldiers on his forecastle were killed by the shock but the *Ark's* rudder was unshipped; she cleared herself of her enemy, but dropped away for the moment unmanageable to leeward, and was immediately surrounded by a number of galleons which attempted to close with her. In an instant her own boats had her in tow; her sails filled as they pulled her head round, and when the galleons had assured themselves of their prize, she slipped away between them so fast that a Spanish spectator says, "though the swiftest ships in the whole Armada pursued her, they seemed in comparison to be at anchor."

The action continued afterwards for several hours. The English had not suffered at all. Hardly a man had been wounded. But neither had they any captures to boast of.

Calderon leaves it uncertain whether de Leyva recovered the store-ships; the English writers do not mention having taken them. The only visible result had been the expenditure of powder. But the invisible result to the Armada had been far more serious. The four feet of timber had been no defence against the English shot. The soldiers had been sent below for security, and the balls ripping through the oak had sent the splinters flying among them like shell. Many had been killed, many more had been wounded; masts, yards, rigging, all had suffered. They had expected that one engagement would annihilate the power of their enemies, and battle followed upon battle and there was as yet no sign of an end.

XIV

They began to be afraid of the English. There was something devilish in the rapid manœuvres of their ships and the torrents of shot which plunged into their tall sides, while their own flew wild and harmless. Their ammunition too, slowly as they had fired, was giving out as well as the English's and it was less easy for them to supply themselves. The duke resolved to fight no more if he could help it, and to make the best of his way to the Prince of Parma, to whom he again wrote without attempting to conceal his perplexities.

"The enemy pursue me," he said. "They fire upon me most days from morning till nightfall; but they will not close and grapple. I have given them every opportunity. I have purposely left ships exposed to tempt them to board; but they decline to do it, and there is no remedy for they are swift and we are slow. They have men and ammunition in abundance, while these actions have almost consumed ours; and if these calms last, and they continue the same tactics, as they assuredly will, I must request your excellency to send me two shiploads of shot and powder immediately. I am in urgent need of it. I trust to find you ready on my arrival to come out and join me."

The day following, Friday, the duke was allowed a respite. The fine weather continued, and the Spaniards inclined away towards the coast of France, while Howard bore up for Dover for the supplies of all kinds which he so frightfully needed. The Earl of Sussex, who was in command at the castle, gave him all the powder that he had. The stores came in which had been taken from the prizes: every barrel of powder, every shot, whether of stone or iron, having been first carefully registered for the severe account which it was known that the queen would demand. The victuallers had not arrived, but were supposed to be at the mouth of the Thames; and having obtained as much as he could get, if less than he wanted, Howard returned in the evening to his place in the rear of the Armada.

On Saturday the weather broke. After less than a week of calm and sunshine, squalls and driving showers again came up from the westward. The Armada was then off Boulogne, the English fleet a league behind it. The duke, with the prospect of a rising sea, without pilots who knew the coast, afraid of the Downs for fear of the Goodwin Sands, and of Margate on account of the banks and shoals in the mouth of the river, determined to bring up in Calais roads and wait there till Parma was ready. The wind was to the west of south, and as long as it held in that quarter the roadstead was tolerably secure. Coming up with a rising tide, he let fall his anchors suddenly, hoping that his pursuers would be unprepared, and would be swept past him; but his movements had been observed by eyes which were skilful to interpret them. The English anchors fell simultaneously with his own two miles astern, and the two fleets lay watching each other, almost within cannon-shot of the shore.

There were still some hours of daylight remaining, and M. Gourdain, the governor of Calais, drove down with his wife to the parade, in the hope of seeing a battle. The duke sent an officer on shore to intimate his arrival and request the hospitalities of the port, while a boat went on to Dunkirk with another despatch to the prince.

It was brief, uneasy, and impatient: Sidonia was irritated at finding no answer to his former letters. He again confessed himself helpless against the repeated assaults of the enemy. He trusted Parma was ready to cross. If not, and if there was to be more delay, he begged him to send immediately thirty or forty flyboats or gunboats, which could move quickly and keep the English at bay. He was uncomfortable at the position of the fleet, and painfully anxious to remove to some more secure anchorage.

It is needless to say that the prince had not been idle. His expenses were so enormous that he had been once more in ex-

tremity for money—his army had been in as bad case as the
English fleet at Plymouth, and at the point of breaking up
through famine. He had kept his men together only by the
expectation of the supplies which were coming with the fleet.
Medina Sidonia's letters had reached him one after the other,
and the troops were in perfect readiness to go on board the
transports. The officer who came from Calais expressed impatience that they were not already embarked. The duke, it
seems, had expected that Parma would have met him on the
sea, and that they could fight the English with their united
force. Farnese explained that this was impossible. To come
out while the enemy's fleet was undispersed would be certain
destruction. His transports could not protect themselves.
The Armada must clear the Channel, and, weather permitting,
he was then prepared to fulfil his majesty's commands. As
to sending gunboats to protect Medina Sidonia, he could not
do it, for he had none belonging to him. Medina Sidonia must
protect him. Ammunition he would provide, "so far as his
own penury would allow."

That the majestic fleet which was to overwhelm opposition
should arrive at the scene of action so helpless as itself to require
assistance was not particularly encouraging. Parma however
promised that his army should go on board immediately. He
would be ready, he said, by the middle of the following week.
He admitted that the Armada must not remain a day longer
than necessary in Calais roads, and was as anxious as the duke
could be to see it in some better shelter. Only he reiterated—
and as the duke was evidently unconvinced, he sent a special
messenger to Philip to insist upon it—that to risk his barges in
a naval engagement would be simple madness. They could not
encounter even the slightest roll of the sea, and if there was no
enemy to fear could only pass safely in a calm.

Parma's answer did not diminish Medina Sidonia's uneasiness. More than half of his shot was expended and with the
enemy's fleet so near the promised supply from Dunkirk could
not easily reach him. On the night of his arrival too the few
Flemish pilots that he had slipped overboard in the darkness,
stole the cockboats, set their shirts for sails, and made for Flushing, leaving him dependent on the imperfect knowledge of the
Spanish shipmasters and their still more imperfect charts.

XIV

Grave however as may have been the anxiety of the Spanish commander, Lord Howard and the English officers had cause for deeper disquiet. Their spirits were unshaken, their resolution firm as ever, but they could not conceal from themselves that they had severe and dangerous work before them, and that on their conduct only it depended to save their country, if not from conquest yet from being the scene of a bloody and desperate struggle. Notwithstanding all that they could do, the enemy's fleet had arrived at its destination, how much injured they could not tell, but to appearance with its strength not materially impaired, and in communication with the Prince of Parma's army.

Lord Henry Seymour joined them with the squadron of the Straits an hour after they anchored, and forty London privateers were reported to be in the mouth of the Thames. But ships and men were of no use without food and ammunition. Seymour "was victualled but for one day's full meal." Howard and Drake, after sharing all they had in their respective divisions, eked out as it had been by short rations, fish, and voluntary fasting, could provide their crews but with five scanty dinners and one breakfast more. The provisions said to be on the way had not arrived and of powder, after all that Sussex had been able to furnish out of Dover Castle, they had only sufficient for one day's fighting. Burghley had laboured in vain with the queen. He had tried to borrow money in the city, but his credit in the city had sunk with the appearance of the Spaniards and the prudent merchants had drawn their purse-strings till the cloud over the future should be raised. The treasury was not empty. There is no record that the half million of reserve had been touched. The Burgundian diamonds had been neither restored nor disposed of; but to the money and the jewels, which, as Howard said, would never save her, Elizabeth clung with the maddened grasp of passionate avarice. It was known that there was powder in the Tower. A messenger had galloped up from Dover stating the condition of the fleet and pressing for an instant supply. The most tape-bound constitutional government could not have sent a more helpless answer than Walsingham was obliged to return. The admiral was lying with empty magazines, with an enemy twice his strength almost within gunshot, and he was required to specify exactly "the proportion of shot and powder that he wanted."

Deserters may perhaps have comforted him with the knowledge that the Spaniards were no better provided; but Parma's magazines were at hand, and delay at all events was ruin. Starvation, if nothing else, would drive every English ship from the seas in another week, and the Channel would be in the enemy's possession.

XV

Sunday was fine, with the wind still from the southwest. The boats of the Armada passed backwards and forwards between the galleons and Calais, bringing fresh vegetables, medicines, and other conveniences. In the afternoon, as the breeze freshened, five large English ships drove their anchors and fouled each other, but they were separated without serious hurt and securely moored again, and at five in the evening a council of war was held in Howard's cabin. If we are to believe Camden, "the foresight of Queen Elizabeth" prescribed the course which was resolved upon.

The Spanish fleet was anchored close on the edge of the shoal water, and to attack it where it lay was impossible. It was determined to drive them out into the Channel with fire-ships, of which they were known to be afraid. Sir Henry Palmer proposed to cross to Dover and fetch over some worthless hulks but time would be lost, and there was not a day nor an hour to spare. Among the volunteer vessels which had attached themselves to the fleet there were many that would be useless in action, and as fit as the best for the service for which they were now needed. Eight were taken, the rigging smeared rapidly with pitch, the hulls filled with any useless material which could be extemporised that would contribute to the blaze. The sky was cloudy. The moon was late in its last quarter, and did not rise till morning and the tide, towards midnight, set directly down from the English position to where the ships of the Armada, seeking shelter from the bend of the coast, lay huddled dangerously close. Long, low, sighing gusts from the westward promised the rising of a gale. The crews of the condemned vessels undertook to pilot them to their destination and then belay the sheets, lash the helm, fire, and leave them.

Thus, when the Spanish bells were striking midnight and, save the watch on deck, soldiers and seamen lay stretched in sleep, certain dark objects which had been seen dimly drifting on the tide near where the galleons lay thickest, shot suddenly into pyramids of light, flames leaping from ruddy sail ·to sail, flickering on the ropes, and forecastles, foremasts, and bowsprits, a lurid blaze of conflagration. A cool commander might have ordered out his boats and towed the fireships clear; but Medina Sidonia, with a strain already upon him beyond the strength of his capacity, saw coming upon him some terrible engines of destruction, like the floating mine which had shattered Parma's bridge at Antwerp.

Panic spread through the entire Armada; the enemy they most dreaded was upon them. The galleons were each riding with two anchors; for their misfortune few of them were provided with a third. A shot was fired from the *San Martin* as a signal to cut or slip their cables and make to sea. Amidst cries and confusion, and lighted to their work by the blaze, they set sail and cleared away, congratulating themselves, when they had reached the open water and found that all or most of them were safe, on the skill with which · they had defeated the machinations of the enemy. They lay-to six miles from shore, intending to return with the daylight, recover their anchors and resume their old position.

The English meanwhile, having accomplished at least part of their purpose in starting the Armada out of its berth, weighed at leisure, and stood off after it into the Channel, Drake, with half the fleet, hanging on the skirts of the Spaniards; Howard, with the rest, hovering nearer to Calais, endeavouring to drive in upon the sands or the fire-ships the last loiterers of the Armada which had been slower than the rest in getting. out. The first object which the admiral saw at daybreak was the largest of the four galleasses, with de Moncada himself on board, aground on Calais bar. Her helm had been entangled in a cable, she had become ungovernable, and the tide had forced her ashore within shot of the French batteries at back of the sandbank which forms the harbour.

The tide had ebbed, the water was still round her, but she had fallen over towards the bank, and Howard, whose notion was to "pluck the feathers of the Spaniards one by one," sent his own launch with some other boats to take her. She was powerfully manned; between soldiers, sailors, and slaves, she carried seven hundred men. In the position in which she was lying however her large guns were useless, and the galley slaves, with the prospect of liberty before them, did not make the defence more easy. The Spaniards fought gallantly; several of the English were killed, but at last two musket-balls struck Monçada at the same moment. He fell dead on the deck. The slaves sprang overboard, and, half in panic and half in pursuit, the crew and the troops followed. "Some swam, some waded to shore, many were drowned." The English swarmed up over the bulwarks, took possession of the galleass, and intended to wait for the tide to carry her off.

XVI

The French meanwhile were watching the scene in crowds from the top of the Rysbank. M. Gourdain, as the ship was on the French shore, might have disputed if he had pleased the lawfulness of the capture. He contented himself with sending off a boat with a message that the English deserved the spoil for their courage, and might have it; but the ship itself he required them to leave where it lay. The language was perfectly friendly, and Gourdain, having been appointed by the king, was better disposed to England than to Spain. National antipathy however proved too strong to be controlled. "Our rude men," says an English officer who was present, "knowing no difference between friend and foe," began to ill use the French who had come on board, "spoiling them," and probably pitching them into the sea. Their friends on shore took up their quarrel. The Rysbank battery opened upon the galleass in return, and the English had to scramble into their boats in haste, carrying with them what plunder they could seize.

It was well that no more time was wasted over so small a matter. Lord Howard had delayed already too long for his fame. It was no time for the admiral of the fleet to be loitering over a stray plume which had dropped from the enemy's wing, when every ship was imperiously needed for a far more important service.

The wind was still rising and threatened a storm. He had seen enough of the sailing powers of the galleons to be assured that until it shifted they could make no way against it; and once in the North Sea, they would be in unknown waters without a harbour into which they could venture to run, and at all events for a time cut off from their communication with Dunkirk. They had drifted in the night further than they intended, and when the sun rose they were scattered over a large surface off Gravelines. Signals were sent up for them to collect and make back for Calais; but Drake with his own squadron and Henry Seymour with the squadron of the Straits, having the advantage of wind, speed, and skill, came on them while they were still dispersed.

Seymour opened the action at eight in the morning with a cluster of galleons on the Spaniards' extreme right. Reserving their fire till within a hundred and twenty yards, and wasting no cartridges at any longer distance, the English ships continued through the entire forenoon to pour into them one continuous rain of shot. They were driven in upon their own centre, where they became entangled in a confused and helpless mass, a mere target to the English guns, Sir William Winter alone delivering five hundred shot into them, "never out of harquebuz range, and often within speaking distance."

Drake himself meanwhile had fallen on Medina Sidonia and Oquendo, who, with a score of galleons better handled than the rest, were endeavouring to keep sea room, and retain some command of themselves. But their wretched sailing powers put them at a disadvantage for which skill and courage could not compensate. The English were always to windward of them, and hemmed in at every turn, they too were forced back upon their consorts, hunted together as a shepherd hunts sheep upon a common, and the whole mass of them forced slowly towards the shoals and banks on the Flanders coast.

Howard came up at noon to join in the work of destruction. The English accounts tell a simple story. The Spaniards' gun practice, which had been always bad, was helpless beyond past experience. Their want of ammunition was not suspected, for they continued to fire throughout the day after their slow awkward fashion; but their guns, worked on rolling platforms by soldiers unused to the sea, sent their shot into the air or into the water while the English fired into them without intermission from eight in the morning till sunset, "when almost the last cartridge was spent, and every man was weary with labour."

They took no prizes and attempted to take none. Their orders were to sink or destroy. They saw three large galleons go down. Three others, as the wind fell westerly, they saw reeling helplessly towards Ostend and the fate of these they heard of afterwards; but of the general effect of the fire, neither at the time nor afterwards did they know anything beyond its practical and broad results. Some details however of that terrible day can be gathered from the narratives of the few Spaniards who fought through it and survived to tell the tale.

Being always to leeward and the wind blowing hard, the hulls of the galleons as they heeled over were exposed below the waterline. The massive timbers which were to have furnished so secure a shelter added only to the effect of the shot. The middle decks were turned into slaughter-houses and in one ship blood was seen streaming from the lee scuppers. Their guns were most of them dismounted or knocked in pieces, and their chief work was to save themselves from sinking by nailing sheets of lead over the shot holes. The action was on so large a scale and there was so much smoke and confusion that individuals could only see what was immediately near them.

Don Pedro Coco Calderon, purser of the fleet, (in his ship) lay most of the day at the side of Medina Sidonia, himself exposed to the tempest of balls. Alonzo de Leyva with the *Rata* was next to him, and close by were the *San Matteo* and the *San Felipe,* commanded by Don Diego de Pimentel and Don Francisco de Toledo. They were opposed to Drake in person and, frightful as was their disadvantage, they fought with conspicuous courage. With men falling in all directions, and heads and arms flying in the smoke, they still manned their maintops, keeping up a fire of musket-balls. Don Francisco finding, as he supposed, that the *San Felipe* was sinking, attempted to grapple with the English ship that was nearest to him. He had fought so well that one of the English officers, seeing his apparently desperate condition, sprung upon his forecastle and called to him in Spanish complimenting his valour and bidding him save the lives of his brave crew by an honourable surrender. One of the Spaniards replied with a shot from a musket. The officer fell; the English ship filled her sails and backed away, leaving the *San Felipe* to her fate, the Spanish crew shouting after them that they were cowards and Lutheran hens, and daring them to come on once more.

It was an idle bravado: soon after the *San Felipe* sent up signals of distress. A barque called the *Doncella* went to her assistance, but was herself shot through and through while the crew of the *San Felipe* were going on board her, and she filled so rapidly that they returned into their own galleon, made for the shore and contrived to keep afloat till they touched the sands between Nieuport and Ostend. The Nieuport boatmen carried them into a friendly harbour, from whence they made their way to the Prince of Parma. The *San Antonio* of Padua, another of the three which the English observed to fall away, crawled into Ostend, where she was taken possession of by the English garrison.

The *San Matteo* had a sadder fortune. She too, finding that she was filling, sent to Medina Sidonia for assistance. Medina Sidonia had work enough to save himself, and could not help her. She was put before the wind and followed the *San Felipe,* but falling more to leeward grounded between Ostend and the Sluys. She was seen by a Dutch lugger, and Lord Willough-by, who was in Flushing, sent three vessels to take possession of her. She again made a gallant fight, and for two hours kept at bay her new assailants, but she was carried by boarding at last. Don Diego and two or three noblemen were reserved alive for their ransom; all the rest, the survivors of five hundred who went into action in the morning, were either killed or flung into the sea. Among the bodies were found those of two English refugees, one of them a brother of Lord Montague.

Outside meanwhile the battle, if battle it could be called which was but the rending and tearing of a scarce resisting enemy, continued till evening. Towards sunset the wind shifted to the north-west with an increasing sea. The wounded ships were driving in a mass towards the banks, and, had the English powder held out for a few hours more, the entire Armada must have been either sunk or driven ashore. Gun after gun how-ever fell gradually silent. A few provision ships came off from the Thames with a day or two's rations. The men were ex-hausted with toil and hunger combined, and the fleet hauled off to take on board the supplies so sorely needed.

XVII

Sidonia, left to himself, extricated his miserable vessels, and made sail for the North Sea, the *Santa Maria* going down with all hands as the sun went under the horizon. When the ships' companies were called over, it was found that four thousand men had been killed or drowned. The wounded were not mentioned, but were perhaps at least as many more. The galleons pierced and shattered were leaking in all directions, the rigging cut up, the masts splintered, the sails torn, rudders, yards, and bowsprits shot away, and still more unfortunately most of the water-butts destroyed. The men had been kept hard at work the day before cleaning and polishing up the guns. Through some accident they had missed their evening meal. The fire-ships had spoilt their night's rest, and through the long day's desperate engagement there had been no leisure to serve out food. Nature could endure no more. To remain where they were was certain wreck, to attempt to recover Calais was to invite a fresh attack, and they fled away into the German Ocean, as close to the wind as their crippled state would bear, "generally frighted and dismayed."

The condition to which they were reduced was imperfectly conjectured by the English. Had the fairest weather come to their relief that English August ever knew, their crews could not have been induced to face Drake again, while they could scarcely have had round shot left to load each gun in the fleet for a single discharge. Howard, who had been present at only half the action, imagined that they "were still wonderful great and strong." Drake saw more clearly that "the day's service had much appalled them," and that some days at least would have to pass "before Parma and Sidonia would shake hands." Still it was thought certain that they would come back if they were not pursued, and though both Drake's and Howard's magazines were almost empty, and they believed those of the Spaniards to be full, they determined "to put on a brag," and "give chase as though they had wanted nothing."

Thus, when morning once more dawned on the miserable Armada, they again saw on their weather beam, almost within cannon-shot, and clinging to them like their shadow, the dreaded English fleet. It was the eve of St. Lawrence's day, Philip's patron saint, whose precious shoulder-bone he had added to the treasures of the Escorial. But St. Lawrence, though he might save his worshippers' souls in the other world, seemed to want either power or will to aid them in the present.

To windward was the enemy, to leeward and clear within

sight the seas were breaking on the endless shoals which fringe the low coast of Holland. The lead gave but seven fathoms, and for each mile they sailed the depth grew less and less, as the north-west wind edged them nearer to the line of yellow foam. Crippled as they were, their masts would not bear a weight of sail sufficient to draw them off. To tack was impossible; there was still room to wear round, but only to fall into the enemy's hands or venture another engagement. Pilots they had none. Their most experienced officers were gone. De Valdez and Francisco of Toledo were prisoners; Pimentel had been flung on the coast of Flanders; Monçada lay dead at Calais; Diego Florez, the Castilian admiral, had lost heart and nerve. The men generally were sick with despondency, and a seaman, taken afterwards in Ireland, said if the English had that day offered to board them, they would all have struck. Sidonia in his extremity summoned the young Miguel de Oquendo to advise him.

"Señor Oquendo," he exclaimed, "what are we to do? We are lost—what are we to do?"

Oquendo gave a brave man's answer.

"Let Diego Florez talk of being lost," he said. "Let your excellency bid me order up the cartridges."

An opportune shift of wind came to the duke's relief, sent, as was fondly imagined, by "the Lord." Swinging suddenly to the east it smoothed the sea and lifted him away from the banks to the open water. The English being no longer to windward fell back, and the Spaniards, with scanty sail, and refitting as they could their shattered spars and stays, crawled out of danger. They had now a fair wind to return to Calais. The sea having gone down, Parma could come out of Dunkirk, and seeing the enemy retiring, Sidonia partially rallied his spirits and called a council of war.

Martinez de Recalde, Diego Florez, Alonzo da Leyva, with the best of the sailing masters, and among them Coco Calderon, who tells the story, came on board the *San Martin;* and Diego Florez asked for the opinions of all of them, what it would be best to do? His own he probably indicated in the tone in which he put the question. There was the alternative of a return into the Channel or a return to Spain by the Orkneys and Ireland. The first was the way of courage, the second of imagined safety, and they chose the last. The proud Castilian spirit which had

presumed to match the world in arms was broken. A de
Leyva or an Oquendo might prefer death to what they might
deem dishonour. The common men would not face a repetition
of the scene of the preceding day.

Calderon, who was an experienced navigator, said that the
west of Ireland was dangerous; but terror of the English fleet
was more real than the unsubstantial perils of an untried sea.
He was overruled. The supply of water in the fleet was examined into, and a sufficient quantity to support life was allotted
to each person, and all that day and all the next day the Armada
pursued its tedious way into the North Sea.

Howard, too, with the change of wind, called his officers
about him. The Prince of Parma depended for what he called
"the sinews of the enterprise," on the Spanish troops which
Sidonia was bringing, and he had made up his mind distinctly
that cross he would not unless the Armada returned to support
him. But the English only knew that Dunkirk was unguarded,
the water smooth, and the defence of the country left to the incapacity of Leicester. It was decided that Lord Henry Seymour's
squadron must return to its post in "the narrow seas." They
waited till dark that their departure might not be seen by the
Spaniards; and bitterly against their will, for another action was
confidently looked for, though "in a manner famished for want
of victuals," thirty vessels turned round outside Brill and made
the best of their way back to the Straits. In a few hours the
uncertain weather had again changed. They were met by a returning south-wester and were driven into Harwich; the
Channel was once more made impassable, and the alarm on the
score of Parma was at an end.

Meantime Drake and the lord admiral, with ninety sail and
five days' provisions, clung to the rear of the enemy. "We have
the army of Spain before us," wrote Drake to Walsingham, "and
mean, by the grace of God, to wrestle a fall with it. There was
never anything pleased me better than seeing the enemy flying
with a southerly wind to the northwards. God grant ye have
a good eye to the Duke of Parma, for with the grace of God,
if we live, I doubt not ere it be long so to handle the matter
with the Duke of Sidonia as he shall wish himself at St. Mary
Port among his orange trees."

The Spaniards, finding that they were not attacked, and observing that the number of their pursuers was reduced, flattered

themselves that the English too must have suffered severely in the action of Monday, and that if they were afraid themselves, they were also an object of fear. The ignominy of returning to Spain, having accomplished nothing, became more obvious the more it was considered, and Sidonia once more began to gather up his courage and to think again of trying to recover Calais. But the black south-wester scattered his reviving spirits. Without pilots, in a strange sea, with the autumn storms prematurely upon him, and with no friendly port for which to run, he became utterly unmanned. The very elements had turned against him, the special prerogative of the Almighty, and he could think of nothing now but of hastening home by the ocean road, where, let the dangers be what they might, there was no English enemies in his path.

On therefore the Armada sped before the rising breeze, the English still following in expectation every moment that they would bear up and engage, and unable to believe that Castilians would yield so easily and go back to their own country with dishonour and shame. Harder and harder blew the wind, and as the sea rose, their distressed condition became more apparent. The pursuing fleet began now to pass drowned and drowning bodies of mules and horses flung over to save the scanty water-casks.

XVIII

There had been some uneasiness about Scotland. Lord Maxwell had been at Lisbon in the spring, and it was supposed that they might possibly be making for the Forth. But they passed on without attempting to enter it; and there seemed no probability that if they let the Forth escape them they would try for any other Scotch harbour. It was now blowing a gale. The English had but three days' provisions left, and to follow further so ill provided, with the prospect of a continuing storm, was to run into needless danger.

Drake thought that the Armada would make for Denmark, refit in the Cattegat, and return at its leisure. Two pinnaces were detached to watch its course, and sending an express to London from Dunbar, to beg that food and ammunition might be dispatched to Margate for them, they turned back before they were overtaken by famine. It was a sore disappointment, for they knew that, had they been fairly provided, not a Spanish

ship would have carried home the tale of the Armada's discomfiture. The hope now was that the elements might complete
the work of the guns. "The long foul weather might be followed by a later summer." But if the gales continued to blow
from the south-west, it was uncertain whether, torn and crippled
as they were, they would be able to fetch Denmark. "Their
great ships were so light" that, even when sound and in fair
weather, "they could hardly bear their sails." The climate of
the North Sea was also likely to try the sailors who had been
trained in lower latitudes, and the opinion in the English fleet,
soundly formed as it proved, was "that many of them would
never see Spain again."

Hunger however was an enemy that would not fly. Storm
or no storm, unless Howard could recover the Thames his case
would be as bad as Sidonia's; and he beat back in the face of
the gale, Hawkins's spars and cordage standing proof against
all trials. Off the Norfolk coast, the wind became so furious
that the fleet was scattered. Howard, with the largest of the
ships, reached Margate as he intended. Others were driven
into Harwich, and rejoined him when the weather moderated.

The greatest service ever done by an English fleet had been
thus successfully accomplished by men whose wages had not
been paid from the time of their engagement, half-starved,
with their clothes in rags and falling off their backs, and so
ill-found in the necessaries of war that they had eked out their
ammunition by what they could take in action from the enemy
himself. "In the desire for victory they had not stayed for the
spoil of any of the ships that they lamed. It were marvellous
good a thousand pounds' worth of hose, doublets, shoes, shirts,
and such like were sent down with all expedition, else in a
very short time I look to see most of the mariners go naked,"
Howard wrote to Burghley. There was no prize-money coming
to them to reward their valour. Their own country was the
prize for which they had fought and conquered. They had
earned, if ever Englishmen had earned anywhere, the highest
honour and the highest recompense which the government
could bestow.

The reward which in fact they received will be very briefly
told. Food had been provided, and was sent down the river
on the 9th—19th of August. The one month's victuals taken
in at Plymouth on the 23rd of June had been stretched over

seven weeks. The three days' rations with which the fleet had left the Forth had been made to serve for eight days. Entire crews had thus been absolutely famishing. The next point to be determined was if the ships were to be paid off or were to remain in commission. "Sure bind, sure find," was the opinion of Lord Howard. It was still possible that the Armada might return. "A kingdom was a great wager, and security was dangerous, as they would have found had not God been their friend." Drake "would not advise her majesty to hazard a kingdom with saving a little charge." "The Prince of Parma," he said, "was a bear robbed of his whelps; and for his credit's sake, being so good a soldier, would try to do something." The queen, on the other hand, thought of nothing but the expense, and was only eager to stop the drain on the exchequer at the earliest possible moment. The question was answered, and the uncertainty was ended, by causes independent of the will either of herself or her advisers. The strain of the last few months was taken off, and with it the spur to the hearts and spirits of the exhausted seamen.

Even at Plymouth short food and poisonous drink had brought dysentery among them; and in one vessel, "the *Elizabeth Jonas,* which had done as well as any ship in any service had ever done," there had been "a dangerous infection from the beginning." Want of food, want of clothes, want of the relief which, if they had been paid their wages, they might have provided for themselves, had aggravated the tendencies to disease, and a frightful mortality now set in through the entire fleet.

Boatloads of poor fellows were carried on shore at Margate, and were laid down to die in the streets, "there being no place in the town to receive them." The officers did what they could. Howard's and Drake's purses were freely opened—some sort of shelter was provided at last in barns and outhouses, but the assistance which they could provide out of their personal resources was altogether inadequate. "It would grieve any man's heart," wrote Lord Howard, "to see men who had served so valiantly to die so miserably."

The fear of Parma's coming soon died away. In a few days news came that the camp at Dunkirk was broken up, the stores taken out of the transports, and the sailors paid off: the pinnaces sent in pursuit of the Armada returned with clear tidings that it had passed westward round the Orkneys, but the havoc among the brave men who had driven it from the shores of England became daily more and more terrible. They sickened one day; they died the next. In the battle before Gravelines not sixty in all had been killed; before a month was out, there was hardly a ship which had enough men left to weigh the anchors.

It was characteristic of the helplessness at headquarters produced by Elizabeth's hardness that, notwithstanding the disorder was traced definitely to the poisonous beer, it continued to be served out. Nothing better was allowed till it was consumed. The sick required fresh meat and vegetables. Within a few hours as they were of London, they continued to be dieted with the usual salt beef and fish. The men expected that, at least, after such a service they would be paid their wages in full. The queen was cavilling over the accounts, and would give no orders for money till she had demanded the meaning of every penny that she was charged. It was even necessary for Sir John Hawkins to remind the government that the pay of those who died was still due to their relatives.

From the severe nature of the service, Lord Howard had been obliged to add to the number of officers. He was challenged for the extra pay, and was obliged to petition for some small assistance from the queen in defraying it himself. "The matter is not great," he said. "Five hundred pounds, with the help of my own purse, will do it. However it fall out, I must see them paid."

XIX

There had been expenses in the fleet which could not be avoided, and in the destitution in which he had been left Howard had used three thousand pistoles out of the treasure taken in the ship of Pedro de Valdez. So keen an account was exacted of him that the lord admiral of England, the conqueror of the Armada, had to defend himself against a charge of peculation. "I did take them," he wrote to Walsingham, "as I told you I would: for, by Jesus, I had not three pounds left in the world, and have not anything could get money in London—my plate was gone before. But I will repay it within ten days after my coming home. I pray you let her majesty know so; and, by the Lord God of heaven, I had not one crown more, and had it not been mere necessity I would not have touched one; but if I had not some to have bestowed upon some poor miserable men, I should have wished myself out of the world."

The worst meanness was yet to come. A surcharge appeared in the accounts of six hundred and twenty pounds, for "extraordinary kinds of victual, wine, cider, sugar, oil, and fresh fish," distributed among the ships while at Plymouth by the order of Howard and Drake. The lord admiral explained that a few delicacies had been thought necessary for the relief of men who, being sick or wounded, might be unable to digest salt meat. He admitted that he had done what was unusual; he said that he had made the allowances "in regard of the greatness of the service for the encouragement of those on whose forwardness and courage success depended." He might have added that their legitimate food had been stolen from them by the queen's own neglect. He petitioned humbly that she would pass the charge. It is uncertain whether she consented or not. It is certain that a further sum for the same purpose Lord Howard felt obliged to take upon himself. He struck the entry out of his account book. "I will myself make satisfaction as well as I may," he said, "so that her majesty shall not be charged withal."

Lord Howard perhaps, as a nobleman whose father had received large benefactions from the crown, and to whom the queen afterwards was moderately liberal, might be expected to contribute at a time of difficulty out of his private resources. The same excuse will not cover the treatment of Sir John Hawkins, who owed nothing to any crowned head, and was the architect of his own fortunes. Hawkins had not only been at the head of the dockyards, but he had been the person employed in collecting the ships' companies, and afterwards in settling the wages with them. No English vessels ever sailed out of port in better condition. No English sailors ever did their duty better.

But Elizabeth had changed her mind so often in the spring, engaging seamen and then dismissing them and then engaging others, that between charges and discharges the accounts had naturally grown intricate. Hawkins worked hard to clear them, and spent his own fortune freely to make the figures satisfactory; but she, who had been herself the cause of the confusion, insisted on an exactness of statement which it was difficult if not impossible to give; and Hawkins, in a petition in which he described himself as a ruined man, sued for a year's respite to disentangle the disorder.

The two statesmen fared no better who had furnished the brain of England, while the fleet had been its right arm. Burghley and Walsingham (Sir Francis, diplomat and a secretary of state) were the soul of the policy which had placed Elizabeth in triumph at last at the head of Protestant Europe. For them, in the hour of victory, there was only abuse, scattered freely and in all presences. They who had never wavered, who had steadily advised a single course, who had never ceased to urge the necessity of providing in time for exigencies which they knew to be approaching—they it was who were made responsible for what had been wanting in the service, and for the shifts of purpose which had been the cause of the neglect. "All irresolutions and lacks," Burghley wrote to Walsingham, "are thrown upon us two in all her speeches to everybody. The wrong is intolerable."

But did Elizabeth show no consciousness of the glorious work which had been done for herself and for the commonwealth? Was there not one of those illustrious sons of England on whom as his sovereign she conferred the honours which were due from his country's gratitude? It was not so altogether. The nation knew Elizabeth only by her public acts. The harassed hours of her ministers, the struggles by which the measures were forced out of her by which England had been barely saved, these of course were unrevealed to the world, and altogether undreamt of. The misery of the dying seamen was set down to the hand of God or to the incapacity of inferior officers.

To her people she was always plausible; always to appearance frank and free-spoken. She was now the heroine of the hour. The wreath of victory which her subjects had won for her they laid at the feet of their sovereign; and that sovereign with gracious condescension bestowed it upon her Leicester. Leicester had saved England, and England was required to do homage to the bravest of her sons. The queen visited the favoured earl at the camp at Tilbury. She rode along the lines of her army with Leicester at her side scattering gracious speeches which none better understood how to make than she, and then, as she had given the great seal to her second favourite, her "Mutton," Sir Christopher Hatton, on Leicester she meditated conferring the far more serious office of lieutenant-general of England and

Ireland. The letters patent were drawn out, and would have
been issued, so Camden says, but for the remonstrances of
Burghley and Hatton, and for misgivings excited at the last
moment in herself on the prudence of the wild act which she
was meditating.

Her fondness likely enough would have carried the day in
the end had not the earl, at the moment of his anticipated
greatness, suddenly died. Scandal of course suggested poison;
more authentic evidence says that he was carried off by a fever
on his way to Kenilworth. (This is the Leicester (1532-1588),
husband of Amy Robsart, whose murder he was suspected of
arranging in order that he might be free to wed Elizabeth. Scott
based his *Kenilworth* upon the romatic historical material provided by the relations between the queen and Leicester.)

XX

When Howard bore up for the Forth the Spaniards for the
first time breathed freely, and began to examine into their
condition. An inquiry was held on board the *San Martin* into
the causes of their misfortunes. Officers who had shown cowardice in action were degraded and set to row in the galleasses;
and Don Christobal de Avila, captain of the *Santa Barbara,*
was hanged. The stores had probably been injured by the
salt water which had made its way through the shot-holes. In
some ships the wine as well as the water-casks had been pierced,
and it was found necessary to reduce the allowances throughout
the fleet. Eight ounces of bread, half a pint of wine, and a
pint of water was all that could be afforded for each man.
Sidonia promised two thousand ducats to a French pilot if he
would bring the Armada into a Spanish port. Calderon sketched
a chart of the route which he submitted to the duke's council.
The wounded began to fail rapidly, and each day in every
galleon there was the sad ceremony of flinging the dead into the
sea. Calderon's ship contained the medicines and delicacies for
the sick, and passing daily from galleon to galleon, he knew
the condition of them all.

Of the hundred and fifty sail which had left Coruña, a hundred and twenty could still be counted when Howard left them.
For five days they were in the gale which he met on his way
back to the Thames, and which he described as so peculiarly

violent. The unusual cold brought with it fog and mist, and
amidst squalls and driving showers, and a sea growing wilder
as they passed the shelter of the Scotch coast, they lost sight
of each other for nearly a week. On the 9th the sky lifted,
and Calderon found himself with the *Almirante* of Don Martinez de Recalde, the galleon of Don Alonzo, the *San Marcos,*
and twelve other vessels. Sick signals were flying all round,
and the sea was so high that it was scarcely possible to lower a
boat. The large ships were rolling heavily. Their wounded
sails had been split by the gusts, and masts and yards carried
away.

That night it again blew hard. The fog closed in once more,
and the next morning Calderon was alone in the open sea without a sail in sight, having passed between the Orkneys and
the Shetlands. Recalde and de Leyva had disappeared with
their consorts, having as Calderon conjectured gone north. He
himself stood on west and south-west. On the 12th, he saw
a number of sails on the horizon; on the 13th—23rd he found
himself with Sidonia and the body of the fleet and Sidonia
signalled to him to come on board. Observations showed that
they were then in 58° 30′ north latitude. Their longitude they
did not know. They were probably a hundred and fifty miles
west-north-west of Cape Wrath. Sidonia asked anxiously for
Recalde and de Leyva. Calderon could only say where he had
last seen him. He supposed that they had gone to the Faroe
Isles or to Iceland, where there were German fishing stations
which had a trade with Spain.

Again a council was held. The sickness had become frightful.
Those who had escaped unwounded were falling ill from want
and cold and the wounded were dying by hundreds, the incessant storms making care and attention impossible. Calderon
and the French pilot insisted that at all costs and hazards they
must keep off the Irish coast. Diego Florez, distressed for the
misery of the men, to whose sufferings want of water had become a fearful aggravation, imagined that along the west shore
there must be a harbour somewhere and that they would find
rest and shelter among a hospitable Catholic people. The
Bishop of Killaloe, a young Fitzmaurice, and a number of Irish
friars were in the fleet. Diego Florez had possibly heard them
speak of their country and countrymen, and there were fishing
connections between Cadiz and Valencia and Galway, which he

and many others must have known of, though they had not been on the coast in person.

But the Irish themselves were with Alonzo de Leyva, and Sidonia happily took the opinion of the pilots. The day was fine and the sick were divided; those which could be moved were transferred wherever there was most room for them, and as Calderon passed to and fro among the galleons with his medicines and his arrowroot, he was received everywhere with the eager question, where was Alonzo de Leyva? There was scarcely a man who did not forget his own wretchedness in anxiety for the idol of them all.

The calm had been but an interlude in the storm. The same night the wild west wind came down once more, and for eleven consecutive days they went on in their misery, unable to communicate except by signals, holding to the ocean as far as their sailing powers would let them and seeing galleon after galleon, Oquendo's among them, falling away to leeward amidst driving squalls and rain, on the vast rollers of the Atlantic. An island, which he supposed to be ten leagues from the coast, Calderon passed dangerously near. It was perhaps Achill, whose tremendous cliffs fall sheer two thousand feet into the sea, or perhaps Innisbofin or Innishark. On the 4th of September he with Sidonia and fifty vessels, fifty-two ships only out of a hundred and fifty, leaking through every seam, and their weary crews ready to lie down and die from exhaustion, crawled past the Blaskets, and were out of danger.

XXI

Don Martinez and de Leyva, with five-and-twenty of them, had steered north after passing the Orkneys. They went on to latitude 62°, meaning, as Calderon had rightly conjectured, to make for the settlement in Iceland. They had suffered so severely in the action that they probably doubted their ability to reach Spain at all. The storms however, which grew worse as the air became colder, obliged them to abandon their intention. One galleon was driven on the Faroe Isles; the rest turned about, and, probably misled by the Irish, made for the Shannon or Galway. As they braced to the wind, their torn rigging gave way; spar after spar, sail after sail, was carried away. Those which had suffered most dropped first to leeward.

A second was lost on the Orkneys; a third fell down the coast of Scotland and drifted on the Isle of Mull. It was one of the largest ships in the whole fleet. The commander (his name is unknown) was a grandee of the first rank, always "served in silver." He had made his way into some kind of harbour where he was safe from the elements; but the Irish Scots of the Western Isles were tempted by the reports of the wealth which he had with him. The fainting crew could not defend themselves and the ship was fired and burnt, with almost every one that it contained.

Their companions holding a better, but only rather better course, rolled along upon the back of Ireland, groping for the hoped-for shelter. The coming of the Spaniards had been long dreamt of by the Irish as the era of their deliverance from tyranny. It had been feared as their most serious danger by the scanty English garrison. The result of the fight in the Channel, if known at all, was known only by vague report; and the country was thrown into a ferment of excitement when, in the first week of September, Spanish sails were reported in numbers as seen along the western coast, off Donegal, off Sligo, in Clew Bay, at the mouth of the Shannon; in fact everywhere.

At first there was a universal panic. Seven ships were at Carrigafoyle. The mayor of Limerick, in sending word of their appearance to the council, converted them into seven score. Twenty-four men were said to have landed at Tralee. Sir William Fitzwilliam, who had returned to be deputy, and was more infirm and incapable than ever, described them as twenty-four galleons. Rumour gradually took more authentic form. Beyond doubt, Spaniards were on the coast, distressed, but likely notwithstanding to be extremely dangerous if they were allowed to land in safety and to distribute arms and powder among the Irish clans.

With one consent, but without communicating with each other, the English officers seem to have concluded that there was but one course for them to pursue. The party at Tralee were Sidonia's household servants, who had been driven into the bay in a small frigate, had surrendered, and had been brought on shore half dead. They begged hard for life; they had friends at Waterford, they said, who would pay a handsome ransom for them. But fear and weakness could not afford to be magnanimous. Sir Edward Denny, who commanded at

Tralee Castle, gave orders for their execution, and they were all put to the sword.

Two days before, two large galleons had rounded the point of Kerry and had put into Dingle. They belonged to Recalde's squadron: one of them was the *Almirante* herself, with Don Martinez on board, who was dying from toil and anxiety. They wanted water; they had not a drop on board but the dregs of the putrid puddle which they had brought with them from Spain, and they sent boats on shore to beg for a supply. The boats' crews gave so piteous an account of Recalde's condition, the Catholic cause was so clearly now the losing one, that it was decided they should have no relief at Dingle. The boats were seized, the men who had landed imprisoned, and those on board the galleons, hunted already within a hair's-breadth of destruction, and with death making daily havoc among them, hoisted their ragged sails and went again to sea.

One of the prisoners taken at Dingle, thus describes the condition of Recalde's galleon:—

"There died four or five in the ship every day of hunger and thirst, and yet this ship was one of the best furnished for victuals which he knoweth, for out of some other ship people were sent to be relieved out of this ship. There remain five hundred men, one hundred of them are very sick, and do lie down and die daily, all the rest very weak, and the captain very sad and weak. Twenty-five pipes of wine are left in the ship, and very little bread, and no water but what they brought out of Spain, which stinketh marvellously, and their flesh meat they cannot eat, the drought is so great. No part of the navy touched land anywhere or had any relief of water since the English fleet left them."

Another galleon of a thousand tons, named *Our Lady of the Rosary*, which Calderon had watched sadly falling away before the waves, had also nearly weathered the headland of Kerry. She had all but escaped. Clear of the enormous cliffs of the Blasket Islands she had no more to fear from the sea. Between the Blaskets and the mainland there is a passage which is safe in moderate weather, but the gale, which had slightly moderated, had risen again. The waves as they roll in from the Atlantic on the shallowing shores of Ireland boil among the rocks in bad weather with a fury unsurpassed in any part of the ocean.

Strong tidal currents add to the danger, and when *Our Lady of the Rosary* entered the sound it was a cauldron of boiling foam. There were scarcely hands to work the sails. Out of seven hundred, five hundred were dead, and most of the survivors were gentlemen, and before she was half way through, she struck among the breakers upon the island. A maddened officer ran the pilot (a Genoese) through the heart, "saying he had done it by treason." Some of the gentlemen tried to launch a boat, but no boat could live for a moment in such a sea. The pilot's son lashed himself to a plank, and was washed on shore alone of the whole company, and all the rest lay among cannon and doubloon chests amidst the rocks in Blasket Sound.

The same 10th of September witnessed another and more tremendous catastrophe in Thomond. The seven ships in the mouth of the Shannon sent their cockboats with white flags into Kilrush, asking permission for the men to come on land. There were no English there, but there were local authorities who knew that the English would hold them answerable, and the request was refused. Here, as everywhere, the Spaniards' passionate cry was for water. They offered a butt of wine for every cask of water; they offered money in any quantity that the people could ask. Finally, they offered the sheriff of Clare "a great ship, with all its ordnance and furniture," for licence to take as much water as would serve their wants.

All was in vain. The sheriff was afraid of an English gallows, and not one drop could the miserable men obtain for themselves by prayer or purchase. They were too feeble to attempt force. A galleass landed a few men, but they were driven back empty-handed; so abandoning and burning one of the galleons which was no longer seaworthy, the other six went despairingly out into the ocean again. But it was only to encounter their fate in a swifter form. They were caught in the same gale which had destroyed *Our Lady of the Rosary*. They were dashed to pieces on the rocks of Clare, and out of all their crews a hundred and fifty men struggled through the surf, to be carried as prisoners immediately to Galway.

Two other galleons were seen at the Isle of Arran. The end of one was unknown, save that it never returned to Spain. The other, commanded by Don Luis of Cordova, who had his nephew and several other Spanish nobles with him, threatened to founder, and Don Luis, trusting to the Spanish connections

of Galway, carried her up opposite to the town and sent a
strong party, or what would have been a strong party had it
been composed of healthy men and not of tottering skeletons,
to the quay. They were made prisoners on the spot, and Don
Luis, under whose eyes they were taken, offered to surrender
if he could have a promise of life for himself and his companions.
The mayor said that they must give up their arms.

While they were hesitating, they saw the Irish snatching the
chains and tearing off the clothes of their comrades, and with
feeble hands they vainly attempted to weigh anchor.

XXII

Other vessels went on shore at different points of Connemara.
Sir Richard Bingham, the governor of Connaught, sent round
orders that every one who came to land alive must be brought
into Galway. Armed searching parties were detached through
Clare and Connemara to see that the command was obeyed;
and several hundred half-dead wretches were added to those
who had been already taken. Bingham was a fine soldier and
a humane man, and that he could see but one way of dealing
with so large and so dangerous a body of prisoners must be
accepted as some evidence that nothing else could have been
easily done with them. Rest and food would only give them
back their strength, and the feeble garrisons were scarce in
sufficient strength to restrain the Irish alone.

Directions were therefore given that they should be all put
to death, and every one of the unfortunate creatures was deliberately shot or hanged, except Don Luis and nine others,
whose ransoms, it was hoped, might be found valuable. George
Bingham, Sir Richard's son, or brother, went up into Mayo to
see the same. work done there also; and "thus," wrote Sir
Richard himself, "having made a clean despatch of them, both
in town and country, we rested Sunday all day, giving praise
and thanks to Almighty God for her majesty's most happy
success and deliverance from her dangerous enemies." Don
Luis, with his nephew and the rest whose lives had been
spared, were ordered to Drogheda, to be carried thence to
England. Don Luis only arrived: the others either died on

the road, or being unable to march, were killed by their escort
to save the trouble of carrying them.

Young Bingham's presence proved unnecessary in Mayo.
The native Irish themselves had spared him all trouble in inquiring after prisoners. The fear that they might show sympathy with the Spaniards was well founded so long as there
was a hope that the Spaniards' side might be the winning one;
but as the tale of their defeat spread abroad, and the knowledge
with it that they were too enfeebled to defend themselves, the
ties of a common creed and a common enmity to England
were not strong enough to overcome the temptation to plunder.

The Castilian gentlemen were richly dressed, and their velvet
coats and gold chains were an irresistible attraction. The
galleon of Don Pedro de Mendoza had made Clew Bay in a
sinking state, and was brought up behind Clare Island. Don
Pedro went ashore with a hundred companions, carrying his
chests of treasures with him. The galleon was overtaken by
the gale of the 10th of September, which had made the havoc
at the mouth of the Shannon. She was dashed on the rocks,
and all who had been left on board were drowned. "Dowdany
O'Malley, chief of the island," completed the work, by setting
upon Don Pedro and the rest. They were killed to the last
man, and their treasure taken.

A consort of Don Pedro was driven past Clare Island into
the bay and wrecked at Burrishoole. The savages flocked like
wolves to the shore. The galleon went to pieces. The crew
were flung on the sands, some drowned, some struggling still
for life; but whether they were dead or alive made no difference
to the hungry rascals who were watching to prey upon them.
A stroke of a club brought all to a common state and, stripped
of the finery which had been their destruction, they were left
to the wash of the tide.

More appalling still, like the desolation caused by some
enormous flood or earthquake, was the scene between Sligo
and Ballyshannon. A glance at the map will explain why there
was a concentration of havoc on those few miles of coast. The
coast of Mayo trends directly westward from Sligo for seventy
miles and crippled vessels, which had fallen upon a lee shore,
were met by a wall of cliff stretching across their course for a
degree and a half of longitude. Their officers had possibly
heard that there was shelter somewhere in the bay. Many

ships were observed for days hovering between Rossan Point and Killala, but without experienced pilots they could not have found their way in the finest weather among the shoals and islands. They too were overtaken by the same great storm. The numbers that perished are unknown; there are no means to distinguish between those that foundered out in deep water and those that went to pieces on the beach. The actual scene however, as described by two English witnesses, was as frightful as human eye ever looked upon.

"When I was at Sligo," wrote Sir Geoffrey Fenton, "I numbered on one strand of less than five miles in length eleven hundred dead bodies of men which the sea had driven upon the shore. The country people told me the like was in other places, though not to the like number."

Sir William Fitzwilliam made a progress to the west coast from Dublin shortly after. "As I passed from Sligo," he said, "I held on towards Bundroys, and so to Ballyshannon, the uttermost part of Connaught that way. I went to see the bay where some of those ships were wrecked, and where, as I heard, lay not long before twelve or thirteen hundred of the dead bodies. I rode along upon that strand near two miles, but left behind me a long mile or more, and then turned off from the shore, leaving before me a mile and better; in both which places they said that had seen it, there lay as great store of the timber of wrecked ships as was in that place which myself had viewed; being, in my opinion, more than would have built five of the greatest ships that ever I saw, besides mighty great boats, cables and other cordage answerable, thereunto, and some such masts for bigness and length as I never saw any two could make the like."

The sea was not answerable for all. The cruelty of nature was imitated by the cruelty of man, and those lines of bodies showed gashes on them not made by rock or splintered spar. "The miseries they sustained upon this coast," wrote Sir George Carew, "are to be pitied in any but Spaniards. Of those that came to the land by swimming or enforced thereto by famine, very near three thousand were slain." "They were so miserably distressed coming to land," reported another, "that one man, named Melaghlin M'Cabbe, killed eighty with his gallowglass axe." The nobler or wiser O'Neil wrung his hands over the disgrace of his country, but could not hinder it; and the

English looked on with a not unnatural satisfaction at work which was dissolving in murder an alliance which they had so much cause to fear.

The harvest was reaped by the Irish. Sir Richard Bingham and his kindred were at hand to glean the ears that were left. Including the execution at Galway, Bingham claimed to have killed eleven hundred. "Divers gentlemen of quality" had been spared for their ransom, but special orders came down from Dublin to execute all, and the gentlemen followed the rest. Of the whole number that fell into the hands of the English, Don Luis Cordova was the only survivor.

Such was the fate of the brilliant chivalry of Spain, the choicest representatives of the most illustrious families in Europe. They had rushed into the service with an emotion pure and generous as ever sent Templar to the sepulchre of Christ. They believed that they were the soldiers of the Almighty. Pope and bishop had commended them to the charge of the angels and the saints. The spell of the names of the apostles had been shattered by English cannon. The elements, which were deemed God's peculiar province—as if to disenchant Christendom, were disenchantment possible, of so fond an illusion—whirled them upon a shore which the waves of a hundred million years had made the most dangerous in the world; there as they crawled half drowned through the surf to fall into the jaws of the Irish wolves.

XXIII

One more tragical story remains to be told. When Calderon recovered the main body of the fleet off Cape Wrath, and the anxious question was asked him from every ship, where was Alonzo de Leyva?—it was not for de Leyva's sake alone, though no officer in the Armada was more loved and honoured; it was because the freight of the vessel which bore him was more than usually precious. The noblest youths in Castile, whose families had been hardly persuaded to let them accompany the expedition, had been placed specially under Don Alonzo's care. His ship had been in the thickest of every fight. She had suffered severely and could not bear her sails. She had not gone north with Recalde when Calderon left her; but with another galleon she had drifted away to leeward.

With extreme difficulty she had cleared the extreme point of Mayo, but unable to go further she had made her way into Blacksod Bay and anchored outside Balloroy. That she had reached so intricate a spot undestroyed was perhaps explained by the presence on board of young Maurice Fitzgerald, the son of Sir James "the traitor," whose pirate habits may have taught him many secrets of the western coast. Fitzgerald died while she lay there, and "was cast into the sea in a cypress chest with great solemnity." It was the country of the MacWilliams, the home and nest of the famous Granny O'Malley. Fourteen Italians were set on shore to try the disposition of the people. They fell in with one Richard Burke, called "the Devil's Hook," or "Devil's Son," who robbed them and took them prisoners. This was on the 9th of September. In the storm of the 10th the ship, which had left her best anchors at Calais, fell helplessly on shore. The sea was broken by a headland which covers the bay; de Leyva and his companions reached the sands, and were able to carry arms with them.

They found an old castle at no great distance from the water and attempted to put it in a state of defence. Report said that Sidonia himself was in this party. Bingham was making haste to the spot when he heard that they had re-embarked in another galleon, and were beating out again to sea. The south-west wind was still so heavy that it was thought impossible they could escape. Many shots were heard from the offing the night after they sailed, and the ship with all it contained was supposed to have gone to the bottom. The galleon was left to be plundered. Casks of wine and oil were rolled on shore. Trunks and mails of the young hidalgos were dragged out and rifled by the experienced "Devil's Hook," and the sands of Ballycroy were strewed with velvets and gold brocade. The sheriff came to the rescue in the queen's name; but the jackals were too strong for him, or the constables put on jackals' skins and scrambled with the rest for the prey. Not a rag or a coin was rescued.

Meanwhile the shots were not de Leyva's, but came from another straggler which was dashed in pieces upon the rocks of Erris. De Leyva, finding the wind heading him, had determined to run back and try for Scotland, trusting rather to the humanity of the heretic James than to the orthodox cruelties of the Irish. He fell in with a second galleon off the coast and the last of the four galleasses, and together they laboured hard to draw off from the shore. But Rossan Point stood out too far for them to clear, and they made for Callibeg or Killibeg harbour. The galleass got in "sore broken," but still able to float. The two galleons ran on the rocks at the opening, and de Leyva was wrecked a second time.

Again however no lives were lost. Fourteen hundred men from the ships got safe on land. The galleass contained six hundred more, and they were all well provided with arms. Arms however were not food and they were starving. The Bishop of Killaloe and an Irish friar who had been with Don Alonzo and had been saved with the rest, undertook that they should be hospitably treated, and a few hundreds of them marched inland with the bishop for a guide. They fell in with a party of Anglo-Irish sent by Fitzwilliam from the Pale and led by two brothers named Ovington. It was night; the Ovingtons fell upon them, killed twenty and wounded more. In the morning they found they were dealing with men who were half dead already. The Spaniards had laid down their harquebuses and had not strength to lift them again. "The best," it was observed, "seemed to carry some kind of majesty; the rest were men of great calling." Perhaps natural pity—perhaps the fear of O'Neil who was in the neighborhood—perhaps respect for the bishop, so far influenced the Ovingtons that they did not kill them. They contented themselves with stripping some of them naked and letting them go.

In the extreme north of Ulster—where O'Neil and O'Donnell were still virtual sovereigns, where the MacSweenies ruled under them with feudal authority and appear in the Elizabethan maps as giants sitting in mail upon their mountains, battle-axe in hand—the fear of the English was less felt than in other parts of Ireland. O'Neil, who was furious at the savagery which had been perpetrated on the coast, when he heard of these new comers, sent orders that the strangers should be hospitably entertained; and, escaped out of the hands of the Ovingtons, both the party that they had fallen in with and those which remained at Callibeg were supplied with food and allowed to rest and recover themselves.

O'Neil was not at the time in rebellion. Fitzwilliam sent a command that every Spaniard who had landed should be taken or killed. O'Neil sheltered, fed, and clothed his guests till they had recovered strength, and then pretended that they were too powerful for him to meddle with. It was suspected that he meant to use their service in an insurrection, and two thousand soldiers were shipped in hot haste from England to make head against them./

(Hugh O'Neill, second Earl of Tyrone, powerful in the west and northwest of Ireland, was intermittently friend and foe of the English, especially in the reigns of Elizabeth and James I.)

But if the Irish chief had any such intention, de Leyva did not encourage it. His one thought was to escape, if escape were possible, from a country which had been the scene of such horrible calamities to Spain, and to carry back the precious treasures which had been entrusted to his care. Either for this reason, or influenced privately by threats or promises from Fitzwilliam, MacSweeney Banagh, on whom the Spaniards depended for their meat, began after a few weeks to shorten the supplies. The galleass at Callibeg—she was called the *Gerona*—was not hopelessly unseaworthy. The October weather appeared to have settled, and Don Alonzo had repaired her so far that he thought she could carry him safely to the western isles of Scotland. She would hold only half the party; but many Spaniards had found friends in Ulster who undertook to take care of them through the winter months, and had no objection to be left behind. The rest, with Don Alonzo at their head, prepared to tempt once more the fortunes of the sea. He had been hurt in the leg by a capstan when the galleon went on the rocks and was still unable to walk. He was carried on board and in the middle of October the *Gerona* sailed.

She crept along the coast for several days without misadventure. Rossan Point was passed safely, and Tory Island, and Lough Swilly, and Lough Foyle. The worst of the voyage was over; a few hours more and they would have been saved. But the doom of the Armada was on them. They struck upon a rock off Dunluce; the galleass broke in pieces, and only five out of the whole number were saved. Thrice wrecked, Don Alonzo and the young Castilian lords perished at last. Two hundred and sixty of their bodies were washed ashore and committed undistinguished to the grave.

With this concluding catastrophe the tragedy of the Armada in Ireland was ended. It was calculated that in the month of September alone, before de Leyva and his companions were

added to the list, eight thousand Spaniards perished between
the Giant's Causeway and Blasket Sound: eleven hundred
were put to death by Bingham; three thousand were murdered
by the Irish; the rest, more fortunate, were drowned.

But the tale of misery was still incomplete, and those who
seemed to have escaped were attended to the last by the same
strang fatality. The ships which remained with Sidonia, and
suceeded in weathering Kerry, made all sail for Spain, and the
wind still hanging to the south of west, they were still obliged
to keep as close to it as possible and dragged on but slowly.
They passed Cape Clear in company on the 4th of September, after which each vessel shifted for itself with general
directions to make if possible for Coruña.

Calderon held his course till the 12th, when his last drop
of water was consumed. The wind and the sea showed no signs
of abatement and the remains of his crew, wearied and worn
out, could no longer work the vessel. He had lost his reckoning,
and only knew that he was somewhere in the Bay of Biscay.
He had made up his mind to run before the wind, and take
his chance of the land to which it would carry him, when
towards evening he saw a ship crawling along, having lost
her topmasts. She fired a gun, to which Calderon replied. She
proved to be one of the finest of the galleons, though so
shattered that he had not recognised her. He learned however
from her captain that the coast of Spain was but a few leagues
distant and that Santander lay directly under their lee. They
both reached the harbour there the next evening.

Sidonia had arrived the day before, and one after another
the survivors dropped in throughout the following week.
Recalde only, with the other vessel which was with him in
Dingle, succeeded in fetching Coruña; some were as far to leeward as St. Sebastian. Fifty-four vessels in all came back, and
between nine and ten thousand still living men. So wretched
was their state that an officer sent from Madrid said that it was
piteous to see them. Foul and stinking as the ships were, the
crews were obliged at Santander to remain in their berths at
the risk of pestilence, for there was no hospital large enough
to receive so many and the owners of private houses feared
infection. Sidonia abandoned himself to misery, shut himself
up in his room, refusing to attend to business, and as soon as
he could move, fled and hid himself in his country house. At

St. Sebastian and at Coruña an accident, singularly the same at
both places, finished the horror of the story. (Involving the
burning of a hospital and the blowing up of a ship, which cost
many lives.)

The cry that went up from the Iberian peninsula was as the
cry of the Egyptians when the destroying angel had passed over
the land. There was not a house where there was not one
dead, and that the best and bravest. When the Armada first
reached the Channel, rumour, at its common work, had spread
news of a glorious victory. The English corsairs had fallen
under the wrath of Don Alonzo's sword; the usurping queen
had stooped her dishonoured head before the legions of Parma
and Sidonia.

A few days dispelled the pleasant dream. The true story came
of the scene at Calais, the fireships, the action, and the fight
of the Armada: and then for some weeks there was the prolonged
agony of uncertainty, till the remnants of the shattered ships
reappeared, bringing "testimonial on their sides from what
banquet they came, with loss of half their men in fight, famine,
and sickness, crying out on Sir Francis Drake, saying he was
a devil and no man."

Drake's was the name in every mouth. Drake, against whom
saints and angels had no more power than mortals: an in-
carnated spirit of evil let loose to afflict the Spanish race
throughout the globe.

XXIV

On Philip himself the news broke slowly. Pictures have
been drawn of him sitting in his study in the Escorial and
hearing with Castilian composure that his fleet was destroyed.
Such a scene was in the nature of things impossible. Line by
line and incident by incident the story reached him.

The Prince of Ascoli, said falsely to be Philip's bastard son,
who had accompanied the fleet and had gone on shore at Calais,
sent a diary of his own adventures, and Juan de Manrique,
the officer whom Sidonia had sent to Dunkirk, filled sheets with
complaints of Parma, to whose unreadiness he attributed the
threatened failure of the enterprise. At the end of August
Parma reported further that the Armada had passed the north
of Scotland and was gone he knew not whither, perhaps to

Norway. He did not conceal the magnitude of the disaster,
so far as it was known to him, and Philip's anxious side-notes
may be read upon his letter, counting and commenting on the
various losses. The English, Parma said, had won a great
victory, and so far as he could learn bore their success with
modesty. Their ships were reported to have suffered, but
none had been sunk or taken. The honour belonged to Drake.
The admiral was supposed to have been backward.

The next instalment of the truth was the return of Sidonia
with a third of the fleet. It affected Philip so much that "he
shut himself up in the Escorial, and no one dared to speak to
him." Still there were hopes of the rest. More than sixty
ships remained yet unaccounted for, besides those whose fate
Sidonia could tell. Reports came dropping in of disasters in
Ireland, but with them accounts also of Spaniards landed and
safe among the Irish chiefs.

Months passed away before the calamity was realised in its
appalling extent, and then it seemed for the moment as if the
sceptre of the monarchy was broken, and its scattered empire
was laid open as a prey to the corsairs. The famous mariners
of the peninsula were wholly destroyed. The great officers on
whom Philip most relied were dead or taken. De Valdez,
Recalde, Conçada, Oquendo, de Leyva—all were gone. "There
was not one man left in all Spain," wrote Palmer, "whom the
king might put in place for matters of the sea, for those whom
his trust was in were dead and drowned." "Great lamentation"
especially "was made for Don Alonzo de Leyva, with whom
were all the nobles that went."

(In his *The Great O'Neil* it is said by Sean O'Faolain that
there is no way of "estimating accurately the numbers of
Spaniards drowned or dispatched; just as there is no evidence
at all that the people murdered them by thousands . . . To
this day, amongst the people in the Blaskets and about Dingle
the folk legend still lives of the King of Spain's son . . . who
drowned in the bay with '500 tall men.' He was the King's
illegitimate son, the Prince of Asculum, who had embarked in
the galleon *St. Martin* with the Duke of Medina Sidonia; he
had gone ashore at Calais and come back to the quays to find
that the Duke had cut his cables when Drake suddenly appeared
from the north. By that fatal chance . . . Asculum boarded
the *Santa Maria de la Rosario* . . . which struck the rocks in

the Blasket Sound and sank. . . . When Don Pedro de Mendoza's crew was cast away off Clare Island and Dowdary O'Malley's kerns fell on the poor wretches limping ashore exhausted, battering them down on the rocks or slashing their blood into the sandy shorewater, they were all as much maniacs as murderers. . . . Three ships tried to land at Killybegs; one was lost, the second battered on the jags of the rocks and only the third escaped serious damage. Twenty miles across the boggy side of the same peninsula, at Loughros, Don Alonso de Leyva, Lieutenant General of the Armada, was cast up in the *Santa Anna.* His leg being crushed by a capstan and his ship stove in, he came ashore and set up a regular camp. When he heard about his compatriots across at Killybegs who were trying to float their third ship, the *Gerona,* he joined them and presently sailed away with as many as the *Gerona* could carry. She ran on the Rock of Bunboys and was wrecked with all hands. . . . (O'Neil, the Earl of Tyrone, standing on his right as an independent nobleman . . . came with a great herd of cattle to feed the castaways of Inishowen . . . and got more than 2000 Spaniards away to Scotland. . . . In the wintry weather of '89 . . . the Lord Deputy Fitzwilliam . . . riding along the western seacoast (saw) enough great hulks on the beaches of Tyrconnel alone to build fifteen ships, with tangled cordage, cables 'great mighty boats,' masts rolling in the surf fit to make any normal two.")

SYNOPSIS OF EVENTS BETWEEN THE DEFEAT OF THE SPANISH ARMADA, 1588; AND THE BATTLE OF BLENHEIM, 1704.

1594. Henry IV. of France conforms to the Roman Catholic Church, and ends the civil wars that had long desolated France.

1598. Philip II. of Spain dies, leaving a ruined navy and an exhausted kingdom.

1603. Death of Queen Elizabeth. The Scotch dynasty of the Stuarts succeeds to the throne of England under James I.

1619. Commencement of the Thirty Years' War in Germany.

1624-1642. Cardinal Richelieu is minister of France. He breaks the power of the nobility, reduces the Huguenots to complete subjection; and by aiding the Protestant German princes in the latter part of the Thirty Years' War, he humiliates France's ancient rival, Austria.

1630. Gustavus Adolphus, King of Sweden, marches into Germany to the assistance of the Protestants, who were nearly crushed by the Austrian armies. He gains several great victories, and, after his death Sweden, under his statesmen and generals, continues to take a leading part in the war.

1640. Portugal throws off the Spanish yoke: and the House of Braganza begins to reign.

1642. Commencement of the civil war in England between Charles I. and his parliament.

1648. The Thirty Years' War in Germany ended by the treaty of Westphalia.

1649. Charles I. of England deposed and executed.

1653. Oliver Cromwell lord-protector of England.

1660. Restoration of the Stuarts to the English throne.

1661. Louis XIV. takes the administration of affairs in France into his own hands.

1667-1668. Louis XIV. makes war in Spain, and conquers a large part of the Spanish Netherlands.

1672. Louis makes war upon Holland, and almost overpowers it. Charles II. of England is his pensioner, and England helps the French in their attacks upon Holland until 1674. Heroic resistance of the Dutch under the Prince of Orange.

1674. Louis conquers Franche-Comté.

1679. Peace of Nimeguen.

1681. Louis invades and occupies Alsace.

1682. Accession of Peter the Great to the throne of Russia.

1685. Louis commences a merciless persecution of his Protestant subjects. Charles II. of England dies; James II. succeeds.

1688. Revolution in England. Expulsion of James II. William of Orange is made King of England. James takes refuge at the French court, and Louis undertakes to restore him. General war in the west of Europe.

1697. Treaty of Ryswick. Charles XII. becomes King of Sweden.

1700. Charles II., of Spain, dies, having bequeathed his dominions to Philip of Anjou, Louis XIV.'s grandson. Defeat of the Russians at Narva, by Charles XII.

1701. William III. forms a "Grand Alliance" of Austria, the Empire, the United Provinces, England, and other powers, against France.

1702. King William dies; but his successor, Queen Anne, adheres to the Grand Alliance, and war is proclaimed against France.

-⟦ ELEVEN ⟧-

Blenheim, 1704

WHY DECISIVE: *"The decisive blow struck at Blenheim resounded through every part of Europe; it at once destroyed the
vast fabric of power which it had taken Louis XIV . . . so
long to construct."* [Alison] *"Blenheim had dissipated forever Louis' visions of almost universal conquest."* [Creasy.]

I

THOUGH more slowly moulded and less imposingly vast
than the empire of Napoleon, the power which Louis XIV
had acquired and was acquiring at the commencement of the
eighteenth century, was almost equally menacing to the general
liberties of Europe. If tested by the amount of *permanent*
aggrandisement which each procured for France, the ambition
of the royal Bourbon was more successful than were the
enterprises of the imperial Corsican. All the provinces that
Bonaparte conquered, were rent again from France within
twenty years from the date when the very earliest of them
was acquired. France is not stronger by a single city or a
single acre for all the devastating wars of the Consulate and
the Empire. But for long she still retained the extended
boundaries which Louis XIV gave her.

When Louis XIV took the reins of government into his
own hands, after the death of Cardinal Mazarin (an Italian
who rose to great power in France as a statesman, 1602-61)
there was a union of ability with opportunity, such as France
had not seen since the days of Charlemagne. Moreover, Louis's
career was no brief one. For upwards of forty years, for a
period nearly equal to the duration of Charlemagne's reign,
Louis steadily followed an aggressive and a generally successful policy. He passed a long youth and manhood of
triumph, before the military genius of Marlborough made him
acquainted with humiliation and defeat. The great Bourbon
lived too long. He should not have outstayed our two English
kings—one his dependant, James II, the other his antagonist,
William III. Had he died in the year within which they died,
his reign would be cited as unequalled in the French annals

for its prosperity. But he lived on to see his armies beaten, his cities captured, and his kingdom wasted by disastrous war. It is as if Charlemagne had survived to be defeated by the Northmen, and to witness the misery and shame that actually fell to the lot of his descendants.

Still, Louis XIV, had forty years of success; and from the permanence of their fruits we may judge what the results would have been if the last fifteen years of his reign had been equally fortunate. Had it not been for Blenheim, all Europe might at this day suffer under the effect of French conquests resembling those of Alexander in extent, and those of the Romans in durability.

When Louis XIV began to govern, he found all the materials for a strong government ready to his hand. Richelieu (French cardinal and statesman, 1585-1642) had completely tamed the turbulent spirit of the French nobility, and had subverted the *imperium in imperio* of the Huguenots. The faction of the Frondeurs (a political party in opposition to the Court and Mazarin) in Mazarin's time had had the effect of making the Parisian parliament utterly hateful and contemptible in the eyes of the nation. The Assemblies of the States-General were obsolete. The royal authority alone remained. The King was the State. Louis knew his position. He fearlessly avowed it, and he fearlessly acted up to it.

Not only was his government a strong one, but the country which he governed was strong; strong in its geographical situation, in the compactness of its territory, in the number and martial spirit of its inhabitants, and in their complete and undivided nationality. Louis had neither a Hungary nor an Ireland in his dominions. And it was not till late in his reign, when old age had made his bigotry more gloomy, and had given fanaticism the mastery over prudence, that his persecuting intolerance caused the civil war in the Cevennes (an ancient district of southern France).

Like Napoleon in after-times, Louis XIV saw clearly that the great wants of France were "ships, colonies, and commerce." But Louis did more than see these wants; by the aid of his great minister, Colbert, he supplied them. One of the surest proofs of the genius of Louis was his skill in finding out genius in others, and his promptness in calling it into action. Under him, Louvois organised, Turenne, Condé, Villars, and Berwick, led the armies of France; and Vauban fortified her frontiers. Throughout his reign, French diplomacy was marked by skilfulness and activity, and also by comprehensive far-sightedness such as the representatives of no other nation possessed.

Guizot's testimony to the vigour that was displayed through every branch of Louis XIV's government, and to the extent to which France at present is indebted to him, is remarkable. He says, that, "taking the public services of every kind, the finances, the departments of roads and public works, the military administration, and all the establishments which belong to every branch of administration, there is not one that will not be found to have had its origin, its development, or its greatest perfection, under the reign of Louis XIV." And he points out to us, that "the government of Louis XIV was the first that presented itself to the eyes of Europe as a power acting upon sure grounds, which had not to dispute its existence with inward enemies, but was at ease as to its territory and its people, and solely occupied with the task of administering government, properly so called. All the European governments had been previously thrown into incessant wars, which deprived them of all security as well as of all leisure, or so harassed by internal parties or antagonists that their time was passed in fighting for existence. The government of Louis XIV was the first to appear as a busy thriving administration of affairs, as a power at once definitive and progressive, which was not afraid to innovate, because it could reckon securely on the future. There have been in fact very few governments equally innovating.

"Compare it with a government of the same nature, the unmixed monarchy of Philip II in Spain; it was more absolute than that of Louis XIV, and yet it was far less regular and tranquil. How did Philip II succeed in establishing absolute power in Spain? By stifling all activity in the country, opposing himself to every species of amelioration, and rendering the state of Spain completely stagnant. The government of Louis XIV on the contrary, exhibited alacrity for all sorts of innovations and showed itself favourable to the progress of letters, arts, wealth, in short, of civilisation This was the veritable cause of its preponderance in Europe, which arose to such a pitch that it became the type of a government not only to sovereigns, but also to nations, during the seventeenth century."

While France was thus strong and united in herself, and ruled by a martial, an ambitious, and (with all his faults) an enlightened and high-spirited sovereign, what European power was there fit to cope with her, or keep her in check?

"As to Germany, the ambitious projects of the German branch of Austria had been entirely defeated, the peace of the empire had been restored, and almost a new constitution formed, or an old revived, by the treaties of Westphalia; nay, the imperial eagle was not only fallen, but her wings were clipped."

As to Spain, the Spanish branch of the Austrian house had sunk equally low. Philip II left his successors a ruined monarchy. He left them something worse; he left them his example and his principles of government, founded in ambition, in pride, in ignorance, in bigotry, and all the pedantry of state.

It is not, therefore, to be wondered at that France, in the first war of Louis XIV, despised the opposition of both branches of the once predominant house of Austria. Indeed, in Germany the French king acquired allies among the princes of the Empire against the Austrian emperor himself. He had a still stronger support in Austria's misgovernment of her own subjects.

II

If, after having seen the imbecility of Germany and Spain against the France of Louis XIV, we turn to the two only remaining European powers of any importance at that time, to England and to Holland, we find the position of England as to European politics, from 1660 to 1688, most painful to contemplate. From 1660 to 1688, "England, by the return of the Stuarts, was reduced to a nullity." The words are Michelet's, and though severe they are just. They are, in fact, not severe enough: for when England, under her restored dynasty of the Stuarts, did take any part in European politics, her conduct, or rather her king's conduct, was almost invariably wicked and dishonourable.

Bolingbroke rightly says that, previous to the Revolution of 1688, during the whole progress that Louis XIV made in obtaining such exhorbitant power as gave him well-grounded hopes of acquiring at last to his family the Spanish monarchy,

England had been either an idle spectator of what passed on the Continent, or a faint and uncertain ally against France, or a warm and sure ally on her side, or a partial mediator between her and the powers confederated together in their common defence. But though the court of England submitted to abet the usurpations of France, and the King of England stooped to be her pensioner, the crime was not national. On the contrary, the nation cried out loudly against it even whilst it was being committed.

Holland alone, of all the European powers, opposed from the very beginning a steady and uniform resistance to the ambition and power of the French king. It was against Holland that the fiercest attacks of France were made, and though often apparently on the eve of complete success, they were always ultimately baffled by the stubborn bravery of the Dutch, and the heroism of their leader, William of Orange. When he became king of England, (in 1689, after the downfall of James II), the power of this country was thrown decidedly into the scale against France; but though the contest was thus rendered less unequal, though William acted throughout "with invincible firmness, like a patriot and a hero," France had the general superiority in every war and in every treaty; and the commencement of the eighteenth century found the last league against her dissolved, all of the forces of the confederates against her dispersed, and many disbanded; while France continued armed, with her veteran forces by sea and land increased, and held in readiness to act on all sides, whenever the opportunity should arise for seizing on the great prizes which, from the very beginning of his reign, had never been lost sight of by her king.

This is not the place for any narrative of the first essay which Louis XIV made of his power in the war of 1667; of his rapid conquest of Flanders and Franche-Comté; of the treaty of Aix-la-Chapelle, which "was nothing more than a composition between the bully and the bullied; of his attack on Holland in 1672; of the districts and barrier-towns of the Spanish Netherlands which were secured to him by the treaty of Nimeguen in 1678; of how, after this treaty, he "continued to vex both Spain and the Empire, and to extend his conquests in the Low Countries and on the Rhine, both by the pen and the sword; how he took Luxembourg by force, stole Strasburg, and bought Casal;" of how the league of Augsburg was formed against him in 1686, and the election of William of Orange to the English throne in 1688 gave a new spirit to the opposition which France encountered; of the long and chequered war that followed, in which the French armies were generally victorious on the Continent, though his fleet was beaten at La Hogue, and his dependant, James II, was defeated at the Boyne; or of the treaty of Ryswick, which left France in possession of Roussillon, Artois, and Strasburg, which gave Europe no security against her claims on the Spanish succession, and which Louis regarded as a mere truce, to gain breathing-time before a more decisive struggle.

It must be borne in mind that the ambition of Louis in these years was twofold. It had its immediate and its ulterior objects. Its immediate object was to conquer and annex to France the neighbouring provinces and towns that were most convenient for the increase of her strength; but the ulterior object of Louis, from the time of his marriage to the Spanish Infanta in 1659, was to acquire for the house of Bourbon the whole empire of Spain. A formal renunciation of all right to the Spanish succession had been made at the time of the marriage; but such renunciations were never of any practical effect, and many casuists and jurists of the age even held them to be intrinsically void. As time passed on, and the prospect of Charles II of Spain dying without lineal heirs became more and more certain, so did the claims of the house of Bourbon to the Spanish crown after his death become matters of urgent interest to French ambition on the one hand, and to the other powers of Europe on the other.

At length the unhappy King of Spain died. By his will he appointed Philip, Duke of Anjou, one of Louis XIV's grandsons, to succeed him on the throne of Spain, and strictly forbade any partition of his dominions. Louis well knew that a general European war would follow if he accepted for his house the crown thus bequeathed. But he had been preparing for this crisis throughout his reign. He sent his grandson into Spain as King Philip V of that country, addressing to him on his departure the memorable words, "There are no longer any Pyrenees."

The empire, which now received the grandson of Louis as its king, comprised, besides Spain itself, the strongest part of the Netherlands, Sardinia, Sicily, Naples, the principality of

Milan, and other possessions in Italy, the Philippines and Manila Islands in Asia, and, in the New World, besides California and Florida, the greatest part of central and of southern America. Philip was well received in Madrid, where he was crowned as King Philip V in the beginning of 1701. The distant portions of his empire sent in their adhesion; and the house of Bourbon, either by its French or Spanish troops, now had occupation both of the kingdom of Francis I and of the fairest and amplest portion of the empire and of the great rival of Francis, Charles V.

Loud was the wrath of Austria, whose princes were the rival claimants of the Bourbons for the empire of Spain. The indignation of our William III, though not equally loud, was far more deep and energetic. By his exertions a league against the house of Bourbon was formed between England, Holland, and the Austrian Emperor, which was subsequently joined by the Kings of Portugal and Prussia, by the Duke of Savoy, and by Denmark. Indeed, the alarm throughout Europe was now general and urgent. It was clear that Louis aimed at consolidating France and the Spanish dominions into one preponderating empire.

At the moment when Philip was departing to take possession of Spain, Louis had issued letters-patent in his favour to the effect of preserving his rights to the throne of France. And Louis had himself obtained possession of the important frontier of the Spanish Netherlands, with its numerous fortified cities, which were given up to his troops under pretence of securing them for the young King of Spain. Whether the formal union of the two crowns was likely to take place speedily or not, it was evident that the resources of the whole Spanish monarchy were now virtually at the French king's disposal.

The peril that seemed to menace the empire, England, Holland, and the other independent powers, is well summed up by Alison: "Spain had threatened the liberties of Europe in the end of the sixteenth century, France had all but overthrown them in the close of the seventeenth. What hope was there of their being able to make head against them both, united under such a monarch as Louis XIV?"

Our knowledge of the decayed state into which the Spanish power had fallen, ought not to make us regard their alarms as chimerical. Spain possessed enormous resources, and her strength was capable of being regenerated by a vigorous ruler.

The death of King William on the 8th of March, 1702, at first seemed likely to paralyse the league against France, for "notwithstanding the ill-success with which he made war generally, he was looked upon as the sole centre of union that could keep together the great confederacy then forming; and how much the French feared from his life, had appeared a few years before, in the extravagant and indecent joy they expressed on a false report of his death. A short time showed how vain the fears of some, and the hopes of others were."

Queen Anne, within three days after her accession, went down to the House of Lords, and there declared her resolution to support the measures planned by her predecessor, who had been "the great support, not only of these kingdoms, but of all Europe." Anne was married to Prince George of Denmark, and by her accession to the English throne the confederacy against Louis obtained the aid of the troops of Denmark; but Anne's strong attachment to one of her female friends led to far more 'important advantages to the the anti-Gallican confederacy, than the acquisition of many armies, for it gave them Marlborough as their Captain-General.

III

There are few successful commanders on whom Fame has shone so unwillingly as upon John Churchill, Duke of Marlborough, Prince of the Holy Roman Empire, victor of Blenheim, Ramilies, Oudenarde, and Malplaquet; captor of Liege, Bonn, Limburg, Landau, Ghent, Bruges, Antwerp, Oudenarde, Ostend, Menin, Dendermonde, Ath, Lille, Tournay, Mons, Douay, Aire, Bethune, and Bouchain; who never fought a battle that he did not win, and never besieged a place that he did not take.

Marlborough's own private character is the cause of this. Military glory may, and too often does, dazzle both contemporaries and posterity, until the crimes as well as the vices of heroes are forgotten. But even a few stains of personal meanness will dim a soldier's reputation irreparably; and Marlborough's faults were of a peculiarly base and mean order. Our feelings towards historical personages are in this respect like our feelings towards private acquaintances. There are actions of so shabby a nature, that, however much they may be outweighed by a man's good deeds on a general estimate of his character, on account of them we never can feel any cordial liking for the person who has been guilty of them. Thus, with respect to the Duke of Marlborough, it goes against our feelings to admire the man, who owed his first advancement in life to the court-favour which he and his family acquired through his sister becoming one of the mistresses of the Duke of York.

It is repulsive to know that Marlborough laid the foundation of his wealth by being the paid lover of one of the fair and frail favourites of Charles II. His treachery and ingratitude to his patron and benefactor, James II, stood out in dark relief, even in that age of thankless perfidy. He was almost equally disloyal to his new master, King William; and a more un-English act cannot be recorded than Godolphin's and Marlborough's betrayal to the French court in 1694 of the expedition then designed against Brest, an act of treason which caused some hundreds of English soldiers and sailors to be helplessly slaughtered on the beach in Camaret Bay. (The "fair and frail favorite" referred to was Barbara Villiers, who was made by Charles I countess of Castlemaine and Duchess of Cleveland.)

It is, however, only in his military career that we have now to consider him; and there are very few generals, of either ancient or modern times, whose campaigns will bear a comparison with those of Marlborough, both for the masterly skill with which they were planned, and for the bold yet prudent energy with which each plan was carried into execution. Marlborough had served while young under Turenne, and had obtained the marked praise of that great tactician. It would be difficult, indeed, to name a single quality which a general ought to have and with which Marlborough was not eminently gifted. What principally attracted the notice of contemporaries was the imperturbable evenness of his spirit. Voltaire says of him:—

"He had, to a degree above all other generals of his time, that calm courage in the midst of tumult, that serenity of soul in danger, which the English call *a cool head,* and it was perhaps, this quality, the greatest gift of nature for command, which formerly gave the English so many advantages over the French in the plains of Cressy, Poictiers, and Agincourt."

King William's knowledge of Marlborough's high abilities, though he knew his faithlessness equally well, is said to have

caused that sovereign in his last illness to recommend Marlborough to his successor as the fittest person to command her
armies: but Marlborough's favour with the new queen by means
of his wife, was so high, that he was certain of obtaining the
highest employment: and the war against Louis opened to him
a glorious theatre for the display of those military talents, which
he had before only had an opportunity of exercising in a subordinate character, and on far less conspicuous scenes.

He was not only made captain-general of the English forces
at home and abroad, but such was the authority of England in
the council of the Grand Alliance, and Marlborough was so
skilled in winning golden opinions from all whom he met with,
that, on his reaching the Hague, he was received with transports
of joy by the Dutch, and it was agreed by the heads of that republic and the minister of the emperor, that Marlborough
should have the chief command of all the allied armies.

It must, indeed, in justice to Marlborough, be borne in mind,
that mere military skill was by no means all that was required
of him in this arduous and invidious station. Had it not been
for his unrivalled patience and sweetness of temper, and his
marvellous ability in discerning the character of those with
whom he had to act, his intuitive perception of those who were
to be thoroughly trusted, and of those who were to be amused
with the mere semblance of respect and confidence—had not
Marlborough possessed and employed, while at the head of the
allied armies, all the qualifications of a polished courtier and
a great statesman, he never would have led the allied armies
to the Danube. The Confederacy would not have held together
for a single year.

IV

War was formally declared by the Allies against France on
the 4th of May, 1702. The principal scenes of its operation
were, at first, Flanders, the upper Rhine, and north Italy.
Marlborough headed the allied troops in Flanders during the
first two years of the war, and took some towns from the enemy,
but nothing decisive occurred. Nor did any actions of importance take place during this period, between the rival armies
in Italy. But in the centre of that line from north to south,
from the mouth of the Scheldt to the mouth of the Po, along
which the war was carried on, the generals of Louis XIV ac-

quired advantages in 1703, which threatened one chief member
of the Grand Alliance with utter destruction.   France had obtained the important assistance of Bavaria, as her confederate
in the war.   The elector of this powerful German state made
himself master of the strong fortress of Ulm and opened a
communication with the French armies on the upper Rhine.
By this junction, the troops of Louis were enabled to assail the
emperor in the very heart of Germany.

In the autumn of the year 1703, the combined armies of the
elector and French king completely defeated the Imperialists
in Bavaria; and in the following winter they made themselves
masters of the important cities of Augsburg and Passau.   Meanwhile the French army of the upper Rhine and Moselle had
beaten the allied armies opposed to them, and taken Treves and
Landau.   At the same time the discontents in Hungary with
Austria again broke out into open insurrection, so as to distract the attention and complete the terror of the emperor and
his council at Vienna.

Louis XIV ordered the next campaign to be commenced by
his troops on a scale of grandeur and with a boldness of enterprise, such as even Napoleon's military schemes have seldom
equalled.   On the extreme left of the line of the war, in the
Netherlands, the French armies were to act only on the defensive.   The fortresses in the hands of the French there were
so many and so strong that no serious impression seemed likely
to be made by the Allies on the French frontier in that quarter
during one campaign; and that one campaign was to give
France such triumphs elsewhere as would (it was hoped) determine the war.   Large detachments were, therefore, to be
made from the French force in Flanders and they were to be
led by Marshal Villeroy to the Moselle and upper Rhine.   The
French army already in the neighborhood of those rivers was
to march under Marshal Tallard through the Black Forest, and
join the elector of Bavaria and the French troops that were
already with the elector under Marshal Marsin.

Meanwhile the French army of Italy was to advance through
the Tyrol into Austria, and the whole forces were to combine
between the Danube and the Inn.   A strong body of troops
was to be despatched into Hungary, to assist and organise the
insurgents in that kingdom; and the French grand army of
the Danube was then, in collected and irresistible might, to

march upon Vienna, and dictate terms of peace to the emperor. High military genius was shown in the formation of this plan, but it was met and baffled by a genius higher still.

V

Marlborough had watched, with the deepest anxiety the progress of the French arms on the Rhine and in Bavaria, and he saw the futility of carrying on a war of posts and sieges in Flanders, while death-blows to the empire were being dealt on the Danube. He resolved therefore to let the war in Flanders languish for a year, while he moved with all the disposable forces that he could collect to the central scenes of decisive operations. Such a march was in itself difficult, but Marlborough had, in the first instance, to overcome the still greater difficulty of obtaining the consent and cheerful co-operation of the Allies, especially of the Dutch, whose frontier it was proposed thus to deprive of the larger part of the force which had hitherto been its protection.

Fortunately, among the many slothful, the many foolish, the many timid, and the not few treacherous rulers, statesmen, and generals of different nations with whom he had to deal, there were two men, eminent both in ability and integrity, who entered fully into Marlborough's projects, and who, from the stations which they occupied, were enabled materially to forward them. One of these was the Dutch statesman Heinsius, who had been the cordial supporter of King William, and who now, with equal zeal and good faith, supported Marlborough in the councils of the allies; the other was the celebrated general, Prince Eugene, whom the Austrian cabinet had recalled from the Italian frontier, to take the command of one of the emperor's armies in Germany. To these two great men, and a few more, Marlborough communicated his plan freely and unreservedly; but to the general councils of his allies he only disclosed part of his daring scheme.

He proposed to the Dutch that he should march from Flanders to the upper Rhine and Moselle, with the British troops and part of the foreign auxiliaries, and commence vigorous operations against the French armies in that quarter, whilst General Auverquerque, with the Dutch and the remainder of the auxiliaries, maintained a defensive war in the

Netherlands. Having with difficulty obtained the consent of the Dutch to this portion of his project, he exercised the same diplomatic zeal, with the same success, in urging the King of Prussia, and other princes of the empire, to increase the number of the troops which they supplied, and to post them in places convenient for his own intended movements.

Marlborough commenced his celebrated march on the 19th of May. The army, which he was to lead, had been assembled by his brother, General Churchill, at Bedburg, not far from Maestricht on the Meuse: it included sixteen thousand English troops and consisted of fifty-one battalions of foot and ninety-two squadrons of horse. Marlborough was to collect and join with him on his march the troops of Prussia, Luneburg, and Hesse, quartered on the Rhine, and eleven Dutch battalions that were stationed at Rothweil. He had only marched a single day, when the series of interruptions, complaints, and requisitions from the other leaders of the allies began, to which he seemed doomed throughout his enterprise and which would have caused its failure in the hands of any one not gifted with the firmness and the exquisite temper of Marlborough.

One specimen of these annoyances and of Marlborough's mode of dealing with them may suffice. On his encamping at Kupen on the 20th, he received an express from Auverquerque pressing him to halt, because Villeroy, who commanded the French army in Flanders, had quitted the lines which he had been occupying, and crossed the Meuse at Namur with thirty-six battalions and forty-five squadrons, and was threatening the town of Huys. At the same time Marlborough received letters from the Margrave of Baden and Count Wratislaw, who commanded the imperialist forces at Stollhoffen near the left bank of the Rhine, stating that Tallard had made a movement, as if intending to cross the Rhine, and urging him to hasten his march towards the lines of Stollhoffen.

Marlborough was not diverted by these applications from the prosecution of his grand design. Conscious that the army of Villeroy would be too much reduced to undertake offensive operations, by the detachments which had already been made towards the Rhine, and those which must follow his own march, he halted only a day to quiet the alarms of Auverquerque. To satisfy also the margrave, he ordered the troops of Hompesch and Bulow to draw towards Philipsburg, though with private injunctions not to proceed beyond a certain distance. He even exacted a promise to the same effect from Count Wratislaw, who at the juncture arrived at the camp to attend him during the whole campaign.

Marlborough reached the Rhine at Coblentz, where he crossed that river, and then marched along its right bank to Broubach and Mentz. His march, though rapid, was admirably conducted, so as to save the troops from all unnecessary fatigue; ample supplies of provisions were ready, and the most perfect discipline was maintained. By degrees Marlborough obtained more reinforcements from the Dutch and other confederates, and he also was left more at liberty by them to follow his own course. Indeed, before even a blow was struck, his enterprise had paralysed the enemy, and had materially relieved Austria from the pressure of the war. Villeroy, with his detachments from the French-Flemish army, was completely bewildered by Marlborough's movements; and, unable to divine where it was that the English general meant to strike his blow, wasted away the early part of the summer between Flanders and the Moselle without effecting anything.

Marshal Tallard, who commanded forty-five thousand men at Strasburg, and who had been destined by Louis to march early in the year into Bavaria, thought that Marlborough's march along the Rhine was preliminary to an attack upon Alsace; and the marshal therefore kept his forty-five thousand men back in order to support France in that quarter. Marlborough skilfully encouraged his apprehensions, by causing a bridge to be constructed across the Rhine at Philipsburg, and by making the Landgrave of Hesse advance his artillery at Manheim, as if for a siege of Landau.

Meanwhile the Elector of Bavaria and Marshal Marsin, suspecting that Marlborough's design might be what it really proved to be, forbore to press upon the Austrians opposed to them, or to send troops into Hungary; and they kept back so as to secure their communications with France. Thus, when Marlborough, at the beginning of June, left the Rhine and marched for the Danube, the numerous hostile armies were uncombined, and unable to check him.

"With such skill and science had this enterprise been concerted, that at the very moment when it assumed a specific direction, the enemy was no longer enabled to render it abortive. As the march was now to be bent towards the Danube, notice was given for the Prussians, Palatines, and Hessians, who were stationed on the Rhine, to order their march so as to join the main body in its progress. At the same time directions were sent to accelerate the advance of the Danish auxiliaries, who were marching from the Netherlands." (W. Coxe, biographer of Marlborough).

VI

Crossing the river Neckar, Marlborough marched in a south-eastern direction to Mundelshene, where he had his first personal interview with Prince Eugene, who was destined to be his colleague on so many glorious fields. Thence, through a difficult and dangerous country, Marlborough continued his march against the Bavarians, whom he encountered on the 2nd of July on the heights of Schullenberg, near Donauwert. Marlborough stormed their entrenched camp, crossed the Danube, took several strong places in Bavaria, and made himself completely master of the Elector's dominions, except the fortified cities of Munich and Augsburg.

But the Elector's army, though defeated at Donauwert was still numerous and strong; and at last Marshal Tallard, when thoroughly apprised of the real nature of Marlborough's movements, crossed the Rhine. He was suffered, through the supineness of the German general at Stollhoffen, to march without loss through the Black Forest, and united his powerful army at Biberach near Augsburg, with that of the Elector and the French troops under Marshal Marsin, who had previously been co-operating with the Bavarians. On the other hand, Marlborough re-crossed the Danube, and on the 11th of August united his army with the Imperialist forces under Prince Eugene. The combined armies occupied a position near Hochstadt, a little higher up the left bank of the Danube than Donauwert, the scene of Marlborough's recent victory, and almost exactly on the ground where Marshal Villars and the Elector had defeated an Austrian army in the preceding year. The French marshals and the Elector were now in position a little farther to the east, between Blenheim and Lutzingen, and with the little stream of the Nebel between them and the troops of Marlborough and Eugene. The Gallo-Bavarian army consisted of about sixty thousand men, and they had sixty-one pieces of artillery. The army of the Allies was about fifty-six thousand strong, with fifty-two guns. A short time before the War of the Succession the musquet and bayonet had been made the arms of all the French infantry. It had formerly been usual to mingle pikemen with musqueteers. The other European nations followed the example of France and the weapons used at Blenheim were substantially the same as those still employed.

Although the French army of Italy had been unable to penetrate into Austria, and although the masterly strategy of Marlborough had hitherto warded off the destruction with which the cause of the Allies seemed menaced at the beginning of the campaign, the peril was still most serious. It was absolutely necessary for Marlborough to attack the enemy, before Villeroy should be roused into action. There was nothing to stop that general and his army from marching into Franconia, whence the Allies drew their principal supplies; and besides thus distressing them, he might, by marching on and joining his army to those of Tallard and the Elector, form a mass which would overwhelm the force under Marlborough and Eugene. On the other hand, the chances of a battle seemed perilous, and the fatal consequences of a defeat were certain. The inferiority of the Allies in point of number was not very great, but still it was not to be disregarded; and the advantages which the enemy seemed to have in the composition of their troops was striking.

Tallard and Marsin had forty-five thousand Frenchmen under them, all veterans, and all trained to act together: the Elector's own troops also were good soldiers. Marlborough, like Wellington at Waterloo, headed an army, of which the larger proportion consisted not of English, but of men of many different nations, and many different languages. He was also obliged to be the assailant in the action, and thus to expose his troops to comparatively heavy loss at the commencement of the battle, while the enemy would fight under the protection of the villages and lines which they were actively engaged in strengthening.

VII

The consequences of a defeat of the confederated army must have broken up the Grand Alliance, and realised the proudest hopes of the French king. Mr. Alison, in his admirable military history of the Duke of Marlborough, has truly stated the effects which would have taken place if France had been successful in the war. And, when the position of the Confederates at the time when Blenheim was fought is remembered; when we recollect the exhaustion of Austria, the menacing insurrection of Hungary, the feuds and jealousies of the German princes, the strength and activity of the Jacobite party in England, the imbecility of nearly all of the Dutch statesmen of the time and the weakness of Holland if deprived of her allies, we may adopt his words in speculating on what would have ensued, if France had been victorious in the battle, and "if a power, animated by the ambition, guided by the fanaticism, and directed by the ability of that of Louis XIV, had gained the ascendancy in Europe. Beyond all question, a universal despotic dominion would have been established over the bodies, a cruel spiritual thralldom over the minds of men. France and Spain united under Bourbon princes, and in a close family alliance—the empire of Charlemagne with that of Charles V—the power which revoked the edict of Nantes, and perpetrated the massacre of St. Bartholomew, with that which banished the Moriscoes, and established the Inquisition, would have proved irresistible, and beyond example destructive to the best interests of mankind.

"The Protestants might have been driven, like the pagan heathens of old by the son of Pepin, beyond the Elbe; the Stuart race, and with them Romish ascendancy, might have been reestablished in England; the fire lighted by Latimer and Ridley might have been extinguished in blood; and the energy breathed by religious freedom into the Anglo-Saxon race might have expired. The destinies of the world would have been changed. Europe instead of a variety of independent states, whose mutual hostility kept alive courage, while their national rivalry stimulated talent, would have sunk into the slumber attendant on universal dominion. The colonial empire of England would have withered away and perished, as that of Spain had done in the grasp of the Inquisition. The Anglo-Saxon race would have been arrested in its mission to overspread the earth and subdue it. The centralised despotism of the Roman Empire would have been renewed on Continental Europe; the chains of Romish tyranny, and with them the general infidelity of France before the Revolution, would have extinguished or perverted thought in the British Islands."

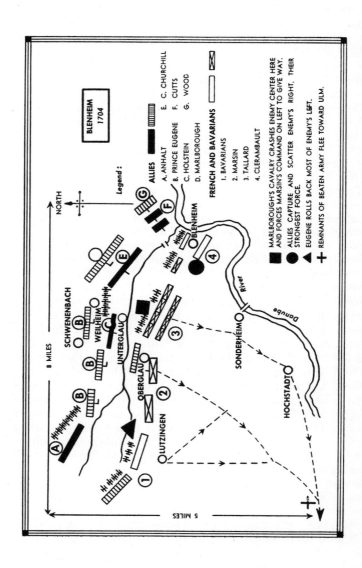

BLENHEIM
1704

Legend:

ALLIES
A. ANHALT
B. PRINCE EUGENE
C. HOLSTEIN
D. MARLBOROUGH
E. C. CHURCHILL
F. CUTTS
G. WOOD

FRENCH AND BAVARIANS
1. BAVARIANS
2. MARSIN
3. TALLARD
4. CLERAMBAULT

MARLBOROUGH'S CAVALRY CRASHES ENEMY CENTER HERE AND FORCES MARSIN'S COMMAND ON LEFT TO GIVE WAY.

ALLIES CAPTURE AND SCATTER ENEMY'S RIGHT, THEIR STRONGEST FORCE.

EUGENE ROLLS BACK MOST OF ENEMY'S LEFT.

REMNANTS OF BEATEN ARMY FLEE TOWARD ULM.

NORTH

8 MILES

5 MILES

SCHWENENBACH

WEILHEIM

UNTERGLAU

OBERGLAU

LUTZINGEN

BLENHEIM

SONDERHEIM

HOCHSTADT

Danube River

Marlborough's words at the council of war, when a battle was resolved on, are remarkable, and they deserve recording. We know them on the authority of his chaplain, Mr. (afterwards Bishop) Hare, who accompanied him throughout the campaign, and in whose journal the biographers of Marlborough have found many of their best materials. Marlborough's words to the officers who remonstrated with him on the seeming temerity of attacking the enemy in their position, were: "I know the danger, yet a battle is absolutely necessary; and I rely on the bravery and discipline of the troops, which will make amends for our disadvantages." In the evening orders were issued for a general engagement, and received by the army with an alacrity which justified his confidence.

VIII

The French and Bavarians were posted behind a little stream called the Nebel, which runs almost from north to south into the Danube immediately in front of the village of Blenheim. The Nebel flows along a little valley, and the French occupied the rising ground to the west of it. The village of Blenheim was the extreme right of their position and the village of Lutzingen, about three miles north of Blenheim, formed their left. Beyond Lutzingen are the rugged high grounds of the Godd Berg, and Eich Berg, on the skirts of which some detachments were posted so as to secure the Gallo-Bavarian position from being turned on the left flank. The Danube protected their right flank; and it was only in front that they could be attacked. The villages of Blenheim and Lutzingen had been strongly palisadoed and entrenched.

Marshal Tallard, who held the chief command, took his station at Blenheim: Prince Maximilian the Elector, and Marshal Marsin commanded on the left. Tallard garrisoned Blenheim with twenty-six battalions of French infantry, and twelve squadrons of French cavalry. Marsin and the Elector had twenty-two battalions of infantry, and thirty-six squadrons of cavalry in front of the village of Lutzingen. The centre was occupied by fourteen battalions of infantry, including the celebrated Irish Brigade. These were posted in the little hamlet of Oberglau, which lies somewhat nearer to Lutzingen than to Blenheim. Eighty squadrons of cavalry and seven battalions

of foot were ranged between Oberglau and Blenheim. Thus
the French position was very strong at each extremity, but was
comparatively weak in the centre. Tallard seems to have relied
on the swampy state of the part of the valley that reaches from
below Oberglau to Blenheim for preventing any serious attack
on this part of his line.

The army of the Allies was formed into two great divisions,
the largest being commanded by the duke in person, and being
destined to act against Tallard, while Prince Eugene led the
other division, which consisted chiefly of cavalry, and was intended to oppose the enemy under Marsin and the Elector.
As they approached the enemy, Marlborough's troops formed
the left and the centre, while Eugene's formed the right of the
entire army. Early in the morning of the 13th of August, the
Allies left their own camp and marched towards the enemy.
A thick haze covered the ground, and it was not until the
allied right and centre had advanced nearly within cannon-
shot of the enemy that Tallard was aware of their approach.
He made his preparations with what haste he could, and about
eight o'clock a heavy fire of artillery was opened from the
French right on the advancing left wing of the British. Marlborough ordered up some of his batteries to reply to it, and
while the columns that were to form the allied left and centre
deployed and took up their proper stations in the line, a warm
cannonade was kept up by the guns on both sides.

The ground which Eugene's columns had to traverse was
peculiarly difficult, especially for the passage of the artillery;
and it was nearly midday before he could get his troops into
line opposite to Lutzingen. During this interval, Marlborough
ordered divine service to be performed by the chaplains at the
head of each regiment and then rode along the lines and
found both officers and men in the highest spirits and waiting impatiently for the signal for the attack. At length an
aide-de-camp galloped up from the right with the welcome news
that Eugene was ready. Marlborough instantly sent Lord Cutts,
with a strong brigade of infantry, to assault the village of Blenheim, while he himself led the main body down the eastward
slope of the valley of the Nebel, and prepared to effect the
passage of the stream.

The assault on Blenheim, though bravely made, was repulsed
with severe loss; and Marlborough, finding how strongly that

village was garrisoned, desisted from any further attempts to carry it, and bent all his energies to breaking the enemy's line between Blenheim and Oberglau. Some temporary bridges had been prepared and planks and fascines had been collected; and by the aid of these, and a little stone bridge which crossed the Nebel, near a hamlet called Unterglau, that lay in the centre of the valley, Marlborough succeeded in getting several squadrons across the Nebel, though it was divided into several branches and the ground between them was soft and in places little better than a mere marsh.

But the French artillery was not idle. The cannon-balls plunged incessantly among the advancing squadrons of the Allies; and bodies of French cavalry rode frequently down from the western ridge, to charge them before they had time to form on the firm ground. It was only by supporting his men by fresh troops, and by bringing up infantry, who checked the advance of the enemy's horse by their steady fire, that Marlborough was able to save his army in this quarter from a repulse which, following the failure of the attack upon Blenheim, would probably have been fatal to the Allies. By degrees, his cavalry struggled over the blood-stained streams; the infantry were also now brought across, so as to keep in check the French troops who held Blenheim, and who, when no longer assailed in front, had begun to attack the Allies on their left with considerable effect.

Marlborough had thus at last succeeded in drawing up the whole left wing of his army beyond the Nebel, and was about to press forward with it, when he was called away to another part of the field by a disaster that had befallen his centre. The Prince of Holstein-Beck had, with eleven Hanoverian battalions, passed the Nebel opposite to Oberglau, when he was charged and utterly routed by the Irish brigade which held that village. The Irish (fighting with the French) drove the Hanoverians back with heavy slaughter, broke completely through the line of the Allies, and nearly achieved a success as brilliant as that which the same brigade afterwards gained at Fontenoy. But at Blenheim their ardour in pursuit led them too far. Marlborough came up in person, and dashed in upon their exposed flank with some squadrons of British cavalry. The Irish reeled back, and as they strove to regain the height of Oberglau their column was raked through and through by the fire of three

battalions of the Allies which Marlborough had summoned up from the reserve. Marlborough having re-established the order and communications of the Allies in this quarter, now, as he returned to his own left wing, sent to learn how his colleague fared against Marsin and the Elector and to inform Eugene of his own success.

Eugene had hitherto not been equally fortunate. He had made three attacks on the enemy opposed to him, and had been thrice driven back. It was only by his own desperate personal exertions, and the remarkable steadiness of the regiments of Prussian infantry which were under him, that he was able to save his wing from being totally defeated. But it was on the southern part of the battle-field, on the ground which Marlborough had won beyond the Nebel with such difficulty, that the crisis of the battle was to be decided.

IX

Like Hannibal, Marlborough relied principally on his cavalry for achieving his decisive successes, and it was by his cavalry that Blenheim, the greatest of his victories, was won. The battle had lasted till five in the afternoon. Marlborough had now eight thousand horsemen drawn up in two lines, and in the most perfect order for a general attack on the enemy's line along the space between Blenheim and Oberglau. The infantry was drawn up in battalions in their rear, so as to support them if repulsed, and to keep in check the large masses of the French that still occupied the village of Blenheim. Tallard now interlaced his squadrons of cavalry with battalions of infantry; and Marlborough, by a corresponding movement, brought several regiments of infantry, and some pieces of artillery, to his front line at intervals between the bodies of horse.

A little after five, Marlborough commenced the decisive movement, and the allied cavalry, strengthened and supported by foot and guns, advanced slowly from the lower ground near the Nebel up the slope to where the French cavalry, ten thousand strong, awaited them. On riding over the summit of the acclivity, the Allies were received with so hot a fire from the French artillery and small arms that at first the cavalry recoiled, but without abandoning the high ground. The guns and the infantry which they had brought with them, maintained the contest with spirit and effect. The French fire seemed to slacken. Marlborough instantly ordered a charge along the line. The allied cavalry galloped forward at the enemy's squadrons, and the hearts of the French horsemen failed them. Discharging their carbines at an idle distance, they wheeled round and spurred from the field, leaving the nine infantry battalions of their comrades to be ridden down by the torrent of the allied cavalry.

The battle was now won. Tallard and Marsin, severed from each other, thought only of retreat. Tallard drew up the squadrons of horse which he had left, in a line extended towards Blenheim, and sent orders to the infantry in that village to leave and join him without delay. But long ere his orders could be obeyed, the conquering squadrons of Marlborough had wheeled to the left and thundered down on the feeble array of the French marshal. Part of the force which Tallard had drawn up for this last effort was driven into the Danube; part fled with their general to the village of Sonderheim, where they were soon surrounded by the victorious Allies and compelled to surrender.

Meanwhile, Eugene had renewed his attack upon the Gallo-Bavarian left, and Marsin, finding his colleague utterly routed, and his own right flank uncovered, prepared to retreat. He and the Elector succeeded in withdrawing a considerable part of their troops in tolerable order to Dilligen; but the large body of French who garrisoned Blenheim were left exposed to certain destruction. Marlborough speedily occupied all the outlets from the village with his victorious troops and then, collecting his artillery round it, he commenced a cannonade that speedily would have destroyed Blenheim itself and all who were in it. After several gallant but unsuccessful attempts to cut their way through the Allies, the French in Blenheim were at length compelled to surrender at discretion; and twenty-four battalions and twelve squadrons, with all their officers, laid down their arms, and became the captives of Marlborough.

"Such," says Voltaire, "was the celebrated battle, which the French call the battle of Hochstet, the Germans Plentheim, and the English Blenheim. The conquerors had about five thousand killed and eight thousand wounded, the greater part being on the side of Prince Eugene. The French army was almost entirely destroyed: of sixty thousand men, so long victorious, there never reassembled more than twenty thousand effectives. About twelve thousand killed, fourteen thousand prisoners, all the cannon, a prodigious number of colours and standards, all the tents and equipages, the general of the army, and one thousand two hundred officers of mark, in the power of the conqueror, signalised that day!"

Ulm, Landau, Treves, and Traerbach surrendered to the Allies before the close of the year. Bavaria submitted to the emperor, and the Hungarians laid down their arms. Germany was completely delivered from France; and the military ascendancy of the arms of the Allies was completely established. Throughout the rest of the war Louis fought only in defence. Blenheim had dissipated for ever his once proud visions of almost universal conquest.

SYNOPSIS OF EVENTS BETWEEN THE BATTLE OF BLENHEIM, 1704, AND THE BATTLE OF PULTOWA, 1709.

1705. The Archduke Charles lands in Spain with a small English army under Lord Peterborough, who takes Barcelona.

1706. Marlborough's victory at Ramilies.

1707. The English army in Spain is defeated at the battle of Almanza.

1708. Marlborough's victory at Oudenarde.

⊰[TWELVE]⊱

Pultowa, 1709

WHY DECISIVE: *"The decisive triumph of Russia over Sweden at Pultowa was all important to the world on account of what it overthrew as well as for what it established; and it is more deeply interesting because it was not merely the crisis of a struggle between the two states, but it was a trial of strength between two great races of mankind. It was the work of a single ruler [Peter the Great] . . . who at Pultowa taught them [the Russians] to face and beat the previously invincible Swedes; and who made stubborn valor and implicit subordination from that time forth the distinguishing characteristics of the Russian soldiery which had before been a mere disorderly and irresolute rabble."* [Creasy.]

I

NAPOLEON prophesied at St. Helena, that all Europe would soon be either Cossack or Republican. It was truly stated, twelve years ago (in 1839) that, "the acquisitions which Russia has made within the [then] last sixty-four years, are equal in extent and importance to the whole empire she had in Europe before that time; that the acquisitions she had made from Sweden are greater than what remains of that ancient kingdom; that her acquisitions from Poland are as large as the whole Austrian empire; that the territory she has wrested from Turkey in Europe, is equal to the dominions of Prussia, exclusive of her Rhenish provinces; and that her acquisitions from Turkey in Asia are equal in extent to all the smaller states of Germany, the Rhenish provinces of Prussia, Belgium, and Holland taken together; that the country she has conquered from Persia is about the size of England; that her acquisitions in Tartary have an area equal to Turkey in Europe, Greece, Italy, and Spain.

"In sixty-four years she has advanced her frontier eight hundred and fifty miles towards Vienna, Berlin, Dresden, Munich, and Paris; she has approached four hundred and fifty miles nearer to Constantinople; she has possessed herself of the capital of Poland, and has advanced to within a few miles of the capital of Sweden, from which, when Peter the Great mounted the throne, her frontier was distant three hundred miles. Since that time she has stretched herself forward about one thousand miles towards India, and the same distance towards the capital of Persia."

Such, at that period, had been the recent aggrandisement of Russia; and the events of the last few years, by weakening and disuniting all her European neighbours, (had) immeasurably augmented the relative superiority of the Muscovite empire over all the other Continental powers.

With a population exceeding sixty millions, all implicitly obeying the impulse of a single ruling mind; with a territorial area of six millions and a half of square miles; with a standing army eight hundred thousand strong; with powerful fleets on the Baltic and Black Seas; with a skilful host of diplomatic agents planted in every court, and among every tribe; with the confidence which unexpected success creates, and the sagacity which long experience fosters, Russia (then, in 1851, grasped) with an armed right hand the tangled thread of European politics, and issued her mandate as the arbitress of the movements of the age.

Yet, a century and a half (had) hardly elapsed since she was first recognised as a member of the drama of modern European history; previously to the battle of Pultowa, Russia played no part. Charles V and his great rival, our Elizabeth and her adversary Philip of Spain, the Guises, Sully, Richelieu, Cromwell, De Witt, William of Orange, and the other leading spirits of the sixteenth and seventeenth centuries, thought no more about the Muscovite czar, than we now think about the King of Timbuctoo. Even as late as 1735, Lord Bolingbroke, in his admirable *"Letters on History,"* speaks of the history of the Muscovites, as having no relation to the knowledge which a practical English statesman ought to acquire." It may be doubted whether a Cabinet Council often takes place now in our Foreign Office, without Russia being uppermost in every English statesman's thoughts.

But, though Russia remained thus long unheeded amid her snows, there *was* a northern power, the influence of which was acknowledged in the principal European quarrels, and whose good-will was sedulously courted by many of the boldest chiefs and ablest councillors of the leading States. This was Sweden, on whose ruins Russia had risen, but whose ascendancy over her semi-barbarous neighbours was complete, until Pultowa.

As early as 1542 France had sought the alliance of Sweden to aid her in her struggle against Charles V. And the name of Gustavus Adolphus is of itself sufficient to remind us that in the great contest for religious liberty, of which Germany was for thirty years the arena, it was Sweden that rescued the falling cause of Protestantism; and it was Sweden that principally dictated the remodelling of the European state-system at the peace of Westphalia. (1648, ending the Thirty Years War.)

From the proud pre-eminence in which the valour of the "Lion of the North," and of Torstenston, Bannier, Wrangel, and the other generals of Gustavus, guided by the wisdom of Oxenstiern, had placed Sweden, the defeat of Charles XII (1682-1718) at Pultowa hurled her down at once and for ever. Her efforts during the wars of the French Revolution to assume a leading part in European politics, met with instant discomfiture, and almost provoked derision. But the Sweden, whose sceptre was bequeathed to Christina (queen from 1644 to 1654. Abdicated and after a wildly romantic life died in Rome in 1689, a Papal pensioner.) and whose alliance Cromwell valued so highly, was a different power from the Sweden of the present day. Finland, Ingria, Livonia, Esthonia, Carelia, and other districts east of the Baltic then were Swedish provinces, and the possession of Pomerania, Rugen, and Bremen, made her an important member of the Germanic empire. These territories are now all reft from her; and the most valuable of them form the staple of her victorious rival's strength. Could she resume them, could the Sweden of 1648 be reconstructed, we should have a first-class Scandinavian state in the north, well qualified to maintain the balance of power, and check the progress of Russia; whose power, indeed, never could have become formidable to Europe, save by Sweden becoming weak.

II

The decisive triumph of Russia over Sweden at Pultowa was therefore all important to the world, on account of what it overthrew as well as for what it established; and it is the more deeply interesting because it was not merely the crisis of a struggle between two states, but it was a trial of strength between two great races of mankind. We must bear in mind that while the Swedes, like the English, the Dutch, and others, belong to the Germanic race, the Russians are a Slavonic people. Nations of Slavonian origin have long occupied the greater part of Europe eastward of the Vistula, and the populations also of Bohemia, Croatia, Servia, Dalmatia, and other important regions westward of that river, are Slavonic. In the long and varied conflicts between them and the Germanic nations that adjoin them, the Germanic race had, before Pultowa. almost always maintained a superiority.

With the single, but important exception of Poland, no Slavonic state had made any considerable figure in history before the time when Peter the Great won his great victory over the Swedish king. What Russia has done since that time we know and we feel. And some of the wisest and best men of our own age and nation, who have watched with deepest care the annals and the destinies of humanity, have believed that the Slavonic element in the population of Europe has as yet only partially developed its powers: that, while other races of mankind (our own, the Germanic, included) have exhausted their creative energies, and completed their allotted achievements, the Slavonic race has yet a great career to run: and that the narrative of Slavonic ascendancy is the remaining page that will conclude the history of the world.

Let it not be supposed that in thus regarding the primary triumph of Russia over Sweden as a victory of the Slavonic over the Germanic race, we are dealing with matters of mere ethnological pedantry, or with themes of mere speculative curiosity. The fact that Russia is a Slavonic empire, is a fact of immense practical influence at the present moment. Half the inhabitants of the Austrian empire are Slavonian. The population of the larger part of Turkey in Europe is of the same race. Silesia, Posen, and other parts of the Prussian dominions are principally Slavonic. And during late years an enthusiastic zeal for blending all Slovanians into one great united Slavonic empire, has been growing up in these countries, which, however, we may deride its principle, is not the less real and active, and of which Russia, as the head and the champion of the Slavonic race, knows well how to take her advantage.

It is a singular fact that Russia owes her very name to a band of Swedish invaders who conquered her a thousand years ago. They were soon absorbed in the Slavonic population, and every trace of the Swedish character had disappeared in Russia for many centuries before her invasion by Charles XII. She was long the victim and the slave of the Tartars; and for many considerable periods of years the Poles held her in subjugation. Indeed, if we except the expeditions of some of the early Russian chiefs against Byzantium, and the reign of Ivan Vasilovitch, the history of Russia before the time of Peter the Great is one long tale of suffering and degradation.

But whatever may have been the amount of national injuries that she sustained from Swede, from Tartar, or from Pole in the ages of her weakness, she has certainly retaliated tenfold during the century and a half of her strength. Her rapid transition at the commencement of that period from being the prey of every conqueror to being the conqueror of all with whom she comes into contact, to being the oppressor instead of the oppressed, is almost without a parallel in the history of nations. It was the work of a single ruler; who, himself without education, promoted science and literature among barbaric millions; who gave them fleets, commerce, arts, and arms; who at Pultowa taught them to face and beat the previously invincible Swedes and who made stubborn valour and implicit subordination from that time forth the distinguishing characteristics of the Russian soldiery, which had before been a mere disorderly and irresolute rabble.

The career of Philip of Macedon resembles most nearly that of the great Muscovite czar; but there is this important difference, that Philip had, while young, received in southern Greece the best education in all matters of peace and war that the ablest philosophers and generals of the age could bestow. Peter was brought up among barbarians, and in barbaric ignorance. He strove to remedy this when a grown man, by leaving all the temptations to idleness and sensuality, which his court offered, and by seeking instruction abroad. He laboured with his own hands as a common artisan in Holland and England, that he might return and teach his subjects how ships, commerce, and civilisation could be acquired. There is a degree of heroism here superior to anything that we know of in the Macedonian king.

But Philip's consolidation of the long disunited Macedonian empire—his raising a people, which he found the scorn of their civilised southern neighbours, to be their dread—his organisation of a brave and well-disciplined army, instead of a disorderly militia—his creation of a maritime force, and his systematic skill in acquiring and improving seaports and arsenals—his patient tenacity of purpose under reverses—his personal bravery— and even his proneness to coarse amusement and pleasures—all mark him out as the prototype of the imperial founder of the Russian power. In justice, however, to the ancient hero, it ought to be added that we find in the history of Philip no examples of that savage cruelty which deforms so grievously the character of Peter the Great.

III

In considering the effects of the overthrow which the Swedish arms sustained at Pultowa, and in speculating on the probable consequences that would have followed if the invaders had been successful, we must not only bear in mind the wretched state in which Peter found Russia at his accession, compared with her present grandeur, but we must also keep in view the fact, that, at the time when Pultowa was fought, his reforms were yet incomplete and his new institutions immature. He had broken up the Old Russia; and the New Russia, which he ultimately created, was still in embryo. Had he been crushed at Pultowa, his mighty schemes would have been buried with him; and (to use the words of Voltaire) "the most extensive empire in the world would have relapsed into the chaos from which it had been so lately taken."

It is this fact that makes the repulse of Charles XII the critical point in the fortunes of Russia. The danger which she incurred a century afterwards from her invasion by Napoleon was in reality far less than her peril when Charles attacked her, though the French emperor, as a military genius, was infinitely superior to the Swedish king, and led a host against her compared with which the armies of Charles seem almost insignificant. But, as Fouché well warned his imperial master, when he vainly endeavoured to dissuade him from his disastrous expedition against the empire of the czars, the difference between the Russia of 1812 and the Russia of 1709 was greater than the disparity between the power of Charles and the might of Napoleon. "If that heroic king," said Fouché, "had not, like your imperial Majesty, half Europe in arms to back him, neither had his opponent, the Czar Peter, 400,000 soldiers, and 50,000 Cossacks."

The historians, who describe the state of the Muscovite empire when revolutionary and imperial France encountered it, narrate with truth and justice, how "at the epoch of the French Revolution this immense empire, comprehending nearly half of Europe and Asia within its dominions, inhabited by a patient and indomitable race, ever ready to exchange the luxury and adventure of the south for the hardships and monotony of the north, was daily becoming more formidable to the liberties of Europe. The Russian infantry had then long been celebrated for its immovable firmness. Her immense population, amounting then in Europe alone to nearly thirty-five millions, afforded an inexhaustible supply of men. Her soldiers, inured to heat and cold from their infancy, and actuated by a blind devotion to their czar, united the steady valour of the English to the impetuous energy of the French troops."

So, also, we read how the haughty aggressions of Bonaparte "went to excite a national feeling, from the banks of the Borysthenes to the wall of China, and to unite against him the wild and uncivilised inhabitants of an extended empire, possessed by a love of their religion, their government, and their country, and having a character of stern devotion, which he was incapable of estimating." But the Russia of 1709 had no such forces to oppose to an assailant. Her whole population then was below sixteen millions; and, what is far more important, this population had neither acquired military spirit, nor strong nationality; nor was it united in loyal attachment to its ruler.

Peter had wisely abolished the old regular troops of the empire, the Strelitzes; but the forces which he had raised in their stead on a new and foreign plain, and principally officered with foreigners, had, before the Swedish invasion, given no proof that they could be relied on. In numerous encounters with the Swedes, Peter's soldiery had run like sheep before inferior numbers. Great discontent, also, had been excited among all classes of the community by the arbitrary changes which their great emperor introduced, many of which clashed with the most cherished national prejudices of his subjects.

A career of victory and prosperity had not yet raised Peter above the reach of that disaffection, nor had superstitious obedience to the czar yet become the characteristic of the Muscovite mind. The victorious occupation of Moscow by Charles XII would have quelled the Russian nation as effectually, as

had been the case when Batou Khan, and other ancient invaders, captured the capital of primitive Muscovy. How little
such a triumph could effect towards subduing modern Russia,
the fate of Napoleon demonstrated at once and for ever.

IV

The character of Charles XII has been a favourite theme with
historians, moralists, philosophers, and poets. But it is his
military conduct during the campaign in Russia that alone requires comment here. Napoleon, in the memoirs dictated by
him at St. Helena, has given us a systematic criticism on that,
among other celebrated campaigns, his own Russian campaign
included. He labours hard to prove that he himself observed
all the true principles of offensive war: and probably his censures of Charles's generalship were rather highly coloured, for
the sake of making his own military skill stand out in more
favourable relief.

Yet, after making all allowances, we must admit the force of
Napoleon's strictures on Charles's tactics and own that his
judgment, though severe, is correct, when he pronounces that
the Swedish king, unlike his great predecessor Gustavus, knew
nothing of the art of war, and was nothing more than a brave
and intrepid soldier. Such, however, was not the light in which
Charles was regarded by his contemporaries at the commencement of his Russian expedition. His numerous victories, his
daring and resolute spirit, combined with the ancient renown
of the Swedish arms, then filled all Europe with admiration and
anxiety.

As Johnson expresses it, his name was then one at which the
world grew pale. Even Louis *le Grand* earnestly solicited his
assistance; and our own Marlborough, then in the full career
of his victories, was specially sent by the English court to the
camp of Charles, to propitiate the hero of the north in favour
of the cause of the Allies, and to prevent the Swedish sword
from being flung into the scale in the French king's favour.
But Charles at that time was solely bent on dethroning the
sovereign of Russia, as he had already dethroned the sovereign
of Poland, and all Europe fully believed that he would entirely
crush the czar, and dictate conditions of peace in the Kremlin.
Charles himself looked on success as a matter of certainty

and the romantic extravagance of his views was continually increasing. "One year, he thought, would suffice for the conquest of Russia. The court of Rome was next to feel his vengeance, as the pope had dared to oppose the concession of religious liberty to the Silesian Protestants. No enterprise at that time appeared impossible to him. He had even despatched several officers privately into Asia and Egypt, to take plans of the towns and examine into the strength and resources of those countries."

Napoleon thus epitomises the earlier operations of Charles's invasion of Russia:—

"That prince set out from his camp at Aldstadt, near Leipsic, in September, 1707, at the head of 45,000 men, and traversed Poland; 20,000 men, under Count Lewenhaupt, disembarked at Riga and 15,000 were in Finland. He was therefore in a condition to have brought together 80,000 of the best troops in the world. He left 10,000 men at Warsaw to guard King Stanislaus, and in January, 1708, arrived at Grodno, where he wintered. In June, he crossed the forest of Minsk, and presented himself before Borisov; forced the Russian army, which occupied the left bank of the Beresina; defeated 20,000 Russians who were strongly entrenched behind marshes; passed the Borysthenes at Mohiloev, and vanquished a corps of 16,000 Muscovites near Smolensko, on the 22nd of September. He was now advanced to the confines of Lithuania, and was about to enter Russia proper: the czar, alarmed at his approach, made him proposals of peace.

"Up to this time all his movements were conformable to rule, and his communications were well secured. He was master of Poland and Riga, and only ten days' march distant from Moscow: and it is probable that he would have reached that capital, had he not quitted the high-road thither, and directed his steps towards the Ukraine, in order to form a junction with Mazeppa, who brought him only 6000 men. By this movement his line of operations, beginning at Sweden, exposed his flank to Russia for a distance of four hundred leagues, and he was unable to protect it, or to receive either reinforcements or assistance."

Napoleon severely censures this neglect of one of the great rules of war. He points out that Charles had not organised his war like Hannibal, on the principle of relinquishing all communications with home, keeping all his forces concentrated, and creating a base of operations in the conquered country. Such has been the bold system of the Carthaginian general; but Charles acted on no such principle inasmuch as he caused Lewenhaupt, one of his generals who commanded a considerable detachment and escorted a most important convoy, to follow him at a distance of twelve days' march. By this dislocation of his forces he exposed Lewenhaupt to be overwhelmed separately by the full force of the enemy, and deprived the troops under his own command of the aid which that general's men and stores might have afforded, at the very crisis of the campaign.

V

The Czar had collected an army of about a hundred thousand effective men and though the Swedes, in the beginning of the invasion, were successful in every encounter, the Russian troops were gradually acquiring discipline; and Peter and his officers were learning generalship from their victors, as the Thebans of old learned it from the Spartans. When Lewenhaupt, in the October of 1708, was striving to join Charles in the Ukraine, the czar suddenly attacked him near the Borysthenes with an overwhelming force of fifty thousand Russians.

Lewenhaupt fought bravely for three days, and succeeded in cutting his way through the enemy, with about four thousand of his men, to where Charles awaited him near the river Desna; but upwards of eight thousand Swedes fell in these battles; Lewenhaupt's cannon and ammunition were abandoned and the whole of his important convoy of provisions, on which Charles and his half-starved troops were relying, fell into the enemy's hands. Charles was compelled to remain in the Ukraine during the winter; but in the spring of 1709 he moved forward towards Moscow, and invested the fortified town of Pultowa, on the river Vorskla, a place where the czar had stored up large supplies of provisions and military stores, and which commanded the roads leading towards Moscow. The possession of this place would have given Charles the means of supplying all the wants of his suffering army, and would also have furnished him with a secure base of operations for his advance against the Muscovite capital. The siege was therefore hotly pressed by the Swedes; the garrison resisted obstinately and the Czar, feeling the importance of saving the town, advanced in June to its relief, at the head of an army from fifty to sixty thousand strong.

Both sovereigns now prepared for the general action, which each perceived to be inevitable, and which each felt would be decisive of his own and of his country's destiny. The czar, by some masterly manœuvres, crossed the Vorskla and posted his army on the same side of that river with the besiegers, but a little higher up. The Vorskla falls into the Borysthenes about fifteen leagues below Pultowa, and the czar arranged his forces in two lines, stretching from one river towards the other; so that if the Swedes attacked him and were repulsed, they would be driven backwards into the acute angle formed by the two streams at their junction. He fortified these lines with several redoubts, lined with heavy artillery; and his troops, both horse and foot, were in the best possible condition, and amply provided with stores and ammunition.

Charles's forces were about twenty-four thousand strong. But not more than half of these were Swedes, so much had battle, famine, fatigue, and the deadly frosts of Russia, thinned the gallant bands which the Swedish king and Lewenhaupt had led to the Ukraine. The other twelve thousand men under Charles were Cossacks and Wallachians, who had joined him in that country. On hearing that the czar was about to attack him, he deemed that his dignity required that he himself should be the assailant; and leading his army out of their entrenched lines before the town, he advanced with them against the Russian redoubts.

He had been severely wounded in the foot in a skirmish a few days before and was borne in a litter along the ranks, into the thick of the fight. Notwithstanding the fearful disparity of numbers and disadvantage of position, the Swedes never showed their ancient valour more nobly than on that dreadful day. Nor do their Cossack and Wallachian allies seem to have been unworthy of fighting side by side with Charles's veterans. Two of the Russian redoubts were actually entered, and the Swedish infantry began to raise the cry of victory.

But on the other side, neither general nor soldiers flinched in their duty. The Russian cannonade and musketry were kept up; fresh masses of defenders were poured into the fortifications, and at length the exhausted remnants of the Swedish columns recoiled from the blood-stained redoubts. Then the czar led the infantry and cavalry of his first line outside the works, drew them up steadily and skilfully, and the action was renewed along the whole fronts of the two armies on the open ground. Each sovereign exposed his life freely in the world-winning battle; and on each side the troops fought obstinately and eagerly under their ruler's eye. It was not till two hours from the commencement of the action that, overpowered by numbers, the hitherto invincible Swedes gave way. All was then hopeless disorder and irreparable rout. Driven downward to where the rivers join, the fugitive Swedes surrendered to their victorious pursuers, or perished in the waters of the Borysthenes. Only a few hundreds swam that river with their king and the Cossack Mazeppa, and escaped into the Turkish territory. Nearly ten thousand lay killed and wounded in the redoubts and on the field of battle.

In the joy of his heart the czar exclaimed, when the strife was over that "the son of the morning has fallen from heaven; and that the foundations of St. Petersburg at length stood firm." Even on that battle-field, near the Ukraine, the Russian emperor's first thoughts were of conquests and aggrandisement on the Baltic. The peace of Nystadt, which transferred the fairest provinces of Sweden to Russia, ratified the judgment of battle which was pronounced at Pultowa. Attacks on Turkey and Persia by Russia commenced almost directly after that victory. An though the czar failed in his first attempts against the Sultan, the successors of Peter have one and all, carried on an uniformly aggressive and uniformly successful system of policy against Turkey, and against every other state, Asiatic as well as European, which has had the misfortune of having Russia for a neighbour.

SYNOPSIS OF EVENTS BETWEEN THE BATTLE OF PULTOWA, 1709,
AND THE DEFEAT OF BURGOYNE AT SARATOGA, 1777.

1713. Treaty of Utrecht. Philip is left by it in possession of the throne of Spain. But Naples, Milan, the Spanish territories on the Tuscan coast, the Spanish Netherlands, and some parts of the French Netherlands, are given to Austria. France cedes to England Hudson's Bay and Straits, the Island of St. Christopher, Nova Scotia, and Newfoundland in America. Spain cedes to England Gibraltar and Minorca, which the English had taken during the war. The King of Prussia and the Duke of Savoy both obtain considerable additions of territory to their dominions.

1714. Death of Queen Anne. The House of Hanover begins to reign in

England with George I. A rebellion in favour of the Stuarts is put down. Death of Louis XIV.

1718. Charles XII. killed at the siege of Frederickshall.

1725. Death of Peter the Great of Russia.

1740. Frederick II., King of Prussia, begins his reign. He attacks the Austrian dominions, and conquers Silesia.

1742. War between France and England.

1743. Victory of the English at Dettingen.

1745. Victory of the French at Fontenoy. Rebellion in Scotland in favour of the House of Stuart: finally quelled by the battle of Culloden in the next year.

1748. Peace of Aix-la-Chapelle.

1756-1763. The Seven Years' War, during which Prussia makes an heroic resistance against the armies of Austria, Russia, and France. England, under the administration of the elder Pitt (afterwards Lord Chatham), takes a glorious part in the war in opposition to France and Spain. Wolfe wins the battle of Quebec, and the English conquer Canada, Cape Breton, and St. John. Clive begins his career of conquest in India. Cuba is taken by the English from Spain.

1763. Treaty of Paris: which leaves the power of Prussia increased, and its military reputation greatly exalted.

France by the treaty of Paris, ceded Canada to England, and the island of Cape Breton, with the islands and coasts of the gulf and river of St. Lawrence. The boundaries between the two nations in North America were fixed by a line drawn along the middle of the Mississippi, from its source to its mouth. All on the left or eastern bank of that river, was given up to England, except the city of New Orleans, which was reserved to France; as was also the liberty of the fisheries on a part of the coasts of Newfoundland and the Gulf of St. Lawrence. The islands of St. Peter and Miquelon were given them as a shelter for their fishermen, but without permission to raise fortifications. The islands of Martinico, Guadaloupe, Marie-galante, Desirada, and St. Lucia, were surrendered to France; while Grenada, the Grenadines, St. Vincent, Dominica, and Tobago, were ceded to England. This latter power retained her conquests on the Senegal, and restored to France the island of Goree, on the coast of Africa. France was put in possession of the forts and factories which belonged to her in the East Indies, on the coasts of Coromandel, Orissa, Malabar, and Bengal under the restriction of keeping up no military force in Bengal.

In Europe, France restored all the conquests she had made in Germany; as also the island of Minorca. England gave up to her Belle Isle, on the coast of Brittany; while Dunkirk was kept in the same condition as had been determined by the peace of Aix-la-Chapelle. The island of Cuba, with the Havannah, were restored to the King of Spain, who, on his part, ceded to England Florida, with Port Augustine and the Bay of Pensacola. The King of Portugal was restored to the same state in which he had been before the war. The colony of St. Sacrament in America, which the Spaniards had conquered, was given back to him.

The peace of Paris, began an era of great prosperity for England. Her commerce and navigation extended over all parts of the globe, and were supported by a naval force so much the more imposing, as it was no longer counterbalanced by the maritime power of France, which had been almost annihilated in the preceding war. The immense territories which that peace had secured her, both in Africa and America, opened up new channels for her industry: and what deserves specially to be remarked is, that she acquired at the same time vast and important possessions in the East Indies.

-◄[THIRTEEN]►-

Saratoga, 1777

WHY DECISIVE: *"Even of those great conflicts, in which hundreds of lives have been engaged and tens of thousands have fallen, none has been more fruitful of results than this surrender of thirty-five hundred fighting men at Saratoga. It not merely changed the relations of England and the feelings of Europe toward these insurgent colonies, but it has modified for all times to come the connection between every colony and every parent state."* [Lord Mahon]. *"Nor can any military event be said to have exercised more important influence on the future fortunes of mankind than the complete defeat of Burgoyne's expedition; a defeat which rescued the revolted colonists from certain subjection and which, by inducing the courts of France and Spain to attack England in their behalf, ensured the independence of the United States and the formation of that trans-Atlantic power which, not only America, but both Europe and Asia, now see and feel."* [Creasy.]

I

OF the four great powers that now (1850) principally rule the political destinies of the world, France and England are the only two whose influence can be dated back beyond the last century and a half. The third great power, Russia, was a feeble mass of barbarism before the epoch of Peter the Great; and the very existence of the fourth great power, as an independent nation, commenced within the memory of living men. By the fourth great power of the world I mean the mighty commonwealth of the western continent, which now commands the admiration of mankind. That homage is sometimes reluctantly given, and accompanied with suspicion and ill-will. But none can refuse it.

All the physical essentials for national strength are undeniably to be found in the geographical position and amplitude of territory which the United States possess; in their almost inexhaustible tracts of fertile, but hitherto untouched, soil; in their stately forests, in their mountain-chains and their rivers, their beds of coal, and stores of metallic wealth; in their extensive sea-board along the waters of two oceans, and in their already numerous and rapidly increasing population.

And, when we examine the character of this population, no one can look on the fearless energy, the sturdy determination, the aptitude for local self-government, the versatile alacrity, and the unresting spirit of enterprise, which characterise the Anglo-Americans, without feeling that he here beholds the true moral elements of progressive might.

Three quarters of a century have not yet passed away since the United States ceased to be mere dependencies of England. And even if we date their origin from the period, when the first permanent European settlements, out of which they grew, were made on the western coast of the North Atlantic, the increase of their strength is unparalleled, either in rapidity or extent.

The ancient Roman boasted, with reason, of the growth of Rome from humble beginnings to the greatest magnitude which the world had then ever witnessed. But the citizen of the United States is still more justly entitled to claim this praise. In two centuries and a half his country has acquired ampler dominion than the Roman gained in ten. And, even if we credit the legend of the band of shepherds and outlaws with which Romulus is said to have colonised the Seven Hills, we find not there so small a germ of future greatness as we find in the group of a hundred and five ill-chosen and disunited emigrants who founded Jamestown in 1607, or in the scanty band of the Pilgrim-Fathers, who, a few years later (1620), moored their bark on the wild and rock-bound coast of the wilderness that was to become New England.

Nothing is more calculated to impress the mind with a sense of the rapidity with which the resources of the American republic advance, than the difficulty which the historical inquirer finds in ascertaining their precise amount. If he consults the most recent works, and those written by the ablest investigators of the subject, he finds in them admiring comments on the change which the past few years, before those books were written, had made; but when he turns to ápply the estimates in those books to the present moment, he finds them wholly inadequate. Before a book on the subject of the United States has lost its novelty, those states have outgrown the description which it contains. The celebrated work of the French statesman, De Tocqueville, appeared about fifteen years ago. In the passage which I am about to quote, it will be seen that he predicts the constant increase of the Anglo-American power, but he looks on the Rocky Mountains as their extreme western limit for many years to come. He had evidently no expectation of himself seeing that power dominant along the Pacific as well as along the Atlantic coast. He says: "It must not, . . . be imagined that the impulse of the British race in the New World can be arrested. The dismemberment of the Union, and the hostilities which might ensue, the abolition of republican institutions, and the tyrannical government which might succeed it, may retard this impulse, but they cannot prevent it from ultimately fulfilling the destinies to which that race is reserved. No power upon earth can close upon the emigrants that fertile wilderness, which offers resources to all industry, and a refuge from all want. Future events, of whatever nature they may be, will not deprive the Americans of their climate or of their inland seas, or of their great rivers, or of their exuberant soil. Nor will bad laws, revolutions, and anarchy be able to obliterate that love of prosperity and that spirit of enterprise which seem to be the distinctive characteristics of their race, or to extinguish that knowledge which guides them on their way.

"Thus, in the midst of the uncertain future, one event at least is sure. At a period which may be said to be near (for we are speaking of the life of a nation), the Anglo-Americans will alone cover the immense space contained between the polar regions and the tropics, extending from the coast of the Atlantic to the shores of the Pacific Ocean; the territory which will probably be occupied by the Anglo-Americans at some future time, may be computed to equal three quarters of Europe in extent. The climate of the Union is upon the whole preferable to that of Europe, and its natural advantages are not less great; it is therefore evident that its population will at some future time be proportionate to our own. Europe, divided as it is between so many different nations, and torn as it has been by incessant wars and the barbarous manners of the Middle Ages, has notwithstanding attained a population of 410 inhabitants to the square league. What cause can prevent the United States from having as numerous a population in time?

"The time will therefore come when one hundred and fifty millions of men will be living in North America, equal in condition, the progeny of one race, owing their origin to the same cause, and preserving the same civilisation, the same language, the same religion, the same habits, the same manners, and imbued with the same opinions, propagated under the same forms. The rest is uncertain, but this is certain; and it is a fact new to the world, a fact fraught with such portentous consequences as to baffle the efforts even of the imagination." (In 1950, a hundred fifteen years after de Tocqueville wrote, the population of continental United States was 150 million, in round numbers.)

II

An Englishman may look, and ought to look, on the growing grandeur of the Americans with no small degree of generous sympathy and satisfaction. They, like ourselves, are members of the great Anglo-Saxon nation, "whose race and language are now overrunning the world from one end of it to the other." And whatever differences of form of government may exist between us and them; whatever reminiscences of the days when, though brethren, we strove together, may rankle in the minds of us, the defeated party; we should cherish the bonds of common nationality that still exist between us.

We should remember, as the Athenians remembered of the Spartans at a season of jealousy and temptation, that our race is one, being of the same blood, speaking the same language, having an essential resemblance in our institutions and usages, and worshipping in the temples of the same God. All this may and should be borne in mind. And yet an Englishman can hardly watch the progress of America, without the regretful thought that America once was English, and that, but for the folly of our rulers, she might be English still. It is true that the commerce between the two countries has largely and beneficially increased; but this is no proof that the increase would not have been still greater had the States remained integral portions of the same great empire. By giving a fair and just participation in political rights, these, "the fairest possessions" of the British crown, might have been preserved to it. "This ancient and most noble monarchy" would not have been, dismembered; nor should we see that which ought to be the right arm of our strength, now menacing us in every political crisis, as the most formidable rival of our commercial and maritime ascendancy.

The war which rent away the North American colonies of England is, of all subjects in history, the most painful for an Englishman to dwell on. It was commenced and carried on by the British Ministry in iniquity and folly, and it was concluded in disaster and shame. But the contemplation of it cannot be evaded by the historian, however much it may be abhorred. Nor can any military event be said to have exercised more important influence on the future fortunes of mankind, than the complete defeat of Burgoyne's expedition in 1777; a defeat which rescued the revolted colonists from certain subjection; and which, by inducing the courts of France and Spain to attack England in their behalf, ensured the independence of the United States, and the formation of that translantic power which, not only America, but both Europe and Asia, now see and feel.

Still, in proceeding to describe this "decisive battle of the world," a very brief recapitulation of the earlier events of the war may be sufficient; nor shall I linger unnecessarily on a painful theme.

The five northern colonies of Massachusetts, Connecticut, Rhode Island, New Hampshire, and Vermont, usually classed together as the New England colonies, were the strongholds of the insurrection against the mother-country. The feeling of resistance was less vehement and general in the central settlement of New York; and still less so in Pennsylvania, Maryland, and the other colonies of the south, although everywhere it was formidably active.

Virginia should, perhaps, be particularised for the zeal which its leading men displayed in the American cause; but it was among the decendants of the stern Puritans that the spirit of Cromwell and Vane breathed in all its fervour; it was from the New Englanders that the first armed opposition to the British crown had been offered; and it was by them that the most stubborn determination to fight to the last, rather than waive a single right or privilege, had been displayed. In 1775, they had succeeded in forcing the British troops to evacuate Boston; and in 1776 the royalists made New York the principal basis of operations for the armies of the mother-country.

A glance at the map will show that the Hudson River, which falls into the Atlantic at New York, runs down from the north at the back of the New England states, forming an angle of about forty-five degrees with the line of the coast of the Atlantic, along which the New England states are situated. Northward of the Hudson, we see a small chain of lakes communicating with the Canadian frontier. It is necessary to attend closely to these geographical points, in order to understand the plan of the operations which the English attempted in 1777, and which was defeated at the battle of Saratoga.

III

The English had a considerable force in Canada; and in 1776 had completely repulsed an attack which the Americans had made upon that province. The British Ministry resolved to avail themselves, in the next year, of the advantage which the occupation of Canada gave them, not merely for the purpose of defense, but for the purpose of striking a vigorous and crushing blow against the revolted colonies. With this view, the army in Canada was largely reinforced. Seven thousand veteran troops were sent out from England, with a corps of artillery abundantly supplied, and led by select and experienced officers. Large quantities of military stores were also furnished for the equipment of the Canadian volunteers, who were expected to join the expedition. It was intended that the force thus collected should march southward by the line of the lakes, (Champlain and George) and thence along the banks of the Hudson river. The British army in New York (or a large detachment of it) was to make a simultaneous movement northward, up the line of the Hudson, and the two expeditions were to unite at Albany, a town on that river. By these operations all communication between the northern colonies and those of the centre and south would be cut off. An irresistible force would be concentrated, so as to crush all further opposition in New England; and when this was done, it was believed that the other colonies would speedily submit.

The Americans had no troops in the field that seemed able to baffle these movements. Their principal army, under Washington, was occupied in watching over Pennsylvania and the south. At any rate it was believed that in order to oppose the plan intended for the new campaign the insurgents must risk a pitched battle, in which the superiority of the royalists, in numbers, in discipline, and in equipment, seemed to promise to the latter a crowning victory. Without question the plan was ably formed; and had the success of the execution been equal to the ingenuity of the design, the re-conquest or submission of the thirteen United States must, in all human probability, have followed; and the independence which they proclaimed in 1776 would have been extinguished before it existed a second year.

No European power had as yet come forward to aid America. It is true that England was generally regarded with jealousy and ill will, and was thought to have acquired, at the treaty of Paris a preponderance of dominion which was perilous to the balance of power; but though many were willing to wound, none had yet ventured to strike; and America, if defeated in 1777, would have been suffered to fall unaided.

In Lord Albemarle's "Memoirs of the Marquis of Rockingham" is contained the following remarkable state paper, drawn up by King George III. himself respecting the plan of Burgoyne's expedition. The original is in the king's own hand.

"REMARKS ON THE CONDUCT OF THE WAR FROM CANADA

"The outlines of the plan seem to be on a proper foundation. The rank and file of the army now in Canada (including the 11th Regiment of British, M'Clean's corps, the Brunswicks and Hanover), amount to 10,527; add the eleven additional companies and four hundred Hanover Chasseurs, the total will be 11,443.

"As sickness and other contingencies must be expected, I should think not above 7,000 effectives can be spared over Lake Champlain; for it would be highly imprudent to run any risk in Canada.

"The fixing the stations of those left in the province may not be quite right, though the plan proposed may be recommended. Indians must be employed, and this measure must be avowedly directed, and Carleton must be in the strongest manner directed that the Apollo shall be ready by that day, to receive Burgoyne.

"The magazines must be formed with the greatest expedition, at Crown Point.

"If possible, possession must be taken of Lake George, and nothing but and absolute impossibility of succeeding in this can be an excuse for proceeding by South Bay and Skeenborough.

"As Sir W. Howe does not think of acting from Rhode Island into the Massachusetts, the force from Canada must join him in Albany.

"The diversion on the Mohawk River ought at least to be strengthened by the addition of the four hundred Hanover Chasseurs.

"The Ordnance ought to furnish a complete proportion of intrenching tools.

"The provisions ought to be calculated for a third more than the effective soldiery, and the General ordered to avoid delivering these when the army can be subsisted by the country. Burgoyne certainly greatly undervalues the German recruits.

"The idea of carrying the army by sea to Sir W. Howe, would certainly require the leaving a much larger part of it in Canada, as in that case the rebel army would divide that province from the immense one under Sir W. Howe. I greatly dislike this last idea."

IV

Burgoyne had gained celebrity by some bold and dashing exploits in Portugal during the last war; he was personally as brave an officer as ever headed British troops; he had considerable skill as a tactician and his general intellectual abilities and acquirements were of a high order. He had several very able and experienced officers under him, among whom were Major-General Phillips and Brigadier-General Frazer. His regular troops amounted, exclusively of the corps of artillery, to about seven thousand two hundred men, rank and file. Nearly half of these were Germans. He had also an auxiliary force of from two to three thousand Canadians. He summoned the warriors of several tribes of the Indians near the western lakes to join his army.

Much eloquence was poured forth, both in America and in England, in denouncing the use of these savage auxiliaries. Yet Burgoyne seems to have done no more than Montcalm, Wolfe, and other French, American, and English generals had done before him. But, in truth, the lawless ferocity of the Indians, their unskilfulness in regular action, and the utter impossibility of bringing them under any discipline, made their services of little or no value in times of difficulty, while the indignation which their outrages inspired went far to rouse the whole population of the invaded districts into active hostilities against Burgoyne's force.

Burgoyne assembled his troops and confederates near the river Bouquet, on the west side of Lake Champlain. He then, in June, 1777, gave his Indians a war feast and harangued them on the necessity of abstaining from their usual cruel practices against unarmed people and prisoners. At the same time he published a pompous manifesto to the Americans, in which he threatened the refractory with all the horrors of war, Indian as well as European. The army proceeded by water to Crown Point, a fortification which the Americans held at the northern extremity of the inlet by which the water from Lake George is conveyed to Lake Champlain. He landed here without opposition, but the reduction of Ticonderoga, a fortification about twelve miles to the south of Crown Point, was a more serious matter, and was supposed to be the critical part of the expedition.

Ticonderoga commanded the passage along the lakes, and was considered to be the key to the route which Burgoyne wished to follow. The English had been repulsed in an attack on it in the war with the French in 1758 with severe loss. But Burgoyne now invested it with great skill; and the American General, St. Clair, who had only an ill-equipped army of about three thousand men, evacuated it on the 5th of July. It seems evident that a different course would have caused the destruction or capture of his whole army; which, weak as it was, was the chief force then in the field for the protection of the New England States. When censured by some of his countrymen for abandoning Ticonderoga, St. Clair truly replied, "that he had lost a post, but saved a province." Burgoyne's troops pursued the retiring Americans, gained several advantages over them, and took a large part of their artillery and military stores.

The loss of the British in these engagements was trifling. The army moved southward along Lake George to Skenesborough; and thence, slowly, and with great difficulty, across a broken country, full of creeks and marshes, and clogged by the enemy with felled trees and other obstacles, to Ft. Edward, on the Hudson river, the American troops continuing to retire before them.

Burgoyne reached the left bank of the Hudson River on the 30th of July. Hitherto he had overcome every difficulty which the enemy and the nature of the country had placed in his way. His army was in excellent order and in the highest spirits; and the peril of the expedition seemed over, when they were once on the bank of the river which was to be the channel of communication between them and the British army in the south.

v

The astonishment and alarm which these events produced among the Americans were naturally great; but in the midst of their disasters none of the colonists showed any disposition to submit. The local governments of the New England states, as well as the Congress, acted with vigour and firmness in their efforts to repel the enemy. General Gates was sent to take the command of the army at Saratoga; and Arnold, a favourite leader of the Americans, was despatched by Washington to act under him, with reinforcements of troops and guns from the main American army.

Burgoyne's employment of the Indians now produced the worst possible effects. Though he laboured hard to check the atrocities which they were accustomed to commit, he could not prevent the occurrence of many barbarous outrages, repugnant both to the feelings of humanity and to the laws of civilised warfare. The American commanders took care that the reports of these excesses should be circulated far and wide, well knowing that they would make the stern New Englanders not droop, but rage. Such was their effect; and though, when each man looked upon his wife, his children, his sisters, or his aged parents, the thought of the merciless Indian "thirsting for the blood of man, woman, and child," of "the cannibal savage torturing, murdering, roasting and eating the mangled victims of his barbarous battles," might raise terror in the bravest breasts, this very terror produced a directly contrary effect to causing submission to the royal army.

It was seen that the few friends of the royal cause, as well as its enemies, were liable to be the victims of the indiscriminate rage of the savages; and thus "the inhabitants of the open and frontier countries had no choice of acting: they had no means of security left, but by abandoning their habitations and taking up arms. Every man saw the necessity of becoming a temporary soldier, not only for his own security, but for the protection and defence of those connections which are dearer than life itself. Thus an army was poured forth by the woods, mountains, and marshes, which in this part were thickly sown with plantations and villages. The Americans recalled their courage; and when their regular army seemed to be entirely wasted, the spirit of the country produced a much greater and more formidable force." (Burke).

While resolute recruits, accustomed to the use of firearms and all partially trained by service in the provincial militias, were thus flocking to the standard of Gates and Arnold at Saratoga; and while Burgoyne was engaged at Fort Edward in providing the means for the further advance of his army through the intricate and hostile country that still lay before him, two events occurred, in each of which the British sustained loss, and the Americans obtained advantage, the moral effects of which were even more important than the immediate result of the encounters.

When Burgoyne left Canada, General St. Leger was detached from that province with a mixed force of about one thousand men, and some light field-pieces, across Lake Ontario against Fort Stanwix, which the Americans held. After capturing this, he was to march along the Mohawk river to its confluence with the Hudson, between Saratoga and Albany, where his force and that of Burgoyne were to unite. But, after some successes, St. Leger was obliged to retreat, and to abandon his tents and large quantities of stores to the garrison.

At the very time that General Burgoyne heard of this disaster, he experienced one still more severe in the defeat of Colonel Baum with a large detachment of German troops at Bennington, whither Burgoyne had sent them for the purpose of capturing some magazines of provisions, of which the British army stood greatly in need. The Americans, augmented by continual accessions of strength, succeeded, after many attacks, in breaking this corps, which fled into the woods and left its commander mortally wounded on the field. They then marched against a force of five hundred grenadiers and light infantry, which was advancing to Colonel Baum's assistance, under Lieutenant-Colonel Breyman; who, after a gallant resistance, was obliged to retreat on the main army. The British loss in these two actions exceeded six hundred men and a party of American loyalists, on their way to join the army, having attached themselves to Colonel Baum's corps, were destroyed with it.

VI

Notwithstanding these reverses, which added greatly to the spirit and numbers of the American forces, Burgoyne determined to advance. It was impossible any longer to keep up his communications with Canada by way of the lakes, so as to supply his army on his southward march; but having by unremitting exertions collected provisions for thirty days, he crossed the Hudson by means of a bridge of rafts, and, marching a short distance along its western bank, he encamped on the 14th of September on the heights of Saratoga, about sixteen miles from Albany. The Americans had fallen back from Saratoga, and were now strongly posted near Stillwater, about half-way between Saratoga and Albany, and showed a determination to recede no farther.

Meanwhile Lord Howe, with the bulk of the British army that had lain at New York, had sailed away to the Delaware, and there commenced a campaign against Washington, in which the English general took Philadelphia, and gained other showy, but unprofitable successes. But Sir Henry Clinton, a brave and skilful officer, was left with a considerable force at New York; and he undertook the task of moving up the Hudson to co-operate with Burgoyne. Clinton was obliged for this purpose to wait for reinforcements which had been promised from England, and these did not arrive till September. As soon as he received them, Clinton embarked about 3000 of his men on a flotilla, convoyed by some ships of war under Commander Hotham, and proceeded to force his way up the river, but it was long before he was able to open any communication with Burgoyne.

The country between Burgoyne's position at Saratoga and that of the Americans at Stillwater was rugged, and seamed with creeks and water-courses; but after great labour in making bridges and temporary causeways, the British army moved forward. About four miles from Saratoga, on the afternoon of the 19th of September, a sharp encounter took place between part of the English right wing, under Burgoyne himself, and a strong body of the enemy, under Gates and Arnold. The conflict lasted till sunset. The British remained masters of the field; but the loss on each side was nearly equal (from five hundred to six hundred men); and the spirits of the Americans were greatly raised by having withstood the best regular troops of the English army.

Burgoyne now halted again, and strengthened his position by field-works and redoubts and the Americans also improved their defenses. The two armies remained nearly within cannon-shot of each other for a considerable time, during which Burgoyne was anxiously looking for intelligence of the promised expedition from New York, which, according to the original plan, ought by this time to have been approaching Albany from the south. At last, a messenger from Clinton made his way, with great difficulty, to Burgoyne's camp, and brought the information that Clinton was on his way up the Hudson to attack the American forts which barred the passage up that river to Albany. Burgoyne, in reply, on the 30th of September, urged Clinton to attack the forts as speedily as possible, stating that the effect of such an attack, or even the semblance of it, would be to move the American army from its position before his own troops.

By another messenger, who reached Clinton on the 5th of October, Burgoyne informed his brother general that he had lost his communications with Canada, but had provisions which would last him till the 20th. Burgoyne described himself as strongly posted, and stated that though the Americans in front of him were strongly posted also, he made no doubt of being able to force them and making his way to Albany, but that he doubted whether he could subsist there, as the country was drained of provisions. He wished Clinton to meet him there, and to keep open a communication with New York.

Burgoyne had over-estimated his resources, and in the very beginning of October found difficulty and distress pressing him hard.

The Indians and Canadians began to desert him; while, on the other hand, Gates's army was continually reinforced by fresh bodies of the militia. An expeditionary force was detached by the Americans, which made a bold, though unsuccessful, attempt to retake Ticonderoga. And finding the number and spirit of the enemy to increase daily, and his own stores of provision to diminish, Burgoyne determined on attacking the Americans in front of him, and by dislodging them from their position, to gain the means of moving upon Albany, or at least of relieving his troops from the straitened position in which they were cooped up.

Burgoyne's force was now reduced to less than 6000 men. The right of his camp was on some high ground a little to the west of the river; thence his entrenchments extended along the lower ground to the bank of the Hudson, the line of their front being nearly at a right angle with the course of the stream. The lines were fortified with redoubts and field-works, and on a height on the flank of the extreme right a strong redoubt was reared, and intrenchments, in a horse-shoe form, thrown up. The Hessians, under Colonel Breyman, were stationed here, forming a flank defence to Burgoyne's main army. The numerical force of the Americans was now greater than the British, even in regular troops, and the numbers of the militia and volunteers which had joined Gates and Arnold were greater still.

General Lincoln, with 2000 New England troops, had reached the American camp on the 29th of September. Gates gave him the command of the right wing, and took in person the command of the left wing, which was composed of two brigades under Generals Poor and Leonard, of Colonel Morgan's rifle corps, and part of the fresh New England Militia. The whole of the American lines had been ably fortified under the direction of the celebrated Polish General, Kosciusko, who was now serving as a volunteer in Gates's army.

The right of the American position, that is to say, the part of it nearest to the river, was too strong to be assailed with any prospect of success: and Burgoyne therefore determined to endeavour to force their left. For this purpose he formed a column of 1500 regular troops, with two twelve-pounders, two howitzers, and six six-pounders. He headed this in person, having Generals Phillips, Reidesel, and Frazer under him. The enemy's force immediately in front of his lines was so strong that he dared not weaken the troops who guarded them, by detaching any more to strengthen his column of attack.

VII

It was on the 7th of October that Burgoyne led his column forward and on the preceding day, the 6th, Clinton had successfully executed a brilliant enterprise against the two American forts which barred his progress up the Hudson. He had captured them both, with severe loss to the American forces opposed to him; he had destroyed the fleet which the Americans had been forming on the Hudson, under the protection of their forts and the upward river was laid open to his squadron. He had also, with admirable skill and industry, collected in small vessels, such as could float within a few miles of Albany, provisions sufficient to supply Burgoyne's army for six months. He was now only a hundred and fifty-six miles from Burgoyne and 1700 men actually advanced within forty miles of Albany.

Unfortunately Burgoyne and Clinton were each ignorant of the other's movements; but if Burgoyne had won his battle on the 7th, he must on advancing have soon learned the tidings of Clinton's success, and Clinton would have heard of his. A junction would soon have been made of the two victorious armies, and the great objects of the campaign might yet have been accomplished. All depended on the fortune of the column with which Burgoyne, on the eventful 7th of October, 1777, advanced against the American position. There were brave men, both English and German, in its ranks; and in particular it comprised one of the best bodies of grenadiers in the British service.

Burgoyne pushed forward some bodies of irregular troops to distract the enemy's attention and led his column to within three quarters of a mile from the left of Gates's camp, and then deployed his men into line. The grenadiers under Major Ackland, and the artillery under Major Williams, were drawn up on the left; a corps of Germans, under General Reidesel and some British troops under General Phillips, were in the centre; and the English Light Infantry, and the 24th regiment, under Lord Balcarres and General Frazer, were on the right.

But Gates did not wait to be attacked and directly the British line was formed and began to advance, the American general, with admirable skill, caused General Poor's brigade of New York and New Hampshire troops, and part of General Leonard's brigade, to make a sudden and vehement rush against its left, and at the same time sent Colonel Morgan, with his rifle corps and other troops, amounting to 1500, to turn the right of the English. The grenadiers under Ackland sustained the charge of superior numbers nobly. But Gates sent more Americans forward, and in a few minutes the action became general along the centre, so as to prevent the Germans from detaching any help to the grenadiers. Morgan, with his riflemen, was now pressing Lord Balcarres and General Frazer hard, and fresh masses of the enemy were observed advancing from their extreme left, with the evident intention of forcing the British right, and cutting off its retreat. The English light infantry and the 24th now fell back and formed an oblique second line, which enabled them to baffle this manoeuvre, and also to succour their comrades in the left wing, the gallant grenadiers, who were overpowered by superior numbers, and, but for this aid, must have been cut to pieces.

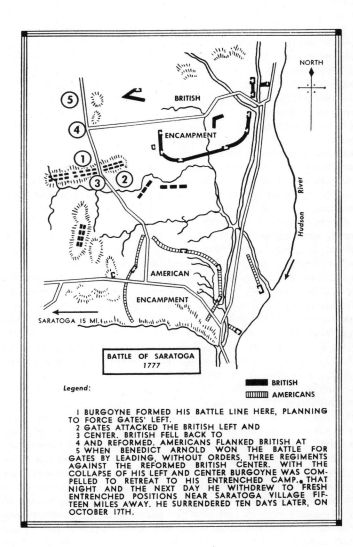

BATTLE OF SARATOGA
1777

Legend:

■■■ BRITISH
▨▨▨ AMERICANS

1 BURGOYNE FORMED HIS BATTLE LINE HERE, PLANNING TO FORCE GATES' LEFT.
2 GATES ATTACKED THE BRITISH LEFT AND
3 CENTER. BRITISH FELL BACK TO
4 AND REFORMED. AMERICANS FLANKED BRITISH AT
5 WHEN BENEDICT ARNOLD WON THE BATTLE FOR GATES BY LEADING, WITHOUT ORDERS, THREE REGIMENTS AGAINST THE REFORMED BRITISH CENTER. WITH THE COLLAPSE OF HIS LEFT AND CENTER BURGOYNE WAS COMPELLED TO RETREAT TO HIS ENTRENCHED CAMP. THAT NIGHT AND THE NEXT DAY HE WITHDREW TO FRESH ENTRENCHED POSITIONS NEAR SARATOGA VILLAGE FIFTEEN MILES AWAY. HE SURRENDERED TEN DAYS LATER, ON OCTOBER 17TH.

The contest now was fiercely maintained on both sides. The English cannon were repeatedly taken and retaken, but when the grenadiers near them were forced back by the weight of superior numbers, one of the guns was permanently captured by the Americans, and turned upon the English. Major Williams and Major Ackland were both made prisoners, and in this part of the field the advantage of the Americans was decided. The British centre still held its ground; but now it was that the American general Arnold appeared upon the scene, and did more for his countrymen than whole battalions could have effected.

Arnold, when the decisive engagement of the 7th of October commenced, had been deprived of his command by Gates, in consequence of a quarrel between them about the action of the 19th of September. He had listened for a short time in the American camp to the thunder of the battle, in which he had no military right to take part, either as commander or as combatant. But his excited spirit could not long endure such a state of inaction. He called for his horse, a powerful brown charger, and springing on it, galloped furiously to where the fight seemed to be the thickest. Gates saw him, and sent an aide-de-camp to recall him, but Arnold spurred far in advance, and placed himself at the head of three regiments which had formerly been under him, and which welcomed their old commander with joyous cheers. He led them instantly upon the British centre and then galloping along the American line, he issued orders for a renewed and a closer attack, which were obeyed with alacrity, Arnold himself setting the example of the most daring personal bravery, and charging more than once, sword in hand, into the English ranks.

On the British side the officers did their duty nobly, but General Frazer was the most eminent of them all, restoring order wherever the line began to waver, and infusing fresh courage into his men by voice and example. Mounted on an iron-grey charger, and dressed in the full uniform of a general officer, he was conspicuous to foes as well as to friends. The American Colonel Morgan thought that the fate of the battle rested on this gallant man's life, and calling several of his best marksmen round him, pointed Frazer out, and said: "That officer is General Frazer; I admire him, but he must die. Our victory depends on it. Take your stations in that clump of bushes, and do your duty." Within five minutes, Frazer fell mortally wounded, and was carried to the British camp by two grenadiers.

Just previously to his being struck by the fatal bullet, one rifleball had cut the crupper of his saddle, and another had passed through his horse's mane close behind the ears. His aide-de-camp had noticed this, and said: "It is evident that you are marked out for particular aim; would it not be prudent for you to retire from this place?" Frazer replied: "My duty forbids me to fly from danger;" and the next moment he fell.

Burgoyne's whole force was now compelled to retreat towards their camp; the left and centre were in complete disorder, but the light infantry and the 24th checked the fury of the assailants, and the remains of the column with great difficulty effected their return to their camp, leaving six of their cannons in the possession of the enemy, and great numbers of killed and wounded on the field; and especially a large proportion of the artillerymen, who had stood to their guns until shot down or bayoneted beside them by the advancing Americans.

VIII

Burgoyne's column had been defeated, but the action was not yet over. The English had scarcely entered the camp, when the Americans, pursuing their success, assaulted it in several places with remarkable impetuosity, rushing in upon the intrenchments and redoubts through a severe fire of grape-shot and musketry. Arnold especially, who on this day appeared maddened with the thirst of combat and carnage, urged on the attack against a part of the intrenchments which was occupied by the light infantry under Lord Belcarres. But the English received him with vigour and spirit. The struggle here was obstinate and sanguinary.

At length, as it grew towards evening, Arnold, having forced all obstacles, entered the works with some of the most fearless of his followers. But in this critical moment of glory and danger, he received a painful wound in the same leg which had already been injured at the assault on Quebec. To his bitter regret he was obliged to be carried back. His party still continued the attack, but the English also continued their obstinate resistance, and at last night fell and the assailants withdrew from this quarter of the British intrenchments.

But in another part the attack had been more successful. A

body of the Americans, under Colonel Brooke, forced their way in through a part of the horseshoe intrenchments on the extreme right, which was defended by the Hessian reserve under Colonel Breyman. The Germans resisted well, and Breyman died in defense of his post; but the Americans made good the ground which they had won, and captured baggage, tents, artillery, and a store of ammunition, which they were greatly in need of. They had, by establishing themselves on this point, acquired the means of completely turning the right flank of the British, and gaining their rear.

To prevent this calamity, Burgoyne effected during the night an entire change of position. With great skill he removed his whole army to some heights near the river, a little northward of the former camp, and he there drew up his men, expecting to be attacked on the following day. But Gates was resolved not to risk the certain triumph which his success had already secured for him. He harassed the English with skirmishes, but attempted no regular attack. Meanwhile he detached bodies of troops on both sides of the Hudson to prevent the British from recrossing that river and to bar their retreat. When night fell, it became absolutely necessary for Burgoyne to retire again, and, accordingly the troops were marched through a stormy and rainy night towards Saratoga, abandoning their sick and wounded, and the greater part of their baggage, to the enemy.

Before the rear-guard quitted the camp, the last sad honours were paid to the brave General Frazer, who expired on the day after the action. He had, almost with his last breath, expressed a wish to be buried in the redoubt which had formed the part of the British lines where he had been stationed, but which had now been abandoned by the English, and was within full range of the cannon which the advancing Americans were rapidly placing in position to bear upon Burgoyne's force. Burgoyne resolved, nevertheless, to comply with the dying wish of his comrade; and the interment took place under circumstances the most affecting that have ever marked a soldier's funeral.

IX

Burgoyne now took up his last position on the heights near Saratoga; and hemmed in by the enemy, who refused any encounter, and baffled in all his attempts at finding a path of escape, he there lingered until famine compelled him to capitulate. The fortitude of the British army during this melancholy period has been justly eulogised by many native historians, but I prefer quoting the testimony of a foreign writer, as free from all possibility of partiality. Botta says:

"It exceeds the power of words to describe the pitiable condition to which the British army was now reduced. The troops were worn down by a series of toil, privation, sickness, and desperate fighting. They were abandoned by the Indians and Canadians; and the effective force of the whole army was now diminished by repeated and heavy losses, which had principally fallen on the best soldiers, and the most distinguished officers, from ten thousand combatants to less than one-half that number. Of this remnant, little more than three thousand were English.

"In these circumstances, and thus weakened, they were invested by an army of four times their own number, whose position extended three parts of a circle round them; who refused to fight them, as knowing their weakness, and who, from the nature of the ground, could not be attacked in any part. In this helpless condition, obliged to be constantly under arms, while the enemy's cannon played on every part of their camp, and even the American rifleballs whistled in many parts of the lines, the troops of Burgoyne retained their customary firmness, and while sinking under a hard necessity, they showed themselves worthy of a better fate. They could not be reproached with an action or a word which betrayed a want of temper or of fortitude."

At length the 13th of October arrived, and as no prospect of assistance appeared, and the provisions were nearly exhausted, Burgoyne, by the unanimous advice of a council of war, sent a messenger to the American camp to treat of a convention.

General Gates in the first instance demanded that the royal army should surrender prisoners of war. He also proposed that the British should ground their arms. Burgoyne replied, "This article is inadmissible in every extremity; sooner than this army will consent to ground their arms in their encampment, they will rush on the enemy, determined to take no quarter." After various messages, a convention for the surrender of the army was settled, which provided that "The troops under General Burgoyne are to march out of their camp with the honours of war, and the artillery of the intrenchments, to the verge of the river, where the arms and artillery are to be left. The arms to be piled by word of command from their own officers. A free passage is to be granted to the army under Lieutenant-General Burgoyne to Great Britain, upon condition of not serving again in North America during the present contest."

The articles of capitulation were settled on the 15th of October; and on that very evening a messenger arrived from Clinton with an account of his successes, and with the tidings that part of his force had penetrated as far as Esopus, within fifty miles of Burgoyne's camp. But it was too late. The public faith was pledged; and the army was, indeed, too debilitated by fatigue and hunger to resist an attack if made; and Gates certainly would have made it, if the convention had broken off. Accordingly, on the 17th, the convention of Saratoga was carried into effect. By this convention 5790 men surrendered themselves as prisoners. The sick and wounded left in the camp when the British retreated to Saratoga, together with the numbers of the British, German, and Canadian troops, who were killed, wounded, or taken, and who had deserted in the preceding part of the expedition, were reckoned to be 4689.

The British sick and wounded who had fallen into the hands of the Americans after the battle of the 7th, were treated with exemplary humanity; and when the convention was executed, General Gates showed a noble delicacy of feeling, which deserves the highest degree of honour. Every circumstance was avoided which could give the appearance of triumph. The American troops remained within their lines until the British had piled their arms; and when this was done, the vanquished officers and soldiers were received with friendly kindness by their victors, and their immediate wants were promptly and liberally supplied. Discussions and disputes afterwards arose as to some of the terms of the convention; and the American Congress refused for a long time to carry into effect the article which provided for the return of Burgoyne's men to Europe; but no blame was imputable to General Gates or his army, who showed themselves to be generous as they had proved themselves to be brave.

Gates, after the victory, immediately despatched Colonel Wilkinson to carry the happy tidings to Congress. On being introduced into the hall, he said, "The whole British army has laid down its arms at Saratoga; our own, full of vigour and courage, expect your order. It is for your wisdom to decide where the country may still have need for their service." Honours and rewards were liberally voted by the Congress to their conquering general and his men; "and it would be difficult (says the Italian historian) to describe the transports of joy which the news of this event excited among the Americans. They began to flatter themselves with a still more happy future. No one any longer felt any doubt about their achieving their independence. All hoped, and with good reason, that a success of this importance would at length determine France, and the other European powers that waited for her example, to declare themselves in favour of America. There could no longer be any question respecting the future; since there was no longer the risk of espousing the cause of a people too feeble to defend themselves."

The truth of this was soon displayed in the conduct of France. When the news arrived at Paris of the capture of Ticonderoga, and of the victorious march of Burgoyne towards Albany, events which seemed decisive in favour of the English, instructions had been immediately despatched to Nants, and the other ports of the kingdom, that no American privateers should be suffered to enter them, except from indispensable necessity, as to repair their vessels, to obtain provisions, or to escape the perils of the sea. The American commissioners at Paris, in their disgust and despair, had almost broken off all negotiations with the French government and they even endeavoured to open communications with the British Ministry.

But the British government, elated with the first successes of Burgoyne, refused to listen to any overtures for accommodation. But when the news of Saratoga reached Paris, the whole scene was changed. Franklin and his brother commissioners found all their difficulties with the French government vanished. The time seemed to have arrived for the house of Bourbon to take a full revenge for all its humiliations and losses in previous wars. In December a treaty was arranged, and formally signed in the February following by which France acknowledged the independent United States of America. This was, of course, tantamount to a declaration of war with England. Spain soon followed France; and before long Holland took the same course. Largely aided by French fleets and troops, the Americans vigorously maintained the war against the armies which England, in spite of her European foes, continued to send across the Atlantic. But the struggle was too unequal to be maintained by this country for many years; and when the treaties of 1783 restored peace to the world, the independence of the United States was reluctantly recognised by their ancient parent and recent enemy, England.

* * * * *

EDITOR'S NOTE: It seems to be generally agreed that treasonous thoughts first began to hag-ride General Benedict Arnold, as the result of the his treatment by Gates at Saratoga and by the Congress before and after Saratoga. Arnold was an excellent soldier. He had proved his worth and the quality of his talents by his successes against the British at Ticonderoga, with Ethan Allen, on Lake Champlain; in Connecticut against Tryon and in the Mohawk Valley. But particularly in his leadership of the American expedition against Quebec and the siege of and assault upon the city. A few months prior to Saratoga, in 1777, the Congress, despite "Washington's protests and Arnold's brilliant services, promoted five brigadier generals of junior rank to major-generalships over Arnold's head." (The Columbia Encyclopedia.) Gates had already been made a major-general.

Gates battened upon the glory that came to him, and largely through Arnold's work, at Saratoga. Arnold did much to contribute to the defeat of Burgoyne. Gates did little or nothing. There is slight reliable and objective evidence to gainsay this. Gates and Arnold were enemies. Before the battle they had quarreled. Gates deprived Arnold of his command. It was touch-and-go, so far as the outcome of the battle was concerned, with Gates taking his ease in his headquarters and contenting himself with sending out orders, which apparently provided slight aid to the progress of his troops. As Lossing, a reliable, even though romantically-inclined, historian tells the story in his Field-Book of the Revolution:

"General Arnold had watched with eager eye and excited spirit the course of the battle thus far. Deprived of all command, he had no authority to fight, much less to order . . . leaping upon his large brown horse, he started off on a full gallop for the field battle. Gates immediately sent Major Armstrong after him, to order him back. Arnold saw him approaching and, anticipating his errand, spurred his horse and left his pursuer far behind, while he placed himself at the head of three regiments of Learned's brigade, who received their former commander with loud huzzas.

"He immediately led them against the British center . . . rushed into the thickest of the fight or 1ode along the lines in rapid and erratic movements, brandishing his broadsword above his head and delivering his orders everywhere in person. The Hessians . . . broke and fled in dismay. . . . Arnold and Morgan were the ruling spirits that controlled the storm on the part of the Americans. [Arnold's] voice, clear as a trumpet, animated the soldiers and, as if ubiquitous, he seemed to be everywhere amid the perils at the same moment. . . . The Germans, who had seen him on his steed in the thickest of the fight for more than two hours, terrified at his approach, fled, delivering a volley in their retreat, which killed Arnold's horse under him and wounded the general himself very severely, in the same leg that had been badly lacerated by a musket-ball at the storming of Quebec two years before.

"Here, wounded and disabled, at the head of conquering troops led on by his valor to the threshold of victory, Arnold was overtaken by Major Armstrong, who delivered to him Gates' order to return to camp, fearing he "might do some rash thing." He indeed did a rash thing in the eyes of military discipline. He led troops to victory without an order from his commander. . . . His conduct was rash indeed, compared with the stately method of General Gates, who directed by orders from his camp what his presence should have sanctioned.

"While Arnold was wielding the fierce sickle of war without orders, and reaping golden sheaves for Gates' garner, the latter, according to Wilkinson [Gates' aide] was within his camp, more intent upon discussing the merits of the Revolution with Sir Francis Clarke, Burgoyne's aide-de-camp, who had been wounded and taken prisoner, . . . than upon winning a battle, all-important to the ultimate triumph of those principles for which he professed so warm an attachment. When one of Gates' aides came up from the field of battle for orders, he found the general very angry because Sir Francis would not allow the force of his arguments. He left the room and calling his aide after him, asked as they went out: 'Did you ever hear so impudent a son of a ———?' "

Gates, and his army, received the thanks of the Congress, which voted Gates a gold medal. The medal bears a portrait of Gates. His expression, as graved thereon, fails to impress one as being that of a man who would go far in being kind to his wife and family, let alone considerate to Arnold or Washington or anyone else who might stand in the path of the man's ambition.

Gates later was mixed up in the currish Conway cabal, which had as its object the deposition, by the Congress of Washington as commander-in-chief and the naming of Gates as his successor.

SYNOPSIS OF EVENTS BETWEEN THE DEFEAT OF BURGOYNE AT SARATOGA, 1777, AND THE BATTLE OF VALMY, 1792.

1781. Surrender of Lord Cornwallis and the British army to Washington.

1782. Rodney's victory over the Spanish fleet. Unsuccessful siege of Gibraltar by the Spaniards and French.

1783. End of the American war.

1788. The States-General are convened in France; beginning of the Revolution.

-=[FOURTEEN]=-

Valmy, 1792

WHY DECISIVE: *"Valmy . . . [was] the primal victory of revolutionary France and prevented the armies [of Prussia and Austria] and the emigrant bands of Condé [who commanded a considerable anti-revolutionary French force] . . . from destroying the immature democracy in its cradle."* [Creasy.]
"From this place and from this day forth commences a new era in the world's history; and you can all say you were present at its birth." [Goethe (who witnessed the battle.)]

I

A few miles distant from the little town of St. Menehould, in the north-east of France, are the village and hill of Valmy; and near the crest of that hill a simple monument points out the burial-place of the heart of a general of the French republic, and a marshal of the French empire.

The elder Kellerman (father of the distinguished officer of that name, whose cavalry charge decided the battle of Marengo) held high commands in the French armies throughout the wars of the Convention, the Directory, the Consulate, and the Empire. He survived those wars, and the empire itself, dying in extreme old age in 1820. The last wish of the veteran on his death-bed was that his heart should be deposited in the battle-field of Valmy, there to repose among the remains of his old companions in arms, who had fallen at his side on that spot twenty-eight years before, on the memorable day when they won the primal victory of revolutionary France, and prevented the armies of Brunswick and the emigrant bands of Condé from marching on defenceless Paris, and destroying the immature democracy in its cradle.

The Duke of Valmy (for Kellerman, when made one of Napoleon's military peers in 1802, took his title from this same battle-field) had participated, during his long and active career, in the gaining of many a victory far more immediately dazzling than the one, the remembrance of which he thus cherished. He had been present at many a scene of carnage, where blood flowed in deluges, compared with which the libations of slaughter poured out at Valmy would have seemed scant and insignificant. But he rightly estimated the paramount importance of the battle with which he thus wished his appellation while living, and his memory after his death, to be identified.

The successful resistance, which the new Carmagnole levies and the disorganised relics of the old monarchy's army, then opposed to the combined hosts and chosen leaders of Prussia, Austria, and the French refugee noblesse, determined at once and for ever the belligerent character of the revolution. The raw artisans and tradesmen, the clumsy burghers, the base mechanics and low peasant churls, as it had been the fashion to term the middle and lower classes in France, found that they could face cannon-balls, pull triggers, and cross bayonets, without having been drilled into military machines, and without being officered by scions of noble houses. They awoke to the consciousness of their own instinctive soldiership. They at once acquired confidence in themselves and in each other; and that confidence soon grew into a spirit of unbounded audacity and ambition. "From the cannonade of Valmy may be dated the commencement of that career of victory which carried their armies to Vienna and the Kremlin."

One of the gravest reflections that arises from the contemplation of the civil restlessness and military enthusiasm which the close of the last century saw nationalised in France, is the consideration that these disturbing influences have become perpetual. No settled system of government, that shall endure from generation to generation, that shall be proof against corruption and popular violence, seems capable of taking root among the French. (When Creasy wrote, the Second Empire, created by Napoleon III's *coup d'etat* of 1852 was about to succeed the Second Republic, 1848-52. The Second Empire fell in 1870 and was followed by the Third Republic. This collapsed with the victory of the Germans in 1940 and gave way to the Vichy government. This was abolished after the war and the present Fourth Republic established.)

France first assumed the title of republic on the 20th of September 1792, on the very day on which the battle of Valmy was fought and won. To that battle the democratic spirit which in 1848, as well as in 1792, proclaimed the Republic in Paris, owed its preservation, and it is thence that the imperishable activity of its principles may be dated.

Far different seemed the prospects of democracy in Europe on the eve of that battle; and far different would have been the present position and influence of the French nation, if Brunswick's columns had charged with more boldness, or the lines of Dumouriez resisted with less firmness. When France, in 1792, declared war against the great powers of Europe, she was far from possessing that splendid military organisation which the experience of a few revolutionary campaigns taught her to assume, and which she has never abandoned. The army of the old monarchy had, during the latter part of the reign of Louis XV., sunk into gradual decay, both in numerical force, and in efficiency of equipment and spirit. The laurels gained by the auxiliary regiments which Louis XVI. sent to the American war did but little to restore the general tone of the army.

The insubordination and licence, which the revolt of the French guards, and the participation of other troops in many of the first excesses of the Revolution introduced among the soldiery, were soon rapidly disseminated through all the ranks. Under the Legislative Assembly every complaint of the soldier against his officer, however frivolous or ill-founded, was listened to with eagerness, and investigated with partiality, on the principles of liberty and equality. Discipline accordingly became more and more relaxed; and the dissolution of several of the old corps, under the pretext of their being tainted with an aristocratic feeling, aggravated the confusion and inefficiency of the war department. Many of the most effective regiments during the last period of the monarchy had consisted of foreigners. These had either been slaughtered in defence of the throne against insurrections, like the Swiss; or had been disbanded, and had crossed the frontier to recruit the forces which were assembling for the invasion of France.

Above all, the emigration of the noblesse had stripped the French army of nearly all its officers of high rank, and of the greatest portion of its subalterns. More than twelve thousand of the high-born youth of France, who had been trained to regard military command as their exclusive patrimony, and to whom the nation had been accustomed to look up to as its natural guides and champions in the storm of war, were now marshalled beneath the banner of Condé and the other emigrant princes, for the overthrow of the French armies, and the reduction of the French capital. Their successors in the French regi-

ments and brigades had as yet acquired neither skill nor experience, self-reliance nor the respect of the men under them.

II

Such was the state of the wreck of the old army; but the bulk
of the forces with which France began the war consisted of raw
insurrectionary levies, which were even less to be depended on.
The Carmagnoles, as the revolutionary volunteers were called,
flocked, indeed, readily to the frontier from every department
when the war was proclaimed, and the fierce leaders of the
Jacobins shouted that the country was in danger. They were
full of zeal and courage, "heated and excited by the scenes of
the Revolution, and inflamed by the florid eloquence, the songs,
dances, and signal-words with which it had been celebrated."
But they were utterly undisciplined, and turbulently impatient
of superior authority, or systematical control.

On one occasion during the campaign of Valmy, eight battalions of federates, intoxicated with massacre and sedition, joined
the forces under Dumouriez, and soon threatened to uproot all
discipline, saying openly that the ancient officers were traitors,
and that it was necessary to purge the army, as they had Paris,
of its aristocrats. Dumouriez posted these battalions apart from
the others, placed a strong force of cavalry behind them, and
two pieces of cannon on their flank. Then, affecting to review
them, he halted at the head of the line, surrounded by all his
staff and an escort of a hundred hussars. "Fellows," said he,
"for I will not call you either citizens or soldiers, you see before
you this artillery, behind you this cavalry; you are stained with
crimes, and I do not tolerate here assassins or executioners. I
know that there are scoundrels amongst you charged to excite
you to crime. Drive them from amongst you, or denounce them
to me, for I shall hold you responsible for their conduct."

Carlyle who narrates this incident, thus apostrophises the
French general:—

"Patience, O Dumouriez, this uncertain heap of shriekers,
mutineers, were they once drilled and inured, will become a
phalanxed mass of fighters; and wheel and whirl to order swiftly,
like the wind or the whirlwind; tanned mustachio-figures; often
barefoot, even barebacked, with sinews of iron; who require
only bread and gunpowder; very sons of fire; the adroitest,
hastiest, hottest, ever seen perhaps since Attila's time."

Such phalanxed masses of fighters did the *Carmagnoles* ultimately become; but France ran a fearful risk in being obliged
to rely on them when the process of their transmutation had
barely commenced. (*Carmagnole,* a coat. The term became
that of a song and a dance which was popular among revolutionary mobs, who affected coats of a style known as *carmagnole*).

The first events, indeed, of the war were disastrous and disgraceful to France, even beyond what might have been expected
from the chaotic state in which it found her armies as well as
her government. In the hopes of profiting by the unprepared
state of Austria, then the mistress of the Netherlands, the
French opened the campaign of 1792 by an invasion of Flanders,
with forces whose muster-rolls showed a numerical overwhelming superiority to the enemy, and seemed to promise a speedy
conquest of that old battlefield of Europe. But the first flash of
an Austrian sabre, or the first sound of an Austrian gun, was
enough to discomfit the French. Their first corps, four thousand strong, that advanced from Lille across the frontier, came
suddenly upon a far inferior detachment of the Austrian garrison of Tournay. Not a shot was fired, not a bayonet levelled.
With one simultaneous cry of panic the French broke and
ran headlong back to Lille, where they completed the specimen
of insubordination·which they had given in the field by murdering their general and several of their chief officers. On the
same day, another division under Biron, mustering ten thousand
sabres and bayonets, saw a few Austrian skirmishers reconnoitring their position. The French advanced posts had scarcely
given and received a volley, and only a few balls from the
enemy's field-pieces had fallen among the lines, when two
regiments of French dragoons raised the cry, "We are betrayed,"
galloped off, and were followed in disgraceful rout by the rest
of the whole army. Similar panics, or repulses almost equally
discreditable, occurred whenever Rochambeau, or Luckner, or
La Fayette, the earliest French generals in the war, brought their
troops into the presence of the enemy.

Meanwhile, the allied sovereigns had gradually collected on
the Rhine a veteran and finely-disciplined army for the invasion
of France, which for numbers, equipment, and martial renown,
both of generals and men, was equal to any that Germany had
ever sent forth to conquer. Their design was to strike boldly

and decisively at the heart of France, and penetrating the country through the Ardennes, to proceed by Chalons upon Paris.

The obstacles that lay in their way seemed insignificant. The disorder and imbecility of the French armies had been even augmented by the forced flight of La Fayette, and a sudden change of generals. The only troops posted on or near the track by which the allies were about to advance, were the twenty-three thousand men at Sedan, whom La Fayette had commanded, and a corps of twenty thousand near Metz, the command of which had just been transferred from Luckner to Kellerman. There were only three fortresses which it was necessary for the allies to capture or mask—Sedan, Longwy, and Verdun. The defences and stores of these three were known to be wretchedly dismantled and insufficient; and when once these feeble barriers were overcome, and Chalons reached, a fertile and unprotected country seemed to invite the invaders to that "military promenade to Paris," which they gaily talked of accomplishing.

III

At the end of July the allied army, having completed all preparations for the campaign, broke up from cantonments, and marching from Luxembourg upon Longwy, crossed the French frontier. Sixty thousand Prussians, trained in the school, and many of them under the eye of the great Frederick, heirs of the glories of the Seven Years' War, and universally esteemed the best troops in Europe, marched in one column against the central point of attack. Forty-five thousand Austrians, the greater part of whom were picked troops, and had served in the recent Turkish war, supplied two formidable corps that supported the flanks of the Prussians. There was also a powerful body of Hessians, and, leagued with the Germans against the Parisian democracy, came fifteen thousand of the noblest and bravest amongst the sons of France.

In these corps of emigrants, many of the highest born of the French nobility, scions of houses whose chivalric trophies had for centuries filled Europe with renown, served as rank and file.

Over this imposing army the allied sovereigns placed as generalissimo the Duke of Brunswick, one of the minor reigning princes of Germany, a statesman of no mean capacity, and who had acquired in the Seven Years' War a military reputation second only to that of the great Frederick himself. He had been deputed a few years before to quell the popular movements which then took place in Holland; and he had put down the attempted revolution in that country with a promptitude and completeness, which appeared to augur equal success to the army that now marched under his orders on a similar mission into France.

Moving majestically forward, with leisurely deliberation, that seemed to show the consciousness of superior strength, and a steady purpose of doing their work thoroughly, the Allies appeared before Longwy on the 20th of August, and the dispirited and dependent garrison opened the gates of that fortress to them after the first shower of bombs. On the 2nd of September the still more important stronghold of Verdun capitulated after scarcely the shadow of resistance.

Brunswick's superior force was now interposed between Kellerman's troops on the left, and the other French army near Sedan, which La Fayette's flight had, for the time, left destitute of a commander. It was in the power of the German general, by striking with an overwhelming mass to the right and left, to crush in succession each of these weak armies, and the allies might then have marched irresistible and unresisted upon Paris. But at this crisis Dumouriez, the new commander-in-chief of the French arrived at the camp near Sedan, and commenced a series of movements, by which he reunited the dispersed and disorganized forces of his country, checked the Prussian columns at the very moment when the last obstacles of their triumph seemed to have given way, and finally rolled back the tide of invasion far across the enemy's frontier.

The French fortresses had fallen; but nature herself still offered to brave and vigorous defenders of the land the means of opposing a barrier to the progress of the allies. A ridge of broken ground, called the Argonne, extends from the vicinity of Sedan towards the south-west for about fifteen or sixteen leagues. (about 45 miles) The country of L'Argonne has now been cleared and drained; but in 1792 it was thickly wooded, and the lower portions of its unequal surface were filled with rivulets and marshes. It thus presented a natural barrier of from four or five leagues broad, which was absolutely impenetrable to an army, except by a few defiles, such as an inferior force might easily fortify and defend. Dumouriez succeeded in marching his army down from Sedan behind the Argonne and in occupying its passes, while the Prussians still lingered on the north-eastern side of the forest line.

Ordering Kellerman to wheel round from Metz to St. Mene-hould, and the reinforcements from the interior and extreme north also to concentrate at that spot, Dumouriez trusted to assemble a powerful force in the rear of the south-west extremity of the Argonne, while, with the twenty-five thousand men under his immediate command, he held the enemy at bay before the passes, or forced him to a long circumvolution round one extremity of the forest ridge, during which favourable opportunities of assailing his flank were almost certain to occur. Dumouriez fortified the principal defiles, and boasted of the Thermopylae which he had found for the invaders; but the simile was nearly rendered fatally complete for the defending force. A pass, which was thought of inferior importance, had been but slightly manned, and an Austrian corps under Clairfayt forced it after some sharp fighting.

Dumouriez with great difficulty saved himself from being enveloped and destroyed by the hostile columns that now pushed through the forest. But instead of despairing at the failure of his plans, and falling back into the interior, to be completely severed from Kellerman's army, to be hunted as a fugitive under the walls of Paris by the victorious Germans, and to lose all chance of ever rallying his dispirited troops, he resolved to cling to the difficult country in which the armies still were grouped, to force a junction with Kellerman, and so to place himself at the head of a force, which the invaders would not dare to disregard, and by which he might drag them back from the advance on Paris, which he had not been able to bar.

Accordingly, by a rapid movement to the south, during which, in his own words, "France was within a hair's-breadth of destruction," and after with difficulty checking several panics of his troops, in which they ran by thousands at the sight of a few Prussian hussars, Dumouriez succeeded in establishing his headquarters in a strong position at St. Menehould, protected by the marshes and shallows of the river Aisne and Aube, beyond which, to the north-west, rose a firm and elevated plateau, called Dampierre's Camp, admirably situated for commanding the road by Chalons to Paris, and where he intended to post Kellerman's army so soon as it came up.

The news of the retreat of Dumouriez from the Argonne

passes, and of the panic flight of some divisions of his troops, spread rapidly throughout the country and Kellerman, who believed that his comrade's army had been annihilated, and feared to fall among the victorious masses of the Prussians, had halted on his march from Metz when almost close to St. Mene-hould. He had actually commenced a retrograde movement, when couriers from his commander-in-chief checked him from that fatal course; and then continuing to wheel round the rear and left flank of the troops at St. Menehould, Kellerman, with twenty thousand of the army of Metz, and some thousands of volunteers who had joined him in the march, made his appear-ance to the west of Dumouriez, on the very evening when West-erman and Thouvenot, two of the staff-officers of Dumouriez galloped in with the tidings that Brunswick's army had come through the upper passes of the Argonne in full force, and was deploying on the heights of La Lune, a chain of eminences that stretch obliquely from south-west to north-east, opposite the high ground which Dumouriez held, and also opposite, but at a shorter distance from, the position which Kellerman was de-signed to occupy.

The Allies were now, in fact, nearer to Paris than were the French troops themselves. Kellerman had laid himself un-necessarily open, by advancing beyond Dampierre's Camp, which Dumouriez had resigned for him, and moving forward across the Aube to the plateau of Valmy, a post inferior in strength and space to that which he had left, and which brought him close upon the Prussian lines, leaving him separated by a dan-gerous interval from the troops under Dumouriez himself. It seemed easy for the Prussian army to overwhelm him while thus isolated, and then they might surround and crush Dumouriez at their leisure.

IV

Accordingly, the right wing of the allied army moved for-ward, in the grey of the morning of the 20th of September, to gain Kellerman's left flank and rear and cut him off from retreat upon Chalons, while the rest of the army, moving from the heights of La Lune, which here converge semicircularly round the plateau of Valmy, were to assail his position in front, and interpose between him and Dumouriez. An unexpected collision between some of the advanced cavalry on each side in the low ground, warned Kellerman of the enemy's approach.

Dumouriez had not been unobservant of the danger of his comrade, thus isolated and involved; and he had ordered up troops
to support Kellerman on either flank in the event of his being
attacked. These troops, however, moved forward slowly and
Kellerman's army, ranged on the plateau of Valmy, "projected
like a cape into the midst of the lines of the Prussian bayonets."

A thick autumnal mist floated in waves of vapour over the
plains and ravines that lay between the two armies, leaving only
the crests and peaks of the hills glittering in the early light.
About ten o'clock the fog began to clear off, and then the French
from their promontory saw emerging from the white wreaths
of mist, and glittering in the sunshine, the countless Prussian
cavalry which were to envelop them as in a net if once driven
from their position, the solid columns of the infantry that
moved forward as if animated by a single will, the bristling
batteries of the artillery, and the glancing clouds of the Austrian
light troops, fresh from their contests with the Spahis of the east.

The best and bravest of the French must have beheld this
spectacle with secret apprehension and awe. However bold
and resolute a man may be in the discharge of duty, it is an
anxious and fearful thing to be called on to encounter danger
among comrades of whose steadiness you can feel no certainty.
Each soldier of Kellerman's army must have remembered the
series of panic routs which hitherto invariably taken place
on the French side during the war and must have cast restless glances to the right and left, to see if any symptoms of
wavering began to show themselves, and to calculate how
long it was likely to be before a general rush of his comrades
to the rear would either hurry him off with involuntary disgrace or leave him alone and helpless, to be cut down by
assailing multitudes.

On that very morning, and at the self-same hour, in which
the allied forces and the emigrants began to descend from La
Lune to the attack of Valmy, and while the cannonade was
opening between the Prussian and the Revolutionary batteries,
the debate in the National Convention at Paris commenced
on the proposal to proclaim France a republic.

The old monarchy had little chance of support in the
hall of the Convention; but if its more effective advocates
at Valmy had triumphed, there were yet the elements existing
in France for a permanent revival of the better part of the

ancient institutions, and for substituting reform for revolution. Only a few weeks before, numerously signed addresses
from the middle classes in Paris, Rouen, and other large cities,
had been presented to the king expressive of their horror of the
anarchists, and their readiness to uphold the rights of the crown,
together with the liberties of the subject. And an armed resistance to the authority of the Convention, and in favour of the
king, was in reality at this time being actively organised in La
Vendée and Brittany, the importance of which may be estimated from the formidable opposition which the Royalists of
these provinces made to the Republican party, at a later period,
and under much more disadvantageous circumstances.

It is a fact peculiarly illustrative of the importance of the
battle of Valmy, that "during the summer of 1792, the gentlemen of Brittany entered into an extensive association for the
purpose of rescuing the country from the oppressive yoke
which had been imposed by the Parisian demagogues. At the
head of the whole was the Marquis de la Rouarie, one of those
remarkable men who rise into pre-eminence during the stormy
days of a revolution, from conscious ability to direct its
current. Ardent, impetuous, and enthusiastic, he was first
distinguished in the American war, when the intrepidity of
his conduct attracted the admiration of the colonial troops,
and the same qualities rendered him at first an ardent supporter of the revolution in France; but when the atrocities
of the people began, he espoused with equal warmth the
opposite side, and used the utmost efforts to rouse the *noblesse*
of Brittany against the plebeian yoke which had been imposed
upon them by the National Assembly. He submitted his plan
to the Count d'Artois, and had organized one so extensive as
would have proved extremely formidable to the Convention,
if the retreat of the Duke of Brunswick, in September, 1792, had
not damped the ardour of the whole of the west of France, then
ready to break out into insurrection."

And it was not only among the zealots of the old monarchy
that the cause of the king would then have found friends.
The ineffable atrocities of the September massacres had just
occurred, and the reaction produced by them among thousands
who had previously been active on the ultra-democratic side,
was fresh and powerful. The nobility had not yet been made
utter aliens in the eyes of the nation by long expatriation and

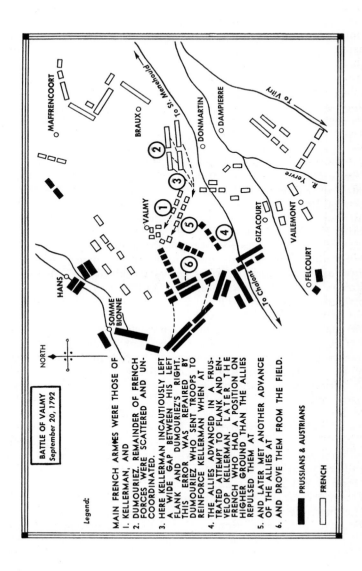

Legend:

BATTLE OF VALMY
September 20, 1792

MAIN FRENCH ARMIES WERE THOSE OF

1. KELLERMAN, AND
2. DUMOURIEZ, REMAINDER OF FRENCH FORCES WERE SCATTERED AND UN-COORDINATED.
3. HERE KELLERMAN INCAUTIOUSLY LEFT A WIDE GAP BETWEEN HIS LEFT FLANK AND DUMOURIEZ'S RIGHT. THIS ERROR WAS REPAIRED BY DUMOURIEZ WHO SENT TROOPS TO REINFORCE KELLERMAN WHEN AT
4. THE ALLIES ADVANCED IN A FRUS-TRATED ATTEMPT TO FLANK AND EN-VELOP KELLERMAN. LATER THE FRENCH WHO HAD A POSITION ON HIGHER GROUND THAN THE ALLIES REPULSED THEM AT
5. AND LATER MET ANOTHER ADVANCE OF THE ALLIES AT
6. AND DROVE THEM FROM THE FIELD.

■ PRUSSIANS & AUSTRIANS

□ FRENCH

civil war. There was not yet a generation of youth educated in revolutionary principles, and knowing no worship save that of military glory. Louis XVI was just and humane, and deeply sensible of the necessity of a gradual extension of political rights among all classes of his subjects. The Bourbon throne, if rescued in 1792, would have had chances of stability, such as did not exist for it in 1814, and seem never likely to be found again in France.

Serving under Kellerman on that day was one who experienced, perhaps the most deeply of all men, the changes for good and for evil which the French revolution had produced. He who, in his second exile, bore the name of the Count de Neuilly in this country, and who lately was Louis Philippe, king of the French, from 1830 to 1848 figured in the French lines at Valmy as a young and gallant officer, cool and sagacious beyond his years, and trusted accordingly by Kellerman and Dumouriez with an important station in the national army. The Duc de Chartres (the title he then bore) commanded the French right, General Valence was on the left, and Kellerman himself took his post in the centre, which was the strength and key of his position.

Besides these celebrated men, who were in the French army, and besides the King of Prussia, the Duke of Brunswick, and other men of rank and power, who were in the lines of the Allies, there was an individual present at the battle of Valmy, of little political note, but who has exercised, and exercises, a greater influence over the human mind, and whose fame is more widely spread, than that of either duke, or general, or king. This was the German poet, Goethe, who had, out of curiosity, accompanied the allied army on its march into France as a mere spectator. He has given us a curious record of the sensations which he experienced during the cannonade.

Contrary to the expectations of both friends and foes, the French infantry held their ground steadily under the fire of the Prussian guns, which thundered on them from La Lune; and their own artillery replied with equal spirit and greater effect on the denser masses of the allied army. Thinking that the Prussians were slackening in their fire, Kellerman formed a column in charging order, and dashed down into the valley, in the hopes of capturing some of the nearest

guns of the enemy. A masked battery opened its fire on
the French column, and drove it back in disorder, Kellerman
having his horse shot under him and being with difficulty
carried off by his men.

The Prussian columns now advanced in turn. The French
artillerymen began to waver and desert their posts, but were
rallied by the efforts and example of their officers; and Kellerman, reorganising the line of his infantry, took his station in
the ranks on foot, and called out to his men to let the enemy
come close up, and then to charge them with the bayonet. The
troops caught the enthusiasm of their general, and a cheerful
shout of *Vive la nation!* taken by one battalion from another,
pealed across the valley to the assailants. The Prussians flinched
from a charge up-hill against a force that seemed so resolute
and formidable; they halted for a while in the hollow, and then
slowly retreated up their own side of the valley.

Indignant at being thus repulsed by such a foe, the King
of Prussia formed the flower of his men in person, and,
riding along the column, bitterly reproached them with
letting their standard be thus humiliated. Then he led them
on again to the attack, marching in the front line, and seeing
his staff mowed down around him by the deadly fire which
the French artillery re-opened. But the troops sent by Dumouriez were now co-operating effectually with Kellerman and
that general's own men, flushed by success, presented a firmer
front than ever. Again the Prussians retreated, leaving eight
hundred dead behind, and at nightfall the French remained
victors on the heights of Valmy.

All hopes of crushing the revolutionary armies, and of the
promenade to Paris, had now vanished, though Brunswick
lingered long in the Argonne, till distress and sickness wasted
away his once splendid force, and finally but a mere wreck
of it recrossed the frontier. France, meanwhile, felt that
she possesed a giant's strength, and, like a giant, did she
use it. Before the close of that year, all Belgium obeyed the
National Convention at Paris, and the kings of Europe, after
the lapse of eighteen centuries, trembled once more before a
conquering military republic.

Goethe's observation to his comrades in the camp of the
Allies, at the end of the battle, deserves citation. It shows that
the poet felt (and, probably, he alone of the thousands there

assembled felt) the full importance of that day. He describes the consternation and the change of demeanour which he observed among his Prussian friends that evening. He tells us that "most of them were silent; and, in fact, the power of reflection and judgment was wanting to all. At last I was called upon to say what I thought of the engagement; for I had been in the habit of enlivening and amusing the troop with short sayings. This time I said: 'From this place, and from this day forth, commences a new era in the world's history; and you can all say that you were present at its birth.'"

SYNOPSIS OF EVENTS BETWEEN THE BATTLE OF VALMY, 1792, AND THE BATTLE OF WATERLOO, 1815.

1793. Trial and execution of Louis XVI., at Paris. England and Spain declare war against France. Second invasion of France by the Allies.

1794. Lord Howe's victory over the French fleet. Final partition of Poland by Russia, Prussia, and Austria.

1795. The French armies, under Pichegru, conquer Holland.

1796. Bonaparte commands the French army of Italy and gains repeated victories over the Austrians.

1797. Victory of Jervis, off Cape St. Vincent. Peace of Campo Formio between France and Austria. Defeat of the Dutch off Camperdown by Admiral Duncan.

1798. Rebellion in Ireland. Expedition of the French under Bonaparte to Egypt. Lord Nelson destroys the French fleet at the Battle of the Nile.

1799. Renewal of the war between Austria and France. The Russian emperor sends an army in aid of Austria, under Suvorov. The French are repeatedly defeated in Italy. Bonaparte returns from Egypt and makes himself First Consul of France. Massena wins the battle of Zurich. The Russian emperor makes peace with France.

1800. Bonaparte passes the Alps and defeats the Austrians at Marengo. Moreau wins the battle of Hohenlinden.

1801. Treaty of Luneville, between France and Austria.

1802. Peace of Amiens.

1803. War between England and France renewed.

1804. Napoleon Bonaparte is made Emperor of France.

1805. Great preparations of Napoleon to invade England. Austria, supported by Russia, renews war with France. Napoleon marches into Germany, takes Vienna, and gains the battle of Austerlitz. Lord Nelson destroys the combined French and Spanish fleets, and is killed at the battle of Trafalgar.

1806. War between Prussia and France. Napoleon conquers Prussia in the battle of Jena.

1807. Obstinate warfare between the French and Russian armies in East Prussia and Poland. Peace of Tilsit.

1808. Napoleon endeavours to make his brother Joseph King of Spain. Rising of the Spanish nation against him. England sends troops to aid the Spaniards. Battles of Vimiera and Coruna.

1809. War renewed between France and Austria. Battles of Asperne and Wagram. Peace granted to Austria. Lord Wellington's victory of Talavera, in Spain.

1810. Marriage of Napoleon and the Archduchess Maria Louisa. Holland annexed to France.

1812. War between England and the United States. Napoleon invades Russia. Battle of Borodino. The French occupy Moscow, which is burned. Disastrous retreat and almost total destruction of the great army of France.

1813. Prussia and Austria take up arms again against France. Battles of Lutzen, Bautzen, Dresden, Culm, and Leipzig. The French are driven out of Germany. Lord Wellington gains the great battle of Vittoria, which completes the rescue of Spain from France.

1814. The Allies invade France on the eastern, and Lord Wellington invades it on the southern frontier. Battles of Laon, Montmirail, Arcis-sur-Aube, and others in the north-east of France; and of Toulouse in the south. Paris surrenders to the Allies, and Napoleon abdicates in favor of Louis XVIII. First restoration of the Bourbons. Napoleon goes to the isle of Elba, which is assigned to him by the Allies. Treaty of Ghent, between the United States and England.

1815. Napoleon suddenly escapes from Elba, and lands in France. The French soldiery join him, and Louis XVIII. is obliged to fly from the throne.

-⟨ FIFTEEN ⟩-

Waterloo, 1815

WHY DECISIVE: *"The great battle which ended the twenty-three years' war of the first French revolution and which quelled the man whose genius and ambition had so long disturbed and desolated the world deserves to be regarded . . . with peculiar gratitude for the repose it secured . . . for the greater part of the human race."* [Creasy.]

I

ONE good test for determining the importance of Waterloo, is to ascertain what was felt by wise and prudent statesmen before that battle, respecting the return of Napoleon from Elba to the Imperial throne of France, and the probable effects of his success. For this purpose, I will quote the words, not of any of our vehement anti-Gallican politicians of the school of Pitt, but of a leader of our Liberal party, of a man whose reputation as a jurist, a historian, and a far-sighted and candid statesman, was, and is, deservedly high, not only in this country, but throughout Europe. Sir James Mackintosh, in the debate in the British House of Commons, on the 20th April 1815, spoke thus of the return from Elba:

"Was it in the power of language to describe the evil? Wars which had raged for more than twenty years throughout Europe; which had spread blood and desolation from Cadiz to Moscow, and from Naples to Copenhagen; which had wasted the means of human enjoyment, and destroyed the instruments of social improvement; which threatened to diffuse among the European nations, the dissolute and ferocious habits of a predatory soldiery,—at length, by one of those vicissitudes which bid defiance to the foresight of man, had been brought to a close, upon the whole, happy beyond all reasonable expectation, with no violent shock to national independence, with some tolerable compromise between the opinions of the age and reverence due to ancient institutions; with no too signal or mortifying triumph over the legitimate interests or avowable feelings of any numerous body of men, and, above all, without those retaliations against nations or parties, which beget new convulsions, often as horrible as those which they close and perpetuate revenge and hatred and bloodshed, from age to age. Europe seemed to breathe after her sufferings.

"In the midst of this fair prospect, and of these consolatory hopes, Napoleon Bonaparte escaped from Elba; his three small vessels reached the coast of Provence; our hopes are instantly dispelled; the work of our toil and fortitude is undone; the blood of Europe is spilt in vain."

The congress of emperors, kings, princes, generals, and statesmen, who had assembled at Vienna to remodel the world after the overthrow of the mighty conqueror in 1814 after the fatal Russian campaign and who thought that Napoleon had passed away forever from the great drama of European politics, had not yet completed their triumphant festivities, and their diplomatic toils, when Talleyrand, on the 11th of March 1815, rose up among them and announced that the ex-emperor had escaped from Elba, and was Emperor of France once more. It is recorded by Sir Walter Scott, as a curious physiological fact, that the first effect of the news of an event which threatened to neutralise all their labours, was to excite a loud burst of laughter from nearly every member of the Congress. But the jest was a bitter one: and they soon were deeply busied in anxious deliberations.

Napoleon sought to disunite the formidable confederacy, which he knew would be arrayed against him, by endeavouring to negotiate separately with each of the allied sovereigns. It is said that Austria and Russia were at first not unwilling to treat with him. Disputes and jealousies had been rife among several of the Allies on the subject of the division of the conquered countries; and the cordial unanimity with which they had acted during 1813 and the first months of 1814, had grown chill during some weeks of discussions. But the active exertions of Talleyrand, (French statesman, 1754-1838 who represented Louis XVIII at the congress, and who both hated and feared Napoleon (whom for years he had ably, and often ignobly served) with all the intensity of which his powerful spirit was capable, prevented the secession of any member of the Congress from the new great league against their ancient enemy. Still it is highly probable that, if Napoleon had triumphed in Belgium over the Prussians and the English, he would have succeeded in opening negotiations with the Austrians and Russians; and he might have thus gained advantages similar to those which he had obtained on his return from Egypt, when he induced the Czar Paul to withdraw the Russian armies from co-operating with the other enemies of France in the extremity of peril to which she seemed reduced in 1799. But fortune now had deserted him both in diplomacy and in war.

II

On the 13th of March, 1815, the ministers of the seven powers, Austria, Spain, England, Portugal, Prussia, Russia, and Sweden, signed a manifesto, by which they declared Napoleon an outlaw; and this denunciation was instantly followed up by a treaty between England, Austria, Prussia, and Russia (to which other powers soon acceded), by which the rulers of those countries bound themselves to enforce that decree, and to prosecute the war until Napoleon should be driven from the throne of France and rendered incapable of disturbing the peace of Europe.

The Duke of Wellington was the representative of England at the Congress of Vienna, and he was immediately applied to for his advice on the plan of military operations against France. It was obvious that Belgium would be the first battlefield; and by the general wish of the Allies, the Duke proceeded thither to assemble an army from the contingents of Dutch, Belgian, and Hanoverian troops, that were most speedily available, and from the English regiments which his own government was hastening to send over from this country.

A strong Prussian corps was near Aix-la-Chapelle, having remained there since the campaign of the preceding year. This was largely reinforced by other troops of the same nation; and Marshal Blucher, the favourite hero of the Prussian soldiery, and the deadliest foe of France, assumed the command of this army, which was termed the army of the Lower Rhine; and which, in conjunction with Wellington's forces, was to make the van of the armaments of the Allied powers. Meanwhile Prince Swartzenburg was to collect 130,000 Austrians, and 124,000 troops of other Germanic States, as the army of the Upper Rhine; and 168,000 Russians, under the command of Barclay de Tolly, were to form the army of the Middle Rhine, and to repeat the march from Muscovy to that river's banks.

The exertions which the Allied powers thus made at this crisis to grapple promptly with the French emperor have truly been termed gigantic; and never were Napoleon's genius and activity more signally displayed, than in the celerity and skill by which he brought forward all the military resources of France, which the reverses of the three preceding years and the pacific policy of the Bourbons during the months of their first restoration, had greatly diminished and disorganized.

He re-entered Paris on the 20th of March and by the end of May, besides sending a force into La Vendée to put down the armed risings of the royalists in that province, and besides providing troops under Massena and Suchet for the defence of the southern frontiers of France, Napoleon had an army assembled in the north-east for active operations under his own command which amounted to between one hundred twenty and one hundred thirty thousand men, with a superb park of artillery and in the highest possible state of equipment, discipline, and efficiency.

The approach of the multitudinous Russian, Austrian, Bavarian, and other foes of the French emperor to the Rhine was necessarily slow; but the two most active of the Allied powers had occupied Belgium with their troops, while Napoleon was organizing his forces. Marshal Blucher was there with one hundred sixteen thousand Prussians; and, before the end of May, the Duke of Wellington was there also with about one hundred six thousand troops, either British or in British pay. Napoleon determined to attack these enemies in Belgium. The disparity of numbers was indeed great, but delay was sure to increase the proportionate numerical superiority of his enemies over his own ranks.

The French emperor considered also that "the enemy's troops were now cantoned under the command of two generals, and composed of nations differing both in interest and in feelings." His own army was under his own sole command. It was composed exclusively of French soldiers, mostly of veterans, well acquainted with their officers and with each other, and full of enthusiastic confidence in their commander. If he could separate the Prussians from the British, so as to attack each singly, he felt sanguine of success, not only against these the most resolute of his many adversaries, but also against the other masses that were slowly labouring up against his eastern dominions.

The triple chain of strong fortresses, which the French possessed on the Belgian frontier, formed a curtain, behind which Napoleon was able to concentrate his army, and to conceal till the very last moment the precise line of attack which he intended to take. On the other hand, Blucher and Wellington were obliged to canton their troops along a line of open country of considerable length, so as to watch for the outbreak of Napoleon from whichever point of his chain of strongholds he should please to make it.

Blucher, with his army, occupied the banks of the Sambre and the Meuse, from Liege on his left, to Charleroi on his right; and the Duke of Wellington covered Brussels, his cantonments being partly in front of that city and between it and the French frontier and partly on its west; their extreme right reaching to Courtray and Tournay, while the left approached Charleroi and communicated with the Prussian right. It was upon Charleroi that Napoleon resolved to level his attack, in hopes of severing the two allied armies from each other, and then pursuing his favourite tactic of assailing each separately with a superior force on the battle-field, though the aggregate of their numbers considerably exceeded his own.

The first French *corps d'armée,* commanded by Count d'Erlon, was stationed in the beginning of June in and around the city of Lille, near to the north-eastern frontier of France. The second corps, under Count Reille, was at Valenciennes, to the right of the first one. The third corps, under Count Vandamme, was at Mezières. The fourth, under Count Gérard, had its headquarters at Metz, the fifth under Count Rapp was at Strasburg and the sixth, under Count Lobau, was at Laon. Four corps of reserve cavalry, under Marshal Grouchy, were also near the frontier, between the rivers Aisne and Sambre. The Imperial Guard remained in Paris until the 8th of June, when it marched towards Belgium, and reached Avesnes on the 13th; and in the course of the same and the following day, the five *corps d'armée,* not including Rapp's, with the cavalry reserves which have been mentioned, were in pursuance of skilfully combined orders rapidly drawn together and concentrated in and around the same place, on the right bank of the river Sambre. On the 14th Napoleon arrived among his troops, who were exulting at the display of their commander's skill in the celerity and precision with which they had been drawn together, and in the consciousness of their collective strength.

Although Napoleon too often permitted himself to use language unworthy of his own character respecting his great English adversary, his real feelings in commencing this campaign may be judged from the last words which he spoke, as he stepped into his travelling-carriage to leave Paris for the army. "I go," he said, "to measure myself with Wellington."

The enthusiasm of the French soldiers at seeing their Emperor among them, was still more excited by the "Order of the Day," in which he thus appealed to them, in his customary use of rodomontade:

"Napoleon, by the Grace of God, and the Constitution of the Empire, Emperor of the French, &c., to the Grand Army.
"AT THE IMPERIAL HEADQUARTERS, *Avesnes, June* 14th, 1815.

"Soldiers! this day is the anniversary of Marengo and of Friedland, which twice decided the destiny of Europe. Then, as after Austerlitz, as after Wagram, we were too generous! We believed in the protestations and in the oaths of princes, whom we left on their thrones. Now, however, leagued together, they aim at the independence and the most sacred rights of France. They have commenced the most unjust of aggressions. Let us, then, march to meet them. Are they and we no longer the same men?

"Soldiers! at Jena, against these same Prussians, now so arrogant, you were one to three, and at Montmirail one to six!

"Let those among you who have been captives to the English describe the nature of their prison-ships, and the frightful miseries they endured.

"The Saxons, the Belgians, the Hanoverians, the soldiers of the Confederation of the Rhine, lament that they are compelled to use their arms in the cause of princes, the enemies of justice and of the rights of all nations. They know that this coalition is insatiable! After having devoured twelve millions of Poles, twelve millions of Italians, one million of Saxons, and six millions of Belgians, it now wishes to devour the states of the second rank in Germany.

"Madmen! one moment of prosperity has bewildered them. The oppression and the humiliation of the French people are beyond their power. If they enter France they will there find their grave.

"Soldiers! we have forced marches to make, battles to fight, dangers to encounter; but, with firmness, victory will be ours. The rights, the honour, and the happiness of the country will be recovered!

"To every Frenchman who has a heart, the moment is now arrived to conquer or to die!

"NAPOLEON,"
"THE MARSHAL DUKE OF DALMATIA,
"MAJOR-GENERAL."

III

The 15th of June had scarcely dawned before the French army was in motion for the decisive campaign, and crossed the frontier in three columns, which were pointed upon Charleroi and its vicinity. The French line of advance upon Brussels, which city Napoleon resolved to occupy, thus lay right through the centre of the cantonments of the Allies.

Much criticism has been expended on the supposed surprise of Wellington's army in its cantonments by Napoleon's rapid advance. These comments would hardly have been made if sufficient attention had been paid to the geography of the Waterloo campaign; and if it had been remembered that the protection of Brussels was justly considered by the Allied generals a matter of primary importance. If Napoleon could, either by manœuvring or fighting, have succeeded in occupying that city, the greater part of Belgium would unquestionably have declared in his favour; and the results of such a success, gained by the Emperor at the commencement of the campaign, might have decisively influenced the whole after-current of events.

A glance at the map will show the numerous roads that lead from the different fortresses on the French north-eastern frontier, and converge upon Brussels; any one of which Napoleon might have chosen for the advance of a strong force upon that city. The Duke's army was judiciously arranged, so as to enable him to concentrate troops on any one of these roads sufficiently in advance of Brussels to check an assailing enemy. The army was kept thus available for movement in any necessary direction, till certain intelligence arrived on the 15th of

June that the French had crossed the frontier in large force near Thuin, that they had driven back the Prussian advanced troops under General Ziethen, and were also moving across the Sambre upon Charleroi.

Marshal Blucher now rapidly concentrated his forces, calling them in from the left upon Ligny, which is to the north-east of Charleroi. Wellington also drew his troops together, calling them in from the right. But even now, though it was certain that the French were in large force at Charleroi, it was unsafe for the English general to place his army directly between that place and Brussels, until it was certain that no corps of the enemy was marching upon Brussels by the western road through Mons and Hal.

The Duke, therefore, collected his troops in Brussels and its immediate vicinity, ready to move due southward upon Quatre Bras, and co-operate with Blucher, who was taking his station at Ligny, but also ready to meet and defeat any manoeuvre that the enemy might make to turn the right of the Allies, and occupy Brussels by a flanking movement. The testimony of the Prussian general, Baron Müffling, who was attached to the Duke's staff during the campaign, and who expressly states the reasons on which the English general acted, ought for ever to have silenced the "weak inventions of the enemy" about the Duke of Wellington having been deceived and surprised by his assailant, which some writers of our own nation, as well as foreigners, have incautiously repeated.

It was about three o'clock in the afternoon of the 15th, that a Prussian officer reached Brussels, whom General Ziethen had sent to Müffling to inform him of the advance of the main French army upon Charleroi. Müffling immediately communicated this to the Duke of Wellington and asked him whether he would now concentrate his army, and what would be his point of concentration; observing that Marshal Blucher in consequence of this intelligence would certainly concentrate the Prussians at Ligny. The Duke replied:

"If all is as General Ziethen supposes, I will concentrate on my left wing, and so be in readiness to fight in conjunction with the Prussian army. Should, however, a portion of the enemy's force come by Mons, I must concentrate more towards my centre. This is the reason why I must wait for positive news from Mons before I fix the rendezvous. Since however

it is certain that the troops *must* march, though it is uncertain
upon what precise spot they must march, I will order
all to be in readiness, and will direct a brigade to move at once
towards Quatre Bras."

Later in the same day a message from Blucher himself was
delivered to Müffling, in which the Prussian field-marshal informed the Baron that he was concentrating his men at
Sombref and Ligny, and charged Müffling to give him speedy
intelligence respecting the concentration of Wellington. Müffling
immediately communicated this to the Duke, who expressed his
satisfaction with Blucher's arrangements, but added that he
could not even then resolve upon his own point of concentration
before he obtained the desired intelligence from Mons. About
midnight this information arrived. The Duke went to the
quarters of General Müffling, and told him that he now had
received his reports from Mons, and was sure that no French
troops were advancing by that route, but that the mass of
the enemy's force was decidedly directed on Charleroi. He informed the Prussian general that he had ordered the British
troops to move forward upon Quatre Bras, but with characteristic coolness and sagacity resolved not to give the appearance
of alarm by hurrying on with them himself.

A ball was to be given by the Duchess of Richmond at
Brussels that night, and the Duke proposed to General Müffling
that they should go to the ball for a few hours and ride forward in the morning to overtake the troops at Quatre Bras.

To hundreds, who were assembled at that memorable ball,
the news that the enemy was advancing, and that the time
for battle had come, must have been a fearfully exciting surprise, and the manificent stanzas of Byron are as true as they
are beautiful:

> There was a sound of revelry by night,
> And Belgium's capital had gather'd then
> Her Beauty and her Chivalry, and bright
> The lamps shone o'er fair women and brave men,
> A thousand hearts beat happily; and when
> Music arose with its voluptuous swell,
> Soft eyes look'd love to eyes which spake again,
> And all went merry as a marriage-bell;
> But hush! hark! a deep sound strikes like a rising knell.
>
> Did ye not hear it?—no; 'twas but the wind,
> Or the car rattling o'er the stony street;

On with the dance! let joy be unconfined;
No sleep till morn, when Youth and Pleasure meet
To chase the glowing Hours with flying feet—
But, hark!—that heavy sound breaks in once more,
As if the clouds its echo would repeat;
And nearer, clearer, deadlier than before!
Arm! Arm! it is—it is—the cannon's opening roar!

Within a window'd niche of that high hall
Sate Brunswick's fated chieftan; he did hear
That sound the first amidst the festival,
And caught its tone with Death's prophetic ear;
And when they smiled because he deem'd it near,
His heart more truly knew that peal too well
Which stretch'd his father on a bloody bier,
And roused the vengeance blood alone could quell:
He rush'd into the field, and, foremost fighting, fell.

Ah! then and there was hurrying to and fro,
And gathering tears, and tremblings of distress,
And cheeks all pale, which but an hour ago
Blush'd at the praise of their own loveliness;
And there were sudden partings, such as press
The life from out young hearts, and choking sighs
Which ne'er might be repeated. Who could guess
If ever more should meet those mutual eyes,
Since upon night so sweet such awful morn could rise?

And there was mounting in hot haste: the steed,
The mustering squadron, and the clattering car,
Went pouring forward with impetuous speed,
And swiftly forming in the ranks of war;
And the deep thunder peal on peal afar;
And near, the beat of the alarming drum
Roused up the soldier ere the morning star;
While throng'd the citizens with terror dumb,
Or whispering, with white lips—"The foe! They come! they come!"

And Ardennes waves above them her green leaves,
Dewy with nature's tear-drops, as they pass,
Grieving, if aught inanimate e'er grieves,
Over the unreturning brave,—alas!
Ere evening to be trodden like the grass
Which now beneath them, but above shall grow
In its next verdure, when this fiery mass
Of living valour, rolling on the foe
And burning with high hope, shall moulder cold and low.

Last noon beheld them full of lusty life,
Last eve in Beauty's circle proudly gay,
The midnight brought the signal-sound of strife,
The morn the marshalling in arms,—the day
Battle's magnificently-stern array!
The thunder-clouds close o'er it, which when rent
The earth is covered thick with other clay,
Which her own clay shall cover, heap'd and pent,
Rider and horse,—friend, foe—in one red burial blent!

But the Duke and his principal officers knew well the stern termination to that festive scene which was approaching. One by one, and in such a way as to attract as little observation as possible, the leaders of the various corps left the ball-room, and took their stations at the head of their men, who were pressing forward through the last hours of the short summer night to the arena of anticipated slaughter.

IV

Napoleon's operations on the 15th had been conducted with signal skill and vigour; and their results had been very advantageous for his plan of the campaign. With his army formed in three vast columns, he had struck at the centre of the line of cantonments of his allied foes; and he had so far made good his blow, that he had effected the passage of the Sambre, he had beaten with his left wing the Prussian corps of General Ziethen at Thuin, and with his centre he had in person advanced right through Charleroi upon Fleurus, inflicting considerable loss upon the Prussians that fell back before him. His right column had with little opposition moved forward as far as the bridge of Chatelet.

Napoleon had thus a powerful force immediately in front of the point which Blucher had fixed for the concentration of the Prussian army, and that concentration was still incomplete. The French Emperor designed to attack the Prussians on the morrow in person, with the troops of his centre and right columns, and to employ his left wing in beating back such English troops as might advance to the help of their allies, and also in aiding his own attack upon Blucher. He gave the command of this left wing to Marshal Ney.

Napoleon seems not to have originally intended to employ this celebrated general in the campaign. It was only on the night of the 11th of June, that Marshal Ney received at Paris an order to join the army. Hurrying forward to the Belgian frontier he met the Emperor near Charleroi. Napoleon immediately directed him to take the command of the left wing, and to press forward with it upon Quatre Bras by the line of the road which leads from Charleroi to Brussels, through Gosselies, Frasne, Quatre Bras, Genappe, and Waterloo. Ney immediately proceeded to the post assigned him; and before

ten on the night of the 15th he had occupied Gosselies and
Frasne, driving out without much difficulty some weak Belgian
detachments which had been stationed in those villages. The
lateness of the hour, and the exhausted state of the French
troops, who had been marching and fighting since ten in the
morning, made him pause from advancing further, to attack
the much more important position of Quatre Bras.

In truth, the advantages which the French gained by their
almost superhuman energy and activity throughout the long
day of the 15th of June, were necessarily bought at the price
of more delay and inertness during the following night and
morrow, than would have been observable if they had not
been thus overtasked. Ney has been blamed for want of promptness in his attack upon Quatre Bras and Napoleon has been
criticised for not having fought at Ligny before the afternoon
of the 16th, but their censors should remember that soldiers are
but men; and that there must be necessarily some interval of
time before troops that have been worn and weakened by
twenty hours of incessant fatigue and strife can be fed, rested,
reorganized, and brought again into action with any hope of
success.

Having on the night of the 15th placed the most advanced
of the French under his command in position in front of
Frasne, Ney rode back to Charleroi, where Napoleon also
arrived about midnight, having returned from directing the
operations of the centre and right column of the French. The
Emperor and the Marshal supped together, and remained
in earnest conversation till two in the morning. An hour or
two afterwards Ney rode back to Frasne, where he endeavoured
to collect tidings of the numbers and movements of the enemy
in front of him; and also busied himself in the necessary duty
of learning the amount and composition of the troops which
he himself was commanding. He had been so suddenly appointed to his high station that he did not know the strength
of the several regiments under him, or even the names of their
commanding officers. He now caused his aides-de-camp to prepare the requisite returns, and drew together the troops, whom
he was thus learning before he used them.

Wellington remained at the Duchess of Richmond's ball
at Brussels till about three o'clock in the morning of the
16th, "showing himself very cheerful," as Baron Müffling,

who accompanied him, observes. At five o'clock the Duke and the Baron were on horseback, and reached the position at Quatre Bras about eleven. As the French, who were in front of Frasne, were perfectly quiet, and the Duke was informed that a very large force under Napoleon in person was menacing Blucher, it was thought possible that only a slight detachment of the French was posted at Frasne in order to mask the English army. In that event Wellington, as he told Baron Müffling, would be able to employ his whole strength in supporting the Prussians: and he proposed to ride across from Quatre Bras to Blucher's position, in order to concert with him personally the measures which should be taken in order to bring on a decisive battle with the French.

Wellington and Müffling rode accordingly towards Ligny, and found Marshal Blucher and his staff at the windmill of Bry, near that village. The Prussian army, 80,000 strong, was drawn up chiefly along a chain of heights, with the villages of Sombref, St. Amand, and Ligny in their front. These villages were strongly occupied by Prussian detachments, and formed the keys of Blucher's position. The heads of the columns which Napoleon was forming for the attack, were visible in the distance. The Duke asked Blucher and General Gneisenau (who was Blucher's adviser in matters of strategy) what they wished him to do. Müffling had already explained to them in a few words the Duke's earnest desire to support the Field-Marshal, and that he would do all that they wished, provided they did not ask him to divide his army, which was contrary to his principles.

The Duke wished to advance with his army (as soon as it was concentrated) upon Frasne and Gosselies, and thence to move upon Napoleon's flank and rear. The Prussian leaders preferred that he should march his men from Quatre Bras by the Namur Road, so as to form a reserve in rear of Blucher's army. The Duke replied, "Well, I will come if I am not attacked myself," and galloped back with Müffling to Quatre Bras, where the French attack was now actually raging.

V

Marshal Ney began the battle about two o'clock in the afternoon. He had at this time in hand about 16,000 infantry, nearly 2000 cavalry, and 38 guns. The force which Napoleon nominally placed at his command exceeded 40,000 men. But more than one half of these consisted of the first French corps d'armée, under Count d'Erlon; and Ney was deprived of the use of this corps at the time that he most required it, in consequence of its receiving orders to march to the aid of the Emperor at Ligny. A magnificent body of heavy cavalry under Kellerman, nearly 5000 strong, and several more battalions of artillery were added to Ney's army during the battle of Quatre Bras; but his effective infantry force never exceeded 16,000.

When the battle began, the greater part of the Duke's army was yet on its march towards Quatre Bras from Brussels and the other parts of its cantonments. The force of the Allies, actually in position there, consisted only of a Dutch and Belgian division of infantry, not quite 7000 strong, with one battalion of foot, and one of horse-artillery. The Prince of Orange commanded them. A wood, called the Bois de Bossu, stretched along the right (or western) flank of the position of Quatre Bras; a farmhouse and building, called Gemiancourt, stood on some elevated ground in its front; and to the left (or east), were the inclosures of the village of Pierremont.

The Prince of Orange endeavoured to secure these posts, but Ney carried Gemiancourt in the centre and Pierremont on the east, and gained occupation of the southern part of the wood of Bossu. He ranged the chief part of his artillery on the high ground of Gemiancourt, whence it played throughout the action with most destructive effect upon the Allies. He was pressing forward to further advantages, when the fifth infantry division under Sir Thomas Picton, and the Duke of Brunswick's corps appeared upon the scene. Wellington (who had returned to Quatre Bras from his interview with Blucher shortly before the arrival of these forces) restored the fight with them; and, as fresh troops of the Allies arrived, they were brought forward to stem the fierce attacks which Ney's columns and squadrons continued to make with unabated gallantry and zeal.

The only cavalry of the Anglo-Allied army that reached Quatre Bras during the action consisted of Dutch and Belgians, and a small force of Brunswickers, under their Duke, who was killed on the field. These proved wholly unable to encounter Kellerman's cuirassiers and Piré's lancers; the Dutch and Belgian infantry also gave way early in the engagement so that the whole brunt of the battle fell on the British and German infantry. They sustained it nobly. Though repeatedly charged by the French cavalry, though exposed to the murderous fire of the French batteries, which from the heights of Gemiancourt sent shot and shell into the devoted squares whenever the French horsemen withdrew, they not only repelled their assailants, but Kempt's and Pack's brigades, led on by Picton, actually advanced against and through their charging foes, and with stern determination made good to the end of the day the ground which they had thus boldly won. Some, however, of the British regiments were during the confusion assailed by the French cavalry before they could form squares, and suffered severely. One regiment, the 92nd, was almost wholly destroyed by the cuirassiers. A French private soldier, named Lami, of the 8th regiment of cuirassiers, captured one of the English colours, and presented it to Ney. It was a solitary trophy.

The arrival of the English Guards about half-past six o'clock, enabled the Duke to recover the wood of Bossu, which the French had almost entirely won, and the possession of which by them would have enabled Ney to operate destructively upon the Allied flank and rear. Not only was the wood of Bossu recovered on the British right, but the inclosures of Pierremont were also carried on the left. When night set in the French had been driven back on all points towards Frasne; but they still held the farm of Gemiancourt in front of the Duke's centre. Wellington and Müffling were unacquainted with the result of the collateral battle between Blucher and Napoleon, the cannonading of which had been distinctly audible at Quatre Bras throughout the afternoon and evening. The Duke observed to Müffling, that of course the two Allied armies would assume the offensive against the enemy on the morrow; and consequently, it would be better to capture the farm at once, instead of waiting till next morning. Müffling agreed in the Duke's views, and Gemiancourt was forthwith attacked by the English and captured with little loss to its assailants.

Meanwhile the French and the Prussians had been fighting in and round the villages of Ligny, Sombref, and St. Amand from three in the afternoon to nine in the evening with a savage inveteracy almost unparalleled in modern warfare. Blucher had in the field, when he began the battle, 83,417 men and 224 guns. Bulow's corps, which was 25,000 strong, had not joined him, but the field-marshal hoped to be reinforced by it, or by the English army before the end of the action. But Bulow, through some error in the transmission of orders, was far in the rear; and the Duke of Wellington was engaged, as we have seen, with Marshal Ney.

Blucher received early warning from Baron Müffling that the Duke could not come to his assistance; but, as Müffling observes, Wellington rendered the Prussians the great service of occupying more than 40,000 of the enemy, who otherwise would have crushed Blucher's right flank. For not only did the conflict at Quatre Bras detain the French troops which actually took part in it, but d'Erlon received orders from Ney to join him, which hindered d'Erlon from giving effectual aid to Napoleon. Indeed, the whole of d'Erlon's corps, in consequence of conflicting directions from Ney and the Emperor, marched and countermarched, during the 16th, between Quatre Bras and Ligny without firing a shot in either battle.

Blucher had, in fact, a superiority of more than 12,000 in number over the French army that attacked him at Ligny. The numerical difference was even greater at the beginning of the battle, as Lobau's corps did not come up from Charleroi till eight o'clock. After five hours and a half of desperate and long-doubtful struggle, Napoleon succeeded in breaking the centre of the Prussian line, at Ligny, and in forcing his obstinate antagonists off the field of battle. The issue was attributable to his skill and not to any want of spirit or resolution on the part of the Prussian troops; nor did they, though defeated, abate one jot in discipline, heart, or hope. As Blucher observed, it was a battle in which his army lost the day but not its honour.

The Prussians retreated during the night of the 16th, and the early part of the 17th, with perfect regularity and steadiness. The retreat was directed not towards Maestricht, where their principal depôts were established, but towards Wavre, so as to be able to maintain their communication with Wellington's army, and still follow out the original plan of the campaign. The heroism with which the Prussians endured and repaired their defeat at Ligny is more glorious than many victories.

VI

The messenger who was sent to inform Wellington of the retreat of the Prussian army was shot on the way and it was not until the morning of the 17th that the Allies, at Quatre Bras, knew the result of the battle of Ligny. The Duke was ready at daybreak to take the offensive against the enemy with vigour, his whole army being by that time fully assembled. But on learning that Blucher had been defeated, a different course of action was clearly necessary. It was obvious that Napoleon's main army would now be directed against Welling-ton, and a retreat was inevitable. On ascertaining that the Prussian army had retired upon Wavre, that there was no hot pursuit of them by the French, and that Bulow's corps had taken no part in the action at Ligny, the Duke resolved to march his army back towards Brussels, still intending to cover that city, and to halt at a point in a line with Wavre, and there restore his communication with Blucher.

An officer from Blucher's army reached the Duke about nine o'clock, from whom he learned the effective strength that Blucher still possessed, and how little discouraged his ally was by the yesterday's battle. Wellington sent word to the Prussian commander that he would halt in the position of Mont St. Jean, and accept a general battle with the French, if Blucher would pledge himself to come to his assistance with a single corps of 25,000 men. This was readily promised; and after allowing his men ample time for rest and refreshment, Well-ington retired over about half the space between Quatre Bras and Brussels. He was pursued, but little molested by the main French army, which about noon of the 17th moved laterally from Ligny, and joined Ney's forces, which had advanced through Quatre Bras when the British abandoned that position.

The Earl of Uxbridge, with the British cavalry, covered the retreat of the Duke's army with great skill and gallantry; and a heavy thunderstorm, with torrents of rain, impeded the opera-tions of the French pursuing squadrons. The Duke still ex-pected that the French would endeavour to turn his right, and march upon Brussels by the high road that leads through Mons and Hal. In order to counteract this anticipated manœuvre, he stationed a force of 18,000 men, under Prince Frederick of the Netherlands, at Hal, with orders to maintain

himself there if attacked as long as possible. The Duke halted
with the rest of his army at the position near Mont St. Jean,
which, from a village in its neighbourhood, has received the
ever-memorable name of the field of Waterloo.

Wellington was now about twelve miles distant, on a line
running from west to east, from Wavre, where the Prussian
army had now been completely reorganised and collected,
and where it had been strengthened by the junction of Bulow's
troops, which had taken no part in the battle of Ligny. Blucher
sent word from Wavre, to the Duke, that he was coming to
help the English at Mont St. Jean, in the morning, not with
one corps, but with his whole army. The fiery old man only
stipulated that the combined armies, if not attacked by
Napoleon on the 18th, should themselves attack him on the
19th. So far were Blucher and his army from being in the
state of annihilation described in the boastful bulletin by which
Napoleon informed the Parisians of his victory at Ligny.

Indeed, the French emperor seems himself to have been
misinformed as to the extent of loss which he had inflicted
on the Prussians. Had he known in what good order and
with what undiminished spirit they were retiring, he would
scarcely have delayed sending a large force to press them in
their retreat until noon on the 17th. Such, however, was the
case. It was about that time that he confided to Marshal
Grouchy the duty of pursuing the defeated Prussians, and
preventing them from joining Wellington. He placed for this
purpose 32,000 men and 96 guns under his orders.

Violent complaints and recriminations passed afterwards between the Emperor and the Marshal respecting the manner in
which Grouchy attempted to perform this duty, and the reasons
why he failed on the 18th to arrest the lateral movement of the
Prussians from Wavre to Waterloo. It is sufficient to remark
here, that the force which Napoleon gave to Grouchy (though
the utmost that the Emperor's limited means would allow) was
insufficient to make head against the entire Prussian army,
especially after Bulow's junction with Blucher. We shall presently have occasion to consider what opportunities were given
to Grouchy during the 18th, and what he might have effected
if he had been a man of original military genius.

But the failure of Grouchy was in truth mainly owing to
the indomitable heroism of Blucher himself; who, though he

had received severe personal injuries in the battle of **Ligny**, was as energetic and ready as ever in bringing his men into action again, and who had the resolution to expose a part of his army, under Thielman, to be overwhelmed by Grouchy at Wavre on the 18th, while he urged the march of the mass of his troops upon Waterloo.

"It is not at Wavre, but at Waterloo," said the old Field-Marshal, "that the campaign is to be decided" and he risked a detachment and won the campaign accordingly. Wellington and Blucher trusted each other as cordially and co-operated as zealously as formerly had been the case with Marlborough and Eugene. It was in full reliance on Blucher's promise to join him, that the Duke stood his ground and fought at Waterloo and those, who have ventured to impugn the Duke's capacity as a general, ought to have had common sense enough to perceive, that to charge the Duke with having won the battle of Waterloo by the help of the Prussians is really to say that he won it by the very means on which he relied, and without the expectation of which the battle would not have been fought.

Napoleon himself has found fault with Wellington for not having retreated further, so as to complete a junction of his army with Blucher's, before he risked a general engagement. But as we have seen, the Duke justly considered it important to protect Brussels. He had reason to expect that his army could singly resist the French at Waterloo until the Prussians came up, and that, on the Prussians joining, there would be a sufficient force united under himself and Blucher, for completely overwhelming the enemy. And while Napoleon thus censures his great adversary, he involuntarily bears the highest possible testimony to the military character of the English, and proves decisively of what paramount importance was the battle to which he challenged his fearless opponent.

Napoleon asks, "If the English army had been beaten at Waterloo, what would have been the use of those numerous bodies of troops, of Prussians, Austrians, Germans, and Spaniards, which were advancing by forced marches to the Rhine, the Alps, and the Pyrenees?"

VII

The strength of the army, under the Duke of Wellington at Waterloo, was 49,608 infantry, 12,402 cavalry, and 5645

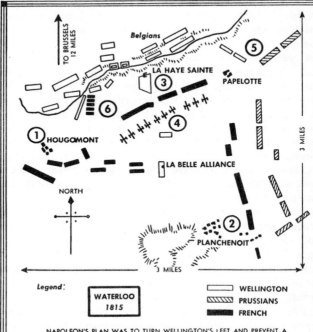

Legend:

WATERLOO 1815

	WELLINGTON
	PRUSSIANS
	FRENCH

NAPOLEON'S PLAN WAS TO TURN WELLINGTON'S LEFT AND PREVENT A UNION BETWEEN HIM AND THE PRUSSIAN ARMIES TO THE EAST. HE BEGAN THE BATTLE IN THE MORNING, BY ATTACKING THE BRITISH STRONG POINT AT

1 HOUGOMONT, WHICH WAS REPELLED ALTHOUGH PERSISTED IN FOR THE GREATER PART OF THE DAY. EARLY IN THE AFTERNOON NAPOLEON MET A THREAT TO HIS RIGHT BY A PRUSSIAN ADVANCE EAST OF

2 PLANCHENOIT BY THROWING IN CAVALRY DIVISIONS. ABOUT THE SAME TIME THE FRENCH BEGAN THEIR MAIN ATTACK UPON WELLINGTON AROUND

3 LA HAYE SAINTE, SUPPORTED BY INTENSE ARTILLERY FIRE FROM

4 THIS ATTACK FAILED, AS DID A LATER CHARGE UPON THE BRITISH CENTER BY NEY WITH 5000 CAVALRY. EARLY IN THE EVENING THE FRENCH REFORMED AND RENEWED THE ATTACK UPON WELLINGTON'S LEFT, WHICH WAS BALKED BY THE ADVANCE OF THE PRUSSIANS AT

5 NAPOLEON'S LAST EFFORT WAS MADE AT

6 BY TEN BATTALIONS OF HIS ELITE CORPS, THE GUARDS. THE BRITISH CHARGED, FLANKED AND ROUTED THE GUARDS. WELLINGTON THEN ADVANCED A COUNTER-OFFENSIVE AGAINST THE WHOLE FRENCH FRONT, WHICH GAVE HIM THE VICTORY.

artillerymen with 156 guns. But of this total of 67,655 men, scarcely 24,000 were British, a circumstance of very serious importance, if Napoleon's own estimate of the relative value of troops of different nations is to be taken. In the Emperor's own words, speaking of this campaign, "A French soldier would not be equal to more than one English soldier, but he would not be afraid to meet two Dutchmen, Prussians, or soldiers of the Confederation." There were about 6000 men, of the old German Legion, with the Duke; these were veteran troops, and of excellent quality. Of the rest of the army the Hanoverians and Brunswickers proved themselves deserving of confidence and praise. But the Nassauers, Dutch, and Belgians were almost worthless; and not a few of them were justly suspected of a strong wish to fight, if they fought at all, under the French eagles rather than against them.

Napoleon's army at Waterloo consisted of 48,950 infantry, 15,765 cavalry, 7232 artillerymen, being a total of 71,947 men, and 246 guns. They were the flower of the national forces of France; and of all the numerous gallant armies which that martial land has poured forth, never was there one braver, or better disciplined, or better led, than the host that took up its position at Waterloo on the morning of the 18th of June, 1815.

Perhaps those who have not seen the field of battle at Waterloo, or the admirable model of the ground, and of the conflicting armies, which was executed by Captain Siborne, may gain a generally accurate idea of the localities, by picturing to themselves a valley between two and three miles long, of various breadths at different points, but generally not exceeding half a mile. On each side of the valley, there is a winding chain of low hills, running somewhat parallel with each other. The declivity from each of these ranges of hills to the intervening valley is gentle, but not uniform, the undulations of the ground being frequent and considerable.

The English army was posted on the northern, and the French army occupied the southern ridge. The artillery of each side thundered at the other from their respective heights throughout the day, and the charges of horse and foot were made across the valley that has been described. The village of Mont St. Jean is situate a little behind the centre of the northern chain of hills, and the village of La Belle Alliance is close behind the centre of the southern ridge. The high road from Charleroi to Brussels (a broad paved causeway) runs through both these villages, and bisects therefore both the English and the French positions. The line of this road was the line of Napoleon's intended advance on Brussels.

There are some other local particulars connected with the situation of each army which it is necessary to bear in mind. The strength of the British position did not consist merely in the occupation of a ridge of high ground. A village and ravine, called Merk Braine, on the Duke of Wellington's extreme right, secured his flank from being turned on that side and on his extreme left two little hamlets called La Haye and Papelotte gave a similar, though a slighter protection. Behind the whole British position is the extensive forest of Soignies. As no attempt was made by the French to turn either of the English flanks, and the battle was a day of straightforward fighting, it is chiefly important to ascertain what posts there were in front of the British line of hills, of which advantage could be taken either to repel or facilitate an attack; and it will be seen that there were two, and that each was of very great importance in the action.

In front of the British right, that is to say, on the northern slope of the valley towards its western end, there stood an old-fashioned Flemish farmhouse called Goumont, or Hougoumont, with out-buildings and a garden, and with a copse of beech trees of about two acres in extent round it. This was strongly garrisoned by the Allied troops; and, while it was in their possession, it was difficult for the enemy to press on and force the British right wing. On the other hand, if the enemy could take it, it would be difficult for that wing to keep its ground on the heights, with a strong post held adversely in its immediate front, being one that would give much shelter to the enemy's marksmen, and great facilities for the sudden concentration of attacking columns. Almost immediately in front of the British centre, and not so far down the slope as Hougoumont, there was another farmhouse, of a smaller size called La Haye Sainte which was also held by the British troops and the occupation of which was found to be of very serious consequence.

With respect to the French position, the principal feature to be noticed is the village of Planchenoit, which lay a little in the rear of their right (*i.e.* on the eastern side), and which proved to be of great importance in aiding them to check the advance of the Prussians.

Napoleon, in his memoirs, and other French writers, have vehemently blamed the Duke for having given battle in such a position as that of Waterloo. They particularly object that the Duke fought without having the means of a retreat, if the attacks of his enemy had proved successful; and that the English army, if once broken, must have lost all its guns and *matériel* in its flight through the forest of Soignies, that lay in its rear. In answer to these censures, instead of merely referring to the event of the battle as proof of the correctness of the Duke's judgment, it is to be observed that many military critics of high authority, have considered the position of Waterloo to have been admirably adapted for the Duke's purpose of protecting Brussels by a battle; and that certainly the Duke's opinion in favour of it was not lightly or hastily formed.

It is a remarkable fact (mentioned in the speech of Lord Bathurst when moving the vote of thanks to the Duke in the House of Lords) that when the Duke of Wellington was passing through Belgium in the preceding summer of 1814, he particularly noticed the strength of the position of Waterloo, and made a minute of it at the time, stating to those who were with him, that if it should be his fate to fight a battle in that quarter for the protection of Brussels, he should endeavour to do so in that position. And with respect to the forest of Soignies, which the French (and some few English) critics have thought calculated to prove so fatal to a retreating force, the Duke on the contrary believed it to be a post that might have proved of infinite value to his army in the event of his having been obliged to give way.

The forest of Soignies had no thicket or masses of close-growing trees. It consisted of tall beeches, and was everywhere passable for men and horses. The artillery could have been withdrawn by the broad road which traverses it toward Brussels; and in the meanwhile a few regiments of resolute infantry could have held the forest and kept the pursuers in check. One of the best writers on the Waterloo campaign, Captain Pringle, well observes that "every person, the least experienced in war, knows the extreme difficulty of forcing infantry from a wood which cannot be turned." The defence of the Bois de Bossu near Quatre Bras on the 16th of June had given a good proof of this; and the Duke of Wellington, when speaking in after years of the possible events that might have followed if he had been beaten back from the open field of Waterloo, pointed to the wood of Soignies as his secure rallying-place, saying, "They never could have beaten us so that we could not have held the wood against them." He was always confident that he could have made good that post until joined by the Prussians, upon whose co-operation he throughout depended.

VIII

As has been already mentioned, the Prussians, on the morning of the 18th, were at Wavre, which is about twelve miles to the east of the field of battle of Waterloo. The junction of Bulow's division had more than made up for the loss sustained at Ligny; and leaving Thielman with about seventeen thousand men to hold his ground, as he best could, against the attack which Grouchy was about to make on Wavre, Bulow and Blucher moved with the rest of the Prussians through St. Lambert upon Waterloo. It was calculated that they would be there by three o'clock, but the extremely difficult nature of the ground which they had to traverse, rendered worse by the torrents of rain that had just fallen, delayed them longer on their twelve miles' march.

An army less animated by bitter hate against the enemy than was the Prussian, and under a less energetic chief than Blucher, would have failed altogether in effecting a passage through the swamps, into which the incessant rain had transformed the greater part of the ground through which it was necessary to move not only with columns of foot, but with cavalry and artillery. At one point of the march, on entering the defile of St. Lambert, the spirits of the Prussians almost gave way. Exhausted in the attempts to extricate and drag forward the heavy guns, the men began to murmur. Blucher came to the spot, and heard cries from the ranks of "We cannot get on." "But you *must* get on," was the old Field-Marshal's answer. "I have pledged my word to Wellington, and you surely will not make me break it. Only exert yourselves for a few hours longer, and we are sure of victory." This appeal from old "Marshal Forward," as the Prussian soldiers loved to call

Blucher, had its wonted effect. The Prussians again moved forward, slowly, indeed, and with pain and toil, but still they moved forward.

The French and British armies lay in the open field during the wet and stormy night of the 17th; and when the dawn of the memorable 18th of June broke the rain was still descending heavily upon Waterloo. The rival nations rose from their dreary bivouacs and began to form, each on the high ground which it occupied. Towards nine the weather grew clearer, and each army was able to watch the position and arrangements of the other on the opposite side of the valley.

The Duke of Wellington drew up his army in two lines; the principal one being stationed near the crest of the ridge of hills already described, and the other being arranged along the slope in the rear of his position. Commencing from the eastward, on the extreme left of the first or main line, were Vivian's and Vandeleur's brigades of light cavalry, and the fifth Hanoverian brigade of infantry, under Von Vincke. Then came Best's fourth Hanoverian brigade. Detachments from these bodies of troops occupied the little villages of Papelotte and La Haye Sainte, down the hollow in advance of the left of the Duke's position.

To the right of Best's Hanoverians, Bylandt's brigade of Dutch and Belgian infantry was drawn up on the outer slope of the heights. Behind them were the ninth brigade of British infantry under Pack; and to the right of these last, but more in advance, stood the eighth brigade of English infantry under Kempt. These were close to the Charleroi road, and to the centre of the entire position. These two English brigades, with the fifth Hanoverian, made up the fifth division, commanded by Sir Thomas Picton.

Immediately to their right, and westward of the Charleroi road, stood the third division, commanded by General Alten, and consisting of Ompteda's brigade of the King's German legion, and Kielmansegge's Hanoverian brigade. The important post of La Haye Sainte, which it will be remembered lay in front of the Duke's centre, close to the Charleroi road, was garrisoned with troops from this division.

Westward, and on the right of Kielmansegge's Hanoverians, stood the fifth British brigade under Halkett; and behind, Kruse's Nassau brigade was posted. On the right of Halkett's men stood the English Guards. They were in two brigades, one commanded by Maitland and the other by Byng. The entire division was under General Cooke.

The buildings and gardens of Hougoumont, which lay immediately under the height, on which stood the British Guards, were principally manned by detachments from Byng's brigade, aided by some brave Hanoverian riflemen, and accompanied by a battalion of a Nassau regiment. On a plateau in the rear of Cooke's division of Guards, and inclining westward towards the village of Merk Braine, were Clinton's second infantry division, composed of Adams's third brigade of light infantry, DuPlat's first brigade of the King's German legion, and the third Hanoverian brigade under Colonel Halkett.

The Duke formed his second line of cavalry. This only extended behind the right and centre of his first line. The largest mass was drawn up behind the brigades of infantry in the centre, on either side of the Charleroi road. The brigade of household cavalry under Lord Somerset was on the immediate right of the road, and on the left of it was Ponsonby's brigade. Behind these were Trip's and Ghingy's brigades of Dutch and Belgian horse. The 3rd Hussars of the King's German Legion were to the right of Somerset's brigade.

To the right of these, and behind Maitland's infantry, stood the 3rd Brigade under Dornberg, consisting of the 23rd English Light Dragoons, and the regiments of Light Dragoons of the King's German Legion. The last cavalry on the right was Grant's brigade, stationed in the rear of the Foot-Guards. The corps of Brunswickers, both horse and foot, and the 10th British brigade of foot, were in reserve behind the centre and right of the entire position. The artillery was distributed at convenient intervals along the front of the whole line. Besides the generals who have been mentioned, Lord Hill, Lord Uxbridge (who had the general command of the cavalry), the Prince of Orange, and General Chassé, were present, and acting under the Duke.

Prince Frederick's force remained at Hal and took no part in the battle of the 18th. The reason for this arrangement (which has been much cavilled at), may be best given in the words of Baron Müffling: "The Duke had retired from Quatre Bras in three columns, by three highways and on the evening of the 17th, Prince Frederick of Orange was at Hal, Lord Hill at Braine la Leud, and the Prince of Orange with the reserve, at Mont St. Jean. This distribution was necessary, as Napoleon could dispose of these three roads for his advance on Brussels.

Napoleon on the 17th had pressed on by Genappe as far as Rossomme. On the other two roads no enemy had yet shown himself. On the 18th the offensive was taken by Napoleon on its greatest scale, but still the Nivelles road was not overstepped by his left wing. These circumstances made it possible to draw Prince Frederick to the army, which would certainly have been done if entirely new circumstances had not arisen. The Duke had, twenty-four hours before, pledged himself to accept a battle at Mont St. Jean if Blücher would assist him there with one corps, of 25,000 men. This being promised, the Duke was taking his measures for defence, when he learned that, in addition to the one corps promised, Blücher was actually already on the march with his whole force, to break in by Planchenoit on Napoleon's flank and rear.

If three corps of the Prussian army should penetrate by the unguarded plateau of Rossomme, which was not improbable, Napoleon would be thrust from his line of retreat by Genappe, and might possibly lose even that by Nivelles. In this case Prince Frederick, with his 18,000 men (who might be accounted superfluous at Mont St. Jean), might have rendered the most essential service. It is also worthy of observation that Napoleon actually detached a force of 2000 cavalry to threaten Hal, though they returned to the main French army during the night of the 17th.

On the opposite heights the French army was drawn up in two general lines, with the entire force of the Imperial Guards, cavalry as well as infantry, in rear of the centre, as a reserve.

The first line of the French army was formed of the two corps commanded by Count d'Erlon and Count Reille. D'Erlon's corps was on the right, that is, eastward of the Charleroi road, and consisted of four divisions of infantry under Generals Durette, Marcognet, Alix, and Donzelot, and of one division of light cavalry under General Jaquinot. Count Reille's corps formed the left or western wing, and was formed of Bachelu's, Foy's, and Jerome Bonaparte's divisions of infantry, and of Pire's division of cavalry.

The right wing of the second general French line was

formed by Milhaud's corps, consisting of two divisions of heavy cavalry. The left wing of this line was formed by Kellerman's cavalry corps, also in two divisions. Thus each of the corps of infantry that composed the first line had a corps of cavalry behind it, but the second line consisted also of Lobau's corps of infantry, and Domont and Subervie's divisions of light cavalry, these three bodies of troops being drawn up on either side of La Belle Alliance, and forming the centre of the second line.

The third, or reserve line, had its centre composed of the infantry of the Imperial Guard. Two regiments of grenadiers and two of infantry formed the foot of the Old Guard under General Friant. The Middle Guard under Count Morand, was similarly composed while two regiments of infantry, and two of sharpshooters, under Duhesme, constituted the Young Guard. The infantry and lancers of the Guard were on the right of the infantry, under Lefebvre Desnouettes; and the grenadiers and dragoons of the Guards, under Guyot, were on the left.

All the French corps comprised, besides their cavalry and infantry regiments, strong batteries of horse artillery; and Napoleon's numerical superiority in guns was of deep importance throughout the action.

Besides the leading generals who have been mentioned as commanding particular corps, Ney and Soult were present, and acted as the Emperor's lieutenants in the battle.

English military critics have highly eulogised the admirable arrangement which Napoleon made of his forces of each arm so as to give him the most ample means of sustaining, by an immediate and sufficient support, any attacks from whatever point he might direct it; and of drawing promptly together a strong force, to resist any attack that might be made on himself in any part of the field. When his troops were all arrayed, he rode along the lines, receiving everywhere the most enthusiastic cheers from his men, of whose entire devotion to him his assurance was now doubly sure. On the northern side of the valley the Duke's army was also drawn up, and ready to meet the menaced attack.

IX

Wellington on the preceding night had caused every brigade and corps to take up its station on or near the part of the ground which it was intended to hold in the coming battle. He had slept a few hours at his headquarters in the village of Waterloo; and rising on the 18th, while it was yet deep night, he wrote several letters to the Governor of Antwerp, to the English Minister at Brussels, and other official personages, in which he expressed his confidence that all would go well, but "as it was necessary to provide against serious losses should any accident occur," he gave a series of judicious orders for what should be done in the rear of the army, in the event of the battle going against the Allies.

He also, before he left the village of Waterloo, saw to the distribution of the reserves of ammunition which had been parked there, so that supplies should be readily forwarded to every part of the line of battle, where they might be required. The Duke, also, personally inspected the arrangements that had been made for receiving the wounded, and providing temporary hospitals in the houses in the rear of the army.

Then, mounting a favourite charger, a small thorough-bred chestnut horse, named "Copenhagen," Wellington rode forward to the range of hills where his men were posted. Accompanied by his staff and by the Prussian general Müffling, he rode along his lines, carefully inspecting all the details of his position. Hougoumont was the object of his special attention. He rode down to the south-eastern extremity of its enclosures, and after having examined the nearest French troops, he made some changes in the disposition of his own men, who were to defend that important post.

Having given his final orders about Hougoumont, the Duke galloped back to the high ground in the right centre of his position and halting there, sat watching the enemy on the opposite heights, and conversing with his staff with that cheerful serenity which was ever his characteristic in the hour of battle.

Not only to those who were thus present as spectators and actors in the dread drama, but to all Europe, the decisive contest then impending between the rival French and English nations, each under its chosen chief, was the object of exciting interest and deepest solicitude. "Never, indeed, had two such generals as the Duke of Wellington and the Emperor Napoleon encountered since the day when Scipio and Hannibal met at Zama."

The two great champions who now confronted each other were equals in years, and each had entered the military profession at the same early age. The more conspicious stage, on which the French general's youthful genius was displayed, his heritage of the whole military power of the French republic, the position on which for years he was elevated as sovereign head of an empire surpassing that of Charlemagne, and the dazzling results of his victories, which made and unmade kings, had given him a formidable pre-eminence in the eyes of mankind. Military men spoke with justly rapturous admiration of the brilliancy of his first Italian campaigns, when he broke through the pedantry of traditional tactics, and with a small but promptly-wielded force, shattered army after army of the Austrians, conquered provinces and capitals, dictated treaties, and annihilated or created states.

The iniquity of his Egyptian expedition was too often forgotten in contemplating the skill and boldness with which he destroyed the Mameluke cavalry at the Pyramids and the Turkish infantry at Aboukir. None could forget the marvellous passage of the Alps in 1800 or the victory of Marengo, which wrested Italy back from Austria, and destroyed the fruit of twenty victories which the enemies of France had gained over her in the absence of her favourite chief. Even higher seemed the glories of his German campaigns, the triumphs of Ulm, of Austerlitz, of Jena, of Wagram. Napoleon's disasters in Russia, in 1812, were imputed by his admirers to the elements; his reverses in Germany, in 1813, were attributed by them to treachery: and even those two calamitous years had been signalised by his victories at Borodino, at Lutzen, at Bautzen, at Dresden, and at Hanau.

His last campaign, in the early months of 1814, was rightly cited as the most splendid exhibition of his military genius, when with a far inferior army he long checked and frequently defeated the vast hosts that were poured upon France. His followers fondly hoped that the campaign of 1815 would open with another "week of miracles," like that which had seen his victories at Montmirail and Montereau. The laurel of Ligny was even now fresh upon his brows. Blucher had not stood before him; and who was the adversary that now should bar the Emperor's way?

That adversary had already overthrown the Emperor's best

generals, and the Emperor's best armies; and, like Napoleon himself, had achieved a reputation in more than European wars. Wellington was illustrious as the destroyer of the Mahratta power, as the liberator of Portugal and Spain, and the successful invader of southern France. In early youth he had held high command in India and had displayed eminent skill in planning and combining movements, and un-rivalled celerity and boldness in execution. On his return to Europe several years passed away before any fitting opportunity was accorded for the exercise of his genius.

In this important respect, Wellington, as a subject, and Napoleon, as a sovereign, were far differently situated. At length his appointment to the command in the Spanish Penin-sula gave him the means of showing Europe that England had a general who could revive the glories of Crecy, of Poictiers, of Agincourt, of Blenheim, and of Ramillies. At the head of forces always numerically far inferior to the armies with which Napoleon overran the Peninsula; thwarted by jealous and incompetent allies; ill-supported by friends, and assailed by factious enemies at home, Wellington maintained the war for seven years unstained by any serious reverse, and marked by victory in thirteen pitched battles, at Vimiera, the Douro, Talavera, Busaco, Fuentes d'Onore, Salamanca, Vittoria, the Pyrenees, the Bidassoa, the Nive, the Nivelle, Orthes, and Toulouse.

Junot, Victor, Massena, Ney, Marmont, and Jourdain, mar-shals whose names were the terrors of continental Europe-, had been baffled by his skill, and smitten down by his energy, while he liberated the kingdoms of the Peninsula from them and their imperial master. In vain did Napoleon at last despatch Soult, the ablest of his lieutenants, to turn the tide of Wellington's success, and defend France against the English invader. Wellington met Soult's manœuvres with superior skill and his boldness with superior vigour. When Napoleon's first abdication, in 1814, suspended hostilities, Wellington was master of the fairest districts of southern France; and had under him a veteran army, with which (to use his own ex-pressive phrase) "he felt he could have gone anywhere and done anything." The fortune of war had hitherto kept separate the orbits in which Napoleon and he had moved. Now, on the ever memorable 18th of June, 1815, they met at last.

It is, indeed, remarkable that Napoleon during his numerous campaigns in Spain as well as other countries not only never encountered the Duke of Wellington before the day of Waterloo, but that he was never until then personally engaged with British troops, except at the siege of Toulon, in 1793, which was the very first incident of his military career. Many, however, of the French generals who were with him in 1815 knew well by sharp experience what English soldiers were and what the leader was who now headed them. Ney, Foy, and other officers who had served in the Peninsula, warned Napoleon that he would find the English infantry "very devils in fight."

The Emperor, however, persisted in employing the old system of attack with which the French generals often succeeded against continental troops, but which had always failed against the English in the Peninsula. He adhered to his usual tactics of employing the order of the column, a mode of attack probably favoured by him (as Sir Walter Scott remarks) on account of his faith in the extreme valour of the French officers by whom the column was headed. It is a threatening formation, well calculated to shake the firmness of ordinary foes; but which, when steadily met, as the English met it, by heavy volleys of musketry from an extended line, followed up by a resolute bayonet charge, has always resulted in disaster to the assailants.

X

It was approaching noon before the action commenced. Napoleon, in his memoirs, gives as the reason of this delay the miry state of the ground through the heavy rain of the preceding night and day, which rendered it impossible for cavalry or artillery to manœuvre on it till a few hours of dry weather had given it its natural consistency. It has been supposed, also, that he trusted to the effect which the sight of the imposing array of his own forces was likely to produce on the part of the Allied army. The Belgian regiments had been tampered with and Napoleon had well-founded hopes of seeing them quit the Duke of Wellington in a body and range themselves under his own eagles. The Duke, however, who knew and did not trust them, had guarded against the risk of this by breaking up the corps of Belgians and distributing them in separate regiments among troops on whom he could rely.

At last, at about half-past eleven o'clock, Napoleon began the battle by directing a powerful force from his left wing under his brother, Prince Jerome, to attack Hougoumont. Column after column of the French now descended from the west of the southern heights and assailed that post with fiery valour, which was countered with the most determined bravery. The French won the copse round the house, but a party of the British Guards held the house itself throughout the day. The whole of Byng's brigade was required to man this hotly-contested post. Amid shell and shot and the blazing fragments of part of the buildings this obstinate contest was continued. But still the English were firm in Hougoumont; though the French occasionally moved forward in such numbers as enabled them to surround and mask it with part of their troops from their left wing, while others pressed onward up the slope and assailed the British right.

The cannonade, which commenced at first between the British right and the French left, in consequence of the attack on Hougoumont, soon became general along both lines; and, about one o'clock Napoleon directed a grand attack to be made under Marshal Ney upon the centre and left wing of the allied army. For this purpose four columns of infantry, amounting to about eighteen thousand men, were collected, supported by a strong division of cavalry under the celebrated Kellerman; and seventy-four guns were brought forward ready to be posted on the ridge of a little undulation of the ground in the interval between the two principal chains of heights, so as to bring their fire to bear on the Duke's line at a range of about seven hundred yards.

By the combined assault of these formidable forces, led on by Ney, "the bravest of the brave," Napoleon hoped to force the left centre of the British position, to take La Haye Sainte and then pressing forward to occupy also the farm of Mont St. Jean. He then could cut the mass of Wellington's troops off from their line of retreat upon Brussels, and from their own left, and also completely sever them from any Prussian troops that might be approaching.

The columns destined for this great and decisive operation descended majestically from the French line of hills, and gained the ridge of the intervening eminence, on which the batteries that supported them were now ranged. As the columns descended again from this eminence the seventy-four guns opened over their heads with terrible effect upon the troops of the Allies that were stationed on the heights to the left of the Charleroi road. One of the French columns kept to the east and attacked the extreme left of the Allies; the other three continued to move rapidly forwards upon the left centre of the allied position. The front line of the Allies here was composed of Bylandt's brigade of Dutch and Belgians. As the French columns move up the southward slope of the height on which the Dutch and Belgians stood and the skirmishers in advance began to open their fire, Bylandt's entire brigade turned and fled in disgraceful and disorderly panic; but there were men more worthy of the name behind.

In this part of the line of the Allies were posted Pack and Kempt's brigades of English infantry, which had suffered severely at Quatre Bras. But Picton was here as general of division, and not even Ney himself surpassed in resolute bravery that stern and fiery spirit. Picton brought his two brigades forward, side by side, in a thin two-deep line. Thus joined together they were not three thousand strong. With these Picton had to make head against the three victorious French columns, upwards of four times that strength and who, encouraged by the easy rout of the Dutch and Belgians, now came confidently over the ridge of the hill.

The British infantry stood firm and as the French halted and began to deploy into line, Picton seized the critical moment. He shouted in his stentorian voice to Kempt's brigade: "A volley, and then charge!" At a distance of less than thirty yards that volley was poured upon the devoted first sections of the nearest column; and then, with a fierce hurrah the British dashed in with the bayonet. Picton was shot dead as he rushed forward, but his men pushed on with the cold steel. The French reeled back in confusion. Pack's infantry had checked the other two columns, and down came a whirlwind of British horse on the whole mass, sending them staggering from the crest of the hill and cutting them down by whole battalions. Ponsonby's brigade of heavy cavalry (the Union Brigade, as it was called, from its being made up of the British Royals, the Scots Greys, and the Irish Inniskillings), did this good service.

On went the horsemen amid the wrecks of the French col-

umns, capturing two eagles and two thousand prisoners; onwards
still they galloped, and sabred the artillerymen of Ney's seventy-
four advanced guns; then severing the traces, and cutting the
throats of the artillery horses, they rendered these guns totally
useless to the French throughout the remainder of the day.
While thus far advanced beyond the British position and disordered by success, they were charged by a large body of French
lancers and driven back with severe loss, till Vandeleur's light
horse came to their aid and beat off the French lancers in their
turn.

Equally unsuccessful with the advance of the French infantry
in this grand attack had been the efforts of the French cavalry
who moved forward in support of it along the east of the
Charleroi road. Somerset's cavalry of the English Household
Brigade had been launched, on the right of Picton's division,
against the French horse, at the same time that the English
Union Brigade of heavy horse charged the French infantry
columns on the left.

Somerset's brigade was formed of the Life Guards, the Blues,
and the Dragoon Guards. The hostile cavalry, which Kellerman led forward, consisted chiefly of cuirassiers. This steel-clad
mass of French horsemen rode down some companies of German
infantry, near La Haye Sainte, and flushed with success, they
bounded onward to the ridge of the British position. The
English Household Brigade, led on by the Earl of Uxbridge
in person spurred forward to the encounter, and in an instant
the two adverse lines of strong swordsmen, on their strong
steeds, dashed furiously together.

A desperate and sanguinary hand-to-hand fight ensued, in
which the physical superiority of the Anglo-Saxons, guided by
equal skill and animated with equal valour, was made decisively
manifest. Back went the chosen cavalry of France; and after
them, in hot pursuit, spurred the English Guards. They went
forward as far and as fiercely as their comrades of the Union
Brigade; and, like them, the Household cavalry suffered severely
before they regained the British position after their magnificent
charge and adventurous pursuit.

Napoleon's grand effort to break the English left centre, had
thus completely failed; and his right wing was seriously
weakened by the heavy loss which it had sustained. Hougoumont was still being assailed, and was still successfully re-

sisting. Troops were now beginning to appear at the edge of the horizon on Napoleon's right, which he too well knew to be Prussian, though he endeavoured to persuade his followers that they were Grouchy's men coming to their aid.

Grouchy was in fact now engaged at Wavre with his whole force against Thielman's single Prussian corps, while the other three corps of the Prussian army were moving without opposition, save from the difficulties of the ground, upon Waterloo. Grouchy believed, on the 17th, and caused Napoleon to believe, that the Prussian army was retreating by lines of march remote from Waterloo upon Namur and Maestricht. Napoleon learned early on the 18th that there were Prussians in Wavre, and felt jealous about the security of his own right. He accordingly, before he attacked the English, sent Grouchy orders to engage the Prussians at Wavre without delay, and to approach the main French army, so as to unite his communication with the Emperor's. Grouchy entirely neglected this last part of his instructions and in attacking the Prussians whom he found at Wavre he spread his force more and more towards his right, that is to say, in the direction most remote from Napoleon. He thus knew nothing of Blucher's and Bulow's flank march upon Waterloo till six in the evening of the 18th, when he received a note which Soult by Napoleon's orders had sent off from the field of battle at Waterloo at one o'clock, to inform Grouchy that Bulow was coming over the heights of St. Lambert, on the Emperor's right flank, and directing Grouchy to approach and join the main army instantly and crush Bulow in the act.

It was then too late for Grouchy to obey, but it is remarkable that as early as noon on the 18th, and while Grouchy had not proceeded as far as Wavre, he and his suite heard the sound of heavy cannonading in the direction of Planchenoit and Mont St. Jean. General Gérard, who was with Grouchy, implored him to march towards the cannonade and join his operations with those of Napoleon, who was evidently engaged with the English. Grouchy refused to do so, or even to detach part of his force in that direction. He said that his instructions were to fight the Prussians at Wavre. He marched upon Wavre and fought for the rest of the day with Thielman accordingly, while Blucher and Bulow were attacking the Emperor.

It has been asserted that Grouchy twice had in his hands the power of changing the destinies of Europe, and twice wanted nerve to act: first when he flinched from landing the French army at Bantry Bay in 1796 (he was second in command to Hoche, whose ship was blown back by a storm), and secondly, when he failed to lead his whole force from Wavre to the scene of decisive conflict at Waterloo. But such were the arrangements of the Prussian general, that even if Grouchy had marched upon Waterloo he would have been held in check by the nearest Prussian corps, or certainly by the two nearest ones, while the rest proceeded to join Wellington. This, however, would have diminished the number of Prussians who appeared at Waterloo, and (what is still more important) would have kept them back to a later hour.

The Prussian writer, General Clausewitz, has been cited as "expressing a positive opinion, in which every military critic but a Frenchman must concur, that, even had the whole of Grouchy's force been at Napoleon's disposal, the Duke had nothing to fear pending Blucher's arrival.

"The Duke is often talked of as having exhausted his reserves in the action. This is another gross error, which Clausewitz has thoroughly disposed of. He enumerates the tenth British brigade, the division of Chassé and the cavalry of Collaert, as having been little or not at all engaged; and he might have also added two brigades of light cavalry." The fact, also, that Wellington did not at any part of the day order up Prince Frederick's corps from Hal is a conclusive proof that the Duke was not so distressed as some writers have represented. Hal is not ten miles from the field of Waterloo.

Napoleon had witnessed with bitter disappointment the rout of his troops,—foot, horse, and artillery,—which attacked the left centre of the English, and the obstinate resistance which the garrison of Hougoumont opposed to all the exertions of his left wing. He now caused the batteries along the line of high ground held by him to be strengthened and for some time an unremitting and most destructive cannonade raged across the valley, to the partial cessation of other conflict. But the superior fire of the French artillery, though it weakened, could not break the British line and more close and summary measures were requisite.

XI

It was now about half-past three o'clock and though Wellington's army had suffered severely by the unremitting cannonade and in the late desperate encounter, no part of the British position had been forced. Napoleon determined therefore to try what effect he could produce on the British centre and right by charges of his splendid cavalry, brought on in such force that the Duke's cavalry could not check them.

Fresh troops were at the same time sent to assail La Haye Sainte and Hougoumont, the possession of these posts being the Emperor's unceasing object. Squadron after squadron of the French cuirassiers accordingly ascended the slopes on the Duke's right, and rode forward with dauntless courage against the batteries of the British artillery in that part of the field. The artillerymen were driven from their guns, and the cuirassiers cheered loudly at their supposed triumph. But the Duke had formed his infantry in squares, and the cuirassiers charged in vain against the impenetrable hedges of bayonets, while the fire from the inner ranks of the squares told with terrible effect on their squadrons. Time after time they rode forward with invariably the same result: and as they receded from each attack the British artillerymen rushed forward from the centres of the squares, where they had taken refuge, and plied their guns on the retiring horsemen.

> On came the whirlwind—like the last
> But fiercest sweep of tempest-blast—
> On came the whirlwind—steel-gleams broke
> Like lightning through the rolling smoke;
>   The war was waked anew,
> Three hundred cannon-mouths roar'd loud,
> And from their throats, with flash and cloud,
>   Their showers of iron threw.
> Beneath their fire, in full career,
> Rush'd on the ponderous cuirassier,
> The lancer couch'd his ruthless spear,
> And hurrying as to havoc near,
>   The cohorts' eagles flew.
> In one dark torrent, broad and strong,
> The advancing onset roll'd along,
> Forth harbinger'd by fierce acclaim,
> That, from the shroud of smoke and flame,
> Peal'd wildly the imperial name.

But on the British heart were lost
The terrors of the charging host;
For not an eye the storm that view'd
Changed its proud glance of fortitude,
Nor was one forward footstep staid,
As dropp'd the dying and the dead.
Fast as their ranks the thunders tear,
Fast they renew'd each serried square;
And on the wounded and the slain
Closed their diminish'd files again,

Till from their line scarce spear's lengths three,
Emerging from the smoke they see
Helmet, and plume, and panoply,—
    Then waked their fire at once!
Each musketeer's revolving knell,
As fast, as regularly fell,
As when they practise to display
Their discipline on festal day.
    Then down went helm and lance,
Down were the eagle banners sent,
Down reeling steeds and riders went,
Corselets were pierced, and pennons rent;
    And, to augment the fray,
Wheel'd full against their staggering flanks
The English horsemen's foaming ranks
    Forced their resistless way.
Then to the musket-knell succeeds
The clash of swords—the neigh of steeds—
As plies the smith his clanging trade,
Against the cuirass rang the blade;
And while amid their close array
The well-served cannon rent their way,
And while amid their scatter'd band
Raged the fierce rider's bloody brand,
Recoil'd in common rout and fear,
Lancer and guard and cuirassier,
Horsemen and foot,—a mingled host,
Their leaders fall'n, their standards lost.—SCOTT.

Nearly the whole of Napoleon's magnificent body of heavy cavalry was destroyed in these fruitless attempts upon the British right. But in another part of the field fortune favoured him for a time. Two French columns of infantry from Donzelot's division took La Haye Sainte between six and seven o'clock, and the means were now given for organising another formidable attack on the centre of the Allies.

There was no time to be lost—Blucher and Bulow were beginning to press hard upon the French right. As early as five o'clock, Napoleon had been obliged to detach Lobau's infantry and Domont's horse to check these new enemies. They succeeded in doing so for a time; but as larger numbers of the Prussians came on the field they turned Lobau's right flank and sent a strong force to seize the village of Planchenoit which, it will be remembered, lay in the rear of the French right.

The design of the Allies was not merely to prevent Napoleon from advancing upon Brussels, but to cut off his line of retreat and utterly destroy his army. The defence of Planchenoit therefore became absolutely essential for the safety of the French, and Napoleon was obliged to send his Young Guard to occupy that village, which was accordingly held by them with great gallantry against the reiterated assaults of the Prussian left, under Bulow. Three times did the Prussians fight their way into Planchenoit and as often did the French drive them out; the contest was maintained with the fiercest desperation on both sides, such being the animosity between the two nations that quarter was seldom given or even asked.

Other Prussian forces were now appearing on the field nearer to the English left whom also Napoleon kept in check by troops detached for that purpose. Thus a large part of the French army was now thrown back on a line at right angles with the line of that portion which still confronted and assailed the English position. But this portion was now numerically inferior to the force under the Duke of Wellington, which Napoleon had been assailing throughout the day, without gaining any other advantage than the capture of La Haye Sainte. It is true that, owing to the gross misconduct of the greater part of the Dutch and Belgian troops, the Duke was obliged to rely exclusively on his English and German soldiers and the ranks of these had been fearfully thinned; but the survivors stood their ground heroically and opposed a resolute front to every forward movement of their enemies.

On no point of the British line was the pressure more severe than on Halkett's brigade in the right centre, which was composed of battalions of the 30th, the 33rd, the 69th, and the 73rd British regiments. We fortunately can quote from the journal of a brave officer of the 30th a narrative of which took place in this part of the field. The late Major Macready served at Waterloo in the light company of the 30th. The extent of the peril and the carnage which Halkett's brigade had to encounter may be judged of by the fact that this light company marched into the field three officers and fifty-one men and emerged with one officer and ten men.

Major Macready's blunt soldierly account of what he actually saw and felt, gives a far better idea of the terrific scene, than can be gained from the polished generalisations which the conventional style of history requires, or even from the glowing stanzas of the poet. During the earlier part of the day Macready and his light company were thrown forward as skirmishers in front of the brigade; but when the French cavalry commenced their attacks on the British right centre, he and his comrades were ordered back. The brave soldier thus himself describes what passed:

"Before the commencement of this attack our company and the Grenadiers of the 73rd were skirmishing briskly in the low ground, covering our guns and annoying those of the enemy. The line of tirailleurs opposed to us was not stronger than our own, but on a sudden they were reinforced by numerous bodies, and several guns began playing on us with canister. Our poor fellows dropped very fast, and Colonel Vigoureux, Rumley, and Pratt, were carried off badly wounded in about two minutes. I was now commander of our company. We stood under this hurricane of small shot till Halkett sent to order us in, and I brought away about a third of the light company; the rest were killed or wounded, and I really wonder how one of them escaped. As our bugler was killed, I shouted and made signals to move by the left, in order to avoid the fire of our guns and to put as good a face upon the business as possible.

"When I reached Lloyd's abandoned guns I stood near them for about a minute to contemplate the scene; it was grand beyond description. Hougoumont and its wood sent up a broad flame through the dark masses of smoke that overhung the field; beneath this cloud the French were indistinctly visible. Here a waving mass of long red feathers could be seen; there, gleams as from a sheet of steel showed that the cuirassiers were moving; 400 cannon were belching forth fire and death on every side; the roaring and shouting were indistinguishably commixed—together they gave me an idea of a labouring volcano. Bodies of infantry and cavalry were pouring down on us, and it was time to leave contemplation, so I moved toward our columns, which were standing up in square. Our regiment and 73rd formed one, and 33rd and 69th another; to our right beyond them were the Guards, and on our left the Hanoverians and German legion of our division. . . .

"In a few minutes after, the enemy's cavalry galloped up and crowned the crest of our position. Our guns were abandoned and they formed between the two brigades, about a hundred paces in our front. Their first charge was magnificent. As soon as they quickened their trot into a gallop, the cuirassiers bent their heads, so that the peaks of their helmets looked like visors, and they seemed cased in armour from the plume to the saddle. Not a shot was fired till they were within thirty yards, when the word was given, and our men fired away at them.

The effect was magical. Through the smoke we could see helmets falling, cavaliers starting from their seats with convulsive springs as they received our balls, horses plunging and rearing in the agonies of fright and pain, and crowds of the soldiery dismounted, part of the squadron in retreat, but the more daring remainder backing their horses to force them on our bayonets. Our fire soon disposed of these gentlemen. The main body re-formed in our front, and rapidly and gallantly repeated their attacks. In fact, from this time (about four o'clock) till near six, we had a constant repetition of these brave, but unavailing charges. There was no difficulty in repulsing them, but our ammunition decreased alarmingly. At length an artillery waggon galloped up, emptied two or three casks of cartridges into the square, and we were all comfortable.

"The best cavalry is contemptible to a steady and well-supplied infantry regiment; even our men saw this, and began to pity the useless perserverance of their assailants, and, as they advanced, would growl out, 'Here come these fools again!' One of their superior officers tried a *ruse de guerre,* by advancing and dropping his sword, as though he surrendered; some of us were deceived by him, but Halkett ordered the men to fire, and he coolly retired, saluting us. Their devotion was invincible.

"One officer whom we had taken prisoner was asked what force Napoleon might have in the field, and replied with a smile of mingled derision and threatening: 'You know very well what his force is, gentlemen.' A private cuirassier was wounded and dragged into the square; and as one of our men dropped dead close to him, he seized his bayonet, and forced it into his own neck; but this not despatching him, he raised up his cuirass, and plunging the bayonet into his stomach, kept working it about till he ceased to breathe.

"Though we constantly thrashed our steel-clad opponents we found more troublesome customers in the round shot and grape, which all this time played on us with terrible effect, and fully avenged the cuirassiers. Often as the volleys created openings in our square would the cavalry dash on, but they were uniformly unsuccessful. A regiment on our right seemed sadly disconcerted, and at one moment was in considerable confusion. Halkett rode out to them, and seizing their colour, waved it over his head, and restored them to something like order, though not before his horse was shot under him.

"At the height of their unsteadiness we got the order to 'right face' to move to their assistance; some of the men mistook it for 'right about face,' and faced accordingly, when old Major M'Laine, 73rd, called out, 'No, my boys, it's "right face;" you'll never hear the right about as long as a French bayonet is in front of you!' In a few moments he was mortally wounded. A regiment of light dragoons, by their facings either the 16th or 23rd, came up to our left and charged the cuirassiers. We cheered each other as they passed us; they did all they could, but were obliged to retire after a few minutes at the sabre.

"A body of Belgian cavalry advanced for the same purpose, but, on passing our square, they stopped short. Our noble Halkett rode out to them and offered to charge at their head; it was of no use; the Prince of Orange came up and exhorted them to do their duty, but in vain. They hesitated till a few shots whizzed through them, when they turned about, and galloped like fury, or, rather, like fear. As they passed the right face of our square the men, irritated by their rascally conduct, unanimously took up their pieces and fired a volley into them.

"The enemy's cavalry were by this time nearly disposed of, and as they had discovered the inutility of their charges, they commenced annoying us by a spirited and well-directed carbine fire. While we were employed in this manner it was impossible to see farther than the columns on our right and left, but I imagine most of the army was similarly situated: all the British

and Germans were doing their duty. About six o'clock I
perceived some artillery trotting up our hill, which I knew
by their caps to belong to the Imperial Guard. I had hardly
mentioned this to a brother officer when two guns unlimbered
within seventy paces of us, and, by their first discharge of
grape, blew seven men into the centre of the square. They
immediately reloaded, and kept up a constant and destructive
fire.

"It was noble to see our fellows fill up the gaps after every discharge. I was much distressed at this moment; having ordered
up three of my men, they had hardly taken their station when
two of them fell horribly lacerated. One of them looked up in
my face and uttered a sort of reproachful groan, and I involuntarily exclaimed, 'I couldn't help it.' We would willinglly
have charged these guns, but, had we deployed, the cavalry
that flanked them would have made an example of us.

"The *vivida vis animi*—the glow which fires one upon
entering into action—had ceased; it was now to be seen which
side had most bottom, and would stand killing longest.

"The Duke visited us frequently at this momentous period:
he was coolness personified. As he crossed the rear face of
our square a shell fell amongst our grenadiers and he checked
his horse to see its effect. Some men were blown to pieces
by the explosion, and he merely stirred the rein of his charger,
apparently as little concerned at their fate as at his own
danger. No leader ever possessed so fully the confidence of his
soldiery—wherever he appeared, a murmur of 'Silence—stand
to your front— here's the Duke,' was heard through the column,
and then all was steady as on a parade. His aides-de-camp,
Colonels Canning and Gordon, fell near our square, and the
former died within it. As he came near us late in the evening,
Halkett rode out to him and represented our weak state,
begging his Grace to afford us a little support. 'It's impossible,
Halkett,' said he. And our general replied, 'If so, sir, you may
depend on the brigade to a man!' "

XII

All accounts of the battle show that the Duke was ever
present at each spot where danger seemed the most pressing;
inspiring his men by a few homely and good-humoured words;

and restraining their impatience to be led forward to attack in their turn. "Hard pounding this, gentlemen: we will try who can pound the longest" was his remark to a battalion, on which the storm from the French guns was pouring with peculiar fury. Riding up to one of the squares, which had been dreadfully weakened, and against which a fresh attack of French cavalry was coming, he called to them: "Stand firm, my lads; what will they say of this in England?"

As he rode along another part of the line where the men had for some time been falling fast beneath the enemy's cannonade, without having any close fighting, a murmur reached his ear of natural eagerness to advance and do something more than stand still to be shot at. The Duke called to them: "Wait a little longer, my lads, and you shall have your wish." The men were instantly satisfied and steady. It was, indeed, indispensable for the Duke to bide his time. The premature movement of a single corps down from the British line of heights, would have endangered the whole position, and have probably made Waterloo a second Hastings.

But the Duke inspired all under him with his own spirit of patient firmness. When other generals besides Halkett sent to him begging for reinforcements, or for leave to withdraw corps which were reduced to skeletons, the answer was the same: "It is impossible; you must hold your ground to the last man, and all will be well." He gave a similar reply to some of his staff, who asked instructions from him, so that, in the event of his falling, his successor might follow out his plan. He answered, "My plan is simply to stand my ground here to the last man." His personal danger was indeed imminent throughout the day; and though he escaped without injury to himself or horse, one only of his numerous staff was equally fortunate.

"As far as the French accounts would lead us to infer," according to one historian, "it appears that the losses among Napoleon's staff were comparatively trifling. On this subject, perhaps the marked contrast afforded by the following anecdotes, which have been related to me on excellent authority, may tend to throw some light. At one period of the battle, when the Duke was surrounded by several of his staff, it is very evident that the group had become the object of the fire of a French battery. The shot fell fast about them, generally striking and turning up the ground on which they stood. Their horses became restive, and 'Copenhagen' himself so fidgety that the Duke, getting impatient, and having reasons for remaining on the spot, said to those about him 'Gentlemen, we are rather too close together—better to divide a little.' Subsequently, at another point of the line, an officer of artillery came up to the Duke, and stated that he had a distinct view of Napoleon, attended by his staff; that he had the guns of his battery well pointed in that direction, and was prepared to fire. His Grace instantly and emphatically exclaimed, 'No! no! I'll not allow it. It is not the business of commanders to be firing upon each other'."

Napoleon had stationed himself during the battle on a little hillock near La Belle Alliance, in the centre of the French position. Here he was seated, with a large table from the neighbouring farmhouse before him, on which maps and plans were spread; and thence with his telescope he surveyed the various points of the field. Soult watched his orders close at his left hand, and his staff was grouped on horseback a few paces in the rear. Here he remained till near the close of the day, preserving the appearance at least of calmness, except some expressions of irritation which escaped him, when Ney's attack on the British left centre was defeated.

But now that the crisis of the battle was evidently approaching, he mounted a white Persian charger, which he rode in action because the troops easily recognised him by the horse's colour. He had still the means of effecting a retreat. His Old Guard had not yet taken part in the action. Under cover of it he might have withdrawn his shattered forces and retired upon the French frontier. But this would only have given the English and Prussians the opportunity of completing their junction; and he knew that other armies were fast coming up to aid them in a march upon Paris, if he should succeed in avoiding an encounter with them, and retreating upon the capital. A victory at Waterloo was his only alternative from utter ruin, and he determined to employ his Guard in one bold stroke more to make that victory his own.

Between seven and eight o'clock, the infantry of the Old Guard was formed into two columns on the declivity near La Belle Alliance. Ney was placed at their head. Napoleon himself rode forward to a spot by which his veterans were to pass; and, as they approached, he raised his arm, and pointed to the position of the Allies, as if to tell them that their path lay there. They answered with loud cries of *"Vive l'Empereur!"* and descended the hill from their own side, into that "valley of the shadow of death," while the batteries thundered with redoubled vigour over their heads upon the British line. The line of march of the columns of the Guard was directed between Hougoumont and La Haye Sainte, against the British right centre; and at the same time the French under Donzelot, who had possession of La Haye Sainte, commenced a fierce attack upon the British centre, a little more to its left.

This part of the battle has drawn less attention than the celebrated attack of the Old Guard; but it formed the most perilous crisis for the Allied army; and if the Young Guard had been there to support Donzelot, instead of being engaged with the Prussians at Planchenoit, the consequences to the Allies in that part of the field must have been most serious. The French tirailleurs, who were posted in clouds in La Haye Sainte, and the sheltered spots near it, picked off the artillerymen of the English batteries near them and, taking advantage of the disabled state of the English guns the French brought some field-pieces up to La Haye Sainte and commenced firing grape from them on the infantry of the Allies, at a distance of not more than a hundred paces.

The allied infantry here consisted of some German brigades who were formed in squares, as it was believed that Donzelot had cavalry ready behind La Haye Sainte to charge them with, if they left that order of formation. In this state the Germans remained for some time with heroic fortitude, though the grape-shot was tearing gaps in their ranks, and the side of one square was literally blown away by one tremendous volley which the French gunners poured into it. The Prince of Orange in vain endeavoured to lead some Nassau troops to the aid of the brave Germans. The Nassauers would not or could not face the French and some battalions of Burnswickers, whom the Duke of Wellington had ordered up as a reinforcement, at first fell back, until the Duke in person rallied them and led them on. Having thus barred the farther advance of Donzelot, the Duke galloped off to the right to head his men who were exposed to the attack of the Imperial

Guard. He had saved one part of his centre from being routed, but the French had gained ground and kept it and the pressure on the Allied line in front of La Haye Sainte was fearfully severe until it was relieved by the decisive success which the British in the right centre achieved over the columns of the Guard.

The British troops on the crest of that part of the position, which the first column of Napoleon's Guard assailed, were Maitland's brigade of British Guards, having Adam's brigade (which had been brought forward during the action) on their right. Maitland's men were lying down, in order to avoid as far as possible the destructive effect of the French artillery, which kept up an unremitting fire from the opposite heights until the first column of the Imperial Guard had advanced so far up the slope towards the British position, that any further firing of the French artillerymen would have endangered their own comrades. Meanwhile the British guns were not idle, but shot and shell ploughed fast through the ranks of the stately array of veterans that still moved imposingly on. Several of the French superior officers were at its head. Ney's horse was shot under him, but he still led the way on foot, sword in hand.

The front of the massive column now was on the ridge of the hill. To their surprise they saw no troops before them. All they could discern through the smoke was a small band of mounted officers. One of them was the Duke himself. The French advanced to about fifty yards from where the British Guards were lying down, when the voice of one of the group of British officers was heard calling, as if to the ground before him, "Up, Guards, and at them!"

It was the Duke who gave the order and at the words, as if by magic, up started before them a line of the British Guards four deep, and in the most compact and perfect order. They poured an instantaneous volley upon the head of the French column, by which no less than three hundred of those chosen veterans are said to have fallen. The French officers rushed forwards; and, conspicuous in front of their men, attempted to deploy them into a more extended line, so as to enable them to reply with effect to the British fire. But Maitland's brigade kept showering in volley after volley with deadly rapidity. The decimated column sought to expand itself into a more efficient formation.

The right word was given at the right moment to the British for the bayonet-charge, and the brigade sprang forward with a loud cheer against their dismayed antagonists. In an instant the compact mass of the French spread out into a rabble, and they fled back down the hill, pursued by Maitland's men, who, however, returned to their position in time to take part in the repulse of the second column of the Imperial Guard.

This column also advanced with great spirit and firmness under the cannonade which was opened on it and passing by the eastern wall of Hougoumont diverged slightly to the right as it moved up the slope towards the British position, so as to approach nearly the same spot where the first column had surmounted the height and been defeated. This enabled the British regiment of Adams's brigade to form a line parallel to the left flank of the French column so that while the front of this column of French Guards had to encounter the cannonade of the British batteries and the musketry of Maitland's Guards, its left flank was assailed with a destructive fire by a four-deep of British infantry extending all along it.

In such a position all the bravery and skill of the French veterans were vain. The second column, like its predecessor, broke and fled, taking at first a lateral direction along the front of the British line towards the rear of La Haye Sainte, so becoming blended with the divisions of French infantry, which under Donzelot had been assailing the Allies so formidably in that quarter. The sight of the Old Guard broken and in flight checked the ardour which Donzelot's troops had hitherto displayed. They, too, began to waver. Adams's victorious brigade was pressing after the flying Guard, and now cleared away the assailants of the allied centre.

But the battle was not yet won. Napoleon had still some battalions in reserve near La Belle Alliance. He was rapidly rallying the remains of the first column of his Guards, and he had collected into one body the remnants of the various corps of cavalry, which had suffered so severely in the earlier part of the day. The Duke instantly formed the bold resolution of now himself becoming the assailant and leading his successful though enfeebled army forward, while the disheartening effect of the repulse of the Imperial Guard on the rest of the French army was still strong and before Napoleon and Ney could rally the beaten veterans themselves for another and a fiercer charge. As the close approach of the Prussians now completely protected the Duke's left, he had drawn some reserves of horse from that quarter, and he had a brigade of Hussars under Vivian fresh and ready at hand. Without a moment's hesitation he launched these against the cavalry near La Belle Alliance. The charge was as successful as it was daring and as there was now no hostile cavalry to check the British infantry in a forward movement, the Duke gave the long-wished-for command for a general advance of the army along the whole line upon the foe.

It was now past eight o'clock and for nearly nine deadly hours had the British and German regiments stood unflinchingly under the fire of artillery, the charge of cavalry and every variety of assault, which the compact columns or the scattered tirailleurs of the enemy's infantry could inflict. As they joyously sprang forward against the discomfited masses of the French, the setting sun broke through the clouds which had obscured the sky during the greater part of the day and glittered on the bayonets of the Allies, while they poured down into the valley and towards the heights that were held by the foe. The Duke himself was among the foremost in the advance and personally directed the movements against each body of the French that essayed resistance. He rode in front of Adam's brigade, cheering it forward, and even galloped among the most advanced of the British skirmishers, speaking joyously to the men, and receiving their hearty shouts of congratulation. The bullets of both friends and foes were whistling fast round him and one of the few survivors of his staff remonstrated with him for thus exposing a life of such value. "Never mind," was the Duke's answer—"never mind, let them fire away; the battle's won, and my life is of no consequence now."

And, indeed, almost the whole of the French host was now in irreparable confusion. The Prussian army was coming more and more rapidly forwards on their right; and the Young Guard, which had held Planchenoit so bravely, was at last compelled to give way. Some regiments of the Old Guard in vain endeavoured to form in squares and stem the current. They were swept away, and wrecked among the waves of the flyers. Napoleon had placed himself in one of these squares. Marshal Soult, Generals Bertrand, Drouot, Corbineau, de

Flahaut, and Gourgaud, were with him. The Emperor spoke of dying on the field, but Soult seized his bridle and turned his charger round, exclaiming, "Sire, are not the enemy already lucky enough?"

With the greatest difficulty, and only by the utmost exertion of the devoted officers round him, Napoleon cleared the throng of fugitives, and escaped from the scene of the battle and the war, which he and France had lost past all recovery. Meanwhile the Duke of Wellington still rode forward with the van of his victorious troops, until he reined up on the elevated ground near Rossomme.

(In the estimation of many, the most graphic narrative of Waterloo, with satisfactory factual presentation, is Victor Hugo's in his *Les Miserables.*)

XIII

The daylight was now entirely gone; but the young moon had risen and the light which it cast, aided by the glare from the burning houses and other buildings in the line of the flying French and pursuing Prussians, enabled the Duke to assure himself that his victory was complete. He then rode back along the Charleroi road toward Waterloo: and near La Belle Alliance he met Marshal Blucher. Warm were the congratulations that were exchanged between the Allied chiefs.

It was arranged that the Prussians should follow up the pursuit and give the French no chance of rallying. Accordingly the British army, exhausted by its toils and sufferings during that dreadful day, did not advance beyond the heights which the enemy had occupied. But the Prussians drove the fugitives before them in merciless chase throughout the night. Cannon, baggage, and all the matériel of the army were abandoned by the French; and many thousands of the infantry threw away their arms to facilitate their escape. The ground was strewn for miles with the wrecks of their host. There was no rearguard; nor was even the semblance of order attempted.

An attempt at resistance was made at the bridge and village of Genappe, the first narrow pass through which the bulk of the French retired. The situation was favourable and a few resolute battalions, if ably commanded, might have held their pursuers at bay there for some considerable time. But despair and panic were now universal in the beaten army. At the first sound of the Prussian drums and bugles, Genappe was given up and nothing thought of but headlong flight. The Prussians, under General Gneisenau, still followed and still slew; nor even when the Prussian infantry stopped in sheer exhaustion was the pursuit given up.

Gneisenau still pushed on with the cavalry and by an ingenious stratagem made the French believe that his infantry were still close on them and scared them from every spot where they attempted to pause and rest. He mounted one of his drummers on a horse which had been taken from the captured carriage of Napoleon, and made him ride along with the pursuing cavalry, and beat the drum whenever they came on any large number of the French. The French thus fled, and the Prussians pursued through Quatre Bras, and even over the heights of Frasne; and when at length Gneisenau drew bridle, and halted a little beyond Frasne with the scanty remnant of keen hunters who had kept up the chase with him to the last, the French were scattered through Gosselies, Marchiennes, and Charleroi; and were striving to regain the left bank of the river Sambre, which they had crossed in such pomp and pride not a hundred hours before.

Part of the French left wing endeavoured to escape from the field without blending with the main body of the fugitives who thronged the Genappe causeway. A French officer who was among those who thus retreated across the country eastward of the high-road has vividly described what he witnessed and what he suffered. Colonel Lemonnier Delafosse served in the campaign of 1815 in General Foy's staff and was consequently in that part of the French army at Waterloo, which acted against Hougoumont and the British right wing. When the column of the Imperial Guard made their great charge at the end of the day, the troops of Foy's division advanced in support of them and Colonel Lemonnier Delafosse describes the confident hopes of victory and promotion with which he marched to that attack and the fearful carnage and confusion of the assailants, amid which he was helplessly hurried back by his flying comrades. He then narrates the closing scene:

"Near one of the hedges of Hougoumont farm, without even a drummer to beat the *rappel,* we succeeded in rallying under the enemy's fire 300 men: they were nearly all that remained of our splendid division. Thither came together a band of generals. There was Reille, whose horse had been shot under him: there were D'Erlon, Bachelu, Foy, Jamin, and others. All were gloomy and sorrowful, like vanquished men. Their words were, 'Here is all that is left of my corps, of my division, of my brigade. I, myself.' We had seen the fall of Duhesme, of Pelet-de-Morvan, of Michel—generals who had found a glorious death. My General, Foy, had his shoulder pierced through by a musket-ball: and out of his whole staff two officers only were left to him, Cahour Duhay and I. Fate had spared me in the midst of so many dangers, though the first charger I rode had been shot and had fallen on me.

"The enemy's horse were coming down on us, and our little group was obliged to retreat. What had happened to our division of the left wing had taken place all along the line. The movement of the hostile cavalry, which inundated the whole plain, had demoralised our soldiers who, seeing all regular retreat of the army cut off, strove each man to effect one for himself. At each instant the road became more encumbered. Infantry, cavalry, and artillery, were pressing along pell-mell: jammed together like a solid mass. Figure to yourself 40,000 men struggling and thrusting themselves along a single causeway. We could not take that way without destruction, so the generals who had collected together near the Hougoumont hedge dispersed across the fields.

"General Foy alone remained with the 300 men whom he had gleaned from the field of battle, and marched at their head. Our anxiety was to withdraw from the scene of action without being confounded with the fugitives. Our general wished to retreat like a true soldier. Seeing three lights in the southern horizon, like beacons, General Foy asked me what I thought of the position of each. I answered 'The first to the left is Genappe, the second is at Bois-de-Bossu, near the farm of Quatre Bras; the third is at Gosselies.' 'Let us march on the second one, then,' replied Foy, 'and let no obstacle stop us—take the head of the column, and do not lose sight of the guiding light.' Such was his order and I strove to obey.

"After all the agitation and the incessant din of a long day of battle, how imposing was the stillness of that night!

We proceeded on our sad and lonely march. We were a prey to the most cruel reflections, we were humiliated, we were hopeless; but not a word of complaint was heard. We walked silently as a troop of mourners, and it might have been said that we were attending the funeral of our country's glory. Suddenly the stillness was broken by a challenge—'*Qui vive?*' 'France!' 'Kellerman!' 'Foy!' 'Is it you, General? come nearer to us.' At that moment we were passing over a little hillock, at the foot of which was a hut in which Kellerman and some of his officers had halted. They came out to join us.

"Foy said to me, 'Kellerman knows the country: he has been along here before with his cavalry; we had better follow him.' But we found that the direction which Kellerman chose was towards the first light, towards Genappe. That led to the causeway which our general rightly wished to avoid. I went to the left to reconnoitre and was soon convinced that such was the case. It was then that I was able to form a full idea of the disorder of a routed army. What a hideous spectacle! The mountain torrent, that uproots and whirls along with it every momentary obstacle, is a feeble image of that heap of men, of horses, of equipages, rushing one upon another; gathering before the least obstacle which dams up their way for a few seconds, only to form a mass which overthrows everything in the path which it forces for itself. Woe to him whose footing failed him in that deluge! He was crushed, trampled to death! I returned and told my general what I had seen, and he instantly abandoned Kellerman and resumed his original line of march.

"Keeping straight across the country over fields and the rough thickets we at last arrived at the Bois-de-Bossu, where we halted. My General said to me, 'Go to the farm of Quatre Bras and announce that we are here. The Emperor or Soult must be there. Ask for orders, and recollect that I am waiting here for you. The lives of these men depend on your exactness.' To reach the farm I was obliged to cross the high-road. I was on horseback, but nevertheless was borne away by the crowd that fled along the road and it was long ere I could extricate myself and reach the farmhouse.

"General Lobau was there with his staff, resting in fancied security. They thought that their troops had halted there; but, though a halt had been attempted, the men had soon fled forwards, like their comrades of the rest of the army. The shots of the approaching Prussians were now heard and I believe that General Lobau was taken prisoner in that farmhouse. I left him to rejoin my general, which I did with difficulty. I found him alone. His men, as they came near the current of flight, were infected with the general panic and fled also.

"What was to be done? Follow that crowd of runaways? General Foy would not hear of it. There were five of us still with him, all officers. He had been wounded at about five in the afternoon and the wound had not been dressed. He suffered severely but his moral courage was unbroken. 'Let us keep,' he said, 'a line parallel to the high-road and work our way hence as we best can.' A foot-track was before us, and we followed it.

"The moon shone out brightly and revealed the full wretchedness of the *tableau* which met our eyes. A brigadier and four cavalry soldiers, with whom we met formed our escort. We marched on; and, as the noise grew more distant, I thought that we were losing the parallel of the highway. Finding that we had the moon more and more on the left, I felt sure of this and mentioned it to the General. Absorbed in thought, he made no reply. We came in front of a windmill and endeavoured to procure some information, but we could not gain an entrance, or make anyone answer, and we continued our nocturnal march. At last we entered a village, but found every door closed against us, and were obliged to use threats in order to gain admission into a single house. The poor woman to whom it belonged, more dead than alive, received us as if we had been enemies. Before asking where we were, 'Food, give us some food!' was our cry. Bread and butter and beer were brought, and soon disappeared before men who had fasted for twenty-four hours. A little revived, we ask, 'Where are we? what is the name of this village?' 'Vieville.'

"On looking at the map, I saw that in coming to that village we had leaned too much to the right, and that we were in the direction of Mons. In order to reach the Sambre at the bridge of Marchiennes, we had four leagues to traverse and there was scarcely time to march the distance before daybreak. I made a villager act as our guide and bound him by his arm to my stirrup. He led us through Roux to

Marchiennes. The poor fellow ran alongside of my horse the whole way. It was cruel, but necessary to compel him, for we had not an instant to spare. At six in the morning we entered Marchiennes.

"Marshal Ney was there. Our general went to see him and to ask what orders he had to give. Ney was asleep, and, rather than rob him of the first repose he had had for four days, our general returned to us without seeing him. And, indeed, what orders could Marshal Ney have given? The whole army was crossing the Sambre, each man where and how he chose; some at Charleroi, some at Marchiennes. We were about to do the same thing. When once beyond the Sambre we might safely halt and both men and horses were in extreme need of rest. We passed through Thuin and finding a little copse near the road we gladly sought its shelter. While our horses grazed we lay down and slept. How sweet was that sleep after the fatigues of the long day of battle, and after the night of retreat more painful still! We rested in the little copse till noon and sat there watching the wrecks of our army defile along the road before us. It was a soul-harrowing sight!

"Yet the different arms of the service had resumed a certain degree of order amid their disorder; and our general, feeling his strength revive, resolved to follow a strong column of cavalry which was taking the direction of Beaumont, about four leagues off. We drew near Beaumont, when suddenly a regiment of horse was seen debouching from a wood on our left. The column that we followed shouted out, 'The Prussians! the Prussians!' and galloped off in utter disorder. The troops that thus alarmed them were not a tenth part of their number, and were in reality our own 8th Hussars, who wore green uniforms.

"But the panic had been brought even thus far from the battle-field, and the disorganised column galloped into Beaumont, which was already crowded with our infantry. We were obliged to follow that *débâcle*. On entering Beaumont we chose a house of superior appearance and demanded of the mistress of it refreshments for the General. 'Alas!' said the lady, 'this is the tenth general who has been to this house since this morning. I have nothing left. Search, if you please, and see.' Though unable to find food for the General, I persuaded him to take off his coat and let me examine his wound.

The bullet had gone through the twists of the left epaulette and penetrating the skin had run round the shoulder without injuring the bone. The lady of the house made some lint for me and without any great degree of surgical skill I succeeded in dressing the wound.

"Being still anxious to procure some food for the General and ourselves, if it were but a loaf of ammunition bread, I left the house and rode out into the town. I saw pillage going on in every direction: open caissons, stripped and half-broken, blocked up the streets. The pavement was covered with plundered and torn baggage. Pillagers and runaways, such were all the comrades I met with. Disgusted at them, I strove, sword in hand, to stop one of the plunderers, but, more active than I, he gave me a bayonet stab in my left arm, in which I fortunately caught his thrust, which had been aimed full at my body. He disappeared among the crowd, through which I could not force my horse. My spirit of discipline had made me forget that in such circumstances the soldier is a mere wild beast. But to be wounded by a fellow-countryman after having passed unharmed through all the perils of Quatre Bras and Waterloo! This did seem hard, indeed.

"I was trying to return to General Foy, when another horde of flyers burst into Beaumont, swept me into the current of their flight, and hurried me out of the town with them. Until I received my wound I had preserved my moral courage in full force; but now, worn out with fatigue, covered with blood, and suffering severe pain from the wound, I own that I gave way to the general demoralisation and let myself be inertly borne along with the rushing mass. At last I reached Landrecies, though I know not how or when. But I found there our Colonel Hurday, who had been left behind there in consequence of an accidental injury from a carriage. He took me with him to Paris, where I retired amid my family and got cured of my wound, knowing nothing of the rest of political and military events that were taking place."

No returns ever were made of the amount of the French loss in the battle of Waterloo, but it must have been immense, and may be partially judged of by the amount of killed and wounded in the armies of the conquerors. On this subject both the Prussian and British official evidence agree.

XIV

Of the army that fought under the Duke of Wellington nearly 15,000 men were killed and wounded on this single day of battle. Seven thousand Prussians also fell at Waterloo. At such a fearful price was the deliverance of Europe purchased.

By none was the severity of that loss more keenly felt than by our great deliverer himself. As may be seen in Major Macready's narrative, the Duke, while the battle was raging, betrayed no sign of emotion at the most ghastly casualties, but, when all was over, the sight of the carnage with which the field was covered, and still more, the sickening spectacle of the agonies of the wounded men who lay moaning in their misery by thousands weighed heavily on the spirit of the victor, as he rode back across the scene of strife.

On reaching his headquarters in the village of Waterloo the Duke inquired anxiously after the numerous friends who had been round him in the morning, and to whom he was warmly attached. Many he was told were dead; others were lying alive, but mangled and suffering, in the houses around him. It is in his own words alone that his feelings can be adequately told. In a letter written by him almost immediately after his return from the field, he thus expressed himself: "My heart is broken by the terrible loss I have sustained in my old friends and companions, and my poor soldiers. Believe me, nothing except a battle lost can be half so melancholy as a battle won. The bravery of my troops has hitherto saved me from the greater evil, but to win such a battle as this of Waterloo, at the expense of so many gallant friends, could only be termed a heavy misfortune, but for the result to the public."

It is not often that a successful general in modern warfare is called on, like the victorious commander of the ancient Greek armies, to award a prize of superior valour to one of his soldiers. Such was to some extent the case with respect to the battle of Waterloo. In the August of 1818, an English clergyman offered to confer a small annuity on some Waterloo soldier, to be named by the Duke. The Duke requested Sir John Byng to choose a man from the 2nd Brigade of Guards, which had so highly distinguished itself in the defence of Hougoumont. There were many gallant candidates, but the election fell on Sergeant James Graham, of the light company of the Coldstreams.

This brave man had signalised himself throughout the day in the defence of that important post, and especially in the critical struggle that took place at the period when the French, who had gained the wood, the orchard, and detached garden, succeeded in bursting open a gate of the courtyard of the château itself and rushed in in large mass, confident of carrying all before them. A hand-to-hand fight, of the most desperate character, was kept up between them and the Guards for a few minutes; but at last the British bayonets prevailed. Nearly all the Frenchmen who had forced their way in were killed on the spot; and, as the few survivors ran back, five of the Guards, Colonel Macdonnell, Captain Wyndham, Ensign Gooch, Ensign Hervey, and Sergeant Graham, by sheer strength closed the gate again in spite of the efforts of the French from without and effectually barricaded it against further assaults.

Over and through the loopholed wall of the courtyard, the English garrison now kept up a deadly fire of musketry which was fiercely answered by the French, who swarmed round the grounds like ravening wolves. Shells, too, from their batteries were falling fast into the besieged place, one of which set part of the mansion and some of the out-buildings on fire.

Graham, who was at this time standing near Colonel Macdonnell at the wall, and who had shown the most perfect steadiness and courage, now asked permission of his commanding officer to retire for a moment. Macdonnell replied, "By all means, Graham; but I wonder you should ask leave now." Graham answered, "I would not, sir, only my brother is wounded, and he is in that out-building there, which has just caught fire." Laying down his musket, Graham ran to the blazing spot, lifted up his brother, and laid him in a ditch. Then he was back at his post, and was plying his musket against the French again, before his absence was noticed, except by his colonel.

Many anecdotes of individual prowess have been preserved: but of all the brave men who were in the British army on that eventful day none deserve more honour for courage and indomitable resolution than Sir Thomas Picton who, as has been mentioned, fell in repulsing the great attack of the French upon the British left centre. It was not until the dead body was examined after the battle, that the full heroism of Picton was discerned. He had been wounded on the 16th, at Quatre Bras, by a musket-ball, which had broken two of his ribs, and caused also severe internal injuries; but he had concealed the circumstance, evidently in expectation that another and greater battle would be fought in a short time and desirous to avoid being solicited to absent himself from the field. His body was blackened and swollen by the wound, which must have caused severe and incessant pain; and it was marvellous how his spirit had borne him up, and enabled him to take part in the fatigues and duties of the field. The bullet which, on the 18th, killed the renowned leader of "the fighting Division" of the Peninsula, entered the head near the left temple, and passed through the brain, so that Picton's death must have been instantaneous.

One of the most interesting narratives of personal adventure at Waterloo, is that of Colonel Frederick Ponsonby, of the 12th Light Dragoons, who was severely wounded when Vandeleur's brigade, to which he belonged, attacked the French lancers in order to bring off the Union Brigade, which was retiring from its memorable charge. The 12th, like those whom they rescued, advanced much further against the French position than prudence warranted. Ponsonby, with many others, was speared by a reserve of Polish lancers, and left for dead on the field. It is well to refer to the description of what he suffered (as he afterwards gave it, when almost miraculously recovered from his numerous wounds), because his fate, or worse, was the fate of thousands more; and because the narrative of the pangs of an individual, with whom we can identify ourselves, always comes more home to us than a general description of the miseries of whole masses. His tale may make us remember what are the horrors of war as well as its glories. It is to be remembered that the operations, which he refers to, took place about three o'clock in the day, and that the fighting went on for at least five hours more. After describing how he and his men charged through the French whom they first encountered, and went against other enemies, he states:

"We had no sooner passed them than we were ourselves attacked, before we could form, by about 300 Polish lancers who had hastened to their relief, the French artillery pouring in among us a heavy fire of grape, though for one of our men they killed three of their own.

"In the *mêlée* I was almost instantly disabled in both arms, losing first my sword and then my reins and followed by a few men, who were presently cut down, no quarter being allowed, asked, or given, I was carried along by my horse, till, receiving a blow from a sabre, I fell senseless on my face to the ground.

"Recovering, I raised myself a little to look around, being at that time, I believe, in a condition to get up and run away; when a lancer passing by, struck his lance through my back. My head dropped, and blood gushed into my mouth, a difficulty of breathing came on, and I thought all was over.

"Not long afterwards (it was impossible to measure time, but I must have fallen in less than ten minutes after the onset), a tirailleur stopped to plunder me, threatening my life. I directed him to a small side-pocket, in which he found three dollars, all I had; but he continued to threaten and I said he might search me; this he did immediately, unloosening my stock and tearing open my waistcoast and leaving me in a very uneasy posture.

"But he was no sooner gone, than an officer bringing up some troops, to which probably the tirailleur belonged, and happening to halt where I lay, stooped down and addressed me, saying he feared I was badly wounded; I said that I was, and expressed a wish to be removed to the rear. He said it was against their orders to remove even their own men; but that if they gained the day (and he understood that the Duke of Wellington was killed, and that some of our battalions had surrendered), every attention in his power would be shown me. I complained of thirst, and he held his brandy-bottle to my lips, directing one of the soldiers to lay me straight on my side, and place a knapsack under my head. He then passed on into action—soon, perhaps, to want, though not to receive, the same assistance; and I shall never know to whose generosity I was indebted, as I believe, for my life. Of what rank he was, I cannot say: he wore a great-coat.

"By-and-by another tirailleur came up, a fine young man, full of ardour. He knelt down, and fired over me, loading and firing many times and conversing with me all the while."

The Frenchman with strange coolness, informed Ponsonby of how he was shooting and what he thought of the progress of the battle. "At last he ran off, exclaiming, 'You will probably not be sorry to hear that we are going to retreat. Good day, my friend.' It was dusk when two squadrons of Prussian cavalry, each of them two deep, came across the valley, and passed over me in full trot, lifting me from the ground, and tumbling me about cruelly. The clatter of their approach, and the apprehensions they excited, may be imagined; a gun taking that direction must have destroyed me.

"The battle was now at an end, or removed to a distance. The shouts, the imprecations, the outcries of *'Vive l'Empereur!'* the discharge of musketry and cannon were over; and the groans of the wounded all around me became every moment more and more audible. I thought the night would never end.

"Much about this time I found a soldier of the Royals lying across my legs: he had probably crawled thither in his agony; and his weight, his convulsive motions, and the air issuing through a wound in his side, distressed me greatly; the last circumstance most of all, as I had a wound of the same nature myself.

"It was not a dark night, and the Prussians were wandering about to plunder. Several stragglers looked at me as they passed by, one after another, and at last one of them stopped to examine me. I told him as well as I could, for I spoke German very imperfectly, that I was a British officer, and had been plundered already; he did not desist, however, and pulled me about roughly.

"An hour before midnight I saw a man in an English uniform walking towards me. He was, I suspect, on the same errand, and he came and looked in my face. I spoke instantly, telling him who I was and assuring him of a reward if he would remain by me. He said he belonged to the 40th, and had missed his regiment; he released me from the dying soldier and being unarmed, took up a sword from the ground and stood over me, pacing backwards and forwards.

"Day broke; and at six o'clock in the morning some English were seen at a distance, and he ran to them. A messenger being sent off to Hervey, a cart came for me, and I was placed in it and carried to the village of Waterloo, a mile and a half off. I had received seven wounds, and I was saved by excessive bleeding."

XV

Major Macready, in the journal already cited, justly praises the deep devotion to their Emperor which marked the French at Waterloo. Never, indeed, had the national bravery of the French people been more nobly shown. One soldier in the French ranks was seen, when his arm was shattered by a cannon-ball, to wrench it off with the other, and throwng it up in the air, he exclaimed to his comrades, "Long live the Emperor, even to death!" Colonel Lemonnier Delafosse mentions in his *Memoirs* that at the beginning of the action a French soldier who had had both legs carried off by a cannon-ball, was borne past the front of Foy's division, and called out to them, "It is nothing, comrades. Long live the Emperor! Glory to France!"

The same officer, at the end of the battle, when all hope was lost, tells us that he saw a French grenadier, blackened with powder and with his clothes torn and stained, leaning on his musket, immovable as a statue. The colonel called to him to join his comrades and retreat; but the grenadier showed him his musket and his hands; and said, "These hands have with this musket used today more than twenty packets of cartridges: it was more than my share: I supplied myself with ammunition from the dead. Leave me to die here on the field of battle. It is not courage that fails me, but strength." Then, as Colonel Delafosse left him, the soldier stretched himself on the ground to meet his fate.

The gallantry of the French officers at least equalled that of their men. Ney, in particular, set the example of the most daring courage. Here, as in every French army in which he ever served or commanded, he was "bravest of the brave." Throughout the day he was in the front of the battle and was one of the very last Frenchmen who quitted the field. His horse was killed under him in the last attack made on the English position; but he was seen on foot, his clothes torn with bullets, his face smirched with powder, striving, sword in hand, first to urge his men forward, and at last to check their flight.

There was another brave general of the French army, whose valour and good conduct on that day of disaster to his nation, should never be unnoticed, when the story of Waterloo is recounted. This was General Pelet, who about seven in the evening, led the first battalion of the 2nd regiment of the

Chasseurs of the Guard to the defence of Planchenoit and on whom Napoleon personally urged the deep importance of maintaining possession of that village. Pelet and his men took their post in the central part of the village, and occupied the church and churchyard in great strength.

There they repelled every assault of the Prussians, who in rapidly increasing numbers rushed forward with infuriated pertinacity. They held their post till the utter rout of the main army of their comrades was apparent, and the victorious allies were thronging around Planchenoit. Then Pelet and his brave chasseurs quitted the churchyard, and retired with steady march, though they suffered fearfully from the moment they left their shelter, and Prussian cavalry as well as infantry dashed fiercely after them. Pelet kept together a little knot of 250 veterans, and had the eagle covered over, and borne along in the midst of them. At one time the inequality of the ground caused his ranks to open a little; and in an instant the Prussian horsemen were on them and striving to capture the eagle. Captain Siborne relates the conduct of Pelet with the admiration worthy of one brave soldier for another:—

"Pelet, taking advantage of a spot of ground which afforded them some degree of cover against the fire of grape by which they were constantly assailed, halted the standard-bearer, and called out, 'To me, men! We will save the eagle or die with it!' The chasseurs immediately pressed around him, forming what is usually termed the rallying square, and, lowering their bayonets, succeeded in repulsing the charge of cavalry. Some guns were then brought to bear upon them and subsequently a brisk fire of musketry, but notwithstanding the awful sacrifice which was thus offered up in defence of their precious charge, they succeeded in reaching the main line of retreat, favoured by the universal confusion as also by the general obscurity which now prevailed, and thus saved alike the eagle and the honour of the regiment."

French writers do injustice to their own army and general, when they revive malignant calumnies against Wellington, and speak of his having blundered into victory. No blunderer could have successfully encountered such troops as those of Napoleon, and under such a leader. It is superfluous to cite against these cavils the testimony which other continental critics have borne to the high military genius of our illustrious chief. I refer to one only, which is of peculiar value, on account of the quarter whence it comes. It is that of the great German writer, Niebuhr, whose accurate acquaintance with every important scene of modern as well as ancient history was unparalleled and who was no mere pedant, but a man practically versed in active life, and had been personally acquainted with most of the leading men in the great events of the early part of this century. Niebuhr, in the passage which I allude to, after referring to the military "blunders" of Mithridates, Frederick the Great, Napoleon, Pyrrhus, and Hannibal, uses these remarkable words, "The Duke of Wellington is, I believe, the only general in whose conduct of war we cannot discover any important mistake."

Not that it is to be supposed that the Duke's merits were simply of a negative order, or that he was merely a cautious, phlegmatic general, fit only for defensive warfare, as some recent French historians have described him. On the contrary, he was bold, even to audacity, when boldness was required. "The intrepid advance and fight at Assaye, the crossing of the Douro, and the movement on Talavera in 1809, the advance to Madrid and Burgos in 1812, the actions before Bayonne in 1813, and the desperate stand made at Waterloo itself, when more tamely-prudent generals would have retreated beyond Brussels, place this beyond a doubt," says Niebuhr.

The overthrow of the French military power at Waterloo was so complete that the subsequent events of the brief campaign have little interest. Lamartine truly says: "This defeat left nothing undecided in future events, for victory had given judgment. The war began and ended in a single battle." Napoleon himself recognised instantly and fully the deadly nature of the blow which had been dealt to his empire.

In his flight from the battle-field he first halted at Charleroi, but the approach of the pursuing Prussians drove him thence before he had rested there an hour. With difficulty getting clear of the wrecks of his own army, he reached Philippeville, where he remained a few hours, and sent orders to the French generals in the various extremities of France, to converge with their troops upon Paris. He ordered Soult to collect the fugitives of his own force, and lead them to Laon. He then hurried forward to Paris, and reached his capital before the news of his own defeat. But the stern truth soon transpired.

At the demand of the Chambers of Peers and Representatives

he abandoned the throne by a second and final abdication on the 22nd of June. On the 29th of June he left the neighbourhood of Paris, and proceeded to Rochefort in the hope of escaping to America: but the coast was strictly watched, and on the 15th of July the ex-Emperor surrendered himself on board of the English man-of-war *Bellerophon*. He later was taken to St. Helena, in exile and died there after six years, in 1821.

Meanwhile the allied armies had advanced steadily upon Paris, driving before them Grouchy's corps, and the scanty force which Soult had succeeded in rallying at Laon. Cambray, Peronne, and other fortresses were speedily captured; and by the 29th of June the invaders were taking their positions in front of Paris. The provisional government, which acted in the French capital after the Emperor's abdication, opened negotiations with the allied chiefs. Blucher, in his quenchless hatred of the French, was eager to reject all proposals for a suspension of hostilities, and to assault and storm the city. But the sager and calmer spirit of Wellington prevailed over his colleague; the entreated armistice was granted; and on the 3rd of July the capitulation of Paris terminated the war of the Battle of Waterloo.

(Wellington died in 1852, in his eighty-third year, after a distinguished career in public life, during which he served as foreign secretary and premier.)

Index

ABDERRAHMAN IBN ABDILLAH ALGHAFEKI, Saracen general, 163; governor in Spain.

AETIUS, Roman general, 143; exertions in collecting his army; effects a junction with his ally Theodoric; commands the right wing of the army at Chalons; his jealousy of the Visigoths.

ALCIBIADES, Athenian general, 45; character; revenge on the Athenians; harangue in the Spartan assembly.

ALEXANDER, 57; character slandered by ancient rhetoricians; Arrian's remarks on; Sir Walter Raleigh's; Napoleon's; important results of his conquests; numbers of his army at Arbela; comes in sight of the Persian army; address to his officers; refuses to attack the Persians by night; great skill shown in his disposition of his army; his personal valour; form of attack; description of his manoeuvres; gains a complete victory; enters Arbela; enters Babylon; victory at Arbela the crisis of his career; his later exploits.

AMERICA, 351; result of the unwise policy of England toward the American colonies; consequences resulting from Burgoyne's defeat, and a brief recapitulation of the early events of the war between England and.

ARBELA, 57; situation of; its importance as a military position; Darius' army at Arbela; his proposed plan of the battle; Alexander's army; its strength and constitution; his instructions to his generals; date of the battle; plan of the battle; the disposition of Alexander's army; description of the battle; Persians defeated; Alexander enters the city and takes possession of the treasure.

ARLETTA, 171; daughter of the tanner of Falaise, influence which events of her life have exercised over the subsequent history of the world; William the Conqueror, her son.

ARMINIUS, 122; his victory over the Roman legions under Varus; his character; perilous nature of the enterprise which immortalised him; state of Rome and her government at the time of; private causes which helped to urge Arminius on to the deliverance of his country; his marriage with Thusnelda; succeeds in blinding Varus as to his schemes; description of the locality chosen by Arminius for his enterprise against Varus; names of several spots in the vicinity still indicate the scene of the battle; Roman army is harassed and its march impeded by; he gives the signal for a general attack; description of the battle; Roman captives slain in sacrifice by the German victors; extreme terror which this decisive victory caused at Rome; terrific portents believed to have occurred at the time; the independence of Germany effectually gained by the victory of; his subsequent contests with the Romans; unhappy fate of his wife and child; fights various battles with the Romans, under Germanicus, and afterwards Cæcina; assembles his army on the banks of the Weser, the Roman army under Germanicus being encamped on the opposite bank; his interview with his brother Flavius, who adhered to the Romans; Arminius wounded in battle, the Romans claim the